Constitutional Debate in Action

Constitutional Debate in Action

Civil Rights & Liberties

SECOND EDITION

H. L. Pohlman

ROWMAN & LITTLEFIELD PUBLISHERS, INC.
Lanham • Boulder • New York • Toronto • Oxford

ROWMAN & LITTLEFIELD PUBLISHERS, INC.

Published in the United States of America
by Rowman & Littlefield Publishers, Inc.
A wholly owned subsidiary of The Rowman & Littlefield Publishing Group, Inc.
4501 Forbes Boulevard, Suite 200, Lanham, MD 20706
www.rowmanlittlefield.com

P.O. Box 317, Oxford OX2 9RU, UK

British Library Cataloguing in Publication Information Available

Library of Congress Cataloging-in-Publication Data

Pohlman, H. L., 1952–
    Constitutional debate in action. Civil rights & liberties / H. L. Pohlman.—2nd ed.
      p.   cm.
    Includes bibliographical references and index.
    ISBN 0-7425-3666-1 (cloth : alk. paper)—ISBN 0-7425-3667-X (pbk. : alk. paper)
    1. Civil rights—United States—Cases.   I. Title: Civil rights & liberties.   II. Title.
  KF4748.P64   2005
  342.7308'5—dc22
                                                                                2004015911

Printed in the United States of America

∞ ™ The paper used in this publication meets the minimum requirements of American National Standard for Information Sciences—Permanence of Paper for Printed Library Materials, ANSI/NISO Z39.48-1992.

Contents

Preface   ix

Acknowledgments   xv

1   Racial Discrimination: *Brown v. Board of Education*   1
    Briefs   13
      Legal Defense Fund's Brief (1952)   13
      Brief for the State of Kansas (1952)   15
    Oral Argument (1952)   16
    Briefs   19
      Legal Defense Fund's Brief (1953)   19
      Brief for the State of Kansas (1953)   22
    Oral Argument (1953)   25
    The Opinion   26
    Postscript   28

2   Affirmative Action: *Regents of University of Calif. v. Bakke* and
    Grutter v. Bollinger (co-authored with Jared Mellott)   35
      I. *Bakke* and Its Background   35
    Briefs   43
      University of California Brief   43
      Allan Bakke's Brief   48
      Polish American Congress *Amicus* Brief   50
      NAACP Legal Defense & Educational Fund *Amicus* Brief   51
      Mexican American Legal Defense & Educational Fund
      Amicus Brief   52
      Anti-Defamation League of B'nai B'rith *Amicus* Brief   53
    Oral Argument   53
    The Opinion   56

II. Developments after *Bakke* 63
Briefs 70
   Grutter's Brief 70
   University of Michigan's Brief 74
   United States' Brief 77
   Brief of Lt. Gen. Julius W. Becton, et al. 78
Oral Argument 79
Opinions 82

3 Abortion: *Roe v. Wade* and *Planned Parenthood v. Casey* 93
  I. *Roe* and Its Background 93
  Briefs 98
    Roe's Brief (1971) 98
    Texas's Brief (1971) 102
  Oral Argument (1971) 104
  Oral Reargument (1972) 107
  The Opinion (1973) 109

  II. Developments after *Roe* 112
  Briefs 121
    Planned Parenthood's Brief 121
    Pennsylvania's Brief 125
  Oral Argument 129
  The Opinion 132
  Postscript 143

4 Hate Speech and Cross Burning: *R.A.V. v. City of St. Paul* and
Virginia v. Black 147
  I. Background to *R.A.V.* 147
  Briefs 155
    R.A.V.'s Brief 155
    St. Paul's Brief 157
  Oral Argument 159
  The Opinion 163

  II. Post–*R.A.V.* Developments 170
  Briefs 177
    Virginia's Brief 177
    Respondent's Brief 182
    Virginia's Reply Brief 187
  Oral Argument 187
  Opinions 193

5 Campaign Finance Regulation and Freedom of Speech: *McConnell
v. Federal Election Commission* 201
  Briefs 214
    Senator McConnell's Brief 214
    Brief for the Federal Election Commission 222

Oral Argument 231
The Opinion 235

6 Peyote Use and Religious Freedom: *Employment Div., Dept. of Human Resources of Oregon v. Smith* (co-authored with Jared Mellott) 249
    Briefs 259
        Oregon's Brief 259
        Smith's Brief 263
    Oral Argument 265
    The Opinion 270
    Postscript 276

Index 285
About the Author 297

Preface

The standard textbook on constitutional law assumes that the United States Constitution is best understood as a set of Supreme Court decisions. *Constitutional Debate in Action* is a series of textbooks that adopts a different premise without denying the value of the traditional approach. At a minimum, the orthodox casebook insightfully shows how the Constitution, from 1789 to the present, has evolved as Supreme Court justices have transformed constitutional doctrine. Yet, it is indisputable that such a text does not capture all the aspects of the U.S. Constitution that deserve to be considered. It is not, for example, especially illuminating in regard either to the process of constitutional adjudication itself or to the surrounding political context of any particular case. The Constitution is presented as what the justices say it is, but the political and intellectual forces that directly shape Supreme Court decisions are often ignored or deemphasized. The result is that doctrinal sophistication is often purchased at the expense of the student's understanding of the nature of constitutional adjudication. The student knows a lot of constitutional law, but he or she knows less about how and why it has grown. *Constitutional Debate in Action* tries to rectify this imbalance by viewing constitutional interpretation as an institutionalized form of debate by which litigants and their lawyers press their political demands and arguments upon the Supreme Court. It is in this fashion, in the wider context of human wants, passions, and values, that judges interpret the Constitution and thereby transform the basic framework of our government and society.

The more political and process-oriented view of the Constitution that is articulated in *Constitutional Debate in Action* has several distinctive features. First, breadth is sacrificed for depth. A case-study approach is used, and therefore this volume explores in depth only eight landmark decisions. Second, each chapter begins with an introduction that describes the legal background as well as the political context. Relevant out-of-courtroom discussions of the constitutional issue in question are excerpted and highlighted in "boxes" set off from the text. These materials will help the student appreciate the political context in which the Supreme Court is operating and assess the degree to which political factors are influencing constitutional adjudication.

The series, however, does not ignore the relevant legal arguments. Rather, it gives a great deal of attention to the process of constitutional argumentation by including sources that deserve more attention than traditional casebooks have given to them: the legal briefs filed in landmark cases and the corresponding oral arguments made before the Supreme Court. These materials, if properly presented, are pedagogically useful.[1] First, the adversarial character of the briefs and oral argument awakens student interest. Students want to figure out for themselves which side has the better argument. And, in general, the time spent reading the briefs is time well spent. The adversarial character of the American approach to constitutional adjudication more or less assumes that the best legal arguments find their way into the actual briefs of the cases, and, in the main (though not always), this assumption is borne out by the quality of the arguments found in the briefs.

As students compare the validity of the opposing arguments in the briefs, they are, in effect, preparing themselves for what comes next: a critical evaluation of the Supreme Court opinion itself. In each chapter, the edited opinion follows the briefs and oral argument. The students, in short, do a lot of thinking about the issues before they have to consider what the Court has said. They are, for this reason, more inclined to analyze, dissect, and digest the opinion than merely to read and summarize it. In this way, reading the briefs and oral arguments not only provides insight into the process of constitutional adjudication, but also encourages students to adopt a more critical perspective on the role that the Supreme Court plays in our constitutional democracy. Is it a court of law? Is it a political policymaker? Is it a little of both? *Constitutional Debate in Action* is designed to underline the significance of these questions by including materials that reveal the important but ambiguous role of the Supreme Court.

Most chapters end with a postscript that briefly describes important developments of constitutional doctrine since the Court decided the landmark case. They are not meant to be comprehensive or detailed discussions. Instead, their primary purpose is to reaffirm the significance of the landmark decision itself. They show how such cases illustrate important moral, constitutional, and philosophical issues that will, in various guises, constantly reappear in our constitutional democracy.

Though *Constitutional Debate in Action* embodies a somewhat novel approach to teaching constitutional law, it is not intended to replace the more orthodox casebook approach but rather to complement it. It is possible to use the series as the main text in a course on American constitutional law, but any particular volume of the series can also function as a supplemental text for a course taught in the traditional manner. The virtue of such a supplement is that it gives students a different perspective from that of the main text. Most casebooks challenge the best students and frequently intimidate the rest. Page after page of abstract and complicated judicial reasoning is often too much for them. A change of pace is at times useful if not necessary. This series was designed with this need in mind. It will enable any class on constitutional law, no matter what major text is being used, to pause occasionally throughout the term to take a closer look—a look from a different perspective—at a landmark case. Such a supplement can improve student morale in a valuable way.

The assumption of this text is that constitutional argumentation before the Supreme Court takes place within a broad political context. In many of the cases that come before the Court, litigants representing distinct political agendas press their claims and arguments. However, not just anyone can litigate before the Court because there are rules that limit access to all courts. Rules governing *ripeness* and *mootness* concern the nature of the "case or controversy" under litigation, whereas *standing* has more to do with the nature of the parties. Courts, including the Supreme Court, will address only "live" controversies. If a dispute has not yet "ripened" or if it has, for whatever reason, resolved itself (become "moot"), then courts—including the Supreme Court—will refuse to hear it. In a similar way, "standing" requires the litigant to have "a sufficient personal interest" in the issue before the Court. Physical injury or economic damage clearly suffices for standing, but courts can deny access to others, not on the ground that the issue is not a "live" one, but rather because the person initiating the suit has not shown that he or she has been sufficiently harmed. The law governing ripeness, mootness, and standing is composed of complicated rules that limit the character of judicial policymaking, including the sort of policymaking inherent in constitutional adjudication.[2] Nevertheless, many litigants representing distinct political agendas satisfy the criteria of these rules, thereby insuring that the Supreme Court plays a political role in the process of constitutional argumentation.

For practical purposes, constitutional argumentation before the Court begins with "the rule of four." Whether the case is coming from the lower federal courts or from a high state court, the party appealing to the Supreme Court must convince four justices to review the case. Throughout most of its history, the Supreme Court has had no lack of cases from which it could pick and choose. At the present time, more than 7,000 cases are appealed to the Supreme Court each year, and the Court hands down decisions with full opinions in only 75 to 90 cases. Therefore, because the Court has so many cases to choose from, it controls its own docket. Though political and institutional factors at times limit the Court's discretion, it is nonetheless true that the Court decides only those cases that four justices want it to decide.

Once the case is accepted for review, the petitioner (who filed the case at the Supreme Court) and the respondent (who answers) submit their constitutional arguments in written briefs. Soon thereafter both sides present their arguments orally in front of the justices. In addition, the Court often permits "friends of the court" (*amici curiae*) to submit briefs and participate in oral argument. These "friends" are individuals, groups, or organizations that are interested in the litigation. The number of *amici* briefs filed varies enormously from case to case and the degree to which they influence the Court is largely unknown. However, the fact that American constitutional adjudication tolerates, if it does

not encourage, the participation of interested third parties is not without significance. It highlights the political aspect of the constitutional process.

After reading the briefs and listening to the oral argument, the justices discuss
the case at a weekly conference and cast their initial votes. Each justice has one
vote. If the chief justice votes with the majority, he or she has the privilege of
deciding which member of the majority should write the majority opinion. If
the chief justice votes in the minority, then the most senior judge in the majority
makes the opinion assignment. However, not all decisions produce a majority
opinion. If a majority of the justices decide in favor of the petitioner but cannot
agree upon an opinion, the result is a plurality opinion or opinions. Moreover,
any justice who agrees with the majority can also write his or her own concurring opinion. Justices who disagree with the majority or the plurality can either
join a dissenting opinion or dissent separately.

In short, every individual justice is free to join any opinion or write one of
his or her own. Therefore, the initial vote at conference is not decisive. The
justices are perfectly free to change their minds. Hence there is often a great
deal of fluidity in the voting as justices circulate, revise, and recirculate opinions
and dissents. What started out as a majority opinion may end up as a dissenting
opinion; a dissent can become the majority opinion. Consequently, the meaning and significance of a decision depends not upon the initial vote but rather
upon how the justices vote when the decision (with any concurring and dissenting opinions) is handed down. The more consensus there is on the Court, the
more definite the meaning of the decision and the greater its potential significance.

An analysis of a Supreme Court case, including those that follow in this
series, requires paying attention to a number of different factors. First, the facts
of a case should be noted: who did what to whom, when, why, how, and
where? What were the political, social, and economic contexts of the litigation?
Second, who are the parties to the litigation? Who initiated the lawsuit against
whom? How did the lawsuit fare in the lower courts? Who is appealing to the
Supreme Court? Third, what are the legal issues of the case and the arguments
on both sides of the question? Which side has the better argument? Why?
Fourth, are there any political influences operating on the Court? What are
they? Are they permissible influences, or do they undermine the legal character
of constitutional adjudication? Fifth, which side does the Supreme Court favor,
and what is the breakdown of the vote? How many concurring and dissenting
opinions are there? Sixth, how do the different justices justify their respective
positions? Which justification is best? Finally, what is your general evaluation
of how the Supreme Court has performed in the particular case under consideration?

Keeping these sorts of questions in mind while reading the following chapters, but at the same time keeping them distinct, will focus attention on the
relevant issues. The present volume is entitled *Civil Rights & Liberties*. It highlights constitutional issues involving racial discrimination, affirmative action,
abortion, hate speech and cross burning, campaign finance regulation and free

speech, and religious freedom. Any number of landmark cases could have been used to explore these important areas of constitutional law. I chose *Brown v. Board of Education, Regents of the University of California v. Bakke, Grutter v. Bollinger, Roe v. Wade, Planned Parenthood v. Casey, R.A.V. v. City of St. Paul, Virginia V. Black, McConnell v. Federal Election Commission,* and *Employment Division, Department of Human Resources of Oregon v. Smith* because they reveal, in an insightful way, how the American system of constitutional adjudication involves the constant interplay of politics and law. Other cases, it is true, could probably have served this purpose just as well, but this fact is not overly significant. The underlying assumption of *Constitutional Debate in Action* is that the question of which cases deserve attention is less important than a deeper awareness of the process of constitutional adjudication itself.

Author's note: Throughout this volume, double brackets indicate my insertions to quoted material. I used double brackets to differentiate these insertions from those made by the original authors of the briefs or opinions, which are enclosed in single brackets.

NOTES

1. Overly technical discussions and the large number of citations that are often found in legal briefs have been eliminated from the excerpts that follow. In addition, for the sake of producing a readable text, stylistic usages peculiar to legal briefs, as well as small grammatical errors and typos, have been adapted to standard English or corrected. The same policy was followed in regard to the "boxes" and the Supreme Court opinions.

2. For a more thorough discussion of these rules and others that limit access to courts, see Henry Abraham, *The Judicial Process,* 6th ed. (New York: Oxford University Press, 1993), chapter 9.

Acknowledgments

First and foremost, I would like to thank Dickinson College, in particular Neil Weissman, Provost and Dean of the College, for all the support I received while revising this series of constitutional law textbooks. It is a privilege to work at an institution that is committed to research and with an administration that honors that commitment so enthusiastically. Secondly, I would like to express my appreciation to all my colleagues in the Political Science Department. I've always been proud to be a member of this productive and conscientious group of wide-ranging iconoclasts. Also, my students deserve recognition, especially those who have ventured into my constitutional law classes. I am especially indebted to Jared Mellott ('04), who has ably assisted me throughout this project, to the point of co-authoring two chapters of the second volume. Jared epitomizes the qualities of Dickinson students that I admire so much: he is analytically very sharp; he works extremely hard; and he writes as if he were born with a pen (or perhaps today it is a keyboard) in his hand. I respect and admire him a great deal. I also wish to thank the professors who have, by using this series of texts in their classes, made this revised edition possible. Since she reviewed the series and advised Rowman & Littlefield to go forward with the project, I am especially grateful to Judith Failer of Indiana University. I owe more than I can say to Victoria Kuhn, the Staff Associate of Dickinson's Political Science Department. She has done so much for me over the years that I fear advancing age makes it impossible for me to balance the account. All that I can do is publicly acknowledge that I am hopelessly (and forever) in her debt. My children Katrina and Nathan, each in their own way, are inspirations for me, though my energy is obviously no longer a match for theirs. Patricia, my wife, has made this second edition possible by ways and means impossible to recount here, except to say that it is she who has kept my body and soul together.

I also wish to take this opportunity to once again thank those who supported my work on the first edition, in particular George Allan, Susan Nichols, Leon Fitts, Jeff Niemitz, Kim Lacy Rogers, and Sue Norman. The staffs at Dickinson Law School Library and Dickinson College Library, especially Tina Maresco and Natalia Chromiak, also provided valuable assistance. I am also very grateful to Bruce Butler ('90), Cindy Mather ('91), Michelle Quinn ('91), and Daniel DeArment ('93). These students helped me put the initial sample chapter together and were wonderful sounding boards for me while I worked on the first edition. For the many hours of typing and proofing that went into this series of textbooks, I gratefully recognize the contributions of Jennifer Williams ('92), Richard Schirmer ('92), Ann Marie Branson ('94), Marc Snyderman ('94), and Tim Grieco ('94). I am also indebted to the Mellon and the Dana Foundations for their support of the student work that went into this series of constitutional law textbooks. I want to thank Eugene Hickok, a friend and former Dickinson colleague, Gary Gildin, a member of the faculty of the Dickinson Law School of Penn State University, D. Grier Stephenson, of Franklin and Marshall College, and Philip B. Kurland and Gerhard Casper, the editors of *Landmark Briefs and Arguments of the Supreme Court of the United States*, published by University Publications of America. I often used this series while working on this project and the editors and the publisher have graciously allowed me to use their designations of which justices asked what questions during oral arguments. In the same vein, I want to thank all those who gave me permission to use copyrighted material.

CHAPTER 1

Racial Discrimination

Brown v. Board of Education
347 U.S. 483 (1954)

Brown v. Board of Education, which declared racial segregation in public education unconstitutional, is arguably the most important and controversial Supreme Court decision of the twentieth century. Before *Brown,* relying upon *Plessy v. Ferguson* (1896), southern and certain border states had confidently assumed that racial segregation complied with the Fourteenth Amendment's Equal Protection Clause. A whole way of life was based upon this "separate-but-equal" principle.

In earlier decisions, the Supreme Court had accepted the legitimacy of "separate but equal," but had not explicitly addressed the constitutionality of racially segregated public education until it ruled that it was "inherently unequal" in *Brown.* Though the decision only required desegregation of public schools "with all deliberate speed," later decisions prohibited all forms of public segregation, from public beaches to public golf courses,[1] and charged southern school boards with "the affirmative duty" to "integrate" their schools with "a plan that promises realistically to work, and promises realistically to work *now.*"[2] During the 1960s, to some extent inspired by what the Supreme Court had done, Congress enacted a range of civil rights laws that ushered in a significantly better, though far from perfect, era of racial equality. Rarely, if ever, has the Supreme Court accomplished so much by its decisions and example.

But the Supreme Court's success in *Brown* is what has produced the controversy. Under what conditions should the Supreme Court revolutionize society by revolutionizing constitutional law and legal precedent? When should the Court compel fundamental changes in society as it adapts the constitutional norms inherited from the past to newly emerging attitudes and perspectives? This is the ultimate question that *Brown* poses.

In 1896, the Supreme Court handed down *Plessy v. Ferguson,* a decision that affirmed the constitutionality of a Louisiana law that required "separate but equal" accommodations for Caucasian and African-American railway passengers. In his majority opinion in *Plessy*, Justice Henry Brown endorsed several propositions that were hotly denied by Justice John Harlan in his famous dissent. First, though Brown admitted that the Fourteenth Amendment's purpose was to "enforce absolute equality of the two races before the law," he claimed that the amendment was not intended to abolish all legal racial distinctions. A racial classification was constitutional, even if it segregated the races, if the treatment was equal and the law was "enacted in good faith for the promotion of the public good, and not for the annoyance or oppression of a particular class." Moreover, Brown reasoned, when a legislature is evaluating the utility of segregation, it may "act with reference to the established usages, customs, and traditions of the people." Accordingly, if a legislature decided to enforce racial segregation for the comfort and safety of both races, the law did not stamp African-Americans with "a badge of inferiority" unless they chose "to put that construction upon it."[3]

Justice Harlan's dissent in *Plessy* totally rejected the assumptions of Brown's defense of the constitutionality of segregation. The Constitution, he insisted, "is colorblind, and neither knows nor tolerates classes among citizens." Racial classifications were therefore unconstitutional per se. Any idea that segregation could be justified on the ground that it served the interests of both races was ludicrous. "Everyone knows that the statute in question had its origin in the purpose, not so much to exclude white persons from railroad cars occupied by blacks, as to exclude colored people from coaches occupied by or assigned to white persons." In this way, segregation placed "a badge of servitude wholly inconsistent with the civil freedom and the equality before the law established by the Constitution. It cannot be justified upon any legal ground." Moreover, Harlan predicted, the results of segregation would be exceedingly unfortunate because the "destinies of the two races . . . are indissolubly linked together, and the interests of both require that the common government of all shall not permit the seeds of race hate to be planted under the sanction of law." The Constitution had to be "colorblind," in Harlan's opinion, if this country was to have any chance of achieving racial peace and harmony.[4]

Harlan's understanding of American race relations eventually triumphed in *Brown v. Board of Education*, but the road to victory was long and slow. The National Association for the Advancement of Colored People (NAACP), in particular its legal arm, the Legal Defense and Educational Fund (LDF), did not formulate its controversial strategy to attack segregation through litigation until the 1930s. The strategy was based on Nathan Margold's recommendation that the attack on segregation in education should be an indirect one. The NAACP should not claim that segregated schools were unequal per se, but should rather bring suits demanding that separate schools be equalized. Since black schools, from the physical plant to the quality of the curriculum, were notoriously unequal to those of whites, Margold calculated that these kinds of suits would have a greater chance of success than those directly challenging the constitutionality of segregation. Victory would give state officials the difficult choice of integrating education or upgrading the black schools. Margold believed that eventually the latter option would prove too costly. The goal of integration would be achieved, but by the indirect means of insisting upon educational institutions for African-Americans that were truly "separate but equal" to those attended by whites.

Since few southern states provided any professional schools for African-Americans, the NAACP first focused on state graduate schools. It was, of course, impossible for the states to claim that a nonexistent black professional school was equal to its functioning white counterpart. In *Missouri ex rel. Gaines v. Canada* (1938), the NAACP claimed that Missouri was denying African-Americans "equal protection" because it had no public black law school within its borders.[5] The Supreme Court agreed, ruling that Missouri had to provide "facilities for legal education substantially equal to those which the State there offered for persons of the white race."[6] If such facilities were not available, Gaines had to be admitted to the white law school.

In *Sweatt v. Painter* (1950), the Court took a huge step beyond *Gaines* by ruling that the University of Texas Law School had to admit African-Americans even though the state had recently established a black law school.[7] According to Chief Justice Fred Vinson's opinion, not only was the white law school superior in "terms of the faculty, variety of courses and opportunity for specialization, size of the student body, scope of the library, availability of law review and similar activities," it also possessed "to a far greater degree those qualities which are incapable of objective measurement but which make for greatness in a law school. Such qualities, to name but a few, include reputation of the faculty, experience of the administration, position and influence of the alumni, standing in the community, traditions and prestige."[8] By focusing on such intangible factors, the Supreme Court came close to denying to the states the option of creating separate black professional schools. Since no *new* black professional school could ever match the traditions and prestige of the white one, states had little choice but to integrate such schools.

Oklahoma reacted to the trend of Supreme Court decisions by forcing an African-American, newly admitted to a white professional school, to sit apart from the other students in classrooms, the library, and the cafeteria. The student attended the same school as his white peers, but the school itself was internally segregated. The Court addressed the constitutionality of this practice in *McLaurin v. Oklahoma* (1950). It ruled that such a form of segregated professional education did not satisfy the requirements of equal protection because the African-American student "is handicapped in his pursuit of effective graduate instruction. Such restrictions impair and inhibit his ability to study, to engage in discussions and exchange views with other students, and, in general, to learn his profession."[9] Accordingly, by 1950 it was difficult to imagine any form of segregated professional education that could be truly equal in the eyes of the Supreme Court. Moreover, in *McLaurin*, the Court had said that racial

segregation could have a pernicious effect upon minority educational performance—a key admission that the NAACP used in their argument in *Brown*.

During the 1940s and 1950s, Thurgood Marshall, who later became the first
African-American to serve on the Supreme Court, directed the attack on segregation in professional education. In this capacity, he played a pivotal role in the
decision to abandon the Margold strategy when the NAACP turned its attention to public primary and secondary education. First, pursuing the Margold
strategy at the level of public school would have necessitated thousands of lawsuits against individual school districts, each suit demanding that the separate
schools be made truly equal—a task far beyond the limited resources of the
LDF. In contrast, a direct attack on the constitutionality of state segregation
statutes would require only a few test cases. Second, equalization suits might
not bring about integration. It seemed probable, if not likely, that some of the
southern and border states would be willing to pay the price for equal segregation. Third, by 1950 the climate of public opinion had changed considerably
since the 1930s. African-Americans, especially those within the NAACP, felt it
was time to condemn segregation explicitly rather than to undermine it indirectly through financial pressure. Even many white Americans were embar-
rassed by the continuation of racial segregation in the United States, the
purported leader of the "free world" after World War II. Reflecting this evolving political climate, Marshall decided that the time for a direct attack on segregation had come.

Though the Supreme Court had never explicitly affirmed the constitutionality of segregated public education, it had endorsed the basic principle several
times. Hence, the NAACP was trying to overturn a body of legal precedent,
and the way of life sheltered by it, that had survived and flourished under the
Constitution for generations. How could something be unconstitutional if its
constitutionality had been upheld by the Supreme Court for the last sixty
years? Marshall's solution to this paradox relied, in part, upon social science.
He tried to convince judges to overturn sixty years of precedent by constructing a sociological argument "proving" that separate but equal education produced within minority students "feelings of inferiority" that prevented them
from realizing their true potential.

Relying on this social-science argument, Marshall and the other attorneys
from the LDF introduced testimony from social scientists at the district court
level.[10] This testimony purported to show that segregated public schools caused
serious harm to African-American children. Of all the scientists who testified,
Kenneth B. Clark, who authored "Effect of Prejudice and Discrimination on
Personality Development," a report he prepared for the Midcentury White
House Conference on Children and Youth in 1950, had the greatest impact.[11]
He testified at three of the trials and recruited other social scientists to testify
that science had proven the harmful character of segregation. Clark himself
used a "doll test" that, in his judgment, showed how segregation caused young
African-American children to distort their own racial identity. After getting the
children to identify white and black dolls that were identical in every other

Box 1.1   KENNETH CLARK'S DOLL TEST

. . . I found that of the children between the ages of six and nine whom I tested, which were a total of sixteen in number, that ten of those children chose the white doll as their preference; the doll which they liked best. Ten of them also considered the white doll a "Nice" doll. And, I think you have to keep in mind that these dolls are absolutely identical in every respect except skin color. Eleven of these sixteen children chose the brown doll as the doll which looked "bad." . . . It may also interest you to know that only one of these children, between six and nine, dared to chose the white doll as looking bad. . . . My opinion is that a fundamental effect of segregation is basic confusion in the individuals and their concepts about themselves conflicting in their self images. That seemed to be supported by the results of these sixteen children. . . . Seven of them, when asked to pick the doll that was like themselves; seven of them picked the white doll. This must be seen as a concrete illustration of the degree to which the pressures which these children sensed against being brown forced them to evade reality—to escape the reality which seems too over-burdening or too threatening to them. . . .

The conclusion which I was forced to reach was that these children in Clarendon County, like other human beings who are subjected to an obviously inferior status in the society in which they live, have been defi-nitely harmed in the development of their personalities; that the signs of instability in their personalities are clear, and I think that every psycholo-gist would accept and interpret these signs as such. . . .

Source: Taken from Clark's testimony in *Briggs v. Elliot*

respect, he would ask the children which was the "nice" doll, which was the doll that "looked bad," and which was the most "like" them. He summarized the results of this test in the testimony that he gave in the lower-court case from South Carolina: *Briggs v. Elliott* (see box 1.1). The test showed, in his judgment, that segregation caused African-American children to accept negative racial ste-reotypes, thereby forcing them to escape from reality by denying their own racial identity.

Edmond Cahn, a professor of law, later criticized Clark's "doll test," claim-ing that it proved little, if anything, and questioned whether social science could or should be the basis for a Supreme Court decision outlawing segregation. In his judgment, the social sciences were "very young, imprecise, and changeful." Their findings therefore had "an uncertain expectancy of life." Accordingly, it was inappropriate to base our "fundamental rights" upon the "latest fashions of psychological literature." After all, the constitutional guarantee of equal pro-tection embodied the principle of equality that has, starting with Justice Harlan's dissent in *Plessy*, slowly become "firmly established" in the American mind. Hence, according to Cahn, segregation was unconstitutional not because it could be shown that it harmed African-Americans, but because it conflicted with evolving moral standards (see box 1.2).

What do you think of Clark's doll test? Is it a valid test? What does it prove? If you were an NAACP attorney involved in the fight for desegregation, would you have introduced Clark's testimony at the trial? What about Cahn's claim that social science is an inadequate basis for fundamental rights? What does he mean? Does the evolving moral consensus of the American people provide a better foundation for fundamental rights? Why? Does it have a more permanent character than the conclusions of social science? Should courts base their decisions on this evolving consensus? What is the relationship of this consensus to the written Constitution and earlier legal precedents? Is the Supreme Court a court of law or of morality?

The southern states that were defending the constitutionality of segregation discounted the significance of the social-science evidence that the NAACP relied upon. They questioned both its credibility and its relevance. It had no bearing, in their opinion, on whether "separate but equal" educational facilities satisfied constitutional requirements. Nonetheless, in *Davis v. County School Board of Prince Edward County*, the desegregation case from Virginia, the state's attorneys produced their own social-science experts who defended the utility of segregated public education. The most prominent witness was Henry Garrett, chairman of the psychology department of Columbia University, who testified that

> in the high school of Virginia, if the Negro child had equal facilities, his own teachers, his own friends, and a good feeling, he would be more likely to develop pride in himself as a Negro, which I think we would all like to see him do—to develop his own potentialities, his sense of duty, his sense of art, his sense of histrionics. . . . They would develop their sense of dramatic art, and music, which they seem to have a talent for—[and] athletics, and they would say, "We prefer to remain as a Negro group." . . .[12]

Garrett's testimony, of course, sharply conflicted with the views of Clark and the other social scientists who claimed that segregation reinforced negative black stereotypes. His testimony clearly implied that integration would endanger African-American racial identity and pride, while segregation would contribute to the formation of both.

The NAACP brief filed in *Brown* in 1952 focused upon the harmful effects of segregation. It noted, for example, that the three-judge district court that had upheld Kansas's segregation statute had nevertheless found (Finding of Fact #8) that segregation harmed the educational development of African-American children. Moreover, the NAACP took the unusual step of attaching (in the form of an appendix) "a social science statement" on the "effects of segregation and the consequences of desegregation." Kenneth Clark, along with two associ-

Box 1.2   EDMOND CAHN'S CRITICISM OF CLARK'S DOLL TEST

. . . We are not provided here with any proof of the numerical adequacy of the sampling [of Clark's doll test] or of its being a representative cross-section. . . .

Moreover, if one follows the arithmetic in Professor Clark's testimony—which is not easy for me—some of his interpretations seem to be predetermined. For example, if Negro children say a *brown* doll is like themselves, he infers that segregation has made them conscious of race; yet if they say a *white* doll is like themselves, he infers that segregation has forced them to evade reality. . . .

. . . What is a "bad doll"? Some children might consider this a term of preference for play purposes: all little "mothers" love to rebuke and punish naughty dolls. Other children . . . would be simply bewildered by the sudden, unexpected introduction of moral or disciplinary references . . . I hope the children asked themselves: Why must there be a "bad" doll at all? . . .

It is noteworthy that seven Negro children picked the white doll "when asked to pick the doll that was like themselves." Professor Clark leaps to infer that they were evading reality. This I doubt. . . . I gather that these seven children were among the ten who had previously chosen the white doll as "nice." Were they wrong, then, to claim that the white doll was very much "like themselves" because they too were "nice"? . . .

. . . Does it really matter whether the Supreme Court relies or does not rely on psychologists' findings? Does it make any practical difference?

I submit it does. In the first place, since the behavioral sciences are so very young, imprecise, and changeful, their findings have an uncertain expectancy of life. Today's sanguine asseveration may be canceled by tomorrow's new revelation—or new technical fad. It would be quite another thing to have our fundamental rights rise, fall, or change along with the latest fashions of psychological literature. Today the social psychologists—at least the leaders of the discipline—are liberal and egalitarian in basic approach. Suppose, a generation hence, some of their successors were to revert to the ethnic mysticism of the very recent past; suppose they were to present us with a collection of racist notions and label them "science." What then would be the state of our constitutional rights? . . .

Source: Taken from Edmond Cahn, "Jurisprudence," 30 *N.Y.U.L. Review* 150 (1955), pp. 163–67. Reprinted with permission of the *New York University Law Review.*

ates, wrote this summary of the evidence of the harmful effects of segregation, but thirty-five prominent social scientists signed it, thereby raising its visibility and credibility. The NAACP wanted the Court to believe that social science had proved, in effect, that it was not possible to implement the "separate-but-equal" doctrine of *Plessy* in public education. *Plessy* itself, the brief argued, did not have to be overruled. It, along with other precedents, only had to be interpreted narrowly, as a ruling that only justified segregation outside the area of public education. According to the NAACP, the Court could act upon the social-science evidence and outlaw segregation without overturning controlling legal precedents.

Kansas's brief disputed the NAACP's contention that segregation in public education could be invalidated without overruling *Plessy*. The majority in *Plessy* had in fact referred to segregation in public education as a form of segregation that did *not* imply "the inferiority of either race to the other." Hence, since the white and black schools were equal in Topeka, there was little doubt that Kansas was in compliance with the Fourteenth Amendment. It is true that the local district court had found that segregation was "detrimental" to African-American children, but that conclusion did not mean that the state was discriminating against the racial minority. White children too might be better off in an integrated school. The Fourteenth Amendment, however, only prohibits racial discrimination; it does not require the state to provide the best education possible. Separate-but-equal schools treated the races equally. They were nondiscriminatory and therefore compatible with the Equal Protection Clause.

During the oral argument of 1952, it became clear that the NAACP's tactic of distancing *Plessy* (and other precedents) from segregation in public education failed to impress certain members of the Supreme Court. Felix Frankfurter tried to get Robert Carter, the NAACP attorney, to admit that he was asking the Court to overturn sixty years of precedent. Justice Hugo Black wondered what would happen if lower district courts, located in different parts of the country, came to conflicting assessments of the social-science evidence? Justice Harold H. Burton wanted to know if it was possible that the country's "social and economic conditions and personal relations" had changed so much in the last seventy-five years that what was a valid interpretation of the Constitution then would no longer be valid today.

When the justices met in conference in December of 1952, they quickly discovered there was no consensus. Four of the justices—Hugo Black, William O. Douglas, Harold Burton, and Sherman Minton—were willing to vote immediately to overturn *Plessy*, but Justice Reed indicated that he would affirm the constitutionality of segregation. The other four justices—Chief Justice Fred M. Vinson, Tom Clark, Robert Jackson, and Felix Frankfurter—were undecided. Given the divided character of the Court, Frankfurter urged delay. The issue of segregation was just too important, he insisted, for the Court to speak with multiple voices. A 5–4 decision reversing *Plessy* would trigger widespread southern resistance to the decision. Such a result, in all likelihood, would not end segregation, but would instead only inflict a serious wound upon the prestige of the Court. Better to delay, Frankfurter reasoned, than to act precipitously.[13]

Frankfurter's plan, which the Court adopted, was to reargue the case the following year, requiring the litigants to address a series of questions concerning the historical intent of the Fourteenth Amendment and the remedial powers of the Supreme Court. It could be said that by following this course the justices were stalling, hoping that the additional year would enable some consensus to develop on the Court. An important question is whether the Court should ever engage in such tactical maneuvers when the constitutional rights of real people are at stake. Is it permissible for a justice who believes that segregation is unconstitutional to vote to delay a decision in a case because he or she is hoping for more consensus on the Court or for a more receptive political climate? Should such political factors influence how the Constitution is interpreted and applied?

In the brief it submitted to the Court the following year, the NAACP argued that the framers of the Fourteenth Amendment intended to outlaw segregation and that the specific intent of the Equal Protection Clause was to provide more protection to the newly freed slaves than what was provided by the Civil Rights Act of 1866. This statute originally contained a clause that forbade any "discrimination" in the civil rights of citizens based upon race, color, or previous condition of servitude. John A. Bingham, one of the leaders of the Radical Republicans, withdrew this clause in the House of Representatives, but he did so, the NAACP brief claimed, only because he believed that Congress did not have the authority to pass such a law in 1866. Hence, after the Civil Rights Act was enacted, Bingham turned immediately to the task of passing the Fourteenth Amendment, which accomplished the goal that Bingham thought Congress could not reach by means of ordinary legislation. Ratified in 1868, the amendment prohibited all forms of racial discrimination, including the kind of "discrimination" inherent in racial segregation of public education. The Jim Crow system of racial segregation arose later in the nineteenth century. Its obvious purpose was to place African-Americans in a subordinate position to whites in violation of the Fourteenth Amendment. Accordingly, the brief concluded, the historical intent of the Fourteenth Amendment and social-science evidence indicating that segregation harmed African-American children converged to form a convincing justification for overturning sixty years of bad precedent.

In response, Kansas and the other states involved in the desegregation litigation claimed that the Equal Protection Clause only protected certain fundamental rights listed in the Civil Rights Act of 1866. The right to an integrated public education was not included among this set of fundamental rights. In addition, the states pointed out that in 1868, the year the amendment was ratified, twenty-four of the thirty-seven states either allowed or required segregation of public schools. Second, at the time that Congress passed the amendment and sent it to the states for ratification, it permitted segregated schools in the District of Columbia. Those who formulated and ratified the Fourteenth Amendment therefore never intended to prohibit segregation in public schools. Since there was no such intent, the brief continued, it would conflict with the "basic theory of written constitutions" for the Supreme Court to overturn sixty years of legal precedent and thereby destroy a workable and valuable system of "separate but equal" public education. Certainly, the controversial claims of "experts" operating on the "frontiers of social science," the Kansas brief concluded, could not justify striking down the long line of precedents governing the constitutionality of segregation in public education.

In the oral argument of 1953, two titans of American constitutional adjudication squared off: John W. Davis, a former president of the American Bar Association who had appeared before the Supreme Court many times during an illustrious career, represented South Carolina, while Thurgood Marshall, the director of the NAACP's effort to end segregated public education, argued the case for the LDF. Davis relied upon the weight of legal precedent supporting the principle of "separate but equal" public schools, rejecting the NAACP's claim that those who ratified the Fourteenth Amendment intended to prohibit segregation. He denigrated the idea that integration would help either African-American or white children, and closed his argument by referring to Aesop's fable about a dog who, while crossing a bridge with a piece of meat in his mouth, plunged for the shadow of meat in the water and lost both "substance and shadow." Marshall countered by emphasizing the irrationality of segregated schools. There was no legitimate reason why white and African-American children who played together should not go to school together. The real reason for segregation was racism—the belief that African-Americans were naturally inferior to whites. "They can't take race out of this case," Marshall insisted. Therefore, if the Court upheld segregation, it would be equivalent to upholding the validity of the Black Codes that southern states enacted after the Civil War, the codes that "the Fourteenth Amendment was intended to deprive the states of power to enforce."

During the fall of 1953, an event occurred that had a monumental impact on how the Supreme Court would ultimately respond to the question of the constitutionality of segregation. On September 8, Chief Justice Fred M. Vinson died of a heart attack. His death not only removed from the Court a justice who in all likelihood would have voted to uphold the constitutionality of segregated public education, it also made way for the appointment of Earl Warren, the governor of California, as the new chief justice. Warren took his seat immediately on an interim basis, pending his confirmation by the Senate early the following year. Warren had no doubt that segregation had to end. "I don't remember," he said twenty years later, "having any great doubts about which way it should go. It seemed to me a comparatively simple case. . . . On the merits, the natural, the logical, and practically the only way the case could be decided was clear."[14]

A unanimous decision overturning *Plessy* was Warren's goal, which he achieved by the force of his personality and by carefully crafting an opinion that was, in his own words, "short, readable by the lay public, non-rhetorical, unemotional and, above all, non-accusatory."[15] By May 1954, Reed was the only justice who still planned to write a dissent, but Warren won him over by appealing to his basic patriotism. "Stan," Warren reportedly said, "you're all by yourself in this now. You've got to decide whether it's really the best thing for the country."[16] Reed, knowing that even a lone dissent would encourage southern opposition and resistance to the decision, placed aside his own constitutional convictions and joined those with whom he disagreed. It is difficult to say whether Reed acted properly by deferring to his colleagues in *Brown*. It may be true that a dissent in *Brown* would have served no useful purpose, that it would only have encouraged harmful but ultimately futile opposition to the Court's decision, but should Supreme Court justices not ignore such political consequences as they go about their job of interpreting the Constitution?

Warren's desire not to antagonize the South precluded a rhetorical justification for overturning racial segregation in public schools. The historical analysis of the intent of the Fourteenth Amendment was set aside as "inconclusive." The precedent of *Plessy v. Ferguson* was formally confined to transportation. To decide the constitutionality of segregation, Warren insisted, the Court had to look to the evolving role of education in American society and "to the effect of segregation itself on public education." In regard to these two issues, Warren responded that education was today "the most important function of state and local governments." No child "may reasonably be expected to succeed in life if he is denied the opportunity of an education." Moreover, whatever the "extent of psychological knowledge at the time of *Plessy v. Ferguson*," today we know that segregated public schools are "inherently unequal."[17] To justify the view that segregation harmed African-Americans, Warren cited Kenneth Clark and a number of other social scientists in Footnote 11 (see page 33, footnote 19)—one of the most famous footnotes in the history of the Supreme Court. The conclusion was that segregation violated the Equal Protection Clause of the Fourteenth Amendment.

Critics of the decision questioned why the Court relied so heavily on what was beyond its expertise. Perhaps education was more important in 1954 than in 1896, but is that a reason to invalidate sixty years of legal precedent? Perhaps a majority of today's psychologists/sociologists would agree that segregation harms African-American children, but do changes in social science require changes in constitutional law?[18] Why did Warren not refer to evolving American moral standards? Would it have been better for Warren to argue that segregation may have been constitutional in 1896, but that the country's evolving ideal of equality required a different answer in 1954? Would such an argument have been too "accusatory," implying that the southern Jim Crow society was immoral in the eyes of the broader American society? Would such a justification for invalidating segregation have been more convincing than the one used by Warren? More honest? Was it appropriate for Warren to let political factors influence the character of his justification in *Brown*? Given the political context, how would you have written the opinion?

Of course, despite the criticism of Warren's reasoning in *Brown*, the main point of contention remained the decision itself. Over a hundred congressmen from southern states signed a declaration that became known as *The Southern Manifesto*. This declaration condemned what the Supreme Court had done in *Brown* as a judicial abuse of power and an invasion of the rights of the states. Judges were substituting their own "personal political and social ideas for the established law of the land." As he entered the *Manifesto* into the Senate record, Senator Strom Thurmond from South Carolina condemned the "troublemakers" from the LDF who were interested in "the mixing of the races," and called upon the South to resist the decision that required the desegregation of public schools. However, Senator Wayne Morse from Oregon responded to Thurmond's charges. Describing May 17, 1954, the day the Supreme Court decided *Brown*, as an "historic" day, Morse praised the Court for finally ushering in an era of racial equality that had long ago been promised, but had not yet been fulfilled.

It is arguable that American race-relations was at a crossroads in 1954, and it is possible that the *Brown* decision was the crucial factor that inclined the country to take one direction rather than another. Though compliance with that decision was painfully slow, it nonetheless functioned as a symbol of hope for the emerging civil rights movement. In 1955, a young black clergyman, Martin Luther King, Jr., led a bus boycott in Montgomery, Alabama, after an African-American woman, Rosa Parks, had been arrested for sitting in the front white section of a municipal bus. Sit-in demonstrations, in which civil rights activists would refuse to leave privately owned restaurants and lunch counters that served only whites, spontaneously erupted around the country. Huge civil rights marches focused national attention on the problem of race. Finally, in 1964, the Civil Rights Act was passed. Prohibiting racial discrimination in public accommodations and employment, it was the most important piece of civil rights legislation enacted since Reconstruction. The Voting Rights Act of 1965 and the Civil Rights Act of 1968 (which prohibited discrimination in housing) followed. By 1968, the country was radically different from what it had been in 1954. Of course, the post-*Brown* era of race relations in the United States is not without its flaws and blemishes. Nevertheless, a revolution had occurred and *Brown v. Board of Education* played an important part in bringing it about.

BIBLIOGRAPHY

Bickel, Alexander. "The Original Understanding and the Segregation Decision," *Harvard Law Review* 69 (1955), pp. 1–65.

Black, Charles. "The Lawfulness of the Segregation Decisions," *Yale Law Journal* 69 (1960), pp. 421–30.

Goodsman, Frank I. "De Facto School Segregation: A Constitutional and Empirical Analysis," *California Law Review* 60 (1972), pp. 275–437.

Hutchinson, Dennis J. "Unanimity and Desegregation: Decisionmaking in the Supreme Court, 1948–1958," *Georgetown Law Journal* 68 (1979), pp. 1–96.

Kluger, Richard. *Simple Justice* (New York: Vintage, 1977).

Pollak, Louis H. "Racial Discrimination and Judicial Integrity: A Reply to Professor Wechsler," *University of Pennsylvania Law Review* 108 (1959), pp. 1–34.

Wolters, Raymond. *The Burden of Brown* (Knoxville: University of Tennessee Press, 1984).

BRIEFS

LEGAL DEFENSE FUND'S BRIEF (1952)

. . . . A racial criterion is a constitutional irrelevance, and is not saved from condemnation even though dictated by a sincere desire to avoid the possibility of violence or race friction. . . .

It follows, therefore, that under this doctrine, the State of Kansas which by statutory sanctions seeks to subject appellants, in their pursuit of elementary education, to distinctions based upon race or color alone, is here attempting to exceed the constitutional limits to its authority. . . .

The court below made the following Finding of Fact [[#8]]:

> Segregation of white and colored children in public schools has a detrimental effect upon the colored children. The impact is greater when it has the sanction of the law; for the policy of separating the races is usually interpreted as denoting the inferiority of the negro group. A sense of inferiority affects the motivation of a child to learn. Segregation with the sanction of law, therefore, has a tendency to retard the educational and mental development of negro children and to deprive them of some of the benefits they would receive in a racially integrated school system.

This finding is based upon uncontradicted testimony that conclusively demonstrates that racial segregation injures infant appellants in denying them the opportunity available to all other racial groups to learn to live, work and cooperate with children representative of approximately 90% of the population of the society in which they live; to develop citizenship skills; and to adjust themselves personally and socially in a setting comprising a cross-section of the dominant population. The testimony further developed the fact that the enforcement of segregation under law denies to the Negro status, power and privilege; interferes with his motivation for learning; and instills in him a feeling of inferiority resulting in a personal insecurity, confusion and frustration that condemns him to an ineffective role as a citizen and member of society. . . .

That these conclusions are the consensus of social scientists is evidenced by the appendix filed herewith. . . .

. . . *Plessy v. Ferguson* . . . is not controlling for the purpose of determining the state's power to enforce racial segregation in public schools. . . .

ROBERT L. CARTER,

SPOTTSWOOD W. ROBINSON, III,

THURGOOD MARSHALL,

CHARLES S. SCOTT,
Counsel for Appellants.

Appendix

*The Effects of Segregation and the Consequences of
Desegregation: A Social Science Statement*

. . . At the recent Midcentury White House Conference of Children and Youth, a fact-finding report on the effects of prejudice, discrimination and segregation on the personality development of children was prepared as a basis for some of the deliberations. This report . . . highlighted the fact that segregation, prejudices and discriminations, and their social concomitants potentially damage the personality of all children—the children of the majority group in a somewhat different way than the more obviously damaged children of the minority group.

The report indicates that as minority group children learn the inferior status to which they are assigned—as they observe the fact that they are almost always segregated and kept apart from others who are treated with more respect by the society as a whole—they often react with feelings of inferiority and a sense of personal humiliation. Many of them become confused about their own personal worth. . . . Under these conditions, the minority group child is thrown into a conflict with regard to his feelings about himself and his group. He wonders whether his group and he himself are worthy of no more respect than they receive. This conflict and confusion leads to self-hatred and rejection of his own group.

The report goes on to point out that these children must find ways with which to cope with this conflict. Not every child, of course, reacts with the same patterns of behavior. . . .

Some children, usually of the lower socio-economic classes, may react by overt aggressions and hostility directed toward their own group or members of the dominant group. Anti-social and delinquent behavior may often be interpreted as reactions to these racial frustrations. . . .

Middle class and upper class minority group children are likely to react to their racial frustrations and conflicts by withdrawl and submissive behavior. Or, they may react with compensatory and rigid conformity to the prevailing middle class values and standards and an aggressive determination to succeed in these terms in spite of the handicap of their minority status.

The report indicates that minority group children of all social and economic classes often react with a generally defeatist attitude and a lowering of personal ambitions. . . .

Many minority group children of all classes also tend to be hypersensitive and anxious about their relations with the larger society. They tend to see hostility and rejection even in those areas where these might not actually exist. . . .

The problem with which we have here attempted to deal is admittedly on the frontiers of scientific knowledge. Inevitably, there must be some differences of opinion among us concerning the conclusiveness of certain items of evidence, and concerning the particular choice of words and placement of emphasis in the preceding statement. We are nonetheless in agreement that this statement is substantially correct and justified by the evidence, and the differences among us, if any, are of a relatively minor order and would not materially influence the preceding conclusions. . . .

[[Signed by 32 social scientists.]]

BRIEF FOR THE STATE OF KANSAS (1952)

. . . Appellants suggest that the Plessy case is not applicable to the situation before us. Admittedly, the question presented in the Plessy case arose out of segregation of white and colored races in railroad cars and not segregation in the public schools. However, the decision of the Court rises above the specific facts in issue and announces a doctrine applicable to any social situation wherein the two races are brought into contact. In commenting upon the purpose and the limitations of the Fourteenth Amendment the Court makes the following statement [[in *Plessy*]]:

> The object of the Amendment was undoubtedly to enforce the absolute equality of the two races before the law, but in the nature of things it could not have been intended to abolish distinctions based upon color, or to enforce social, as distinguished from political, equality, or a commingling of the two races upon terms unsatisfactory to either. Laws permitting and even requiring their separation in places where they are liable to be brought into contact do not necessarily imply the inferiority of either race to the other, and have been generally, if not universally, recognized as within the competency of the state legislatures in the exercise of their police power. The most common instance of this is connected with the establishment of separate schools for white and colored children which has been held to be a valid exercise of the legislative power even by courts of States where the political rights of the colored race have been longest and most earnestly enforced.

Certainly this language refutes appellants' contention that the Plessy case has no application to these facts. . . .

It is undoubtedly true that the separate but equal doctrine is susceptible of abuse. In many instances it has resulted in a separate and unequal rule in practice. However, it is the impossibility of equality under such a doctrine, and not the difficulty of administering and applying the same with equality, that would make such a doctrine unconstitutional *per se*. The situation in Topeka is one where substantial equality has been reached. Such was the finding of the Court below and such is apparently conceded by the appellants. These facts, under authority of decisions heretofore reviewed, compel an inescapable conclusion: Neither the statute of Kansas nor the action of the appellee, Board of Education, offends the Fourteenth Amendment to the Federal Constitution. . . .

We call attention to the fact that the . . . Finding [[of Fact #8]] is couched only in broad and general language; it makes no specific or particular reference to any of the appellants, nor to the grade schools in Topeka, nor to racial groups other than Negroes, nor to inequality of educational opportunities between Negroes and other racial groups. The substance of the finding can be summarized in the following statement: "Generally speaking, segregation is detrimental to colored children, and deprives them of some benefits they would receive in a racial integrated school system." . . .

We believe the court intended the finding to mean simply that colored children would be better off in integrated schools than they are in segregated schools. Conceding that that is the meaning of the finding, it does not amount to a finding of actual discrimination against colored children and in favor of white children upon the facts in this case. White children are not permitted to attend integrated schools in Topeka. The mere fact, if it be a fact, that the Topeka school system could be improved so far as education of colored children is concerned, does not prove discrimination against them. . . .

> Respectfully submitted,
> HAROLD R. FATZER,
> Attorney General,
> State of Kansas.

ORAL ARGUMENT (1952)

MR. JUSTICE FRANKFURTER: . . . I do think we have to face in this case the fact that we are dealing with a long-established historical practice by the states, and the assumption of the exercise of power which not only was written on the statute books, but has been confirmed and adjudicated by state courts, as well as by the expressions of this Court.

MR. CARTER [[Legal Defense Fund Attorney]]: Well, Justice Frankfurter, I would say on that that I was attempting here to take the narrow position with regard to this case, and to approach it in a way that I thought the Court approached the decision in *Sweatt* and *McLaurin*. I have no hesitancy in saying to the Court that if they do not agree that the decision can be handed down in our favor on this basis, . . . [[then]] I have no hesitancy in saying that the issue of "separate but equal" doctrine should be squarely overruled. . . .

FRANKFURTER: Are you saying that we can say that "separate but equal" is not a doctrine that is relevant at the primary school level? Is that what you are saying?

MR. JUSTICE DOUGLAS: I think you are saying that segregation may be all right in street cars and railroad cars and restaurants, but that is all we have decided.

CARTER: That is the only place that you have decided that it is all right.

DOUGLAS: And that education is different, education is different from that.

CARTER: Yes, sir. . . .

FRANKFURTER: But how can that be your argument when the whole basis of dealing with education thus far has been to find out whether it, the "separate but equal" doctrine, is satisfied? . . .

*   *   *

MR. WILSON [[Kansas's attorney]]: . . . [[W]]e think the question before this Court is simply: Is the *Plessy* case and . . . the "separate but equal" doctrine still the law of the land? . . .

MR. JUSTICE BURTON: Don't you recognize it as possible that within seventy-five years the social and economic conditions and the personal relations of the nation may have been changed, so that what may have been a valid interpretation of them seventy-five years ago would not be a valid interpretation of them constitutionally today?

WILSON: We recognize that as a possibility. We do not believe that this record discloses any such change. . . .

*   *   *

CARTER: . . . What I meant to say was that this Court if they . . . agreed with the findings of fact [[#8]] of the court below, and came to the conclusion that the court below had correctly found the facts on its own independent examination, that this Court would—it would necessitate a reversal of that court's judgment. I do not mean that the findings of the court below come here and that you have to accept them. Of course, I do not agree with that.

MR. JUSTICE BLACK: Do you think that there should be a different holding here with reference to the question involved, according to the place where the segregation might occur, and if not, why do you say it depends—why do you say that it depends on the findings of fact at all? . . .

CARTER: I think I agree with the fact that the finding refers to the State of Kansas and to these appellants and to Topeka, Kansas. I think that the findings were made in this specific case referring to this specific case.

BLACK: In other words, if you are going to go on the findings, then you would have different rulings with respect to the places to which this applies; is that true?

CARTER: . . . We think that the court below did . . . what this Court did in *McLaurin* and *Sweatt*, and we think that in the examination of the equality of education offered, that what it did was it found that these restrictions imposed disabilities on Negro children and prevented them from having educational opportunities equal to white, and for these reasons we think that the judgment of the court below should be reversed and the Kansas statute should be struck down. . . .

*   *   *

MR. MOORE [[Virginia's attorney]]: . . . Now, the statement is made here . . . time after time [[that]] there is consensus of opinion among social scientists that segregation is bad. I was interested in the appendix which is signed by some 32 alleged social scientists who say that [the] appendix is out on the frontiers of scientific knowledge; that is the way they describe it. When you examine that appendix you find that five of the persons who signed that appendix were cross-examined in our case, and the appendix is really just an effort—I say this without any lack of respect—but it is just an effort to try to rehabilitate those gentlemen and add to it with some other persons. . . .

FRANKFURTER: Who are these specialists in that field?

MOORE: Well, they described them as sociologists, anthropologists, psychologists, and variations of those groups, principally, Your Honor.

FRANKFURTER: Everybody in the sociological field is an expert in his domain?

MOORE: That is right, Your Honor.

We say it does not mean a thing except as a matter of stating something in the abstract. You might as well be talking about the Sermon on the Mount or something like that, that it would be better—

FRANKFURTER: It is supposed to be a good document.

*   *   *

MR. JUSTICE REED: What if they decided to the contrary?

MOORE: You mean the trial court?

REED: The trial court; and your experts had not been so persuasive as they were, and there were other experts, and the trial court had accepted their conclusion that this was detrimental and was injurious to the ability of the Negro child to learn or of the white child to learn, and created difficulties; what difference does it make which way they decided this particular question?

MOORE: I think you can argue the matter two ways, Your Honor. I think, in the first place, you can argue that the difference, for instance, in the Kansas finding and the Virginia finding point up how important is the legislative policy that is involved. . . . It illustrates how it really is a policy question.

REED: I can understand that. But is it your argument that there are two sides to it?

MOORE: It illustrates there are two sides to it, and it points up that the real crux of the whole matter is that there is involved fundamentally a policy question for legislative bodies to pass on, and not for courts. . . .

BRIEFS

LEGAL DEFENSE FUND'S BRIEF (1953)

[[1. Segregation's Purpose]] . . . Segregation originated as a part of an effort to build a social order in which the Negro would be placed in a status as close as possible to that he had before the Civil War. The separate but equal doctrine furnished a base from which those who sought to nullify the Thirteenth, Fourteenth, and Fifteenth Amendments were permitted to operate in relative security. While this must have been apparent at the end of the last century, the doctrine has become beclouded with so much fiction that it becomes important to consider the matter in historical context to restore a proper view of its meaning and import. . . .

[[After the Civil War,]] control of the Republican Party passed to those who believed that the protection and expansion of their economic power could best be served by political conciliation of the southern irreconcilables, rather than by unswerving insistence upon human equality and the rights guaranteed by the post-war Amendments. In the 1870's those forces that held fast to the notion of the Negro's preordained inferiority returned to power in state after state, and it is significant that one of the first measures adopted was to require segregated schools on a permanent basis in disregard of the Fourteenth Amendment.

In 1877, out of the exigencies of a close and contested election, came a bargain between the Republican Party and the southern leaders of the Democratic Party which assured President Hayes' election, led to the withdrawal of federal troops from the non-redeemed states and left the South free to solve the Negro problem without apparent fear of federal intervention. This agreement preserved the pragmatic and material ends of Reconstruction at the expense of the enforcement of not only the Fourteenth Amendment but the Fifteenth Amendment as well. For it brought in its wake peonage and disfranchisement as well as segregation and other denials of equal protection. . . .

This is the historic background against which the validity of the separate but equal doctrine must be tested. History reveals it as a part of an overriding purpose to defeat the aims of the Thirteenth, Fourteenth, and Fifteenth Amendments. Segregation was designed to insure inequality—to discriminate on account of race and color—and the separate but equal doctrine accommodated the Constitution to that purpose. Separate but equal is a legal fiction. There never was and never will be any separate equality. Our Constitution cannot be used to sustain ideologies and practices which we as a people abhor. . . .

[[2. *Intent of the Fourteenth Amendment*]] . . . The men who wrote the Fourteenth Amendment were themselves products of a gigantic antislavery crusade which, in turn, was an expression of the great humanitarian reform movement of the Age of Enlightenment. This philosophy upon which the Abolitionists had taken their stand had been adequately summed up in Jefferson's basic proposition "that all men are created equal" and "are endowed by their Creator with certain unalienable Rights." . . .

The 39th Congress which was to propose the Fourteenth Amendment convened in December 1865 with the realization that, although slavery had been abolished, the overall objective, the complete legal and political equality for all men, had not been realized. This was dramatically emphasized by the infamous Black Codes being enacted throughout the southern states. . . .

The Black Codes, while they grudgingly admitted that Negroes were no longer slaves, nonetheless used the states' power to impose and maintain essentially the same inferior, servile position which Negroes had occupied prior to the abolition of slavery. These codes thus followed the legal pattern of the antebellum slave codes. Like their slavery forerunners, these codes compelled Negroes to work for arbitrarily limited pay; restricted their mobility; forbade them, among other things, to carry firearms; forbade their testimony in a court against any white man; and highly significant here, contained innumerable provisions for segregation on carriers and in public places. In at least three states these codes prohibited Negroes from attending the public schools provided for white children.

It was this inferior caste position which the Radical Republicans in Congress were determined to destroy. They were equally determined that by federal statutory or constitutional means, or both, Congress would not only invalidate the existing Black Codes but would proscribe any and all future attempts to enforce governmentally-imposed caste distinctions. . . .

[[In this effort, of great]] . . . importance was S.61, "A Bill to Protect All Persons in the United States in Their Civil Rights and Furnish the Means of Vindication." This bill, though introduced through Senator [[Lyman]] Trumbull in his capacity as Chairman of the Judiciary Committee, was in fact a measure sponsored by the entire Radical Republican majority.

The bill forbade any "discrimination in civil rights or immunities" among "the people of the United States on account of race, color, or previous condition of slavery." . . .

After two full days of debate, the Senate passed the Trumbull bill by a vote of 33 to 12. . . .

At this point, Representative [[John A.]] Bingham of Ohio . . . made a notable address to the House [[of Representatives]]. While admitting that perhaps Congress was at that time without constitutional authority to enact so sweeping a bill, he said it was nevertheless true that the bill as it stood was as sweeping as was charged by the Conservatives.

Representative Bingham then made it preeminently clear that he entirely approved of the sweeping objectives of the bill as it came from the Senate. His willingness to accept any modification of the bill was *solely* on the grounds of an overwhelming present constitutional objection which he himself was even then in the process of curing with a proposal for a constitutional amendment. . . . Bringham's prestige as a leader of the Radical Republican majority obliged [[James F.]] Wilson [[of Iowa]] to accept the Ohioan's interpretation. Consequently, the bill was returned to the Judiciary Committee and amended to eliminate the sweeping phrase "there shall be no discrimination in civil rights and immunities." . . .

The bill in its amended form was adopted by Congress and vetoed by President [[Andrew]] Johnson [[but Congress overrode the veto and the bill became the Civil Rights Act of 1866]]. . . .

It must be borne in mind that Representative Bingham, and those who supported his position on the amendment to the Civil Rights Bill of 1866, had already demonstrated that the constitutional amendment under consideration [["H.R.63"]] would be at least as comprehensive in its scope and effect as the original sweeping language of the Trumbull Civil Rights Bill *before* it was amended in the House and that it would be far broader than the scope of the bill as finally enacted into law. On this point, Bingham repeatedly made his intentions clear, both in his discussion on the power limitations on the Civil Rights Bill itself and in his defense of his early drafts of the proposed constitutional amendment. . . .

[[However, "H.R.63" soon "passed into the more extensive proposal which the Joint Committee brought forward at the end of April." In regard to this new "more extensive proposal,"]] . . . Bingham moved that the following be added as a new section of the amendment:

No state shall make or enforce any law which shall abridge the privileges or immunitites of citizens of the United States; nor shall any state deprive any person of life, liberty, or property without due process of law; nor deny to any person within its jurisdiction the equal protection of the laws.

This was substantially Bingham's earlier amendment, submitted to Congress in February as H.R.63 with the addition of the equal protection clause. . . .

On May 10, the House passed the Amendment without modification by a vote of 128 to 37. The measure then went to the Senate. . . .

Senator [[Jacob H.]] Howard [[of Michigan]], among others, asserted categorically that the effect of the due process and equal protection clauses of the Fourteenth Amendment would be to sweep away entirely all caste legislation in the United States. Certainly a number of Conservatives, notably Representative [[Andrew Jackson]] Rogers of New Jersey, a member of the Joint Committee, and Senator [[Garrett]] Davis of Kentucky, were convinced that the effect of the Amendment would be to prohibit entirely all laws classifying or segregating on the basis of race. They believed, and stated, that school laws providing separate systems for whites and Negroes of the kind which existed in Pennsylvania, Ohio, and in several of the Johnson-Reconstructed southern states would be made illegal by the Amendment. . . .

[[3. Conclusion.]] [[The]] . . . historical evidence surrounding the adoption, submission and ratification of the Fourteenth Amendment compels the conclusion that it was the intent, understanding and contemplation that the Amendment proscribed all state-imposed racial restrictions. The Negro children in these cases are arbitrarily excluded from state public schools set apart for the dominant white groups. Such a practice can only be continued on a theory that Negroes, *qua* Negroes, are inferior to all other Americans. The constitutional and statutory provisions herein challenged cannot be upheld without clear determination that Negroes are inferior and, therefore, must be segregated from other human beings. Certainly, such a ruling would destroy the intent and purpose of the Fourteenth Amendment and the very equalitarian basis of our Government. . . .

HAROLD BOULWARE
OLIVER W. HILL
SPOTTSWOOD W. ROBINSON II
ROBERT L. CARTER
THURGOOD MARSHALL
JACK GREENBERG
LOUIS REDDING
CHARLES S. SCOTT

BRIEF FOR THE STATE OF KANSAS (1953)

[[1. Intent of the 14th Amendment.]] . . . There can be no doubt that certain of the Abolitionist leaders demonstrated no tolerance for segregation. At the same time, there can be no doubt that they failed to impress their views upon the majority of their colleagues and to incorporate their philosophy into the legislation of Congress. Charles Sumner of Massachusetts, the most brilliant of them all, had long protested segregation. In 1850 he had urged to the Supreme Judicial Court of Massachusetts that segregation in the public schools of Boston violated the constitutional principle of "equality before the law." He failed, however, to make his point. In 1866, in a new forum, the United States Senate, he contended for a proposition that struck down "all laws and customs . . . establishing any oligarchical prejudices and any distinctions of rights on account of color or race." Doubtless, Sumner's view precluded segregation. But again his view did not prevail. The Fourteenth Amendment, as adopted by the Congress, did not approach Sumner's broad concept of equal protection. . . .

Scholars disagree as to whether all the guaranties of the first eight amendments were incorporated into the 14th Amendment, but they agree unanimously that Section I was intended to place the Civil Rights Bill of 1866 in the Constitution. Says [[Horace E.]] Flack:

> The very men who passed the Civil Rights Bill submitted the 14th Amendment, the first section of which practically incorporated that bill.

[[Charles]] Fairman points out that the Civil Rights Bill in turn rests on the concept of fundamental rights pronounced by Justice [[Bushrod]] Washington in *Corfield v. Coryell*. These were:

> . . . the protection of government, enjoyment of life and liberty, the right to acquire and possess property of all kinds, pursue happiness and safety, the right to move from state to state for trade, agricultural and professional pursuits, the right to the writ of habeas corpus, the right to institute and maintain suits in courts of law and not be subject to unfair taxes.

Thus, the Civil Rights Bill becomes especially significant. Its provisions were in part:

> . . . That all persons born in the United States and not subject to any foreign Power, . . . are hereby declared to be citizens of the United States; and such citizens . . . shall have the same right, in every State and Territory in the United States, to make and enforce contracts, to sue, be parties, and give evidence, to inherit, purchase, lease, sell, hold, and convey real and personal property, and to full and equal benefit of all laws and proceedings for the security of person and property, as is enjoyed by white citizens, and shall be subject to like punishment, pains, and penalties, and to none other. . . .

However liberally we may construe these provisions, we find no evidence that they were intended to preclude segregation. The authors were concerned with protecting personal security and personal rights and were not proposing that every person should enjoy the privilege of exercising those rights at the same time and in the same place and manner as every other citizen. Only in those areas where the safety of the individual and his property were jeopardized was the law to operate. . . .

In the somewhat incomplete debates in Congress as to the meaning of the guarantees of Section 1 of the proposed Fourteenth Amendment, there is nothing from which we can infer that the proponents intended to give it a broader meaning than to protect the basic and fundamental rights about which the abolitionists had spoken theretofore. Abolition of segregation was not one of these. It is significant, perhaps, that a majority of the members of Congress represented states where segregation in the public schools was practiced with sanction of law. The same statement is true of a majority of the members of the Joint Committee on Reconstruction. Had there been an intent to disturb a social pattern so firmly established we believe that that intent would have been reflected in the Congressional debates. . . .

[[2. Segregation in Washington, D.C. and the states.]] However persuasive may be the evidence thus far assembled, it is still circumstantial. It has been adduced by a process of analysis and inference. But there is other testimony that is positive and direct. We refer to the congressional acts establishing racial segregation in the public schools of the District of Columbia.

Congress has exclusive power to legislate for the District of Columbia. The 37th and 38th Congresses, in 1862 and 1864, established segregated public school systems in the District. The 39th Congress, at the very time that the Fourteenth Amendment was being debated, enacted laws to implement and expedite the administration of the segregated system of public schools. Measures specifically designed to end segregation in the District failed to pass in both the 41st and 42d Congresses.

It is hardly credible that the Congress would have disregarded a limitation that it intended to impose on the states. It is equally incredible that the Congress would have denied negro citizens of the District of Columbia rights that it sought to assure elsewhere in the country. . . .

. . . Our researches have disclosed that of the 37 states that comprised the Union at the time of adoption of the Fourteenth Amendment, 24 of them maintained legal segregation in the public schools at the time of adoption or subsequent thereto. In 10 states legislation providing for segregated schools was enacted by the same legislatures at the same sessions at which ratification was accomplished. This we deem positive evidence that none of those 24 states considered that segregation was abolished by the Fourteenth Amendment. . . .

[[3. Purpose of a Written Constitution.]] . . . [[The]] manifest understanding that the Fourteenth Amendment did not abolish segregation in the public schools and did not bring the schools within the scope of national authority precludes any possibility of an understanding that at some undetermined future time Congress or the Judiciary might without further grant of constitutional authority take from the states the power not intended to be granted. Such a suggestion is repugnant to the basic theory of written constitutions. . . .

It is not our intent to disregard the concept of a "living constitution," nor do we deny that changed conditions produce new factual situations and require new interpretations of constitutional provisions. However, it is our view that the present case presents neither a factual situation that did not exist at the time the amendment was adopted, nor a record that reveals a substantial change in the conditions surrounding the situation. It is a fact of history that racial segregation in the public schools was an established pattern in a majority of the states when the amendment was adopted. It is equally well established that there were repeated efforts in the Congress, contemporaneous with the adoption of the amendment, to enact legislation prohibiting segregation in the public schools. . . .

Thus, the record discloses neither new facts nor changed conditions. We have the same problem, the same arguments. To be sure, there is a variation in the language employed, and to the record has been added the somewhat speculative conclusions of a few individuals whose own assertion is that their theses are "admittedly on the frontiers of scientific knowledge." We feel that this court would be going far beyond the limits of the judicial power if, on the basis of such a record, it should reverse the trend of nearly ninety years and strike down a state statute that during all those years has been universally deemed a proper exercise of legislative power. It is not within the province of the federal judiciary to legislate, particularly beyond the limits of the federal constitution. . . .

Respectfully submitted,
HAROLD R. FATZER,
Attorney General.

ORAL ARGUMENT (1953)

MR. DAVIS [[South Carolina's attorney]]: . . . In Clarendon Schools District No. 1 in South Carolina, in which this case alone is concerned, there were in the last report that got into this record, something over a year or year and a half ago, 2,799 Negroes, registered Negro children of school age. There were 295 whites, and the state has now provided those 2,800 Negro children with schools as good in every particular. In fact, because of their being newer, they may even be better. There are good teachers, the same curriculum as in the schools for the 295 whites.

Who is going to disturb that situation: If they were to be reassorted or commingled, who knows how that could best be done? If it is done on the mathematical basis, with 30 children as a maximum, which I believe, is the accepted standard in pedagogy, you would have 27 Negro children and 3 whites in one school room. Would that make the children happier? Would they learn any more quickly? Would their lives be more serene?

Children of that age are not the most considerate animals in the world, as we all know. Would the terrible psychological disaster being wrought, according to some of these witnesses, to the colored child be removed if he had three white children sitting somewhere in the same school room? Would white children be prevented from getting a distorted idea of racial relations if they sat with 27 Negro children? . . .

You say that is racism. Well, it is not racism. Recognize that for 60 centuries and more humanity has been discussing questions of race and race tension, not racism. Say that we make special provisions for the aboriginal Indian population in this country; it is not racism. Say that the 29 states have miscegenation statutes now in force which they believe are of beneficial protection to both races. Disraeli said, "No man," said he, "will treat with indifference the principle of race. It is the key of history." . . .

Let me say this for the State of South Carolina. It does not come here, as Thad Stevens would have wished, in sack cloth and ashes. It believes that its legislation is not offensive to the Constitution of the United States, It is confident of its good faith and intention to produce equality for all of its children of whatever race or color. It is convinced that the happiness, the progress and the welfare of these children is best promoted in segregated schools. . . .

I am reminded—and I hope it won't be treated as a reflection on any-body—of Aesop's fable of the dog and the meat: The dog, with a fine piece of meat in his mouth, crossed a bridge and saw the shadow in the stream and plunged for it and lost both substance and shadow. Here is equal education, not promised, not prophesied, but present. Shall it be thrown away on some fancied question of racial prestige? . . .

*   *   *

MR. MARSHALL [[Legal Defense Fund Attorney]]: . . . I got the feeling [[on hearing the discussion]] yesterday that when you put a white child in a school with a whole lot of colored children, the child would fall apart or something. Everybody knows that is not true. Those same kids in Virginia and South Car-olina—and I have seen them do it—they play in the streets together, they play on their farms together, they go down the road together, they separate to go to school, they come out of school and play ball together. They have to be sepa-rated in school.

There is some magic to it. You can have them voting together, you can have them not restricted because of law in the houses they live in. You can have them going to the same state university and the same college, but if they go to ele-mentary and high school, the world will fall apart. . . .

They can't take race out of this case. From the day this case was filed until this moment, nobody has in any form or fashion, despite the fact I made it clear in the opening argument that I was relying on it, done anything to distinguish this statute from the Black Codes [[that]] . . . the Fourteenth Amendment was intended to deprive the states of power to enforce. . . . We charge that they are Black Codes. They obviously are Black Codes if you read them. They haven't denied that they are Black Codes, so if the Court wants to very narrowly decide this case, they can decide it on that point.

So whichever way it is done, the only way that this Court can decide this case in opposition to our position is that there must be some reason which gives the state the right to make a classification . . . in regard to Negroes; and we submit the only way to arrive at this decision is to find that for some reason Negroes are inferior to all other human beings. Nobody will stand in the Court and urge that, and in order to arrive at the decision that they want us to arrive at, there would have to be some recognition of a reason why of all the multitudinous groups of people in this country, you have to single out Negroes and give them this separate treatment.

. . . The only thing [[it]] can be is an inherent determination that the people who were formerly in slavery, regardless of anything else, shall be kept as near that stage as is possible; and now is the time, we submit, that this Court should make it clear that that is not what our Constitution stands for. . . .

THE OPINION

Mr. Chief Justice delivered the opinion of the Court. . . .

The plaintiffs contend that segregated public schools are not "equal" and cannot be made "equal," and that hence they are deprived of the equal protection of the laws. . . .

Reargument was largely devoted to the circumstances surrounding the adoption of the Fourteenth Amendment in 1868. . . . This discussion and our own investigation convince us that, although these sources cast some light, it is not enough to resolve the problem with which we are faced. At best, they are inconclusive. The most avid proponents of the post-War Amendments undoubtedly intended them to remove all legal distinctions among "all persons born or naturalized in the United States." Their opponents, just as certainly, were antagonistic to both the letter and the spirit of the Amendments and wished them to have the most limited effect. What others in Congress and the state legislatures had in mind cannot be determined with any degree of certainty.

An additional reason for the inconclusive nature of the Amendment's history, with respect to segregated schools, is the status of public education at that time. In the South, the movement toward free common schools, supported by general taxation, had not yet taken hold. Education of white children was largely in the hands of private groups. Education of Negroes was almost nonexistent, and practically all of the race were illiterate. In fact, any education of Negroes was forbidden by law in some states. Today, in contrast, many Negroes have achieved outstanding success in the arts and sciences as well as in the business and professional world. It is true that public school education at the time of the Amendment had advanced further in the North, but the effect of the Amendment on the Northern States was generally ignored in the congressional debates. Even in the North, the conditions of public education did not approximate those existing today. The curriculum was usually rudimentary; ungraded schools were common in rural areas; the school term was but three months a year in many states; and compulsory school attendance was virtually unknown. As a consequence, it is not surprising that there should be so little in the history of the Fourteenth Amendment relating to its intended effect on public education.

In the first cases in this Court construing the Fourteenth Amendment, decided shortly after its adoption, the Court interpreted it as proscribing all state-imposed discriminations against the Negro race. The doctrine of "separate but equal" did not make its appearance in this Court until 1896 in the case of *Plessy v. Ferguson*, involving not education but transportation. . . .

. . . Here, unlike *Sweatt v. Painter*, there are findings below that the Negro and white schools involved have been equalized, or are being equalized, with respect to buildings, curricula, qualifications and salaries of teachers, and other "tangible" factors. Our decision, therefore, cannot turn on merely a comparison of these tangible factors in the Negro and white schools involved in each of the cases. We must look instead to the effect of segregation itself on public education.

In approaching this problem, we cannot turn the clock back to 1868 when the Amendment was adopted, or even to 1896 when *Plessy v. Ferguson* was written. We must consider public education in the light of its full development and its present place in American life throughout the Nation. Only in this way can it be determined if segregation in public schools deprives these plaintiffs of the equal protection of the laws.

Today, education is perhaps the most important function of the state and local governments. Compulsory school attendance laws and the great expenditures for education both demonstrate our recognition of the importance of education to our democratic society. It is required in the performance of our most basic public responsibilities, even service in the armed forces. It is the very foundation of good citizenship. Today it is a principal instrument in awakening the child to cultural values, in preparing him for later professional training, and in helping him to adjust normally to his environment. In these days, it is doubtful that any child may reasonably be expected to succeed in life if he is denied the opportunity of an education. Such an opportunity, where the state has undertaken to provide it, is a right which must be made available to all on equal terms.

We come then to the question presented: Does segregation of children in public schools solely on the basis of race, even though the physical facilities and other "tangible" factors may be equal, deprive children of the minority group of equal educational opportunities? We believe it does.

In *Sweatt v. Painter*, in finding that a segregated law school for Negroes could not provide them equal educational opportunities, this Court relied in large part on "those qualities which are incapable of objective measurement but which make for greatness in a law school." In *McLaurin v. Oklahoma State Regents*, the Court, requiring that a Negro admitted to a white graduate school be treated like all other students, again resorted to intangible considerations: ". . . his ability to study, to engage in discussions and exchange views with other students, and, in general, to learn his profession." Such considerations apply with added force to children in grade and high schools. To separate them from others of similar age and qualifications solely because of their race generates a feeling of inferiority as to their status in the community that may affect their hearts and minds in a way unlikely ever to be undone. . . .

Whatever may have been the extent of psychological knowledge at the time of *Plessy v. Ferguson*, this finding is amply supported by modern authority.[19] Any language in *Plessy v. Ferguson* contrary to this finding is rejected.

We conclude that in the field of public education the doctrine of "separate but equal" has no place. Separate educational facilities are inherently unequal. Therefore, we hold that the plaintiffs and others similarly situated for whom the actions have been brought are, by reason of the segregation complained of, deprived of the equal protection of the laws guaranteed by the Fourteenth Amendment. . . .

POSTSCRIPT

May 17, 2004, marked the fiftieth anniversary of *Brown v. Board of Education*, certainly a time for reflection on the status of race relations in the United States. Though a great deal of racial and ethnic tension yet divides Americans, real progress toward racial fairness has occurred and American courts played an active role in this process by dismantling legal (*de jure*) segregation following the *Brown* decision.[20] However, it is arguable that the ultimate promise of *Brown* has gone unfulfilled in part because courts refused to redress the *de facto* segregation of public schools that resulted from housing patterns: most whites lived in the suburbs; most African-Americans and other minorities lived in the large urban centers. During the 1990s, the Supreme Court extended this passive approach to *de facto* segregation by relaxing judicial supervision of schools that had once been legally segregated. In the end, though *de jure* segregation has largely been eliminated from public education in the United States, racially integrated schools are the exceptions because *de facto* housing segregation is the norm. The underlying question is whether the spirit of *Brown* has been realized if most African-American and other minority children attend non-integrated schools.

Following the groundbreaking decision in 1954, *Brown* was once again scheduled for reargument. The Court asked for guidance on two remedial questions: should the five cases consolidated in *Brown* be sent back to the district courts for them to decide the nature of specific relief and, if they should be sent back, what kind of direction should the Court give to the district judges. A year later the Court decided not to impose immediate or a specific form of relief. Instead, the Court directed the relevant federal district judges to take into account local conditions as they monitored whether the school districts admitted children to schools "on a racially nondiscriminatory basis with all deliberate speed."[21] Specific criteria outlining what a school district had to accomplish were not mentioned in the Court's opinion and no deadline for the end of segregation was imposed.

On remand in the South Carolina case, Chief Judge John J. Parker interpreted *Brown* to mean only that a state could not deny "to any person on account of race the right to attend any school that it maintains." Accordingly, he continued, if the public schools "are open to children of all races, no violation of the Constitution is involved even though the children of different races voluntarily attend different schools. . . ."[22] Parker's opinion, influential throughout the South, permitted states to fulfill their constitutional duties under the Equal Protection Clause by establishing what were called "freedom-of-choice plans."

As long as a school board did not illegally prevent or discourage African-Americans from attending a formerly all-white school, it did not matter if none of the white students enrolled in the African-American school and if only a few "token" African-Americans enrolled in the white one. According to Parker, *Brown* did not require integration, but only the end of legally mandated segregation.

The Supreme Court did not explicitly outlaw freedom-of-choice plans until it decided *Green v. County School Board* in 1968, fourteen years after *Brown*.[23] Of course, much had happened during the interim, including a number of Supreme Court decisions that had invalidated segregated public facilities outside the context of public education.[24] Congress had also enacted the Civil Rights Act of 1964, which allowed the Department of Health, Education, and Welfare to deny federal assistance to school districts that had not yet desegregated. Despite these important developments, southern schools in 1968 were far from being fully integrated. In reaction, Justice William Brennan, in his majority opinion in *Green*, wrote that school districts formerly segregated by law were "clearly charged with the *affirmative duty* to take whatever steps might be necessary to convert to *a unitary system* in which racial discrimination would be *eliminated root and branch*." It had "to come forward with a plan that promises realistically to work, and promises realistically to work *now*."[25] (Emphasis mine.) In other words, southern school districts did not satisfy their constitutional obligations by merely ending segregation. They had an immediate duty to integrate their schools.

The Court described what kind of techniques lower courts could use to achieve integration in *Swann v. Charlotte-Mecklenburg Board of Education* (1971).[26] They could change attendance zones, establish racial quotas, alter the sites of future schools, and order busing of children to schools outside their neighborhood. Soon thereafter the Supreme Court vastly increased the number of school districts subject to the equitable remedies described in *Swann*. In *Keyes v. School District* (1973) it held that northern school districts had a duty to integrate if local officials had *intentionally* kept white and black students in separate schools.[27] Such an intent to segregate, without any legislative authorization, was enough to trigger the *Swann* remedies. Moreover, in his majority opinion, Justice Brennan explained that the intent to discriminate did not have to pervade the school district. Even if the unlawful intent was confined to only a part of the school district, a judge could assume that it had affected the whole district or that unlawful discrimination had also occurred in other parts of the district. In either case, the judge could utilize busing and racial quotas to achieve integrated schools throughout the district.

The final major step that the Supreme Court took in the direction of compulsory integration was in the 1979 cases of *Columbus Board of Education v. Penick* and *Dayton Board of Education v. Brinkman*.[28] Here the Court, in an opinion written by Justice Byron White, ruled that it was not necessary for contemporary school board officials to discriminate before integration could be ordered. The equitable remedies described in *Swann* could be imposed if school boards had intentionally segregated students at any time after *Brown* was decided. *Brown* had imposed on the school boards of Columbus and Dayton a duty not to segregate. If those school districts violated that duty at any time after *Brown*, courts could presume that the violation or the failure to remedy the violation had contributed to the existing racial imbalances in Columbus's and Dayton's schools (some schools being predominantly white and others predominantly black). Accordingly, judges could order children bused out of their neighborhoods so that all schools in the district would have a roughly equal racial composition. These two decisions encouraged large municipal school districts to take immediate steps to integrate their schools. Officials either had to integrate or face the possibility of a lawsuit based upon what their predecessors had done or failed to do.

Academic and public reaction to this line of cases, from *Green* to *Columbus* and *Dayton*, varied over time. At the beginning, prominent elements of the academic community fully supported judicially imposed integration. In 1966, James S. Coleman and a number of other social scientists claimed, in a study entitled *Equality of Educational Opportunity*,[29] that integration would help African-American students without any harm to the educational opportunities of other racial groups. The only downside to compulsory integration was the loss of the neighborhood school through busing and the racial assignments of students—purportedly a small price to pay for improved African-American educational performance. Many white parents, however, did not calculate the advantages and disadvantages of judicially imposed integration in the way that Coleman and his colleagues did. Some withdrew their children from public schools and enrolled them in all-white private schools. Others joined the migration to the predominantly white suburbs—a demographic trend already well underway. As middle-class parents, including some middle-class minority parents, moved to the suburbs, the percentage of minority students in the city's public schools went up, raising new fears and anxieties and unleashing another round of migration. Many large urban school districts were trapped in this vicious cycle.

Extensive white flight could place a federal judge in a difficult position. What if a city school district had engaged in intentional segregation in the past, which made it subject to the *Swann* remedies, but demographic trends had reduced the number of white students within the school district to such a degree that no real integration could be achieved? In such a situation, could a federal judge create a super-large metropolitan school district and bus white middle-class students from suburban schools to inner-city schools and disadvantaged minority students from inner-city schools to suburban schools? In 1974, the Supreme Court considered the constitutionality of such a remedy in *Milliken v. Bradley*.[30] The district court found that intentional segregation had occurred within Detroit, and on this basis issued a multi-district remedy, one which included 53 suburban school districts. The court ordered this kind of relief even though there had been no evidence that the suburban districts had engaged in any intentional segregation within their districts.

The Supreme Court, over sharp dissents, overturned the lower court's decision. The scope of any desegregation remedy, Chief Justice Warren Burger's majority opinion insisted, had to be determined by the "nature and extent of the constitutional violation." Since there was no proof that the predominantly white suburban school districts had participated in any segregation, they could not be forced to remedy Detroit's constitutional violation, even if Detroit could not remedy its violation in any other way. In effect, the Court's decision in *Milliken* meant that a constitutional violation had no remedy because meaningful integration was no longer possible within the boundaries of Detroit.

Milliken marked an important turning point. The line of cases that began with the promise of *Brown* had produced a political reaction to which, some would argue, the Supreme Court bowed in *Milliken* by refusing to compel the predominantly white middle-class children of the suburbs to integrate with the racial minorities that filled the schools of America's inner cities. The results were foreseeable. By 1982, the percentage of African-American children attending substantially mixed schools was only "slightly higher" than in 1968.[31] Schools, were no longer segregated by law (*de jure* segregation), but they were segregated in fact (*de facto* segregation). Was this result consistent with the spirit of *Brown*? What is the moral and constitutional significance of the distinction between *de jure* and *de facto* segregation? Has American society truly remedied the constitutional outrage of legally mandated segregation in public education if its schools remain nonintegrated? On the other hand, if it is coercively imposed, is integration a worthwhile goal? A practical one?[32]

During the 1990s, the Supreme Court continued its relatively passive approach toward integration by authorizing the withdrawal of judicial supervision of local school districts under desegregation orders. In *Board of Education of Oklahoma City v. Dowell* (1991), the Court ruled that a district judge could dissolve a desegregation decree if the school district in question had been in good faith compliance with the decree for "a reasonable period of time" and if the vestiges of intentional discrimination had been eliminated "to the extent practicable." Arguably, the latter criterion meant that the district did not have to eliminate the vestiges of discrimination "root and branch."[33] One year later, in *Freeman v. Pitts* (1992), the Court allowed a partial withdrawal of judicial supervision of a school district even though the district judge in question found that all vestiges of discrimination had not been eliminated, that a "unitary system" had not been achieved, and that *de facto* racial imbalances in the district's schools were greater than they were in 1969. In regard to the last point, the Court concluded that the racial imbalances were the result of demographic changes, unrelated to earlier acts of intentional segregation by the school district. In effect, the Court ruled that white flight to the suburbs was no reason for a district judge to delay returning control of a formerly segregated urban school district to local authorities.[34]

Along with *Milliken*, both *Dowell* and *Freeman* pose difficult questions concerning the Supreme Court's future role in public school desegregation and in American race relations in general. *Brown v. Board of Education* is certainly a milestone in the history of American race relations and the history of the Supreme Court. Real progress toward racial fairness has occurred, even if much remains to be done if true racial equality and harmony are to be achieved. Arguably, de *facto* segregation in housing and public education is one indication that the ultimate promise of *Brown* has gone unfulfilled. Has the Supreme Court in some way failed to deliver on that promise in the post-*Milliken* period? Does *de facto* segregation harm African-American children today as much as *de jure* segregation purportedly did in the past? Does it violate the Equal Protection Clause any less than *de jure* segregation? Why? In *Brown* the Court played an important role in ushering in a new era of race relations. Should it play a similar function in regard to *de facto* segregation? Does the Court have the power to impose racial integration on American public schools? Should it?

NOTES

1. See *Mayor of Baltimore v. Dawson*, 350 U.S. 877 (1955); *Holmes v. Atlanta*, 350 U.S. 879 (1955).
2. See *Green v. County School Board*, 391 U.S. 430, 439 (1968).
3. *Plessy v. Ferguson*, 163 U.S. 537, 544, 550–551 (1896).
4. *Id.* at 553–63.
5. 305 U.S. 337 (1938).
6. *Id.* at 351.
7. 339 U.S. 629 (1950).
8. *Id.* at 633–34.
9. *McLaurin v. Oklahoma*, 339 U.S. 637, 641 (1950).
10. There were five cases consolidated in *Brown*. The NAACP was not directly involved with *Bolling v. Sharpe*, the case from Washington, D.C. The NAACP cases were from Kansas (*Brown v. Board of Education*), South Carolina (*Briggs v. Elliot*), Virginia (*Davis v. Prince Edwards County*), and Delaware (*Gebhart v. Belton*).
11. A revised version of the report was published under the title *Prejudice and Your Child* (New York: Beacon Press, 1955).
12. Henry Garrett's trial testimony in *Davis v. County School Board of Prince Edward County*, cited by Richard Kluger, *Simple Justice* (New York: Random House, 1975), p. 504.
13. This account is taken from Kluger, Chap. 23.
14. *Ibid.*, p. 678.
15. Cited by Kluger, p. 696.
16. *Ibid.*, p. 698.
17. *Brown v. Board of Education of Topeka*, 347 U.S. 483, 492, 493, 495 (1954).
18. See Herbert Wechsler, "Toward Neutral Principles of Constitutional Law," *Harvard Law Review* 73 (1959), pp. 31–35, and Louis H. Pollak, "Racial Discrimination and Judicial Integrity: A Reply to Professor Wechsler," *University of Pennsylvania Law Review* 108 (1959), pp. 24–31; Edmond Cahn, "Jurisprudence," *New York University Law Review* 30 (1955), pp. 150–169. For recent critiques of the *Brown* decision, see Jack M. Balkin, *What Brown v. Board of Education Should Have Said* (New York: New York, 2002).
19. Warren's footnote: K. B. Clark, *Effect of Prejudice and Discrimination on Per-*

sonality Development (Midcentury White House Conference on Children and Youth, 1950); Witmer and Kotinsky, *Personality in the Making* (1952), Chap. VI; Deutscher and Chein, "The Psychological Effects of Enforced Segregation: A Survey of Social Science Opinion," 26 *J. Psychol.* 259 (1948); Chein, "What Are the Psychological Effects of Segregation Under Conditions of Equal Facilities," 3 *Int. J. Opinion and Attitude Res.* 229 (1949); Brameld, "Educational Costs," in *Discrimination and National Welfare* (MacIver, ed., 1949), pp. 44–88; Frazier, *The Negro in the United States* (1949), pp. 674–681. And see generally Myrdal, *An American Dilemma* (New York: Harper & Bros., 1944).

20. Courts played an active role, but it is debatable whether they would have been successful without the cooperation and support of the political branches of the federal government. See Gerald N. Rosenberg, *The Hollow Hope: Can Courts Bring about Social Change* (Chicago: University of Chicago Press, 1991).

21. *Brown v. Board of Education*, 349 U.S. 294, 301 (1955).

22. *Briggs v. Elliott*, 132 F. Supp. 776, 777 (1955).

23. 391 U.S. 430 (1968).

24. See *Mayor of Baltimore v. Dawson*, 350 U.S. 877 (1955) (public beaches); *Holmes v. Atlanta*, 350 U.S. 879 (1955) (public golf courses); *Gayle v. Browder*, 352 U.S. 903 (1956) (public buses); *New Orleans City Park Improvement Association v. Detiege*, 358 U.S. 54 (1958) (public parks); *Turner v. Memphis*, 369 U.S. 350 (1962) (public restaurants).

25. *Id.* at 439.

26. 402 U.S. 1 (1971).

27. 413 U.S. 189 (1973).

28. 443 U.S. 449 (1979); 443 U.S. 526 (1979).

29. (Washington: U.S. Department of Health, Education, and Welfare, 1966).

30. 418 U.S. 717 (1974).

31. Wolters, *The Burden of Brown*, p. 288, citing Gary Orfield, *Desegregation of African-American and Hispanic Students from 1968 to 1980* (Washington: Joint Committee for Political Studies, 1982), p. 11.

32. For recent commentary discussing these and similar questions, see Gary Orfield, *Dismantling Desegregation: The Quiet Reversal of Brown v. Board of Education* (New York: New Press, 1996); Gary Orfield and John T. Yun, *Resegregation in American Schools* (Cambridge, Mass.: Harvard University, The Civil Rights Project [available online], 1999). James T. Patterson, *Brown v. Board of Education: A Civil Rights Milestone and Its Troubled Legacy* (New York: Oxford University Press, 2001).

33. 498 U.S. 237, 249–50 (1991).

34. 503 U.S. 467 (1992). The Supreme Court also limited the remedial powers of federal judges supervising school districts. Such district court judges cannot, unless there is no other alternative, order school districts to raise taxes to pay for desegregation programs. Nor can they order salary increases and remedial education programs on the ground that student achievement scores are low. See *Missouri v. Jenkins*, 495 U.S. 33 (1990) and *Missouri v. Jenkins*, 515 U.S. 70 (1995).

CHAPTER 2

Affirmative Action

Regents of University of Calif. v. Bakke
438 U.S. 265 (1978)

Grutter v. Bollinger
539 U.S. 306 (2003)

I. *BAKKE* AND ITS BACKGROUND

Landmark cases do not always make their "mark" in the same way. Though it took years for *Brown v. Board of Education* to be fully implemented, the Supreme Court in this decision unanimously stood behind the principle that segregation in public education was inherently unequal. Twenty-four years later, in *Regents of University of California v. Bakke* (1978), the Court upheld the constitutionality of affirmative action in a 5-4 decision. Justice Lewis Powell was the pivotal justice. Although he agreed with four justices that a quota program was illegal, he also agreed with four other justices that public universities could use a person's race as a "plus" in admissions practices. In his opinion, Powell reasoned that a diverse student body was a compelling interest that justified the use of racial preferences. Despite the fact that Powell was the only justice who endorsed this rationale, the decision was a landmark because affirmative action policies of the type endorsed by Powell flourished throughout the 1980s and 1990s. However, it was not until *Grutter v. Bollinger* (2003), twenty-five years after *Bakke*, that five justices of the Supreme Court embraced Justice Powell's lone opinion from *Bakke*. Though all three decisions are landmarks, they have all made their "marks" differently: *Brown* placed the Court squarely behind a principle that took many years to realize because opposition to it was strong and steady; *Bakke* established a tiny legal foothold for a policy that elites in higher education pursued aggressively; *Grutter* legally sanctified much of the reality of affirmative action that these elites had produced in higher education over the preceding twenty-five years.

Effective affirmative action programs began in the mid-1960s, a time when African-Americans and other minority groups lagged far behind whites in education, jobs, income, and status. Responding to a growing sense of frustration, President Lyndon Johnson, in 1965, issued Executive Order 11246 directing all federal contractors to use "affirmative action" in their hiring and promotion decisions. At a speech at Howard University, he justified his policy by referring to the metaphor of a race. He said that if a person who had been "hobbled by chains" for years was unshackled, that individual could not fairly compete in a race. Since African-Americans and other minorities were "shackled" by the effects of past discrimination, they were to be given some kind of "head start" in the American race for education, income, and status. Formal equality of opportunity was abandoned in favor of an equality of "fact" and "result."

In May of 1968, the Department of Labor's Office of Federal Contract Compliance, which monitors all federal contracts, issued more specific regulations concerning the type of affirmative action programs mandated for all federal government contractors:

> The contractor's program shall provide in detail for specific steps to guarantee equal employment opportunity keyed to the problems and needs of members of minority groups, including, when there are deficiencies, the development of specific goals and time-tables for the prompt achievement of full and equal employment opportunity. . . . The evaluation of utilization of minority group personnel shall include . . . an analysis of minority group representation in all categories.[1]

All federal contractors were therefore to examine the percentage of minorities in each job category. If the percentage of any particular minority in any category was "low," the company had to come up with a timetable for remedying the deficiency by utilizing racial preferences. The regulations prohibited "rigid and inflexible quotas," but racial preferences were explicitly required.[2]

With these federal regulations as a backdrop, affirmative action in employment became a common practice by the late 1960s and early 1970s because so many corporations had contracts with the federal government. By the early 1970s, many undergraduate and professional schools had also established programs that clearly used race as a factor in admissions and in hiring. Some of these programs created quotas, which set aside a certain number of spaces in each entering class for minority members, or goals, which allowed admissions officers to use a person's race as one of the factors bearing upon his or her admission. In 1974, the constitutionality, legality, and morality of such programs were debated before the Special Subcommittee on Education in the House of Representatives (the O'Hara hearings). Political leaders, educators, and social commentators each had their say in this fascinating example of American constitutional debate (see box 2.1).

In the same year as the O'Hara hearings, Allan Bakke, a thirty-four-year-old white male, filed suit against the medical school of the University of California at Davis on the ground that the school had set aside sixteen spaces of each class of one hundred students for four groups of minority applicants: "Blacks, Chicanos, Asians, and American Indians."[3] Bakke claimed that Davis's policies violated the California Constitution, Title VI of the Civil Rights Act of 1964, and the Equal Protection Clause of the Fourteenth Amendment.[4] The lower California court ruled that Davis's affirmative action was illegal, but refused to order Bakke's admission because he had not proven that he would have been admitted without the plan. In 1976, the California Supreme Court reversed the latter part of the lower court's ruling and ordered Bakke's admission. The Regents of the University of California, however, appealed to the Supreme Court, which granted certiorari on February 22, 1977. Bakke, now 37 years old, had to continue to bide his time.

The number of briefs filed in *Bakke* reveals how this case and the issue of affirmative action had captured the attention of the American public. One hundred seventeen organizations, including the federal government, either alone or collaboratively, submitted fifty-one amici curiae briefs.[5] Such "friend-of-the-court" briefs insure that the Supreme Court will have access to the full spectrum of opinion on any particular constitutional issue. However, with each additional amicus brief, *Bakke* became less a legal dispute between a frustrated white male and the University of California and more of a political confrontation between groups of American citizens that were divided over the legitimacy of affirmative action. The excerpts from the briefs that follow are, of course, no more than a sampling of those that were submitted in *Bakke*. They are nonetheless a revealing window on the constitutional debate over affirmative action that occurred in the *Bakke* case.

The most basic issue debated in the briefs is the question of which standard of equal protection was relevant to the constitutionality of affirmative action. By 1978, the Supreme Court had evolved three standards of equal protection, each standard implying a different level of judicial scrutiny. The lowest standard required that a law must be a "minimally rational" means to some "conceivable" legitimate legislative purpose. If the law under consideration passed this test, which it almost invariably did in those areas in which this "minimal" standard was applied (primarily socioeconomic legislation), then the Court deferred to the legislature. In contrast, for a law to pass the highest standard of equal protection, a test known as "strict scrutiny," the law had to be a "necessary" means for a "compelling" legislative purpose. If what the legislature was trying to accomplish was, in the Court's view, not "compelling," or if there was some other way for the state to obtain its goal other than by using a "suspect" classification, then the Court would invalidate the law. Historically, "suspect" classifications that required such close judicial scrutiny were those utilizing racial or ethnic criteria. In 1976, the Supreme Court endorsed an "intermediate" stan-

Box 2.1   THE PROPONENTS

ANDREW YOUNG, Representative from Georgia:
    . . . One of the things we need to do as a society is break out of the ethnocentric bag in which we find ourselves.

I think education historically and perhaps of necessity has been a predominantly white Anglo-Saxon–Protestant phenomenon and that anybody that doesn't come under that category is automatically discriminated against. . . .

The point I am making is I think we ought to think of our educational system as a part of our society, reflecting the sickness of that society, and that what we call objectivity most of the time . . . has a particular cultural or ethnic frame of reference.

Anytime we try to set up criteria according to that frame of reference, whatever it is, I think we are going to exclude somebody. We are going to exclude some concept of truth that we very definitely need in order for our society to function. . . .

CÉSAR SERESERES, University of California at Irvine:
    . . . The reality of American society consists of the following virtues. Equality of opportunity exists in America if you are male and if you are Anglo. . . .

The male Anglo by far gets the good start in the race for success. Why else do we find 97 percent of the engineers and 85 percent of the lawyers being male Anglos?

. . . [A] fundamental change is taking place in American society—a shift from the rights of individuals to the rights of groups. What this suggests is that the primacy of equality of opportunity must be replaced with the far more important primacy of the equality of results. . . .

CLARENCE MITCHELL, Director, Washington Bureau, NAACP:
    . . . There has been coined a new term, innocent on its face, but deadly in its application. This new term is "reverse discrimination." It is used by those who wish to protect the status quo that we in the NAACP must face each time we seek to change the biased patterns in faculty selection or in admissions to colleges and universities.

We know from bitter experience that those who employ this term are no different from the framers of the so-called southern manifestoes against the 1954 school desegregation decisions, the captains of so-called massive resistance to school desegregation and the propounders of numerous high sounding but scoff-law phrases of "interposition" and "10th amendment guarantees." . . .

(Box 2.1 cont.)   THE OPPONENTS

BERNARD KUTTNER, Chairman, National Discriminations Committee, Anti-Defamation League:
. . . Our basic rule is simply that in each case, we must make sure that every person, male or female, minority or nonminority, is accorded the same right to be free from discrimination as is every other person.

There must be no discrimination against a member of any group in hiring, promotion, admissions, or any other selective process in which some candidates are chosen and others are rejected. Any such act is illegal, since it violates the laws against discrimination, which prohibit all discrimination without exception.

It simply substitutes a new form of discrimination for an old form of discrimination; the victim has changed, but not the act. . . .

SIDNEY HOOK, Emeritus Professor, New York University:
. . . The representatives of HEW confuse themselves and others by saying that numerical goals are not quotas because "good faith efforts" to achieve goals is "an adequate substitute for evidence that goals have been met."

But this is logically equivalent to saying that sincere good faith efforts to achieve quotas are adequate evidence that quotas have been met.

Here is a proposition in ethics. If anything is morally wrong then sincere efforts to bring it about are wrong. If quotas are morally wrong in education then sincere "good faith efforts" to achieve them are also wrong. . . .

. . . Preferential hiring or quotas in education under any disguise is inherently divisive, unjust and undemocratic. It destroys the quest for excellence and opens the door to mediocrity, injurious to students, educational institutions and in the long run to the public good. . . .

JOHN BUNSEL, President, California State University:
. . . Title VII removed the "shackles" from the black and female "runners." Affirmative action wants to let them "catch up." . . . "The affirmative action of [Executive Order] 11246 tells the scorekeeper that he must 'make a good faith effort' to insure that the black runners and the female runners win at least x percent of the races." . . .

Affirmative action in practice has moved from eliminating discrimination to increasing the representation of certain groups over a specified period of time. My quarrel is with a preferential policy aimed at proportionate employment of preferred groups which is supposed to mean equal opportunity. We are apparently asked to believe that equal opportunity means some fixed percentage of the results, and that equality does not mean equal rights. I am not persuaded. . . .

Source: Federal Higher Education Programs Institutional Eligibility, Hearings before the Special Subcommittee on Education, Committee on Education and Labor, House of Representatives, 93rd Cong., 2nd Sess., Part 2A, pp. 219–20, 231–34, 260, 341, 457–59, 615, 708, 725.

dard of equal protection to assess the constitutionality of laws that discriminated on the basis of sex.[6] Such laws, like the one requiring only males to register for the draft, are constitutional if they are "substantially related" to the achievement of "important" governmental objectives.[7] The intermediate standard was therefore easier to meet than strict scrutiny, but more difficult than minimal rationality.

Bakke argued that Davis's affirmative action plan was a form of "reverse discrimination" that could only be constitutional if it passed strict scrutiny; the University of California insisted that its plan was no more than "benign discrimination" that only had to meet the requirements of minimal rationality; certain amici curiae briefs held that the intermediate standard was appropriate. What was the proper view? To what extent does the answer to this question depend upon whether state activities that benefit racial minorities are equivalent to those that discriminate against them?

Besides debating which standard of equal protection should be applied, the briefs also discussed whether Davis's affirmative action program passed the appropriate test. This issue concerned what the goals and the means of the program were. The University of California claimed that its program remedied the pernicious effects of societal discrimination, produced more minority physicians, elevated the quality of medical care in minority communities, and improved medical education by creating a more diverse student body. Were any of these goals compelling, important, or legitimate? And what of the specific means that Davis used to obtain these goals? Was Davis's program a racial quota or a goal, and was there any significant difference between the two? Were the racially conscious means used by Davis similar to or different from those used in public school desegregation? Could Davis have achieved the same results in their admissions process by relying upon nonracial criteria, such as poverty, personal hardship, or educational disadvantage? All of these kinds of questions bear upon any assessment of whether Davis's program passes one of the standards of equal protection mentioned above.

The oral argument that took place before the Supreme Court on September 12, 1977, in *Bakke* was a study in contrasts. The experienced Archibald Cox, a former special Watergate prosecutor and Solicitor General, presented the case for the University of California, while Reynold H. Colvin, Bakke's local California attorney, made his first appearance before the Court. Cox focused upon the general question: Given the history of discrimination and the underrepresentation of minorities in the medical profession, could a public school take race into account in its admissions process? He did not confine himself to the specifics of Davis's program or to the record of the case. In contrast, Colvin perceived himself as Bakke's advocate. First and foremost, Bakke wanted to get into Davis's medical school. He cared less about invalidating all the affirmative action programs that were in operation across the country. Accordingly, Colvin dwelled upon the specific facts of Bakke's case, especially those that suggested how unfairly Davis had treated Bakke. He wanted to give the Court the opportunity to make a narrow decision, one that got Bakke into Davis Medical School without deciding whether every affirmative action program in the country, of whatever type, had to be declared unconstitutional. Which lawyer was the better advocate? Did each attorney pursue a strategy that served his client's interests?

At the first conference at which they discussed *Bakke*, the justices voted to require supplemental briefs on the question of Title VI. This issue was important because four justices eventually decided the case on that basis, upholding the California decision without addressing the constitutionality of Davis's program. The program may or may not be constitutional, but it was illegal because a federal statute prohibited it. In a memo to his colleagues on the Court, Justice John Paul Stevens explained the virtues of resolving *Bakke* on this ground:

> . . . The critical point is that a decision based on Title VI leaves room for legislative and executive flexibility in areas where that is badly needed. . . . While the question of reverse discrimination obviously involves enduring principles, I am convinced that it also poses problems unique in our history and that the faults and virtues of many of the proposed solutions can only be adequately judged on an "empirical" basis. The legislative arena is the proper forum for this sort of experimentation.[8]

According to Stevens, affirmative action was a problem to be handled "experimentally" and "empirically" by legislatures, not "constitutionally" by courts. Chief Justice Warren Burger, along with Justices Potter Stewart and William Rehnquist, joined Stevens's *Bakke* opinion.

Justice Lewis Powell disagreed. In a memo to his colleagues, he claimed that avoiding the constitutional issue "would be viewed by many as a 'self-inflicted wound' on the Court."[9] Davis-type programs would be illegal, but less radical programs of affirmative action would soon be the subject of litigation, ultimately ending up before the Supreme Court. The way to avoid this scenario, according to Powell, was to assume that Title VI only prohibited affirmative action programs that violated the Equal Protection Clause of the Fourteenth Amendment. If Title VI was interpreted in this way, the Court had to decide the constitutional question, thereby giving state universities and colleges ample guidance on what type of program was lawful and what type was not. Which justice, Stevens or Powell, is correct? Would deciding *Bakke* on statutory grounds be a "self-inflicted wound" or a prudent exercise of judicial restraint?

Though Powell insisted that the constitutional issue had to be addressed, he agreed with Stevens that Davis's program was illegal. In his view, the program violated Title VI, but only because it violated the Fourteenth Amendment. Powell came to his conclusion that the program was unconstitutional by, first, deciding that strict scrutiny was the appropriate standard to be used to assess the constitutionality of benign programs of racial preference. Davis's program therefore had to be a "necessary" means to a "compelling" state purpose. In his judgment, it did not matter that such programs were not meant to stigmatize any racial/ethnic group. Racial preferences for minorities discriminated against whites, and that fact alone triggered strict scrutiny. Moreover, after examining the explicit goals of Davis's program, Powell held that only one of them—the goal of creating a diverse student body—was a "compelling" purpose within the purview of a state medical school. However, the means by which the school tried to obtain student diversity—setting aside a quota of sixteen spaces for minorities—were not "necessary," because student diversity could just as well be obtained by a goal, by allowing admissions officers to consider an applicant's race as a "plus," rather than by establishing a quota of sixteen spaces. Since Davis's program was therefore unconstitutional and illegal, Powell, in conjunction with the four justices who based their decision solely upon Title VI, upheld the California court order directing Bakke's admission into the Davis medical school.

Justice William Brennan, along with Justices Byron White, Thurgood Marshall, and Harry Blackmun, sharply disagreed with Powell's approach in *Bakke*. Brennan insisted that strict scrutiny should be reserved for laws that stigmatized racial minorities by discriminating against them. In his separate dissent, Marshall agreed with Brennan and highlighted the tragic history of African-Americans and the historical fact that the intent of the Equal Protection Clause had initially been to help the newly freed slaves. Both justices thought the intermediate standard was the appropriate one to assess the constitutionality of "benign" discrimination. Applying this standard to the case, Brennan concluded that reserving sixteen spaces for minority candidates was "substantially related" to the school's "important" goals of remedying past societal discrimination and providing better medical service to minority communities. Second, Brennan argued, the distinction that Powell drew between a goal and a quota had no constitutional significance. A goal would function in the same way as a quota, depending upon how big a "plus" or "minus" was assigned to a particular applicant's race. White applicants would suffer the same consequences regardless of which type of affirmative action plan was used.

Despite these theoretical differences that divided these two justices from Powell, Brennan pointed out to Powell that since he believed that the race of an applicant could constitute a "plus," he could not uphold the California order in its entirety because it prohibited Davis from using race in any form in its admissions process.[10] Convinced by Brennan's argument, Powell decided to affirm in part and reverse in part the California Supreme Court's decision. Davis's affirmative action program was unconstitutional and the school had to admit Bakke, but that part of the state's judicial order directing the school not to use race at all in their admissions process was reversed. Because Powell voted in this way, Brennan could claim in his opinion that "the central meaning" of *Bakke* was that "Government may take race into account when it acts not to demean or insult any racial group, but to remedy disadvantages cast on minorities by past racial prejudice, at least when appropriate findings have been made by judicial, legislative, or administrative bodies with competence to act in this area" (see opinion below). Brennan's interpretation of the "central holding" of *Bakke* quickly became the reality. Accordingly, though Powell had been the crucial fifth vote (both against quotas and for affirmative action), it can be argued that *Bakke* was a victory for Brennan.[11]

How much of a victory, of course, depended upon how people reacted to *Bakke*. Today we know that affirmative action flourished during the late 1970s and throughout the 1980s and 1990s. The contrast to *Brown v. Board of Education* is striking and perhaps instructive. In *Brown*, the Court unanimously stood behind the clear and simple principle that segregation was inherently unequal, but nothing meaningful was done until the mid-1960s, when the political branches of the federal government began to oppose the southern segregationist elite. On the other hand, *Bakke*, a divided decision that theoretically stood for very little, became a landmark immediately because the proponents of affirmative action had the political and institutional power necessary to exert their will. It can therefore be argued that a comparison of how American elites responded to these two decisions reveals the degree to which political and institutional power has an impact upon how and why any particular Supreme Court decision achieves landmark status.

BIBLIOGRAPHY

Fullinwider, Robert K. *The Reverse Discrimination Controversy.* Totowa, N.J.: Rowman and Littlefield, 1980.
Glazer, Nathan. *Affirmative Discrimination.* New York: Basic Books, 1978.
O'Neil, Timothy J. *Bakke & the Politics of Equality.* Middletown, Conn.: Wesleyan University Press, 1985.
Schwartz, Bernard. *Behind Bakke: Affirmative Action and the Supreme Court.* New York: New York University Press, 1988.
Sindler, Allan P. *Bakke, De Funis, and Minority Admissions.* New York: Longman, 1978.
Symposium. *California Law Review,* 67 (1979).
Wilkinson, J. Harvie, III. *From Brown to Bakke.* Oxford: Oxford University Press, 1979.

BRIEFS

UNIVERSITY OF CALIFORNIA BRIEF

. . . [[1. Past Discrimination.]] Students applying for admission to medical school in 1970, the first year of operation of the Davis Task Force program, would in ordinary course have begun elementary school in 1954, the year this Court decided *Brown v. Board of Education. Brown* eloquently expressed the goal of educational opportunity unimpaired by the effects of racial discrimination, but implementation of the commitment expressed in *Brown* has taken years and is even today not complete. A rectification of such magnitude cannot occur overnight, especially when it encounters resistance at the local level. Minority students entering medical schools in the 1970's are from the generation of minority students who have seen the hope but not the promise of *Brown. . . .*

The ramifications of societal discrimination for minority doctors extend to every aspect of their professional lives. Black doctors have been isolated and constricted by denial of opportunities in their training, their practice, and their professional status. Restrictions on the access of black medical graduates to advanced clinical training and to specialty board certification have resulted in fewer specialists among black physicians than among white. The relative paucity of blacks on the faculties of American medical schools exceeds even the degree of their scarcity in the profession. . . .

The data could be multiplied. But the most important fact about minority doctors is that there are so few of them. The 1970 census reported 6,002 black physicians out of 279,658 physicians in the United States, or 2.1% of the total. The reported ratio of black physicians to blacks is far lower than the physician/non-physician ratio for the nation at large. For blacks, that ratio is 1/4248. For the population generally, it is 1/649. The shortage of black physicians is most acute in the deep South, where in some states the physician/non-physician ratios among blacks has been reported to be in the range of 1/15,000 to 1/20,000. The picture for Mexican Americans and American Indians is almost certainly worse yet. . . .

[[2. Qualifications for Medical School.]] During the past ten years, the vast majority of medical school faculties have taken a much wider view of their role, reemphasizing their responsibilities for educating effective clinicians and practitioners. In selecting among a continually expanding pool of well-qualified applicants, these schools have sought to admit a significant number of applicants with characteristics more directly related to the broad range of needs and responsibilities of medical education and to the varied requirements of effective delivery of health care. The increased relative weight given nonnumerical criteria—such as motivation, character, ability to cope, interest in career patterns for which there is special need, orientation toward human as well as scientific concerns—and the definition and balance of those elements, varied from school to school. But in each the admissions process produced a class in which each student was not only well-qualified cognitively but was further "particularly qualified" for membership, one no less than another, because of personal characteristics judged by that faculty to be relevant to the needs of the educative community and profession.

Special admissions programs like the one at Davis, represent a logical extension of the rejection of an excessive degree of reliance on science-related indicators. . . .

[[3. Goals and Means of the Program.]] The Davis program, like its counterparts nationwide, represents a voluntary effort by a medical school faculty to further the process initiated in *Brown v. Board of Education*. The ends of the program are universally recognized as compelling. The ends include reducing the historic deficit of traditionally disfavored minorities in medical schools and in the medical profession, countering the effects of educational deprivation and societal discrimination, and obtaining the educational and societal benefits that flow from racial and ethnic diversity in a medical school student body. The goals are not restricted to increasing the number of medical school students and doctors from the ranks of minority groups or to obtaining the benefits of the recognition that, in a multiracial world, applicants from minority backgrounds may possess skills not shared broadly by applicants from other backgrounds. Nor are they limited to increasing aspirations among minorities that have viewed medicine as a field closed to them and thus unworthy of pursuit, or to destroying persistent and pernicious stereotypes, among minorities and non-minorities alike, that it is not the proper "place" for minorities to aspire to become physicians. The goals also include increasing the skills of non-minority medical school students and physicians. As a result of the integrated education made possible by the Davis program, white students will develop an enhanced awareness of the medical concerns of minorities and of the difficulties of effective delivery of health care services in minority communities. They will also stand a better chance of developing a rapport with their future minority patients, no matter where they encounter such patients. . . .

The means chosen by the Davis medical school are the means most directly related to the desired ends. The faculty chose racially-conscious means because it concluded nothing else would work. "To have done otherwise would have severely hampered the [faculty's] ability to deal effectively with the task at hand."

The court below based its result largely on the premise that racially-neutral means would further the goals of the Davis program. That premise is wholly false. There are no effective alternatives to attainment of the desired ends. One of the California court's proposals, expanding the number of medical schools is, of course, beyond the control of medical school faculties, but the decisive answer is its unrealism in today's era of dwindling financial resources. Another, "aggressive programs" of identification and recruitment of prospects, simply ignores the great amount of such activity which has been going on for some years, as well as the fact that the known existence of real opportunities for admission to medical school constitutes a far more powerful magnet than—and an essential condition to the success of—any recruiting efforts. Similarly, the proposal for a special admissions program based on disadvantage without regard to race also founders on the rock of reality. A racially "neutral" disadvantaged program would produce results essentially indistinguishable from the total abolition of special-admissions, for at least two reasons. First, whites greatly outnumber minorities at every income level. Second, the gap between numerical indicators exhibited by whites and by minorities remains just as wide when only applicants from lower-income families are considered as it is in the universe of all applicants. Thus, adoption of a truly racially "neutral" disadvantaged approach would do little more than substitute less-affluent whites for more affluent whites. . . .

"Quota" is a label sometimes applied to this case, as by the court below, perhaps because that term stirs such emotions. It evokes memories of an era of deliberate exclusion by the dominant group of more than a limited number of members of certain "classes." Obviously that is not true in the instant case.

Today, the label quota might signify a floor, a ceiling, or both. None of these attributes appears in the Davis program, and it is misleading to use the term quota with regard to that program. The Davis program sets a goal, not a quota. There is no floor below which minority presence is not permitted to fall. The medical school does not admit unqualified applicants in order to insure that each entering class contains a particular number of minorities. Every student admitted to Davis is fully qualified. If in a given year less than sixteen well-qualified Task Force applicants are available for admission to Davis, the goal will not be met. . . . Likewise, there is no ceiling on minorities; the medical school does not restrict them to the number coming through special-admissions. The total of minority students varies from year to year, looking at the entire entering class, no matter how admitted. . . .

. . . [[I]]t is nevertheless said by some that the Davis program threatens to depict minorities as incapable of holding their own. Respondent is plainly in no position to assert this claim. In any event, it is conjectural, deceptive, and an utterly unsound basis for deciding this case. It overlooks the insistence that all students be fully qualified, the intensity of the demand among all groups for a medical education, the refusal to lower academic or curricular requirements in the medical school, and the existence of state and national licensing examinations as a condition of entry into the profession. It also overlooks the fact that the program expresses a judgment by medical educators that minority students "bring to the profession special talents and views which are unique and needed." . . .

The premises underlying the plea to meritocracy in opposition to the Davis program are false. Even if it were possible to get agreement on ranking "the best doctors"—somehow measuring a general practitioner in an underserved rural area against a pathologist in a university hospital—the assumption that students with the highest numerical indicators will necessarily be the best doctors is completely questionable: MCAT scores and college grade-point averages do no correlate *that* well with initial performance in medical school, let alone with subsequent clinical training and experience. . . .

Another of the harms said to support invalidation of the Davis program is the injury to respondent and those in his category. No doubt the existence of the Davis program diminishes the chances that respondent, and those in his position, will attain admission. But it is diminution, not exclusion, which is the issue, and the diminution is both marginal and similar in effect to a host of other factors beyond the control of an applicant that reduce the odds of admission. Special-admissions programs do not "fence out" whites (or imply any racial slur or stigma with respect to them). . . .

[[4. Justifiable Concern about the Program.]] . . . The relevant concern to explore and weigh in assessing the Davis program is the risk of reinforcement of color-consciousness in a society that is striving to put behind it tendencies to make judgments about the relative worth of individuals on racial or ethnic bases. . . .

Having identified the race-related risk truly at issue in this case, it is now appropriate to . . . [[emphasize that the]] medical school was not writing on a clean slate. It did not arouse color consciousness where none had existed before. It acted against the background of an unhealthy and debilitating race consciousness that, despite the enormous strides made in our lives, our society has not yet erased. To an unfortunate degree, stereotypical thinking persists that it is unusual for a minority to be a physician. The Davis faculty sought to attack this lingering and negative color awareness directly with the best tools at its disposal. . . . This recognition by the Davis faculty is the antithesis of counter-educative. It is pro-educative, in the most fundamental sense. . . .

[[5. School Desegregation Precedents.]] Numerous state and lower federal courts have upheld the utilization of racial criteria to increase racial diversity in schools and to counter the effects of discrimination, despite an absence of *de jure* discrimination. In the context of voluntary efforts by state and local officials to overcome the effects of *de facto* discrimination in schools, judicial approval of race-conscious means has been unanimous. . . .

. . . In upholding orders compelling the desegregation of faculties, those cases have approved the use of racial criteria that injure individual whites to a degree that may exceed the injury to individual whites caused by special-admissions programs. For example, in *Carr v. Montgomery County Board of Education*, the district court ordered faculty desegregation, pursuant to a fixed racial ratio, and ordered that the ratio be accomplished by hiring and assignment. . . . This order, which requires hiring by race and which, inevitably, produces instances in which white teaching applicants are rejected in favor of blacks and in which white teachers are compelled, on pain of dismissal to teach in schools they would not attend voluntarily, was affirmed by this Court. Disappointed white teaching applicants in such cases are in a position indistinguishable from that of respondent in this case. . . .

[[6. Proper Standard of Review.]] When race sensitive means are employed against historically disfavored racial minorities, strict judicial scrutiny, an exception in the general scheme of judicial review, is appropriate because of the peculiar susceptibility of such groups to race-related harms. . . .

Obviously respondent and those in his position possess none of the attributes that have led the Court to define suspect classes and to trigger strict scrutiny. Indeed, to apply the suspect classification doctrine to defeat the Davis program would "stand the equal protection clause on its head." Respondent has suffered a diminished chance of obtaining a position in medical school, but the program he attacks "does not add to the burdens of an already disadvantaged discrete minority." Without minimizing the significance to respondent of not attaining admission, it remains true that his non-admission does not carry with it the stigmatic and degrading injury suffered by the discrete and insular groups singled out by the state in cases like *Loving*. The injury to respondent is an isolated incident in his life. It is not a reinforcement of the pervasive discrimination that members of alienated minority groups encounter constantly and repeatedly throughout their lives. It will not engender in respondent's own mind any belief that he is innately inferior, nor will it prompt others to so view him. There is not, in short, invidious discrimination against respondent. . . .

The Davis program does not constitute invidious racial discrimination, does not injure a suspect class, and does not infringe a fundamental right. It follows that the case is governed by the "traditional standard of review, which requires only that a state's system be shown to bear some rational relationship to legitimate state purposes."

The means chosen by the medical school bear not only a rational relationship to the desired ends, they are the means most directly related to those ends, indeed, the only effective means. Since the fit between means and ends is as tight as possible, and since the state ends are not only legitimate but extraordinarily compelling, there can be little doubt that the University prevails under the traditional standard of review. . . .

> Respectfully submitted,
> PAUL J. MISHKIN
> JACK B. OWENS
> DONALD L. REIDHAAR

ALLAN BAKKE'S BRIEF

[[1. Statistical Facts.]] . . . According to statistics published by petitioner, the average applicant admitted under the special-admissions programs possesses academic and other qualifications inferior to those of Bakke and of the average student admitted under the regular procedure. The following chart [see table 2.1] compares Bakke's qualifications with those of applicants who are regularly admitted and with those of applicants admitted under the special admission program.

[[2. Program is a Quota.]] . . . There are 100 places in the first year class at the Davis Medical School. Under normal circumstances, Allan Bakke would be eligible to compete for all of those places. In this case, however, petitioner has formally adopted a preferential racial quota and has set aside 16 of the places for members of designated racial and ethnic minority groups. In so doing, petitioner has prevented Bakke, solely because of his race, from competing for the 16 quota places. Petitioner does not dispute this fact and, under the burden of proof rule announced by the California Supreme Court, concedes that it cannot refute Bakke's claim that he would have been admitted to the medical school had there been no quota. . . .

. . . The mechanism of the quota has grave implications; the evil transcends an individual case of favored treatment, just as it goes beyond an individual case of personal discrimination. It implies that rights to education, training, and consequent career opportunities, ideally open to all on an equal opportunity basis, will now be officially categorized by group membership. One would not become a doctor, lawyer, engineer or accountant, but a Black doctor, a Chicano

Table 2.1   [from Allan Bakke's Brief]

CLASS ENTERING IN FALL, 1973

			MCAT PERCENTILE[o]			
	SGPA[+]	OGPA[x]	Verb.	Quan.	Sci.	Gen. Info.
Allan Bakke	3.45	3.51	96	94	97	72
Average of Regular Admittees	3.51	3.49	81	76	83	69
Average of Special Admittees	2.62	2.88	46	24	35	33

CLASS ENTERING IN FALL, 1974

			MCAT PERCENTILE[o]			
	SGPA[+]	OGPA[x]	Verb.	Quan.	Sci.	Gen. Info.
Allan Bakke	3.45	3.51	96	94	97	75
Average of Regular Admittees	3.36	3.29	69	67	82	72
Average of Special Admittees	2.42	2.62	34	30	37	18

[+] Science Grade Point Average
[x] Overall Grade Point Average
[o] Medical College Admissions Test

lawyer, an Asian engineer, or an American Indian accountant. Admission to each profession or trade would be limited according to the relative size of each ethnic group. . . .

There immediately arises the problem of numbers. A quota in proportion to the national population? The state population? The county or city population? . . .

There also arises the question of numerous groups not covered by petitioner's quota: Filipinos? Samoans? Hawaiians? Moroccans? Lebanese? There are also a wide variety of ethnic sub-groups contained within the so-called "majority," who themselves have been disadvantaged or discriminated against in the past. . . .

And who is a member of a racial group? Need one be a "full-blooded" American Indian to qualify? Or is one grandparent sufficient? Or one greatgrandparent? Are we to become involved in the testing of legal rights according to blood lines?

The questions do not stop there. How extensive a preference should be granted? In this case it is sixteen places at the Davis Medical School. Why not eight, or thirty-two, or sixty-four, or some other number? What is the rational basis for any specific percentage?

For how long is the preference to be continued? And who shall decide when the preference is to be altered or concluded, and on what terms, and by what authority?

These questions illustrate the dilemmas inherent in the quota system. While they might arise case-by-case in the context of heated litigation, their ultimate resolution would lie beyond the prayer of any individual claimant. We would be required to abandon the commitment to a society protective of individual achievement and replace it with a system of rights based upon racial or ethnic group membership. . . .

[[3. The Proper Standard of Review.]] . . . Nearly a generation ago, this Court ruled that the exclusion of a black applicant from a state university solely because of his race was a violation of the Equal Protection Clause. Ever since, the unvaried holding of this Court's decisions and the teaching of contemporary history have been the same: discrimination on the basis of race is illegal, immoral, unconstitutional, inherently wrong and destructive of a democratic society. . . .

Despite the obvious adverse effect of the special admission program upon Bakke, the University claims that he needs no judicial protection. Petitioner says that "[t]he injury to [Bakke] is an isolated incident in his life." Petitioner asserts that Bakke, as a member of the so-called majority, has "life-or-death control over the special-admission program." The record is totally barren of any evidence to support such an argument. Bakke certainly has not chosen to discriminate against himself. It is a state operated medical school which has made that decision. To say that Allan Bakke should resort to the political process for protection is unrealistic insofar as Bakke the individual is concerned, and is wrong insofar as the Constitution is concerned.

Allan Bakke has brought this lawsuit on his own behalf. He claims membership in no group, and represents no class of litigants. He desires to be a physician and he seeks enrollment at the Davis Medical School. He asks only that his application be considered in a racially neutral manner. To tell him at this time that he should stop suing and start campaigning is to tell him to forget entirely about a career in medicine. . . .

Thus when an individual such as Allan Bakke is discriminated against because of his race, he must not be deprived of judicial protection because he is a member of the "majority." Under the Fourteenth Amendment, racial discrimination is inherently suspect regardless of the purpose of the discriminator or the identity of the person victimized. It has always been subject to strict judicial scrutiny and is illegal unless the government demonstrates that the end sought to be achieved is a *compelling state interest* and, further, that the discrimination employed is *strictly necessary* to promote such an objective. . . .

Respectfully submitted,
REYNOLD H. COLVIN

POLISH AMERICAN CONGRESS *AMICUS* BRIEF

. . . We ask this Court whether there is a substantial difference between a Black being called a "Nigger" and a Polish American being called a "Pollack," whether telling a Black or Mexican American he cannot qualify is substantially more degrading than telling a Polish American the same thing; whether the lack of recognition of Blacks and Latins in senior levels of corporate management is more serious than the lack of recognition of Polish and Italian Americans. . . .

The greatest irony of this result is that many Whites who have championed the cause of civil rights have ended up being in this "forgotten and disfavored" group. Why are "Whites" who never practiced discrimination, but fought for and championed equality, and who themselves suffered discrimination obliged to continue to suffer simply because other Whites practice racial discrimination? If Whites are to suffer for the "greater good" then for how long and for whose benefit? . . .

We do not suggest that a "special admissions" program is never constitutionally feasible or that less significance be attached to the problems of Blacks, Chicanos and Asians. We do say that for such a program to be constitutionally permissible it (1) cannot be arbitrary as it is here in giving preference to one kind of White ethnic group (Hispanic) without showing why other White ethnic groups similarly situated have not even been considered, (2) cannot be concerned with race alone but must also provide relief for other groups who have suffered prohibited discrimination such as color, sex, religion and national origin of all types, (3) must demonstrate that those included in the "unfavored" group will not be discriminated in a prohibited manner by the program itself and (4) establish a sufficient data base indicating more precisely why such a program is needed, how long it is to last, and who is to benefit therefrom. . . .

Respectfully submitted,
LEONARD F. WALENTYNOWICZ

NAACP LEGAL DEFENSE & EDUCATIONAL FUND *AMICUS* BRIEF

. . . The propriety of race-conscious remedies was a matter squarely considered by the Congress which fashioned the Fourteenth Amendment, and that Congress believed such remedial programs not merely permissible but necessary. From the closing days of the Civil War until the end of civilian Reconstruction, Congress adopted a series of social welfare laws expressly delineating the racial groups entitled to participate in or benefit from each program. . . . The most far reaching of these programs, the 1866 Freedmen's Bureau Act, was enacted less than a month after Congress approved the Fourteenth Amendment. . . .

[[The Freedmen's Bureau]] . . . was authorized by Congress in 1866 to provide land and buildings and spend designated funds for "the education of the freed people," but could provide no such aid to refugees or other whites. The same statute conveyed a number of disputed lands to "heads of families of the African races" and authorized the sale of some thirty-eight thousand other acres to black families. . . . No comparable federal programs existed for—or were established—for whites. . . .

. . . [[P]]rograms such as those enacted by Congress in the Reconstruction

Era are still needed a century later to alleviate the injuries suffered by blacks and other minorities in the health area. . . .

> Respectfully submitted,
> JACK GREENBERG
> ERIC SCHNAPPER
> BETH J. LIEF
> JAMES M. NABRIT
> DAVID E. KENDALL
> KELLIS PARKER
> CHARLES S. RALSTON
> BILL LANN LEE

MEXICAN AMERICAN LEGAL DEFENSE & EDUCATIONAL FUND *AMICUS* BRIEF

. . . It has been observed that "Mexicans were by far the most segregated group in California public education by the end of the 1920's." Such an observation is equally appropriate today. For example, in the Los Angeles Unified School District in 1974 more than 45% of the Spanish surnamed pupils were in schools in which minorities constituted more than 90% of the student body. . . . These seeds of past acts of intentional segregation, along with the continuing reluctance to deal with the problem, continue to haunt the Mexican American student. . . .

The consequences of these acts have been predictable. In California 85.7% of Anglos reach grade 12, while only 67.3% and 63.8% of black and Mexican American children respectively achieve this level. By the twelfth grade, 8.1% of Anglos read more than three (3) years behind grade level while the comparable figures for blacks are 18.9% and for Mexican Americans, 22.1%. . . .

. . . There is substantial evidence that minority populations are seriously underserved with medical care and that this has been the cause, in part, of a substantial disparity in the quality of health that exists in minority communities. . . .

. . . In California, blacks comprise approximately 7.6% of the population while Mexican Americans comprise approximately 18%. . . .

. . . In California, blacks constitute today 2.2% of the employed physicians while Mexican Americans constitute approximately 1%. Stated another way, while blacks and Mexican Americans constitute approximately 24–25% of the California population, their representation in the medical profession before the inception of special admissions programs was approximately 3%. . . .

> Respectfully submitted,
> VILMA S. MARTINEZ
> PETER D. ROOS
> LINDA HANTEN

ANTI-DEFAMATION LEAGUE OF
B'NAI B'RITH *AMICUS* BRIEF

. . . In what sense can a racial quota be benign so that a racial classification can be immune from the strictures of the Equal Protection Clause? . . . By definition a quota is a means of allocating scarce rights, goods, or services. If there were enough places at California's medical schools for all who wished to take advantage of them, there would be no need for a quota. A quota arbitrarily—i.e., on grounds inconsistent with the equal treatment of equals—grants benefits to some by denying them to others. . . .

A racial quota is, therefore, not benign with regard to the individual who is deprived of benefits he would have had were he only of the preferred racial group. But a racial quota is not necessarily benign even for the individual or the group that is purportedly the beneficiary of the quota. The individual admitted under the quota will bear the stigma of one who could not "make it" under standards applicable to his fellow students. . . .

. . . It is indeed difficult to discover where the benignity of a racial quota is to be found. Not in the deprivation of benefits to the non-preferred race; not in the stigmatization of the preferred race; not in the effects on a given society. A racial quota cannot be benign. It must always be malignant, malignant because it defies the constitutional pronouncement of equal protection of the laws; malignant because it reduces individuals to a single attribute, skin color, and is the very antithesis of equal opportunity; malignant because it is destructive of the democratic society which requires that in the eyes of the law every person shall count as one, none for more, none for less. . . .

> Respectfully submitted,
> PHILIP B. KURLAND
> DANIEL D. POLSBY

ORAL ARGUMENT

MR. COX [[Attorney for Davis Medical School]]: . . . I wanted to emphasize that the designation of sixteen places was not a quota, at least [[not]] as I would use that word. Certainly it was not a quota in the sense of an arbitrary limit put on the number of members of a non-popular group who would be admitted to an institution which was looking down its nose at them.

THE COURT: It did put a limit on the number of white people, didn't it?

COX: I think that it limited the number of non-minority, and therefore essentially white, yes. But there are two things to be said about that: One is that this was not pointing the finger at a group which had been marked as inferior in any sense; and it was undifferentiated, it operated against a wide variety of people. So I think it was not stigmatizing in the sense of the old quota against Jews was stigmatizing, in any way.

THE COURT: But it did put a limit on their number in each class? . . .

COX: It did put a limit, no question about that, and I don't mean to infer that [[it didn't]]. And I will direct myself to it a little later, if I may.

THE COURT: Do you agree, then, that there was a quota of eighty-four?

COX: Well, I would deny that it was a quota. We agree that there were sixteen places set aside for qualified disadvantaged minority students. Now, if that number—if setting aside a number, if the amount of resources—

THE COURT: No, the question is not whether the sixteen is a quota; the question is whether the eighty-four is a quota. And what is your answer to that?

COX: I would say that neither is properly defined as a quota.

THE COURT: And then, why not?

COX: Because, in the first place—because of my understanding of the meaning of "quota." And I think the decisive things are the facts, and the operative facts are: This is not something imposed from outside, as the quotas are in employment, or the targets are in employment sometimes today.

It was not a limit on the number of minority students. Other minority students were in fact accepted through the regular admissions program. It was not a guarantee of a minimum number of minority students, because all of them had to be, and the testimony is that all of them were, fully qualified.

All right. It did say that if there are sixteen qualified minority students, and they were also disadvantaged, then sixteen places shall be filled by them and only eighty-four places will be available to others.

THE COURT: Mr. Cox, the facts are not in dispute. Does it really matter what we call this program?

COX: No, I quite agree with you, Mr. Justice. I was trying to emphasize that the facts here have none of the aspects—that there are none of the facts that lead us to think of "quota" as a bad word. What we call this doesn't matter; and if we call it a quota, knowing the facts, and deciding according to the operative facts and not influenced by the semantics, it couldn't matter less. . . .

✳   ✳   ✳

THE COURT: Mr. Cox, what if Davis Medical School had decided that, since the population of doctors in the—among the minority population of doctors in California was so small, instead of setting aside sixteen seats for minority doctors, they would set aside fifty seats, until that balance were redressed, and the minority population of doctors equalled that of the population as a whole. Would that be any more infirm than the program that Davis has?

COX: Well, I think my answer is . . . that so long as the numbers are . . . reasonably adaptable to the social goal—and I'm thinking of the one you mentioned, Justice Rehnquist—then there is no reason to condemn a program because of the particular number chosen. . . .

I would say that as the number goes up, the danger of invidiousness, or the danger that this is being done not for social purposes but to favor one group as against another group, the risk, if you will, of a finding of an invidious purpose to discriminate against is great[[er]]. And therefore, I think it's a harder case. . . .

THE COURT: Mr. Cox, along this same line of discussion, would you relate the number in any way to the population; and if so, the population of the nation, the state, the city, or to what standard?

COX: Well, the number sixteen here is not in any way linked to population in California.

THE COURT: It's twenty-three, I think, for the minorities.

COX: Well, this was sixteen.

THE COURT: Yes.

COX: I think . . . I would only say, as the number gets higher, I think that it's undesirable to have the number linked to population. . . .

But I think it's quite clear that this program was not of that character; and in fact, of course, if we're speaking of what's going to happen to education all over the country, in fact . . . the minorities admitted to professional schools have not come anywhere near their actual percentage of the population. . . .

*   *   *

THE COURT: Mr. Colvin, you do not dispute the basic finding that everybody admitted under the special program was qualified, do you?

MR. COLVIN [[Attorney for Bakke]]: We certainly do dispute it. Not upon the ground that Mr. Bakke is attempting to tell the school what the qualifications are, nor upon the ground that we as his counsel can somehow set up a rule which will tell us who is qualified to go to medical school. . . .

THE COURT: There is nothing in the record to indicate that they chose the 2.5 figure because they felt that anyone with a lesser score would not be qualified either to do the academic work or to practice medicine.

COLVIN: No, but that was their rule. . . .

THE COURT: But then, how does that go—why do you disagree with the proposition that there is nothing in this record to show that any of the special people were [[not]] qualified to study and to practice?

COLVIN: We simply say that we do not agree, we do not agree that there is a showing that they were qualified. We are not making the argument that they were disqualified, but we are saying: Taking the school's own standards, taking the very thing that the school was talking about, they simply do not measure up on that point.

✳   ✳   ✳

THE COURT: Now, would your argument be the same if one, instead of sixteen, seats were left open?

COLVIN: Most respectfully, the argument does not turn on the numbers.

THE COURT: My question is: Would you make the same argument?

COLVIN: Yes.

THE COURT: If it was one?

COLVIN: If it was one and if there was an agreement, as there is in this case, that he was kept out by his race Whether it is one, one hundred, two—

THE COURT: I didn't say anything about him being—I said that the regulation said that one seat would be left open for an underprivileged minority person.

COLVIN: Yes. We don't think we would ever get to that point—

THE COURT: So numbers are just unimportant?

COLVIN: Numbers are unimportant. It is the principle of keeping a man out because of his race that is important.

THE COURT: You are arguing about keeping somebody out, and the other side is arguing about getting somebody in.

COLVIN: That's right.

THE COURT: So it depends on which way you look at it, doesn't it?

COLVIN: It depends on which way you look at the problem.

THE COURT: It does?

COLVIN: If I may finish. The problem—

THE COURT: You are talking about your client's rights. Don't these underprivileged people have some rights?

COLVIN: They certainly have the right to compete—

THE COURT: To eat cake. . . .

THE OPINION

Mr. Justice Powell announced the judgment of the Court. . . .

In view of the clear legislative intent, Title VI must be held to proscribe only those racial classifications that would violate the Equal Protection Clause or the Fifth Amendment. . . .

Nevertheless, petitioner argues that the court below erred in applying strict scrutiny to the special admissions program because white males, such as respondent, are not a "discrete and insular minority" requiring extraordinary protection from the majoritarian political process. This rationale, however, has never been invoked in our decisions as a prerequisite to subjecting racial or ethnic distinctions to strict scrutiny. Nor has this Court held that discreteness and insularity constitute necessary preconditions to a holding that a particular classification is invidious. These characteristics may be relevant in deciding whether or not to add new types of classifications to the list of "suspect" categories or whether a particular classification survives close examination. Racial and ethnic classifications, however, are subject to stringent examination without regard to these additional characteristics. . . .

Petitioner urges us to adopt for the first time a more restrictive view of the Equal Protection Clause and hold that discrimination against members of the white "majority" cannot be suspect if its purpose can be characterized as "benign." The clock of our liberties, however, cannot be turned back to 1868. It is far too late to argue that the guarantee of equal protection to *all* persons permit the recognition of special wards entitled to a degree of protection greater than that accorded others. "The Fourteenth Amendment is not directed solely against discrimination due to a 'two-class theory'—that is, based upon differences between 'white' and Negro."

Once the artificial line of a "two-class theory" of the Fourteenth Amendment is put aside, the difficulties entailed in varying the level of judicial review according to a perceived "preferred" status of a particular racial or ethnic minority are intractable. The concepts of "majority" and "minority" necessarily reflect temporary arrangements and political judgments. As observed above, the white "majority" itself is composed of various minority groups, most of which can lay claim to a history of prior discrimination at the hands of the State and private individuals. Not all of these groups can receive preferential treatment and corresponding judicial tolerance of distinctions drawn in terms of race and nationality, for then the only "majority" left would be a new minority of white Anglo-Saxon Protestants. There is no principled basis for deciding which groups would merit "heightened judicial solicitude" and which would not. . . .

We have held that in "order to justify the use of a suspect classification, a State must show that its purpose or interest is both constitutionally permissible and substantial, and that its use of the classification is 'necessary . . . to the accomplishment' of its purpose or the safeguarding of its interest." The special admissions program purports to serve the [[following four]] purposes . . .

[[i.]] If petitioner's purpose is to assure within its student body some specified percentage of a particular group merely because of its race or ethnic origin, such a preferential purpose must be rejected not as insubstantial but as facially invalid. Preferring members of any one group for no reason other than race or ethnic origin is discrimination for its own sake. This the Constitution forbids. . . .

[[ii.]] The State certainly has a legitimate and substantial interest in ameliorating, or eliminating where feasible, the disabling effects of identified discrimination. The line of school segregation cases, commencing with Brown, attests to the importance of this state goal and the commitment of the judiciary to affirm all lawful means toward its attainment. In the school cases the States were required by court order to redress the wrongs worked by specific instances of racial discrimination. That goal was far more focused than the remedying of the effects of "societal discrimination," an amorphous concept of injury that may be ageless in its reach into the past.

We have never approved a classification that aids persons perceived as members of relatively victimized groups at the expense of other innocent individuals in the absence of judicial, legislative, or administrative findings of constitutional or statutory violations. . . .

Hence, the purpose of helping certain groups whom the faculty of the Davis Medical School perceived as victims of "societal discrimination" does not justify a classification that imposes disadvantages upon persons like respondent, who bear no responsibility for whatever harm the beneficiaries of the special admissions program are thought to have suffered. . . .

[[iii.]] Petitioner identifies, as another purpose of its program, improving the delivery of health-care services to communities currently underserved. It may be assumed that in some situations a State's interest in facilitating the health care of its citizens is sufficiently compelling to support the use of a suspect classification. But there is virtually no evidence in the record indicating that petitioner's special admissions program is either needed or geared to promote that goal. . . .

[[iv.]] The fourth goal asserted by petitioner is the attainment of a diverse student body. This clearly is a constitutionally permissible goal for an institution of higher education. Academic freedom, though not a specifically enumerated constitutional right, long has been viewed as a special concern of the First Amendment. The freedom of a university to make its own judgments as to education includes the selection of its student body. . . .

Thus, in arguing that its universities must be accorded the right to select those students who will contribute the most to the "robust exchange of ideas," petitioner invokes a countervailing constitutional interest, that of the First Amendment. In this light, petitioner must be viewed as seeking to achieve a goal that is of paramount importance in the fulfillment of its mission. . . .

It may be assumed that the reservation of a specified number of seats in each class for individuals from the preferred ethnic groups would contribute to the attainment of considerable ethnic diversity in the student body. But petitioner's argument that this is the only effective means of serving the interest of diversity is seriously flawed. . . .

The experience of other university admissions programs, which take race into account in achieving the educational diversity valued by the First Amendment, demonstrates that the assignment of a fixed number of places to a minority group is not a necessary means toward that end. An illuminating example is found in the Harvard College program. . . .

In such an admissions program, race or ethnic background may be deemed a "plus" in a particular applicant's file, yet it does not insulate the individual from comparison with all other candidates for the available seats. The file of a particular black applicant may be examined for his potential contribution to diversity without the factor of race being decisive when compared, for example, with that of an applicant identified as an Italian-American if the latter is thought to exhibit qualities more likely to promote beneficial educational pluralism. Such qualities could include exceptional personal talents, unique work or service experience, leadership potential, maturity, demonstrated compassion, a history of overcoming disadvantage, ability to communicate with the poor, or other qualifications deemed important. . . .

This kind of program treats each applicant as an individual in the admissions process. The applicant who loses out on the last available seat to another candidate receiving a "plus" on the basis of ethnic background will not have been foreclosed from all consideration for that seat simply because he was not the right color or had the wrong surname. . . .

In summary, it is evident that the Davis special admissions program involves the use of an explicit racial classification never before countenanced by this Court. It tells applicants who are not Negro, Asian, or Chicano that they are totally excluded from a specific percentage of the seats in an entering class. No matter how strong their qualifications, quantitative and extracurricular, including their own potential for contribution to educational diversity, they are never afforded the chance to compete with applicants from the preferred groups for the special admissions seats. At the same time, the preferred applicants have the opportunity to compete for every seat in the class.

The fatal flaw in petitioner's program is its disregard of individual rights as guaranteed by the Fourteenth Amendment. . . . For this reason, that portion of the California court's judgment holding petitioner's special admissions program invalid under the Fourteenth Amendment must be affirmed. . . .

[[H]]owever, the courts below failed to recognize that the State has a substantial interest that legitimately may be served by a properly devised admissions program involving the competitive consideration of race and ethnic origin. For this reason, so much of the California court's judgment as enjoins petitioner from any consideration of the race of any applicant must be reversed. . . .

Opinion of Mr. Justice Brennan, White, Marshall, and Blackmun, concurring in the judgment in part and dissenting . . .

. . . The difficulty of the issue presented—whether government may use race-conscious programs to redress the continuing effects of past discrimination—and the mature consideration which each of our Brethren has brought to it have resulted in many opinions, no single one speaking for the Court. But this should not and must not mask the central meaning of today's opinions: Government may take race into account when it acts not to demean or insult any racial group, but to remedy disadvantages cast on minorities by past racial prejudices, at least when appropriate findings have been made by judicial legislative, or administrative bodies with competence to act in this area. . . .

In our view, Title VI prohibits only those uses of racial criteria that would violate the Fourteenth Amendment if employed by a State or its agencies; it does not bar the preferential treatment of racial minorities as a means of remedying past societal discrimination to the extent that such action is consistent with the Fourteenth Amendment. . . .

We turn, therefore, to our analysis of the Equal Protection Clause of the Fourteenth Amendment. . . .

. . . [[W]]e have held that a government practice or statute which restricts "fundamental rights" or which contains "suspect classifications" is to be subjected to "strict scrutiny" and can be justified only if it furthers a compelling government purpose and, even then, only if no less restrictive alternative is available. But no fundamental right is involved here. Nor do whites as a class have any of the "traditional indicia of suspectness: the class is not saddled with such disabilities, or subjected to such a history of purposeful unequal treatment, or relegated to such a position of political powerlessness as to command extraordinary protection from the majoritarian political process." . . .

On the other hand, the fact that this case does not fit neatly into our prior analytic framework for race cases does not mean that it should be analyzed by applying the very loose rational-basis standard of review that is the very least that is always applied in equal protection cases. . . . Instead, a number of considerations . . . lead us to conclude that racial classifications designed to further remedial purposes "'must serve important governmental objectives and must be substantially related to achievement of those objectives.'"

First, race, like "gender-based classification too often [has] been inexcusably utilized to stereotype and stigmatize politically powerless segments of society." . . .

Second, race, like gender and illegitimacy, is an immutable characteristic which its possessors are powerless to escape or set aside. While a classification is not per se invalid because it divides classes on the basis of an immutable characteristic, it is nevertheless true that such divisions are contrary to our deep belief that "legal burdens should bear some relationship to individual responsibility or wrongdoing." . . .

In sum, because of the significant risk that racial classifications established for ostensibly benign purposes can be misused, causing effects not unlike those created by invidious classifications, it is inappropriate to inquire only whether there is any conceivable basis that might sustain such a classification. Instead, to justify such a classification an important and articulated purpose for its use must be shown. In addition, any statute must be stricken that stigmatizes any group or that singles out those least well represented in the political process to bear the brunt of a benign program. . . .

[[In regard to the first prong of our test]] . . . Davis' articulated purpose of remedying the effects of past societal discrimination is, under our cases, sufficiently important to justify the use of race-conscious admissions programs where there is a sound basis for concluding that minority underrepresentation is substantial and chronic, and that the handicap of past discrimination is impeding access of minorities to the Medical School. . . .

. . . [[O]]ur prior cases unequivocally show that a state government may adopt race-conscious programs if the purpose of such programs is to remove the disparate racial impact its actions might otherwise have and if there is reason to believe that the disparate impact is itself the product of past discrimination, whether its own or that of society at large. There is no question that Davis' program is valid under this test.

Certainly, on the basis of the undisputed factual submissions before this Court, Davis had a sound basis for believing that the problem of underrepresentation of minorities was substantial and chronic and that the problem was attributable to handicaps imposed on minority applicants by past and present racial discrimination. Until at least 1973, the practice of medicine in this country was, in fact, if not in law, largely the prerogative of whites. In 1950, for example, while Negroes constituted 10% of the total population, Negro physicians constituted only 2.2% of the total number of physicians. . . .

Davis clearly could conclude that the serious and persistent underrepresentation of minorities in medicine depicted by these statistics is the result of handicaps under which minority applicants labor as a consequence of a background of deliberate, purposeful discrimination against minorities in education and in society generally, as well as in the medical profession. . . .

The second prong of our test—whether the Davis program stigmatizes any discrete group or individual and whether race is reasonably used in light of the program's objectives—is clearly satisfied by the Davis program.

It is not even claimed that Davis' program in any way operates to stigmatize or single out any discrete and insular, or even any identifiable, nonminority group. Nor will harm comparable to that imposed upon racial minorities by exclusion or separation on grounds of race be the likely result of the program. . . .

Nor was Bakke in any sense stamped as inferior by the Medical School's rejection of him. . . . Moreover, there is absolutely no basis for concluding that Bakke's rejection as a result of Davis' use of racial preference will affect him throughout his life in the same way as the segregation of the Negro school children in *Brown I* would have affected them. Unlike discrimination against racial minorities, the use of racial preferences for remedial purposes does not inflict a pervasive injury upon individual whites in the sense that wherever they go or whatever they do there is a significant likelihood that they will be treated as second-class citizens because of their color. . . .

We disagree with the lower courts' conclusion that the Davis program's use of race was unreasonable in light of its objectives. First, as petitioner argues, there are no practical means by which it could achieve its ends in the foreseeable future without the use of race-conscious measures. With respect to any factor (such as poverty or family educational background) that may be used as a substitute for race as an indicator of past discrimination, whites greatly outnumber racial minorities simply because whites make up a far larger percentage of the total population and therefore far outnumber minorities in absolute terms at every socioeconomic level. . . . Moreover, while race is positively correlated with difference in GPA and MCAT scores, economic disadvantage is not. Thus, it appears that economically disadvantaged whites do not score less well than economically advantaged whites, while economically advantaged blacks score less well than do disadvantaged whites. These statistics graphically illustrate that the University's purpose to integrate its classes by compensating for past discrimination could not be achieved by a general preference for the economically disadvantaged or the children of parents of limited education unless such groups were to make up the entire class. . . .

Finally, Davis' special admissions program cannot be said to violate the Constitution simply because it has set aside a predetermined number of places for qualified minority applicants rather than using minority status as a positive factor to be considered in evaluating the applications of disadvantaged minority applicants. For purposes of constitutional adjudication, there is no difference between the two approaches. In any admissions program which accords special consideration to disadvantaged racial minorities, a determination of the degree of preference to be given is unavoidable, and any given preference that results in the exclusion of a white candidate is no more or less constitutionally acceptable than a program such as that at Davis. Furthermore, the extent of the preference inevitably depends on how many minority applicants the particular school is seeking to admit in any particular year so long as the number of qualified minority applicants exceeds that number. There is no sensible, and certainly no constitutional, distinction between, for example, adding a set of number of points to the admissions rating of disadvantaged minority applicants as an expression of the preference with the expectation that this will result in the admission of an approximately determined number of qualified minority applicants and setting a fixed number of places for such applicants as was done here. . . .

Mr. Justice Marshall . . .

. . . While I applaud the judgment of the Court that a university may consider race in its admissions process, it is more than a little ironic that, after several hundred years of class-based discrimination against Negroes, the Court is unwilling to hold that a class-based remedy for that discrimination is permissible. In declining to so hold, today's judgment ignores the fact that for several hundred years Negroes have been discriminated against, not as individuals, but rather solely because of the color of their skins. It is unnecessary in 20th century America to have individual Negroes demonstrate that they have been victims of discrimination; the racism of our society has been so pervasive that none, regardless of wealth or position, has managed to escape its impact. The experience of Negroes in America has been different in kind, not just in degree, from that of other ethnic groups. It is not merely the history of slavery alone but also that a whole people were marked as inferior by the law. And that mark has endured. The dream of America as a great melting pot has not been realized for the Negro; because of his skin color he never even made it into the pot. . . .

Mr. Justice Stevens, concurring in the judgment in part and dissenting in part . . .

Both petitioner and respondent have asked us to determine the legality of the University's special admissions program by reference to the Constitution. Our settled practice, however, is to avoid the decision of a constitutional issue if a case can be fairly decided on a statutory ground. . . . [[A]] dispositive statutory claim was raised at the very inception of this case, and squarely decided in the portion of the trial court judgment affirmed by the California Supreme Court, it is our plain duty to confront it. Only if petitioner should prevail on the statutory issue would it be necessary to decide whether the University's admissions program violated the Equal Protection Clause of the Fourteenth Amendment. Section 601 of the Civil Rights Act of 1964 provides:

> No person in the United States shall, on the ground of race, color, or national origin, be excluded from participation in, be denied the benefits of, or be subjected to discrimination under any program or activity receiving Federal financial assistance.

The University, through its special admissions policy excluded Bakke from participation in its program of medical education because of his race. The University also acknowledges that it was, and still is, receiving federal financial assistance The plain language of the statute therefore requires affirmance of the judgment below. . . .

II. DEVELOPMENTS AFTER *BAKKE*

Following *Bakke*, the Supreme Court has revisited the issue of affirmative action a number of times in a variety of contexts. How the Supreme Court has responded to these various cases has depended upon the authority of government that created the program, the type of program it was, and the changing membership and alignment of the Court itself. In two cases from the 1980s, *Wygant v. Jackson Board of Education* (1986)[12] and *Richmond v. J.A. Croson Company* (1989),[13] the Supreme Court struck down two affirmative action programs that local governments had instituted to remedy some form of past racial discrimination against racial minorities. In *Wygant*, a school board and a teacher's union had signed a contract that gave minority teachers with less seniority than white teachers additional protection from layoffs. The Court held that the purpose of remedying general societal discrimination by retaining "minority role model" teachers was not a compelling interest for a local school board and laying off white teachers because of their race was not a necessary means to that objective. Similarly, in *Croson*, Richmond, Virginia, required that 30 percent of all funds devoted to public works projects be subcontracted to "minority business enterprises." Although the Court held that the city did have a compelling interest in remedying the effects of its own past discrimination, the city did not document that it had engaged in such discrimination and it did not have the authority to remedy general societal discrimination. Because the Richmond affirmative action program gave racial preferences to minority enterprises outside of Richmond and to certain minority groups that had not been victims of discrimination inside Richmond (such as Eskimos and Aleuts), the Court concluded that the program failed strict scrutiny.

Until the mid-1990s, the Court was more deferential to affirmative action programs instituted by the federal government, both to remedy past societal discrimination and to promote diversity. In *Fullilove v. Klutznick* (1980), the Court upheld a 10 percent "set aside" of federal funds for local public works projects overseen by minority business enterprises.[14] It reasoned that Section 5 of the Fourteenth Amendment, which gave Congress the power to enforce the Equal Protection Clause, allowed the federal government to remedy all societal discrimination. Therefore, the program did not have to withstand strict scrutiny, despite its quota-like character. Similarly, in *Metro Broadcasting v. F.C.C.* (1990), the Court upheld a Federal Communications Commission (FCC) program that was intended to promote broadcast diversity.[15] The program in question preferred minorities in awarding new broadcast licenses and setting prices for previously revoked licenses. In this decision, a five-justice majority lowered the judicial scrutiny applicable to the FCC program and all other federal programs to intermediate scrutiny. Citing the *Bakke* opinion of Justice Powell, who had just retired from the Court, the Court held that broadcast diversity was an important governmental purpose and that the means used were substantially related to the goal. Therefore the FCC's affirmative action program was constitutional.

The composition of the Court has had a significant impact on how it has assessed the constitutionality of the above affirmative action programs. During most of the 1980s, Chief Justice Burger and Justices White, Powell, and Stevens were "swing" justices who voted to uphold some affirmative action programs and invalidate others. However, in 1986, Burger resigned and Antonin Scalia, a consistent opponent of all race-based affirmative action, joined the Court. In 1988, Anthony Kennedy, who was also generally (though not uniformly) skeptical of affirmative action, replaced Justice Powell. In 1991, shortly after *Metro*, a more pronounced shift in the balance of the Court on this issue occurred when Clarence Thomas, a consistent critic, replaced Thurgood Marshall, a staunch supporter. In 1993, White resigned and was replaced by Ruth Bader Ginsburg, an avowed defender of affirmative action. Lastly, over the years Stevens has gradually become more favorably disposed to affirmative action programs that promote some future benefit, such as diversity. In general, these changes made the Court by the mid-1990s more polarized on affirmative action and somewhat less deferential to such policies than it had been during the 1980s.

This reconstituted Court reformulated its stance on affirmative action in the context of public employment and contracting in *Adarand Constructors, Inc. v. Pena* (1995).[16] Acting under a federal law that presumed all racial minorities were "disadvantaged," the U.S. Department of Transportation's Central Federal Lands Highway Division (CFLHD) paid extra compensation to contractors who hired subcontracting firms run by "socially and economically disadvantaged individuals." Adarand, a highway construction company, submitted the low bid to a federal contractor, but the contract went to a Hispanic-owned firm. Adarand sued, claiming a violation of the Equal Protection Clause. Though the Supreme Court did not specifically invalidate the federal contracting clause, but rather remanded the case back to the district court, it did, in a sharply divided 5-4 decision, endorse three constitutional principles by which the constitutionality of affirmative action policies were to be assessed: skepticism, consistency, congruence. According to Justice O'Conner's majority opinion (joined by Chief Justice Rehnquist and Justices Scalia, Kennedy, and Thomas), all racial discrimination must be viewed with *skepticism* and therefore be evaluated under the severe test of strict scrutiny. This skepticism had to be applied in a *consistent* fashion, subjecting to the same test all governmental policies that used race, including "benign" discrimination that benefited traditionally disfavored racial minorities. Lastly, strict scrutiny also had to be applied in a *congruent* manner, requiring affirmative action programs at all levels of government, from the federal government to local counties and municipalities, to be measured by the same standard. O'Conner's opinion thus explicitly overruled *Metro* and undermined the holding in *Fullilove*, while expanding the import of *Wygant* and *Croson*.

Though *Adarand* did not explicitly invalidate the above contracting provision of the federal law, it clearly raised the constitutional bar for affirmative action programs. Accordingly, it called into question the validity of *Bakke* as a precedent because a majority of the Court had never formally embraced the diversity rationale for affirmative action in colleges and universities. In fact, in *Adarand*, the Court overruled *Metro*, which had been the only time a clear majority of the Court ever considered any kind of diversity to be an acceptable rationale for racial preferences. The controversy surrounding affirmative action programs in higher education mounted in March 1996 after the Fifth Circuit Court of Appeals ruled in *Hopwood v. Texas* that any consideration of race in college admissions was unconstitutional.[17] In response, Texas Governor George W. Bush implemented a race-neutral plan called "affirmative access," which granted the top 10 percent of Texas high school graduates automatic admission to state colleges and universities. In November 1996, the voters of California approved Proposition 209, which eliminated racial and gender preferences in "public employment, public education, or public contracting." In 1998, voters in Washington state overwhelmingly adopted Initiative 200, which contained the same language as California's Proposition 209. In 1999, Florida Governor

Jeb Bush implemented his "One Florida" initiative, which ended consideration of race in state education and guaranteed admission to state universities to the top 20 percent of high school graduates. Efforts to adopt similar policies in other states intensified, reflecting considerable popular opposition to affirmative action.

In 1996, the same year that the Fifth Circuit Court of Appeals struck down affirmative action in *Hopwood*, the University of Michigan Law School denied admission to Barbara Grutter, a white Michigan resident with an undergraduate grade point average (GPA) of 3.8 and a Law School Admissions Test (LSAT) score of 161 (85th percentile.) The Law School's admissions policy that resulted in Grutter's rejection included an affirmative action plan that sought to achieve student body diversity by enrolling a "critical mass" of racial minorities. To accomplish this end, the Law School gave a "plus" to a person's application if he or she was an African-American, a Hispanic, or a Native American. The result was that the Law School therefore admitted a significant number of these minorities who had lower GPAs and LSAT scores than rejected white and other applicants (see table 2.2).

In 1997, Grutter filed suit in federal district court, claiming that the Law School treated race as a "predominant" factor in admissions in violation of the Equal Protection Clause. Holding that Justice Powell's opinion in *Bakke* was not binding because it was the opinion of only one justice, the district court ruled in favor of Grutter. The Law School appealed to the Sixth Circuit Court of Appeals, which upheld Powell's opinion and reversed the lower court's judgment. Grutter appealed to the Supreme Court. For the first time in twenty-five years, the Court would revisit the constitutionality of affirmative action in higher education.[18]

The briefs filed by the litigants in *Grutter v. Bollinger* focused on two main questions: Was diversity a "compelling governmental interest"? Did the Law School's plan use "narrowly tailored" means to achieve the end of diversity?[19] Grutter's attorneys argued in their brief that only remedying clearly identified instances of past discrimination could be compelling under strict scrutiny. Unlike such remedial preferences, preferences to achieve diversity could exist permanently because the concept of "critical mass" was "amorphous" and "indistinguishable from simple racial balancing." On the other side, the Law School's attorneys argued in their brief that, because "race matters," diversity resulted in significant "educational benefits" for both the preferred minority students and for other students who would be exposed to minority viewpoints. Therefore, in their view, diversity was a compelling interest. In regard to whether the Law School's plan was narrowly tailored, Grutter's attorneys argued that it was a disguised quota, which also benefited people who had not suffered from real disadvantage while harming some who had been disadvantaged. The Law School countered that its plan was necessary to achieve a "critical mass" of minority students. Without the plan, minority students would feel isolated and the school would not obtain the educational benefits of substantial diversity.

Table 2.2 University of Michigan Law School LSAT and GPA Admission Grids for 1995 (in each cell: applicants above, admittees below)

African-Americans, Hispanics, and Native Americans

GPA	LSAT Score								
	148–150	151–153	154–155	156–158	159–160	161–163	164–166	167–169	170–180
3.75–4.00	2/0	4/1	2/1	5/3	3/2	3/3	3/3	1/1	1/1
3.50–3.74	7/0	10/5	9/5	9/8	10/8	14/13	3/2	0/0	1/1
3.25–3.49	8/2	7/3	12/7	18/15	5/3	7/7	3/3	4/4	0/0
3.00–3.24	28/2	16/2	8/2	14/8	7/6	11/10	3/3	2/2	2/2

Caucasians

GPA	LSAT Score								
	148–150	151–153	154–155	156–158	159–160	161–163	164–166	167–169	170–180
3.75–4.00	8/0	11/0	12/0	47/4	45/0	93/8	108/46	96/86	121/114
3.50–3.74	19/0	23/0	32/3	57/2	65/2	161/14	163/62	130/96	95/89
3.25–3.49	16/0	24/0	21/0	51/1	61/1	126/5	92/11	78/38	74/55
3.00–3.24	17/0	13/0	15/0	26/0	19/1	42/2	37/3	19/4	17/8

Source: From Petitioner's Brief, *Grutter v. Bollinger,* p. 16.

As in *Bakke*, a large number of organizations filed amicus briefs in *Grutter*. Two amicus briefs were particularly significant. The United States, acting through Solicitor General Theodore Olson, filed a brief in support of Barbara Grutter's position. Though it conceded that higher education had to be "broadly inclusive to our diverse national community" to achieve equal opportunity, and though it noticeably refrained from arguing that racial diversity was not a compelling interest, it extolled various race neutral means of achieving racial and "experiental" diversity. Specifically, it cited the "percent plans" of Texas, California, and Florida that guaranteed admission to state colleges and universities for the top graduates of in-state high schools. On behalf of the Law School, a group of retired military officers, including Lt. General Julius W. Becton, filed another important amicus brief through their attorney, Carter Phillips. The Becton brief argued that a diverse military officer corps was necessary for a "cohesive, and therefore effective, fighting force." In the view of these former officers, racial preferences in the admission practices of the service academies (e.g., West Point) and all public and private universities that supported the Reserve Officer Training Corps (ROTC) were necessary for national security and therefore satisfied strict scrutiny.

At oral argument Kirk Kolbo represented Grutter and Maureen Mahoney represented the University of Michigan Law School. Through the tone and content of their questions, most of the justices left little doubt about their constitutional leanings in the case: Rehnquist, Scalia, and Thomas were opposed to the Law School's policy; Stevens, Souter, Ginsburg, and Breyer were supportive. Two justices, however, were in the middle. As they had been throughout the 1990s and into the twenty-first century, Justices Anthony Kennedy and Sandra Day O'Conner were the crucial swing votes. Though both had voted to invalidate affirmative action programs in hiring, neither had taken an unequivocal stand against all forms of affirmative action. The questions they asked at oral argument revealed their ambivalence. Kennedy seemed open to the possibility that diversity was a compelling interest, while O'Conner, though receptive to some limited use of race in admissions, was bothered by the fact that the Law School's policy had no logical endpoint and for that reason was perhaps not narrowly tailored.

In spite of this concern, O'Conner joined the four steadfast supporters of affirmative action to produce a five-member majority to uphold the Law School's affirmative action policy. O'Conner's opinion for the Court, echoing Powell's opinion in *Bakke*, agreed that the achievement of racial diversity was a compelling interest in higher education and the legal profession. While applying strict scrutiny, she indicated that the Law School's description of the importance of a diverse student body was "one to which we defer." The benefits included increased "cross-racial understanding" for participants in an increasingly diverse workplace and an assurance that "the path to leadership" was "visibly open to talented and qualified individuals of every race and ethnicity." Citing the Becton brief, she underlined the importance of maintaining diversity in the military's officer corps. Since the policy allowed for "truly individualized consideration" and used race in a "flexible, nonmechanical way," she concluded that the Law School's plan was narrowly tailored. Other relevant kinds of diversity received enough consideration so that racial minorities were not insulated from competition with nonminority applicants in the admissions process. However, because racial classifications were "potentially so dangerous," she ended her opinion with the remark that "race-conscious admissions policies must be limited in time" and added, "We expect that 25 years from now, the use of racial preferences will no longer be necessary to further the interest approved today."

Kennedy, the other "swing" justice, "swung" the other way, joining Scalia and Thomas in a dissent written by Chief Justice Rehnquist.[20] While Rehnquist did not explicitly address the issue of diversity as a compelling interest, he believed the Law School's race-conscious admissions policy should have been stricken down because it was not narrowly tailored. Specifically, he viewed the program as a "naked effort to achieve racial balancing." He questioned the definition of "critical mass," especially in light of statistics that showed that Hispanics and Native Americans were admitted in much smaller numbers than African-Americans. How could a "critical mass" of Native Americans be so much lower than the one needed for African-Americans? And why did the percentages of admitted students from each minority group approximate the percentage of each minority in the applicant pool? Noting these discrepancies and coincidences, Rehnquist concluded that the goal of a "critical mass" was "simply a sham." In a separate dissent, Justice Thomas, joined by Justice Scalia, questioned whether diversity really was a compelling interest. In his view, only a "pressing public necessity" that threatened violence or anarchy was sufficiently powerful to override the guarantee of equal protection. The state of Michigan had no such interest in promoting racial diversity in its elite public law school because it could achieve diversity by lowering the academic standards of the school. In fact, Thomas insisted, the state had no compelling interest in maintaining the Michigan Law School at all since most Law School graduates left the state of Michigan.

Which justice had the best argument? Is diversity in education so compelling that it justifies race-conscious programs? What exactly are the benefits associated with racial diversity? Is all this talk about diversity, as Chief Justice Rehnquist suggests, simply a "sham"? Can universities afford not to consider race in a world in which race still matters? Or does diversity no more justify racial preferences than remedying general societal discrimination? Should colleges and universities be allowed to use racial preferences for the latter purpose, if they can use them for the former?

Regardless of the answers to these questions, the Supreme Court in *Grutter*, twenty-five years after *Bakke*, finally resolved the vexing issue of the constitutionality of affirmative action in higher education. In 2003, four years after Justice Powell's death, his opinion in *Bakke* unmistakably commanded five members of the Court, thereby confirming the earlier decision as a landmark precedent. For at least twenty-five more years, racial preferences of the type

Box 2.2   CONGRESSIONAL REACTION TO *GRUTTER*

REPRESENTATIVE JOE BACA (D-California):
    Mr. Speaker, yesterday, [[the]] Supreme Court decided to support the hopes and dreams of millions of Hispanic children. It tells them they will have the same opportunities, the same choices, the same future that others will. The Court was loud and clear when it said that diversity can be used by colleges and universities in their admissions policies. . . .
    This year, black and Hispanic students make up only 16 percent of first-year students at California's five state-run medical schools and public law schools. In contrast, in the final years of race-conscious admissions, black and Hispanics consistently accounted for more that 20 percent of enrollment at these schools. Acceptance rates for Hispanic applicants in the entire University of California system has dropped from 64 percent in 1997 to 47 percent in 2002. What is happening to those other students? They are not just numbers!!! They are people whose lives will be changed forever. . . .
    This loss for the Bush Administration and for its policies is a victory for every child that wants an opportunity for a better education and a better life.

REPRESENTATIVE STEVE KING (R-Iowa):
    . . . I am not a lawyer, but it does not take a lawyer to know that the Supreme Court missed the mark when they upheld the program at the University of Michigan Law School that relies on race and the law school admissions decision-making process. The race-based admissions policy violates Martin Luther King's call for a color-blind society. Admission should be determined based on criteria that reward excellence, not race. It is paternalistic for minority students to be given preferential treatment. All students should have the same opportunities to succeed, regardless of color. . . .
    . . . Justice Thomas hit the nail on the head when he wrote of the lack of principle in the majority opinion. . . . Justice Thomas, I agree. And I agree that the only principle in the majority opinion in Grutter was the principle of expediency to allow racial preferences. Certainly, the constitutional principles were not involved. The Fourteenth amendment prohibits such race-based admissions decisions. Our Constitution is color-blind. Obviously, a majority of the Supreme Court is not.

Source: "Affirmative Action Ruling," June 24, 2003, 108th Congress, 1st Session, *Congressional Record*, p. E1331; "Michigan Affirmative Action Case," June 24, 2003, p. H5799.

used by the University of Michigan Law School can constitutionally be used in higher education. How the Court's decision in *Grutter* will affect affirmative action programs outside higher education is not known. Moreover, it is unclear whether public opposition to affirmative action will continue to grow. There is little doubt that *Grutter* has not ended the public debate over affirmative action, as congressional reaction to the decision shows (see box 2.2). There is also little doubt that state legislatures and Congress have the authority to prohibit or restrict affirmative action, as California, Washington, and Florida have already done. What is uncertain is whether other states and the federal government will follow their example given the fact most politicians are not eager to enter this political minefield.

BIBLIOGRAPHY

George, Robert P. "Symposium: Examining Diversity in Education: Gratz and Grutter: Some Hard Questions." 103 *Columbia Law Review* (2003): 1634–39.
Karst, Kenneth L. "Symposium: The Revival of Forward-Looking Affirmative Action." 104 *Columbia Law Review* (2004): 60–74.
Liu, Goodwin. "Article: Affirmative Action in Higher Education: The Diversity Rationale and the Compelling Interest Test." 33 *Harvard Civil Rights-Civil Liberties Law Review* (1998): 381–442.
McMahan, T. Vance, and Don R. Willett. "Symposium: Hope from Hopwood: Charting a Positive Civil Rights Court for Texas and the Nation." 10 *Stanford Law and Policy Review* (1999): 163–75.
Selmi, Michael. "Essay: The Life of Bakke: An Affirmative Action Retrospective." 87 *Georgetown Law Journal* (1999): 981–1022.

BRIEFS

GRUTTER'S BRIEF

[[1. Diversity as a Compelling Interest.]] Unhinged from any purported constitutional foundation, the Law School's assertion that diversity is a compelling state interest falls away readily in light of the Court's other precedents. This becomes apparent by comparing the Law School's articulated diversity interest to the one interest that the Court has held to be compelling—remedying past or present identified statutory or constitutional violations of the guarantee of equality. . . . A remedy for identified instances of discrimination is inextricably tethered to the purposes of the nondiscrimination guarantee; it seeks to repair the injury and restore the promise of equality broken by the effects of the violation. In its invocation and use, the "deviation from the norm of equal treatment of all racial and ethnic groups is a temporary matter, a measure taken in the service of the goal of equality itself." . . . Such a clearly identified remedial goal permits guidance in determining "the precise scope of the injury" and the "extent of the remedy necessary to cure its effects." Absent these attributes, an interest could be used to "justify a preference of any size or duration.". . .

. . . The concept of "diversity" is itself notoriously ill-defined, and the Law School's defense in this case only illustrates the point. . . . The "mass" reaches the stage of "critical" when it produces the educational benefits claimed by the Law School to flow from it. The point at which this "critical mass" is reached can best be described as a matter for mystical and metaphysical inquiry. On the one hand, the Law School vehemently denies that "critical mass" can be defined with reference to a number or range of numbers of enrolled students, while on the other hand it contends that "critical mass" means the *same thing* as "meaningful numbers" of enrolled students from the specified racial and ethnic minority groups. A rare point of clarity, though, is that however defined, the Law School claims for itself and other educational institutions the unique ability (and hence the right) to determine which particular racial and ethnic minorities are necessary for achievement of "critical mass," and at what point that "critical mass" is reached. . . .

Accordingly, an interest in diversity is as "ill-defined" and "amorphous" as a goal of remedying societal discrimination or providing role models to minority children. . . . Because the nature of the interest is one in which success in achieving it is measured not by remedying past identified injury, but instead by ensuring against "underrepresentation" going forward, it is an interest that could justify preferences "timeless in their ability to affect the future." Its adoption as a compelling interest would give the Nation its first *permanent* justification for racial preferences, and one that is indistinguishable from simple racial balancing. . . .

. . . [[W]]hether diversity actually produces educational benefits is a question entirely distinct from whether it is a *compelling interest* sufficient to support racial preferences in admissions. Few would gainsay that remedying the lingering effects of societal discrimination or providing role models to school children would produce positive benefits. . . . But as important and valuable as those interests are, they cannot be. . . . *compelling interests* justifying state-sponsored racial preferences. Because similar reasoning applies to the amorphous, boundless diversity rationale, it is a non sequitur for the Law School to argue that mere evidence of some educational benefit makes the interest a compelling one. . . .

[[2. Narrow Tailoring of Means.]] Because an interest in diversity is inherently unsuited to "narrowly-tailored" means, it should hardly be surprising that the Law School's racial preferences, which it justifies on diversity grounds, are anything but narrowly tailored. . . .

. . . The Law School's racial preferences . . . are not even facially restricted to those individuals who demonstrate disadvantage of any kind, whether or not arising from discrimination. Because *"race matters"* in the judgment of the Law School, race *by itself* is a sufficient basis for a student to receive a preference if one belongs to a race that has been "historically discriminated against." To the Law School, at least, it is "obvious that 'students from groups which have been historically discriminated against' have experiences that are integral to this mission, *regardless of whether they are rich or poor or 'victims' of discrimination.*" This is a stark use of race, more so than was employed by the program that was *struck down* in *Bakke*. . . .

The way in which the Law School defines its interest in diversity proves how it is tied to crude stereotypes. It deems that *mere membership* in one of the specified racial or ethnic groups will make it "particularly likely" that students will have had "experiences and perspectives of special importance" to the Law School's "mission." Thus, the Law School "impermissibly value[s] individuals because [it] presume[s] that persons think in a manner associated with their race." . . .

In no meaningful sense can the Law School be said to "weigh fairly and competitively" the consideration of race and ethnicity in the admissions process. Applicants from the disfavored races certainly do not compete on the "same footing" as applicants from the preferred racial and ethnic groups. . . .

The Law School's "critical mass," a concept it reserves for students from the "historically discriminated against" racial and ethnic groups is, as the district court found, "practically indistinguishable from a quota system." The fact that it does not set aside each year a "fixed" number of spaces in the class does not make it any less a quota-based system. Justice Powell made clear that a university could not constitutionally maintain the "functional equivalent of a quota system." . . .

Here, the district court found that the Law School's conception of "critical mass" was to ensure enrollment of a minimum of 10–12% of the class from the specified minority groups, with a range of enrollment between 10–17%. The finding has ample support in the record. First, although evasive, the Law School does acknowledge that "critical mass" means the same thing as "meaningful numbers" of students from the preferred minority groups. It reports that it has been able to achieve critical mass with its policy, so that by looking at the admissions data, one can observe what numbers define critical mass. Even with some variations, the numbers demonstrate a remarkable stability, at least as stable as the numbers for enrollment of all students across the years. . . .

Second, the relationship of means to ends is a poor one if the Law School's genuine interest is either intellectual or even racial and ethnic diversity. As the district court noted, "there is no logical basis" for the Law School's choice of the "particular racial groups which receive special attention under the current admissions policy." Thus, the preferences extend to Puerto Ricans born on the United States mainland, but not those born in Puerto Rico. The Law School's bulletin singles out Mexican Americans rather than other Hispanics as receiving "special attention" in the admissions process, and the admissions data confirms the differences in treatment for those two groups. Caucasian Americans and Asian Americans are treated as undifferentiated masses, receiving no preference for race or ethnicity, even though one could easily identify dozens of separate racial or ethnic groups contained in those broad categories. The Law School's daily tracking of the race and ethnicity of its applicants entirely omits many racial and ethnic groups, including, for example, Arab Americans, who receive no preferential treatment.

It is no answer to the haphazard manner of conferring preferences that the Law School has singled out groups that have been "historically discriminated against." The preferences are both overinclusive and underinclusive, and hence there is no close "fit" of means to ends. As discussed above, the preferences to the specified groups are given without regard to whether a student is "rich" or "poor" or the victim of discrimination. At the same time, students who have actually been subject to discrimination, but who belong to racial and ethnic groups not preferred by the Law School, receive no preference for their race or ethnicity. . . . "The chosen means, resting as they do on stereotyping and so indirectly furthering the asserted end, could not plausibly be deemed narrowly tailored." . . .

Respectfully submitted,
Kirk O. Kolbo,
Counsel of Record

UNIVERSITY OF MICHIGAN'S BRIEF

[[1. Diversity as a Compelling Interest.]] . . . America remains both highly segregated by race and profoundly and constantly aware of its significance in our society. . . . "[[T]]o be born black is to know an unchangeable fact about oneself that matters every day." The evidence for that fact, anecdotal and scientific, is beyond serious dispute. . . . African-American men are asked to pay almost twice the markup that white men are asked to pay for automobiles. Recent studies have shown dramatic disparities in the treatment of whites and African-Americans trying to rent an apartment over the telephone. . . .

Against this backdrop, law schools need the autonomy and discretion to decide that teaching about the role of race in our society and legal system, and preparing their students to function effectively as leaders after graduation, are critically important aspects of their institutional missions. And it hardly requires extensive proof that pursuit of those goals is greatly enhanced in ways that white students alone, no matter what their viewpoints are or even what their experiences have been, cannot possibly supply.

. . . At its most successful, the educational process is a productive collision not only of facts and ideas, but also of *people*. . . . The Law School is training lawyers and leaders for a society in which, within the careers of its current students, white citizens will become a minority of the population. These students need to learn how to bridge racial divides, work sensitively and effectively with people of different races, and simply overcome the initial discomfort of interacting with people visibly different from themselves that is a hallmark of human nature. . . .

Effective pursuit of these goals requires more than an isolated handful of minority students, for several reasons. First, the educational benefits of diversity depend on opportunities for interaction—in classrooms, cafeterias, or residential settings. The Law School is a large institution, and a few minority students obviously could not be everywhere at once, or establish meaningful personal ties with more than a small fraction of their classmates.

Second, the presence of more than one or two minority students in a classroom encourages students to think critically and reexamine stereotypes. . . . When there are more than a token number of minority students, "everyone in the class starts looking at people as individuals in their views and experiences, instead of as races."

Third, as the Harvard plan recognized, there is a powerful body of evidence that very low numbers of minority students tend to create a "sense of isolation among the [minority] students themselves" that would "make it more difficult for them to develop and achieve their potential." That sense of isolation particularly inhibits the willingness of many minority students to participate freely in class discussions.

As Justice Powell recognized in *Bakke*, the Law School's interest in educational benefits of a diverse, racially integrated student body is both unquestionably legitimate and "of paramount importance to the fulfillment of its mission.". . .

. . . The Law School does not premise its need for a racially integrated student body on any belief that minority students always (or even consistently) express some characteristic minority viewpoint on any issue. To the contrary, breaking down such stereotypes is a crucial part of its mission, and one that cannot be advanced with only token numbers of minority students. The Law School values the presence of minority students because they will have direct, personal *experiences*, that white students cannot—experiences which are relevant to the Law School's mission.

Finally, petitioner argues that an interest in educational diversity cannot be recognized as compelling because it would "give the Nation its first *permanent* justification for racial preferences." . . . The Law School of course recognizes that race-conscious programs must have reasonable durational limits, and the Sixth Circuit properly found such a limit in the Law School's resolve to cease considering race when genuine race-neutral alternatives become available.

[[2. Narrow tailoring of means.]] Petitioner and the United States assert that there are race-neutral alternatives available to the Law School. . . . [[A]]ll are demonstrably unworkable or would substitute a different institutional mission for the one that the Law School has chosen. . . .

"Percentage Plans." The United States touts admission policies adopted recently by the public undergraduate institutions in Texas, Florida, and California, which guarantee admission to all students above a certain class-rank threshold in every high school in the State. . . . But the United States does not even

attempt to articulate how such a program could work for graduate and professional schools.

No elite law school could responsibly assemble a class by guaranteeing admission to every applicant who had secured a high grade point average in college, without such regard to the institution or course of study. Moreover, such an approach could not produce meaningful diversity. The Law School draws from a national pool and is too small to guarantee admission to even a tiny percentage of graduates from every university in the country. . . .

Abandon academic selectivity. The United States repeatedly suggests that the Law School "eas[e] admissions requirements for all students," and "discard facially neutral criteria that, in practice, tend to skew admissions in a manner that detracts from educational diversity." . . .

. . . There are so many more white and Asian American applicants throughout the upper and middle score ranges that no incremental lowering of standards will create a pool with meaningful racial diversity. Setting the bar so low that academic criteria are nearly irrelevant might . . . produce a racially diverse class, but any such plan would require the Law School to become a very different institution, and to sacrifice a core part of its educational mission.

Socio-economic criteria. The Law School already considers the light that a history of overcoming poverty or disadvantage may shed on *every* applicant's likely contributions. But if petitioner is suggesting that the Law School could enroll a critical mass of minority students by giving even greater weight to socio-economic criteria in an honestly race-blind manner, the problem is, again, the facts.

There is a strong correlation between race and poverty in our country. Nonetheless, there are still many more poor white students than poor minority students in the pool from which the Law School draws. . . . [[T]]his is not a way the Law School could enroll an academically talented class that is diverse in many ways, including race. [[The University of California at Berkeley's]] Boalt Hall recently experimented with admitting more low-income students but abandoned that experiment after one year, concluding that it could not produce racial diversity. . . .

. . . [[T]]he Law School's hope that its admissions policy will produce a critical mass of minority students does not make that policy a quota. . . . [[T]]here is of course "some relationship between numbers and achieving the benefits to be derived from a diverse student body, and between numbers and providing a reasonable environment for those students admitted." If the Law School did not pay attention to these educational concerns, then its policy would not be narrowly tailored to the interests it seeks to promote. But "some attention to numbers" does not transform a flexible admissions system into a rigid quota. . . .

Petitioner contends that the Law School's policy is illogical and "haphazard" in the choice of racial or ethnic groups for which it shows a particular concern. It is not. That policy's objective is to assemble a class that is both academically superior and richly diverse in a variety of ways that include, but certainly are not limited to, race and ethnicity. The Law School therefore pays attention to the racial or ethnic background of *every* applicant, to the extent that it sheds any light on their experiences and "likely contribution to the intellectual and social life of the institution."

But the Law School's desire for meaningful numbers of African-American, Hispanic and Native-American students is, in several important respects, unique. By virtue of our Nation's unfortunate past and ongoing struggle with racial inequality, such students are both uniquely likely to have had experiences of particular importance to the Law School's mission, and uniquely *unlikely* to be admitted in meaningful numbers on criteria which ignore those experiences. The Law School's goal of fostering interaction and understanding across racial lines also particularly requires African-American students, since those are the groups most isolated by racial barriers in our country. . . .

Respectfully submitted,
MAREEN E. MAHONEY,
Counsel of Record

UNITED STATES' BRIEF[21]

Ensuring that public institutions are open and available to all segments of American society, including people of all races and ethnicities, represents a paramount government objective. . . . If undergraduate and graduate institutions are not open to all individuals and broadly inclusive to our diverse national community, then the top jobs, graduate schools, and the professions will be closed to some. . . . Public universities have substantial latitude to tackle such problems and ensure that . . . student bodies are experientially diverse and broadly representative of the public. Schools may . . . adopt admission policies that seek to promote experiental, geographical, political, or economic diversity in the student body, which are entirely appropriate race-neutral governmental objectives. The adoption of such policies, moreover, has led to racially diverse student bodies in other States. . . .

For example, in Texas, which has operated without race-based admissions policies since they were invalidated by the Fifth Circuit in 1996, the undergraduate admissions program focuses on attracting the top graduating students from throughout the State, including students from underrepresented areas. . . . Under this race-neutral admissions policy, "pre-Hopwood diversity levels were restored by 1998 or 1999 in the admitted and enrolled populations and have held steady." Thus, in 1996, the last year race was used in University of Texas admissions decisions, 4% of enrolled freshmen were African Americans, 14% were Hispanic, and less than 1% were Native Americans. In 2002, 3% of enrolled freshmen were African-American (this figure has fluctuated between 4% and 3% since 1997), 14% were Hispanic, and less than 1% were Native

American. . . . Similar race-neutral programs are now in place in California and Florida and have had similar results. . . .

In addition, to the extent the Law School seeks candidates with diverse backgrounds and experiences and viewpoints or "achievements in light of the barriers [an applicant has] had to overcome," it can focus on numerous race-neutral factors including . . . volunteer and work experiences, exceptional personal talents, leadership potential, communication skills, commitment and dedication to particular causes, extracurricular activities, extraordinary expertise in a particular area, and individual outlook as reflected by essays. . . . Such programs have produced school systems to which minorities have meaningful access and are represented in significant numbers, as the experience in Texas, Florida, and California demonstrates. . . . The Law School, however, has not sought to implement its goals through race-neutral means. . . . The use of race in the face of such alternatives demonstrates that respondents have not employed race in a narrowly tailored manner.

Respectfully submitted,
THEODORE B. OLSON,
Solicitor General

BRIEF OF LT. GEN. JULIUS W. BECTON, ET AL[22]

. . . . During the 1960s and 1970s, the military experienced a demoralizing and destabilizing period of internal racial strife. . . . For example, in the 1960s, racial violence among the Marines at Camp Lejeune was not uncommon. . . . "Fights between black and white soldiers were endemic in the 1970s, an era remembered as the 'time of troubles.'" "In Vietnam, racial tensions reached a point where there was an inability to fight." African-American troops, who rarely saw members of their own race in command positions, lost confidence in the military as an institution. . . . The painful lesson slowly learned was that our diverse enlisted ranks rendered integration of the officer corp a military necessity. . . . "[T]he current leadership views complete racial integration as a . . . prerequisite to a cohesive, and therefore effective, fighting force. In short, success with the challenge of diversity is critical to national security." . . .

In order to integrate itself, and hence the Army officer corps, the U.S. Military Academy has self-consciously attempted "to balance the Corps" and therefore has "develop[ed] goals for each class for desired percentages of scholars, leaders, athletes, women, blacks, Hispanics and other minorities." . . . In pursuit of these goals, "[M]inorities [are] consistently offered admission [to West Point] at higher rates than whites [despite] lower academic predictor scores and lower academic, physical education, and military grades." . . . Like West Point, the U.S. Naval Academy aggressively recruits minority applicants and employs a limited race-conscious admission policy. . . . [[The Air Force

Academy also]] has an admissions policy that takes some limited account of race. . . .

Like the service academies, the ROTC employs an aggressive race-conscious admissions program. Each service's ROTC program is tasked to meet its service's minority goals for commissioning officers. . . . ROTC officer candidates are selected from those *already admitted* to host colleges and universities. These institutions must have sufficient minority enrollment so that their ROTC programs can, in turn, train and educate substantial numbers of qualified minority officers and provide officer candidates with a racially diverse educational experience. . . . [[P]]reparing officer candidates for service, let alone *command*, in our racially diverse military is extraordinarily difficult in a racially homogeneous setting. . . . It requires only a small step from this analysis to conclude that our country's other most selective institutions must remain both diverse and selective. Like our military security, our economic security and international competitiveness depend upon it. An alternative that does not preserve both diversity and selectivity is no alternative at all.

Respectfully submitted,
CARTER G. PHILLIPS

ORAL ARGUMENT

JUSTICE KENNEDY: . . . Suppose you have a law school with two or three percent Hispanic and—and black students, is that a legitimate concern for the university and for the State officials?

MR. KOLBO [[Grutter's Attorney]]: We believe not, Your Honor, for the reason that we need to get away from the notion that there's some right number for each racial group.

KENNEDY: So if year after year after year there's an under representation, there is no cause for the State or the Government or its educational experts to be concerned whatsoever?

KOLBO: I wouldn't say not to be concerned, Your Honor, I think the mere fact of under representation, that is to say, blacks are not represented as they are in the population is not a concern that would justify racial preferences. It certainly would justify perhaps broad social and political concerns.

KENNEDY: Well, it's a broad social and political concern that there are not adequate members of—of a profession which is designed to protect our rights and to—and to promote progress. I would—I should think that's a very legitimate concern on the part of the State.

KOLBO: The current concern there, Your Honor, ought to be addressed by—by addressing the problem. If there is some reason that—that particular minority groups are not participating as fully in the fruits of our society such as being represented at the schools, we need to address those problems. But racial preferences don't address those problems. . . .

*   *   *

JUSTICE BREYER: Fine, if you can use race as a criterion for spending money, I take it one argument on the other side, which I'd like you to address, is that we live in a world where more than half of all the minorities—really 75 percent of black students below the college level are at schools that are more than 50 percent minority. And 85 percent of those schools are in areas of poverty.

And many among other things that they tell us on the other side is that . . . the only way to break this cycle is to have a leadership that is diverse. And to have a leadership across the country that is diverse, you have to train a diverse student body for law, for the military, for business, for all the other positions in this country that will allow us to have a diverse leadership in a country that is diverse.

Now, you're familiar with that argument. But if it is reasonable to use race as a criterion, as a plus for spending money, why isn't it also reasonable to use it as a plus to see that—to obtain that set of objectives that I've tried to summarize in a second that you're very familiar with.

KOLBO: Because very simply, Justice Breyer, the Constitution provides the right of individuals with the right of equal protection. And by discriminating on the basis of race at a point of competition, innocent individuals are being injured in their constitutional rights. That's the distinction between that and simply trying to cast a wider net, recruiting, spending money on outreach efforts, a very principal line it seems to me can be drawn between those two things.

BREYER: The reason that the injury is more severe to the white person who doesn't get in when that white person doesn't get in because she's not an athlete or he's not a—he's not a alumnus or he's not any of the other things that fits within these other criteria? What is the difference? . . .

KOLBO: The difference is the Equal Protection Clause, Your Honor, does not apply to alumni preferences in scholarships. It applies to race. . . .

*   *   *

JUSTICE SCALIA: Is two percent a critical mass, Ms. Mahoney?

MS. MAHONEY [[University of Michigan Law School's Attorney]]: I don't think so, Your Honor.

SCALIA: Okay. Four percent?

MAHONEY: No, Your Honor, what—

SCALIA: You have to pick some number, don't you?

MAHONEY: Well, actually what—

SCALIA: Like eight, is eight percent?

MAHONEY: Your Honor.

SCALIA: . . . [[D]]oes it stop being a quota because it's somewhere between 8 and 12, but it is a quota if it's 10? I don't understand that reasoning. Once you use the term critical mass and—you're—you're into quota land?

MAHONEY: Your Honor, what a quota is under this Court's cases is a fixed number. And there is no fixed number here. The testimony was that it depends on the characteristics of the applicant pool. . . .

✳   ✳   ✳

JUSTICE O'CONNOR: . . . In all programs which this Court has upheld in the area of . . . affirmative action, there's been a fixed time period within which it would operate. You could see . . . an end to it, there is none in this, is there? How do we deal with that aspect?

MAHONEY: What the policy says, of course, is that it will only take race into account as long as it is necessary in order to achieve the educational objectives. I don't think that this Court should conclude that this is permanent, because there are two things that can happen that will make this come to an end. The first is that the number of high-achieving minorities will continue to grow and that law school will be able to enroll a sufficient number to have a critical mass or meaningful numbers or substantial presence without having to take race into account.

The second thing that can happen, Your Honor, is that we could reach a point in our society where the experience of being a minority did not make such a fundamental difference in their lives, where race didn't matter so much that it's truly salient to the law school's educational mission.

While . . . I can't say when that will happen, we certainly know that as a nation, we have made tremendous progress in overcoming intolerance. And we certainly should expect that that will occur with respect to minorities.

O'CONNOR: [[Have we ever]] approved any other affirmative action program with such a vague distant termination base?

MAHONEY: Well, in Bakke itself, Your Honor. In Bakke itself, there were five votes to allow the University of California Davis to use a plan modeled on the Harvard plan. It's been in effect for about 25 years. It has reaped extraordinary benefits for this country's educational system. . . .

OPINIONS

Justice O'Connor delivered the opinion of the Court. . . .

[[1. Diversity as a Compelling Interest.]]. . . . Today, we hold that the Law School has a compelling interest in attaining a diverse student body. The Law School's educational judgment that such diversity is essential to its educational mission is one to which we defer. The Law School's assessment that diversity will, in fact, yield educational benefits is substantiated by respondents and their *amici*. Our scrutiny of the interest asserted by the Law School is no less strict for taking into account complex educational judgments in an area that lies primarily within the expertise of the university. Our holding today is in keeping with our tradition of giving a degree of deference to a university's academic decisions, within constitutionally prescribed limits. . . .

These benefits are substantial. As the District Court emphasized, the Law School's admissions policy promotes "cross-racial understanding," helps to break down racial stereotypes, and "enables [students] to better understand persons of different races." These benefits are "important and laudable," because "classroom discussion is livelier, more spirited, and simply more enlightening and interesting" when the students have "the greatest possible variety of backgrounds."

The Law School's claim of a compelling interest is further bolstered by its *amici*, who point to the educational benefits that flow from student body diversity. In addition to the expert studies and reports entered into evidence at trial, numerous studies show that student body diversity promotes learning outcomes, and "better prepares students for an increasingly diverse workforce and society, and better prepares them as professionals."

These benefits are not theoretical but real, as major American businesses have made clear that the skills needed in today's increasingly global marketplace can only be developed through exposure to widely diverse people, cultures, ideas, and viewpoints. What is more, high-ranking retired officers and civilian leaders of the United States military assert that, "[b]ased on [their] decades of experience," a "highly qualified, racially diverse officer corps . . . is essential to the military's ability to fulfill its principle mission to provide national security.". . .

We have repeatedly acknowledged the overriding importance of preparing students for work and citizenship, describing education as pivotal to "sustaining our political and cultural heritage" with a fundamental role in maintaining the fabric of society. This Court has long recognized that "education . . . is the very foundation of good citizenship.". . .

Moreover, universities, and in particular, law schools, represent the training ground for a large number of our Nation's leaders. Individuals with law degrees occupy roughly half the state governorships, more than half the seats in the

United States Senate, and more than a third of the seats in the United States House of Representatives. The pattern is even more striking when it comes to highly selective law schools. A handful of these schools accounts for 25 of the 100 United States Senators, 74 United States Courts of Appeals judges, and nearly 200 of the more than 600 United States District Court judges.

In order to cultivate a set of leaders with legitimacy in the eyes of the citizenry, it is necessary that the path to leadership be visibly open to talented and qualified individuals of every race and ethnicity. All members of our heterogeneous society must have confidence in the openness and integrity of the educational institutions that provide this training. As we have recognized, law schools "cannot be effective in isolation from the individuals and institutions with which the law interacts." Access to legal education (and thus the legal profession) must be inclusive of talented and qualified individuals of every race and ethnicity, so that all members of our heterogeneous society may participate in the educational institutions that provide the training and education necessary to succeed in America. . . .

[[2. Narrow Tailoring of Means.]] We find that the Law School's admissions program bears the hallmarks of a narrowly tailored plan. As Justice Powell made clear in *Bakke*, truly individualized consideration demands that race be used in a flexible, nonmechanical way. It follows from this mandate that universities cannot establish quotas for members of certain racial groups or put members of those groups on separate admissions tracks. Nor can universities insulate applicants who belong to certain racial or ethnic groups from the competition for admission. Universities can, however, consider race or ethnicity more flexibly as a "plus" factor in the context of individualized consideration of each and every applicant. . . .

The Law School's goal of attaining a critical mass of underrepresented minority students does not transform its program into a quota. As the Harvard plan described by Justice Powell recognized, there is of course "some relationship between numbers and achieving the benefits to be derived from a diverse student body, and between numbers and providing a reasonable environment for those students admitted." "[S]ome attention to numbers," without more, does not transform a flexible admissions system into a rigid quota. . . .

That a race-conscious admissions program does not operate as a quota does not, by itself, satisfy the requirement of individualized consideration. When using race as a "plus" factor in university admissions, a university's admissions program must remain flexible enough to ensure that each applicant is evaluated as an individual and not in a way that makes an applicant's race or ethnicity the defining feature of his or her application. The importance of this individualized consideration in the context of a race-conscious admissions program is paramount.

Here, the Law School engages in a highly individualized, holistic review of each applicant's file, giving serious consideration to all the ways an applicant might contribute to a diverse educational environment. The Law School affords this individualized consideration to applicants of all races. There is no policy, either *de jure* or *de facto*, of automatic acceptance or rejection based on any single "soft" variable. Unlike the program at issue in *Gratz v. Bollinger*, the Law School awards no mechanical, predetermined diversity "bonuses" based on race or ethnicity. Like the Harvard plan, the Law School's admissions policy "is flexible enough to consider all pertinent elements of diversity in light of the particular qualifications of each applicant, and to place them on the same footing for consideration, although not necessarily according them the same weight."

We also find that, like the Harvard plan Justice Powell referenced in *Bakke*, the Law School's race-conscious admissions program adequately ensures that all factors that may contribute to student body diversity are meaningfully considered alongside race in admissions decisions. With respect to the use of race itself, all underrepresented minority students admitted by the Law School have been deemed qualified. By virtue of our Nation's struggle with racial inequality, such students are both likely to have experiences of particular importance to the Law School's mission, and less likely to be admitted in meaningful numbers on criteria that ignore those experiences.

The Law School does not, however, limit in any way the broad range of qualities and experiences that may be considered valuable contributions to student body diversity. To the contrary, the 1992 policy makes clear "[t]here are many possible bases for diversity admissions," and provides examples of admittees who have lived or traveled widely abroad, are fluent in several languages, have overcome personal adversity and family hardship, have exceptional records of extensive community service, and have had successful careers in other fields. The Law School seriously considers each "applicant's promise of making a notable contribution to the class by way of a particular strength, attainment, or characteristic—*e.g.*, an unusual intellectual achievement, employment experience, nonacademic performance, or personal background." All applicants have the opportunity to highlight their own potential diversity contributions through the submission of a personal statement, letters of recommendation, and an essay describing the ways in which the applicant will contribute to the life and diversity of the Law School.

What is more, the Law School actually gives substantial weight to diversity factors besides race. The Law School frequently accepts nonminority applicants with grades and test scores lower than underrepresented minority applicants (and other nonminority applicants) who are rejected. This shows that the Law School seriously weighs many other diversity factors besides race that can make a real and dispositive difference for nonminority applicants as well. By this flexible approach, the Law School sufficiently takes into account, in practice as well as in theory, a wide variety of characteristics besides race and ethnicity that contribute to a diverse student body . . .

Petitioner and the United States argue that the Law School's plan is not narrowly tailored because race-neutral means exist to obtain the educational benefits of student body diversity that the Law School seeks. We disagree. Narrow tailoring does not require exhaustion of every conceivable race-neutral alternative. Nor does it require a university to choose between maintaining a reputation for excellence or fulfilling a commitment to provide educational opportunities to members of all racial groups. Narrow tailoring does, however, require serious, good faith consideration of workable race-neutral alternatives that will achieve the diversity the university seeks.

We agree with the Court of Appeals that the Law School sufficiently considered workable race-neutral alternatives. The District Court took the Law School to task for failing to consider race-neutral alternatives such as "using a lottery system" or "decreasing the emphasis for all applicants on undergraduate GPA and LSAT scores." But these alternatives would require a dramatic sacrifice of diversity, the academic quality of all admitted students, or both. . . .

. . . We are satisfied that the Law School adequately considered race-neutral alternatives currently capable of producing a critical mass without forcing the Law School to abandon the academic selectivity that is the cornerstone of its educational mission. . . .

We are mindful, however, that "[a] core purpose of the Fourteenth Amendment was to do away with all governmentally imposed discrimination based on race." Accordingly, race-conscious admissions policies must be limited in time. This requirement reflects that racial classifications, however compelling their goals, are potentially so dangerous that they may be employed no more broadly than the interest demands. Enshrining a permanent justification for racial preferences would offend this fundamental equal protection principle. We see no reason to exempt race-conscious admissions programs from the requirement that all governmental use of race must have a logical end point. The Law School, too, concedes that all "race-conscious programs must have reasonable durational limits."

In the context of higher education, the durational requirement can be met by sunset provisions in race-conscious admissions policies and periodic reviews to determine whether racial preferences are still necessary to achieve student body diversity. Universities in California, Florida, and Washington State, where racial preferences in admissions are prohibited by state law, are currently engaged in experimenting with a wide variety of alternative approaches. Universities in other States can and should draw on the most promising aspects of these race-neutral alternatives as they develop. . . .

. . . It has been 25 years since Justice Powell first approved the use of race to further an interest in student body diversity in the context of public higher education. Since that time, the number of minority applicants with high grades and test scores has indeed increased. We expect that 25 years from now, the use of racial preferences will no longer be necessary to further the interest approved today. . . .

Chief Justice Rehnquist, with whom Justice Scalia, Justice Kennedy, and Justice Thomas join, dissenting.

. . . The Law School claims it must take the steps it does to achieve a "critical mass" of underrepresented minority students. But its actual program bears no relation to this asserted goal. Stripped of its "critical mass" veil, the Law School's program is revealed as a naked effort to achieve racial balancing. . . .

Before the Court's decision today, we consistently applied the same strict scrutiny analysis regardless of the government's purported reason for using race and regardless of the setting in which race was being used. We rejected calls to use more lenient review in the face of claims that race was being used in "good faith" because "'[m]ore than good motives should be required when government seeks to allocate its resources by way of an explicit racial classification system.'" We likewise rejected calls to apply more lenient review based on the particular setting in which race is being used. Indeed, even in the specific context of higher education, we emphasized that "constitutional limitations protecting individual rights may not be disregarded."

Although the Court recites the language of our strict scrutiny analysis, its application of that review is unprecedented in its deference. . . .

From 1995 through 2000, the Law School admitted between 1,130 and 1,310 students. Of those, between 13 and 19 were Native American, between 91 and 108 were African-Americans, and between 47 and 56 were Hispanic. If the Law School is admitting between 91 and 108 African-Americans in order to achieve "critical mass," thereby preventing African-American students from feeling "isolated or like spokespersons for their race," one would think that a number of the same order of magnitude would be necessary to accomplish the same purpose for Hispanics and Native Americans. Similarly, even if all of the Native American applicants admitted in a given year matriculate, which the record demonstrates is not at all the case, how can this possibly constitute a "critical mass" of Native Americans in a class of over 350 students? In order for this pattern of admission to be consistent with the Law School's explanation of "critical mass," one would have to believe that the objectives of "critical mass" offered by respondents are achieved with only half the number of Hispanics and one-sixth the number of Native Americans as compared to African-Americans. But respondents offer no race-specific reasons for such disparities. Instead, they simply emphasize the importance of achieving "critical mass," without any explanation of why that concept is applied differently among the three underrepresented minority groups. . . .

. . . Respondents have *never* offered any race-specific arguments explaining why significantly more individuals from one underrepresented minority group are needed in order to achieve "critical mass" or further student body diversity. They certainly have not explained why Hispanics, who they have said are among "the groups most isolated by racial barriers in our country," should have their admission capped out in this manner. True, petitioner is neither Hispanic nor Native American. But the Law School's disparate admissions practices with respect to these minority groups demonstrate that its alleged goal of "critical mass" is simply a sham. . . .

But the correlation between the percentage of the Law School's pool of applicants who are members of the three minority groups and the percentage of the admitted applicants who are members of these same groups is far too precise to

Table 2.3   University of Michigan Law School Yearly Admissions Statistics by Race (in each cell: percentage of applicants above, percentage of admittees in middle, number of admittees below)

	1995	1996	1997	1998	1999	2000
African-Americans	9.7%	9.3%	9.3%	8.6%	7.3%	7.5%
	9.4%	9.2%	8.3%	7.9%	7.1%	7.3%
	106	108	101	103	91	91
Hispanics	5.1%	5.1%	4.8%	4.2%	4.5%	4.9%
	5.0%	4.6%	3.9%	4.2%	3.8%	4.2%
	56	54	47	55	48	53
Native Americans	1.1%	0.8%	1.1%	1.1%	0.7%	1.0%
	1.2%	1.1%	1.6%	1.4%	1.0%	1.1%
	14	13	19	18	13	14

be dismissed as merely the result of the school paying "some attention to [the] numbers." . . . [[F]]rom 1995 through 2000 the percentage of admitted applicants who were members of these minority groups closely tracked the percentage of individuals in the school's applicant pool who were from the same groups.

[[In his dissent, Chief Justice Rehnquist included three tables that are summarized by table 2.3.]]

For example, in 1995, when 9.7% of the applicant pool was African-American, 9.4% of the admitted class was African-American. By 2000, only 7.5% of the applicant pool was African-American, and 7.3% of the admitted class was African-American. This correlation is striking. Respondents themselves emphasize that the number of underrepresented minority students admitted to the Law School would be significantly smaller if the race of each applicant were not considered. But, as the examples above illustrate, the measure of the decrease would differ dramatically among the groups. The tight correlation between the percentage of applicants and admittees of a given race, therefore, must result from careful race based planning by the Law School. It suggests a formula for admission based on the aspirational assumption that all applicants are equally qualified academically, and therefore that the proportion of each group admitted should be the same as the proportion of that group in the applicant pool.

Not only do respondents fail to explain this phenomenon, they attempt to obscure it. But the divergence between the percentages of underrepresented minorities in the applicant pool and in the *enrolled* classes is not the only relevant comparison. In fact, it may not be the most relevant comparison. The Law School cannot precisely control which of its admitted applicants decide to attend the university. But it can and, as the numbers demonstrate, clearly does employ racial preferences in extending offers of admission. Indeed, the ostensibly flexible nature of the Law School's admissions program that the Court finds appealing appears to be, in practice, a carefully managed program designed to ensure proportionate representation of applicants from selected minority groups. . . .

The Court suggests a possible 25-year limitation on the Law School's current program. Respondents, on the other hand, remain more ambiguous, explaining that "the Law School of course recognizes that race-conscious programs must have reasonable durational limits, and the Sixth Circuit properly found such a limit in the Law School's resolve to cease considering race when genuine race-neutral alternatives become available." These discussions of a time limit are the vaguest of assurances. In truth, they permit the Law School's use of racial preferences on a seemingly permanent basis. Thus, an important component of strict scrutiny—that a program be limited in time—is casually subverted.

The Court, in an unprecedented display of deference under our strict scrutiny analysis, upholds the Law School's program despite its obvious flaws. We have said that when it comes to the use of race, the connection between the ends and the means used to attain them must be precise. But here the flaw is deeper than that; it is not merely a question of "fit" between ends and means. Here the means actually used are forbidden by the Equal Protection Clause of the Constitution.

Justice Thomas, with whom Justice Scalia joins, . . . dissenting. . . .

Where the Court has accepted only national security, and rejected even the best interests of a child, as a justification for racial discrimination, I conclude that only those measures the State must take to provide a bulwark against anarchy, or to prevent violence, will constitute a "pressing public necessity."

The Constitution abhors classifications based on race, not only because those classifications can harm favored races or are based on illegitimate motives, but also because every time the government places citizens on racial registers and makes race relevant to the provision of burdens or benefits, it demeans us all. "Purchased at the price of immeasurable human suffering, the equal protection principle reflects our Nation's understanding that such classifications ultimately have a destructive impact on the individual and our society."

Unlike the majority, I seek to define with precision the interest being asserted by the Law School before determining whether that interest is so compelling as to justify racial discrimination. The Law School maintains that it wishes to obtain "educational benefits that flow from student body diversity." This statement must be evaluated carefully, because it implies that both "diversity" and "educational benefits" are components of the Law School's compelling state interest. Additionally, the Law School's refusal to entertain certain changes in its admissions process and status indicates that the compelling state interest it seeks to validate is actually broader than might appear at first glance.

Undoubtedly there are other ways to "better" the education of law students aside from ensuring that the student body contains a "critical mass" of underrepresented minority students. Attaining "diversity," whatever it means,* is the mechanism by which the Law School obtains educational benefits, not an end of itself. The Law School, however, apparently believes that only a racially mixed student body can lead to the educational benefits it seeks. How, then, is the Law School's interest in these allegedly unique educational "benefits" *not* simply the forbidden interest in "racial balancing" that the majority expressly rejects?

A distinction between these two ideas (unique educational benefits based on racial aesthetics and race for its own sake) is purely sophistic—so much so that the majority uses them interchangeably. The Law School's argument, as facile as it is, can only be understood in one way: Classroom aesthetics yields educational benefits, racially discriminatory admissions policies are required to achieve the right racial mix, and therefore the policies are required to achieve the educational benefits. It is the *educational benefits* that are the end, or allegedly compelling state interest, not "diversity." . . .

While legal education at a public university may be good policy or otherwise laudable, it is obviously not a pressing public necessity when the correct legal standard is applied. Additionally, circumstantial evidence as to whether a state activity is of pressing public necessity can be obtained by asking whether all States feel compelled to engage in that activity. Evidence that States, in general, engage in a certain activity by no means demonstrates that the activity constitutes a pressing public necessity, given the expansive role of government in today's society. The fact that some fraction of the States reject a particular enterprise, however, creates a presumption that the enterprise itself is not a compelling state interest. In this sense, the absence of a public, American Bar Association (ABA) accredited, law school in Alaska, Delaware, Massachusetts, New Hampshire, and Rhode Island, provides further evidence that Michigan's maintenance of the Law School does not constitute a compelling state interest. . . .

The Equal Protection Clause, as interpreted by the Court in *Gaines*, does not permit States to justify racial discrimination on the basis of what the rest of the Nation "may do or fail to do." The only interests that can satisfy the Equal Protection Clause's demands are those found within a State's jurisdiction.

---

*Footnote by Justice Thomas: "[D]iversity," for all of its devotees, is more a fashionable catchphrase than it is a useful term, especially when something as serious as racial discrimination is at issue. Because the Equal Protection Clause renders the color of one's skin constitutionally irrelevant to the Law School's mission, I refer to the Law School's interest as an "aesthetic." That is, the Law School wants to have a certain appearance, from the shape of the desks and tables in its classrooms to the color of the students sitting at them.

I also use the term "aesthetic" because I believe it underlines the ineffectiveness of racially discriminatory admissions in actually helping those who are truly underprivileged. It must be remembered that the Law School's racial discrimination does nothing for those too poor or uneducated to participate in elite higher education and therefore presents only an illusory solution to the challenges facing our Nation.

The only cognizable state interests vindicated by operating a public law school are, therefore, the education of that State's citizens and the training of that State's lawyers. . . .

The Law School today, however, does precious little training of those attorneys who will serve the citizens of Michigan. In 2002, graduates of the University of Michigan Law School made up less than 6% of applicants to the Michigan bar, even though the Law School's graduates constitute nearly 30% of all law students graduating in Michigan. Less than 16% of the Law School's graduating class elects to stay in Michigan after law school. Thus, while a mere 27% of the Law School's 2002 entering class are from Michigan, only half of these, it appears, will stay in Michigan. The Law School's decision to be an elite institution does little to advance the welfare of the people of Michigan or any cognizable interest of the State of Michigan. . . .

The interest in remaining elite and exclusive that the majority thinks so obviously critical requires the use of admissions "standards" that, in turn, create the Law School's "need" to discriminate on the basis of race. . . . The Court never explicitly holds that the Law School's desire to retain the status quo in "academic selectivity" is itself a compelling state interest, and, as I have demonstrated, it is not. Therefore, the Law School should be forced to choose between its classroom aesthetic and its exclusionary admissions system—it cannot have it both ways. . . .

NOTES

1. Title 41. C.F.R., 60-1.40, cited by Nathan Glazer, *Affirmative Discrimination* (New York: Basic Books, 1978), p. 46.
2. Later C.F.R. regulations, issued in 1971, read as follows: "An acceptable affirmative action program must include . . . goals and timetables to which the contractor's good faith efforts must be directed to correct the deficiencies, and thus to increase materially the utilization of minorities and women, at all levels and in all segments of his work force where deficiencies exist." See Glazer, *Affirmative Discrimination*, p. 48.
3. Bakke filed his suit immediately after the Supreme Court had refused, on mootness grounds, to rule on the merits of an earlier case dealing with affirmative action in higher education, *DeFunis v. Odegaard*, 416 U.S. 312 (1974).
4. Title VI: "No person in the United States shall, on the ground of race, color, or national origin, be excluded from participation in, be denied the benefits of, or be subjected to discrimination under any program or activity receiving Federal financial assistance."
5. See Timothy J. O'Neil, *Bakke & the Politics of Equality*, pp. 3–4.
6. See *Craig v. Boren*, 429 U.S. 190 (1976).
7. *Rostker v. Goldberg*, 453 U.S. 57 (1981).
8. Cited by Schwartz, *Behind Bakke*, p. 107.
9. Schwartz, *Behind Bakke*, p. 60.
10. See Schwartz, *Behind Bakke*, p. 96.
11. See Schwartz, *Behind Bakke*, pp. 152–53.
12. 478 U.S. 267 (1986).

13. 488 U.S. 469 (1989).

14. 448 U.S. 448 (1980).

15. 497 U.S. 547 (1990).

16. 515 U.S. 200 (1995).

17. 78 F.3d 932, cert. denied, 518 U.S. 1033 (1996).

18. At the same time that the Court considered *Grutter*, it also reviewed *Gratz v. Bollinger*, 539 U.S. 244 (2003), a case dealing with the University of Michigan's undergraduate admissions policy. In contrast to the result in *Grutter*, the Court invalidated the undergraduate affirmative action program because it used an impersonal "point system," which automatically granted a specific number of points to minority applicants on the basis of their race, without any additional individualized consideration. While *Gratz* informs universities and colleges what forms of affirmative action are impermissible, *Grutter* clarifies what forms universities and colleges can pursue.

19. The phrase "narrowly tailored" had gradually replaced the necessary means requirement of strict scrutiny in the Court's affirmative action cases of the 1980s. It was unclear whether this revision was merely a stylistic change in wording or a relaxation of the severity of the means prong of strict scrutiny.

20. Justice Kennedy also wrote a dissent that is not excerpted below.

21. Paragraphing has been slightly altered in the United States' brief.

22. The paragraphing has been altered slightly in the Becton brief.

CHAPTER 3

Abortion

Roe v. Wade
410 U.S. 113 (1973)

Planned Parenthood v. Casey
505 U.S. 833 (1992)

I. *ROE* AND ITS BACKGROUND

The abortion controversy illustrates, in a profound way, the moral dilemmas that often underlie constitutional adjudication. The Supreme Court is frequently called upon to strike a balance between opposing moral values that have a constitutional dimension. However, in regard to the issue of abortion, a significant number of Americans are unyieldingly committed to the contending values. In recent years, neither side of the controversy would acquiesce to the Court's decisions on abortion. On the one side, pro-life groups, affirming the sacredness of human life, demand that abortion be strictly limited, if not prohibited entirely, while on the other, pro-choice groups, stressing the values of sexual equality, privacy, and autonomy, insist that individual women must decide whether to carry a fetus to term or not. The majority of Americans may think that some kind of compromise is necessary, but both extremes, fearing that any compromise will undermine the very principles that define and justify their outlook, refuse to make substantial concessions. Since neither side will accept any Supreme Court decision that is not compatible with their convictions, the ultimate question is whether abortion is an issue beyond the Court's institutional capacity to resolve. Can the Court decide public-policy issues that sharply divide a significant number of Americans into uncompromising, antagonistic, single-issue constituencies?

Such a fundamental question is not easily answered. It cannot be denied that
Roe did change the political landscape in 1973. In time the decision produced
settled expectations concerning the availability and the propriety of abortion,
especially among young people who grew up under the *Roe* umbrella. Before
the Supreme Court handed down *Roe* only four states—New York, Hawaii,
Alaska, and Washington—permitted abortion. Today many more states than
four would protect the right of abortion. Is it possible that the Supreme
Court's decision in *Roe* was an essential step in this historical trend? On the
other hand, those who objected to the substance of the Court's decision in *Roe*
also disputed its assessment that abortion was a constitutional issue within its
purview. In this way, the pro-life movement garnered its support not only by
claiming that the decision was morally intolerable but also by insisting that
the Supreme Court had abused its power. It is therefore arguable that, if the
Court had stayed out of the hotly contested issue of abortion, political pressure throughout the 1970s would have induced state legislatures to repeal laws
prohibiting abortions. The pro-life movement would have languished because
it would not have had the easy target of *Roe* and the Supreme Court. The right
of a woman to have an abortion would be more secure today without *Roe v.
Wade*.[1] What do you think? Even if the Court could temporarily decide a
hotly contested issue, thereby reshuffling the political deck and stacking it in
favor of one side or the other, should it do so? Is such a maneuver bound to
backfire?

These questions highlight the relationship between the Supreme Court's
institutional ability to resolve controversial public-policy issues and its nor-
mative function. Of course, the pro-choice side insists that the Court had a
duty to address abortion because a constitutional right was at stake: the right
of privacy. Though this right was not mentioned in the Constitution, the
Supreme Court relied on it to invalidate a Connecticut law prohibiting the use
of contraceptives in *Griswold v. Connecticut* (1965). In his majority opinion
in this case, Justice William Douglas argued that the "specific guarantees in
the Bill of Rights have penumbras, formed by emanations from those guarantees that help give them life and substance." In this fashion, Douglas claimed
that the First, Third, Fourth, Fifth, and Ninth Amendments created "zones
of privacy" that could be enforced against the states through the Fourteenth
Amendment's Due Process Clause. The novelty of Douglas's approach was
not that he inferred a constitutional right. The Court had earlier used the First
Amendment to infer a right of association, a right to educate a child, and a
right to study foreign languages.[2] What was unprecedented, however, was the
suggestion that the Court could infer a right of privacy in part from a previously inferred right, the right of association, and the newly inferred right
could be broader, at least in certain respects, than the specific constitutional
guarantees from which it was ultimately derived. Do you think these aspects
of Douglas's approach render his attempt to find a constitutional basis for the
right of privacy invalid?

In their concurring opinions in *Griswold*, Justice Arthur Goldberg relied heavily on the Ninth Amendment to claim that judges had the authority to protect fundamental rights not listed in the Constitution, while Justice John Harlan relied on the Due Process Clause of the Fourteenth Amendment. In contrast, Justice Hugo Black dissented, arguing that the justices in the majority, under the guise of interpreting the Constitution, were injecting their own personal predilections into it, just as the Court had done in *Lochner v. New York* (1905), a controversial decision that had invalidated a state law that had prohibited bakers from working more than ten hours a day or sixty hours a week on the ground that it violated the liberty of contract protected by the Due Process Clause.[3] In Black's view, by referring to the right of privacy as an "inferred" or "fundamental" right, the Court was only trying to disguise what it was actually doing—creating a "new" constitutional right.

Was Black's characterization of *Griswold* correct? If so, was the decision illegitimate? What do you think of Justice Harlan's view that the Court has a duty to protect "fundamental" rights? What is a "fundamental" right? Are there "fundamental" constitutional rights that are not listed in the Constitution? What of Justice Douglas's "penumbra-approach"? Did the Court "create" a new constitutional right of privacy in *Griswold*? Was it legitimate? If it was legitimate, under what circumstances can the Court create a "new" constitutional right?

Griswold established the right of privacy, but did little to define its boundaries. In the late 1960s, no one really knew what kinds of activities this right insulated from governmental control.[4] A number of women's groups around the country responded by initiating litigation to test the constitutionality of various state abortion laws, including a Texas statute that made it a crime for a doctor to perform an abortion unless one was necessary to save the life of the mother. In 1969, a pregnant woman in Texas (Roe), whose name (it later came to be known) was Norma McCorvey, wanted an abortion but could not find a doctor who would perform one. Two recent graduates of the University of Texas Law School, Sarah Weddington and Linda Coffee, came to McCorvey's rescue. These two lawyers were deeply involved with women's issues and were associated with a group that wanted to challenge the constitutionality of the state's abortion laws. On McCorvey's behalf, the two lawyers filed a class action suit asking that the Texas law be declared unconstitutional. A class action suit is one brought on behalf of the plaintiff and "all others similarly situated." Federal rules allow such a suit if a legal right common to the members of the group is claimed and if the group is "so numerous as to make it impractical to bring them all before the court."[5]

Of course, McCorvey delivered her baby before the three-judge district court's decision. The litigation was not mooted because it fit one of the exceptions to the rule that courts hear only "live" controversies. Because the human gestation period is so much shorter than the time that a case normally takes to undergo appellate review, the issue of the constitutionality of abortion was "capable of repetition, yet evading review." Accordingly, the district court heard the case even though McCorvey at the time was no longer pregnant or seeking an abortion. On June 17, 1970, the district court declared Texas's abortion law an unconstitutional violation of the Ninth Amendment, but declined to issue an injunction against the enforcement of the Texas law. Not satisfied, Weddington and Coffee took advantage of a rule that, at the time, allowed immediate appeal to the Supreme Court from decisions of three-judge district courts.

In their 1971 written brief and oral argument, Weddington and Coffee argued that the Texas law violated a woman's right of privacy and autonomy. A second issue concerned the state's interest in prohibiting abortion. Even if it is accepted that the fundamental right of privacy includes within it the right to have an abortion, it is an independent question whether the state has a sufficiently compelling interest to override the right. Weddington and Coffee argued that none of the state's interests, including the interest of protecting human life, could justify any infringement upon a woman' right to have an abortion. Women had a right to terminate their pregnancies even late in the third trimester.

Texas, of course, denied both of these claims. It rejected the notion that marital or personal privacy was an "absolute." In response to the claim that the state's abortion law served no important governmental interest, Texas presented an "unbiased" description of fetal growth and development. Perhaps for rhetorical effect, the state's description of fetal development in the brief dwelled upon aspects of gestation that gave the impression that the fetus was not only a live human being, but a distinct individual. According to the state, the "facts" were such that the state not only had a compelling interest in preserving fetal life, but also a constitutional duty to do so.

On December 13, 1971, when Weddington and Jay Floyd, representing Texas, appeared before the Supreme Court for oral argument, the Court was shorthanded. Justices Hugo Black and John Harlan had retired and their successors—Lewis Powell and William Rehnquist—had not yet been sworn in. Though it was her first appearance before the Court, Weddington was remarkably calm and collected. Even if she was somewhat vague about the constitutional basis for the right to an abortion, she maintained her position that fetuses had no constitutional rights and that even late third trimester abortions were constitutionally protected. The performance of Texas's attorney, Jay Floyd, was less impressive. The Court and the audience met his opening reference to "two beautiful ladies" with stony silence and Floyd had to admit several times that he did not know the answers to the justices' questions.

At the Court's weekly conference, four of the seven justices—William Douglas, Potter Stewart, William Brennan, and Thurgood Marshall—voted to invalidate the Texas law because it violated the right of privacy. Chief Justice Warren Burger, who tentatively wanted to void the law on the ground of its vagueness, exercised his right as the Chief Justice and assigned the opinion to Harry Blackmun, who labored for almost six months on it. On May 18, 1972, he circulated a draft of an opinion that, as Burger had suggested at conference, invalidated the law on the ground of vagueness, not privacy. When Douglas and Brennan objected, Blackmun endorsed Burger's and Justice Byron White's suggestion to reargue the case. The newly appointed Justice Powell, who had not heard the oral argument in *Roe* in 1971, then circulated a memo informing the other members of the Court that he and Rehnquist were going to vote for reargument, despite the Court's tradition that only justices who had heard the initial argument could vote on whether or not to reargue a case. The four-justice majority favoring a privacy-backed right to an abortion in 1971 became a four-justice minority opposing reargument in 1972.[6]

What do you make of these maneuverings? Is it possible that Burger voted at the initial conference in such a way that he could make the opinion assignment?[7] Is it permissible for a Chief Justice to manipulate his vote for the purpose of shaping the majority opinion? Do you think that that is what happened in *Roe*? Why do you think Burger assigned the opinion to Blackmun rather than to Douglas? Since *Roe* was such a politically charged case, do you think Douglas and the other justices who supported the right to an abortion in 1972 should not have resisted rearguing the case? Should Powell and Rehnquist have shown more respect for the Court's traditions? Or were they simply trying to do what was best in a set of difficult circumstances?

The oral argument of 1972 returned to the issue of whether the fetus was a person. Justice Stewart got Weddington to admit that she would have a "very difficult case" if the unborn fetus was deemed a person. On the other side, in response to a similar question from Stewart, Robert C. Flowers, the attorney for Texas, agreed that no state could permit any abortions since the fetus was a person. Perhaps if the life of the mother was in danger, the legislature could permit the option of abortion, but absent that danger, he conceded, the Constitution prohibited all abortions. Lurking in the background of this discussion was the underlying question concerning whether the fetus was a person? In what way was this question a legal one? Is it possible or arguable that the basic underlying question of *Roe* was beyond any court's expertise?

Douglas's fears that Powell's and Rehnquist's participation in the abortion decision might end in an affirmation of the Texas law or its invalidation on some ground other than privacy proved unwarranted. The Court split 7-2, with White and Rehnquist in dissent, and Blackmun's majority opinion invalidated the Texas law on the ground that it violated a woman's right of privacy.[8] However, the right, Blackmun insisted, was "not unqualified." It had to be "considered against important state interests in regulation." The state cannot adopt one theory of when life begins and thereby prohibit all or most abortions. The state did, however, have an interest in the health of the pregnant woman and in the potentiality of human life. Each of these interests grew and became "compelling" at different points during pregnancy. The result was the now familiar trimester framework. During the first trimester, a woman's right to an abortion could not be limited; during the second, it might be limited by regulations that were reasonably related to the health of the pregnant woman; during the third, abortions could be prohibited based upon the state's interest in the potentiality of life.

Justices White and Rehnquist dissented. They insisted that the Court had no authority to create yet another "new" constitutional right. *Roe* was "an exercise of raw judicial power." The Court's actions could not be legitimated by calling abortion a "fundamental" right. After all, throughout the twentieth century, all the states had prohibited most abortions. How, they asked, could the right to an abortion be "fundamental" if abortion itself had been illegal? In Rehnquist's judgment, the right of privacy could not justify what the Court had done because there was nothing "private" about abortion, at least not in a constitutional sense. Abortion was a matter of liberty, which could be restricted by state laws that were "rational means" to "valid objectives." By applying the higher standard of a "compelling interest," the Court was abusing its powers by inventing a new constitutional right. Were White and Rehnquist correct? Was the Court creating a "new" constitutional right? How was the "new" right related to the one created in *Griswold*? Was *Roe* more of a judicial abuse of power than *Griswold*? Why?

BIBLIOGRAPHY

Ely, John Hart. "The Wages of Crying Wolf: A Comment on *Roe v. Wade.*" *Yale Law Journal* 82 (1973), pp. 920–49.
Faux, Marian. *Roe v. Wade.* New York: MacMillan, 1988.
Heymann, Philip B., and Douglas E. Barzelay. "The Forest and the Trees: *Roe v. Wade* and Its Critics." *Boston University Law Review* 53 (1973), pp. 765–84.
Rubin, Eva. *Abortion, Politics, and the Courts.* Westport, Conn.: Greenwood, 1982.

BRIEFS

ROE'S BRIEF (1971)

[[1. The Right of Privacy.]] . . . Recognition of the sanctity of the marital relationship has resulted in recognition of a right of marital privacy, or as the *Griswold* decision states, "notions of privacy surrounding the marriage relationship" and of rights attendant to the marital state. Protection has been extended to such rights as the rights to marry and have offspring because of their fundamental nature, even though such rights are not expressly enumerated in the Bill of Rights. These decisions support the propositions that there is a sphere of marital privacy and that important interests associated with marriage and the family are, and should be, protected from arbitrary government intrusion. . . .

Associated with the right to marry is the right to have children, if one chooses, without arbitrary governmental interference. This Court unanimously held "the right to have offspring" is a constitutionally protected "human right" which cannot be taken away by a discriminatory statute requiring the sterilization of some persons convicted of crime, but not of others similarly situated. The *Skinner* Court recognized a constitutionally protected right *to have* offspring even though such [[a]] right is not mentioned in the Bill of Rights; a right *not to have* offspring should be of equal constitutional stature.

Further cases supporting these family rights include *Pierce v. Society of Sisters* and *Meyer v. Nebraska*, both of which were reaffirmed in *Griswold v. Connecticut*. A unanimous Court in *Pierce* recognized a right to send one's children to private school. This right derived from "the liberty of parents and guardians to direct the upbringing and education of children under their control." This liberty, and the responsibility it implies, suggests a concomitant right of persons to determine the number of children whose "upbringing and education" they will direct. . . .

Taken together, the *Griswold, Loving, Skinner, Pierce* and *Meyer* decisions illustrate that the Constitution protects certain privacy and family interests from governmental intrusion unless a compelling justification exists for the legislation. The right of family to determine whether to have additional children, and terminate a pregnancy in its early stages if a negative decision is reached, is such a right and is fully entitled to protection.

The number and spacing of children obviously have a profound impact upon the marital union. Certainly the members of this Court know from personal experience the emotional and financial expenditures parenthood demands. For those couples who are less fortunate financially and especially for those who are struggling to provide the necessities of life, additional financial responsibilities can be economically disastrous. For families who require two incomes for economic survival, the pregnancy can be ruinous since the wife will generally have to resign her job. In many other situations, such as where husband and wife are working to put themselves through school, pregnancy at a particular time can present a crisis.

Pregnancy can be a significant added problem in marriages. The added pressures of prospective parenthood can be "the last straw." . . .

In addition to rights associated with marital privacy an overlapping body of precedent extends significant constitutional protection to the citizen's sovereignty over his or her own physical person. . . .

Without the right to respond to unwanted pregnancy, a woman is at the mercy of possible contraceptive failure, particularly if she is unable or unwilling to utilize the most effective measures. Failure to use contraceptives effectively, if pregnancy ensues, exacts an exceedingly high price.

The court in *Baird v. Eisenstadt* recognized the inhumane severity of laws which impose continued pregnancy and compulsory parenthood as the cost of inadequate contraception. . . .

Baird involved contraceptives unavailable to unmarried women; this case involves measures unavailable to all women. The impact of the two statutes is identical for the women affected. Moreover, the magnitude of the impact is substantial.

When pregnancy begins, a woman is faced with a governmental mandate compelling her to serve as an incubator for months and then as an ostensibly willing mother for up to twenty or more years. She must often forego further education or a career and often must endure economic and social hardships. Under the present law of Texas she is given no other choice. Continued pregnancy is compulsory, unless she can persuade the authorities that she is potentially suicidal or that her life is otherwise endangered. The law impinges severely upon her dignity, her life plan and often her marital relationship. The Texas abortion law constitutes an invasion of her privacy with irreparable consequences. Absent the right to remedy contraceptive failure, other rights of personal and marital privacy are largely diluted. . . .

Without the ability to control their reproductive capacity, women and couples are largely unable to control determinative aspects of their lives and marriages. If the concept of "fundamental right" means anything, it must surely include the right to determine when and under what circumstances to have children. . . .

. . . [[T]]he Texas abortion laws infringe privacy rights here as much as the Connecticut statute did in *Griswold*. As in that case, the compelling interest test is the proper standard for reviewing the Texas statute.

[[2. Interests of the State.]] As Counsel for appellee admitted during oral argument, "the State only has one interest and that is the protection of the life of the unborn child." The question then becomes when this interest is sufficiently compelling to overcome the couple's or woman's fundamental right to privacy and autonomy. In this regard it is revealing to examine other aspects of the State's attitude toward the fetus. Such an inquiry reveals that only in the area of abortion does the State exhibit an interest in the fetus or treat it as having legal personality.

First, the pregnant woman who searches out a person willing to perform an abortion and who consents to, if not pleads for, the procedure is guilty of no crime. Texas courts have repeatedly held that the woman is neither a principal nor an accomplice. Similarly, the women who travel from Texas to states with less restrictive abortion laws in order to secure medical abortions and avoid the alleged state interest in protecting the fetus are guilty of no crime. Moreover, self-abortion has never been treated as a criminal act. The State has failed to seek to deter through criminal sanctions the person whose interests are most likely to be adverse to those of the fetus. This suggests a statutory purpose other than protecting embryonic life.

An unborn fetus is not a "human being" and killing a fetus is not murder or any other form of homicide. "Homicide" in Texas is defined as "the destruction of the life of one human being by the act, agency, procurement, or culpable omissions of another." . . . Since the common law definition of "human being" is applicable, a fetus neither born nor in the process of birth is not a "human being" within the meaning of those words as they appear in the homicide statute. In *Keller v. Superior Court* . . . a pregnant woman was assaulted by her former husband; a Caesarean section and examination *in utero* revealed that the fetus, of approximately thirty-five weeks gestation, had died of a severely fractured skull and resultant hemorrhaging. The California Supreme Court held the man could not be guilty of murder; the same result would apply in Texas. A fetus is not considered equal to a "human being," and its destruction involves a significantly lesser penalty.

The State does not require that a pregnant woman with a history of spontaneous abortion go into seclusion in an attempt to save the pregnancy. No pregnant woman having knowingly engaged in conduct which she reasonably could have foreseen would result in injury to the fetus (such as skiing in late pregnancy) has ever been charged with negligent homicide. . . .

It is sometimes argued that scientific discoveries show that human life exists in the fetus. Scientific studies in embryology have greatly expanded our understanding of the process of fertilization and development of the fetus and studies relating to the basic elements of life have shown that life is not only present in the fertilized egg, sperm and ova but that each cell contains elements which could conceivably constitute the beginning of a new human organism. Such studies are significant to science but only confuse the problem of defining human life. . . .

Once the fact that science can offer no guidance on the question of when human life begins is conceded, arguments concerning preservation of the fetus almost always fall back to the proposition of potential life. Despite disagreements as to when human characteristics are assumed by the fetus, its would-be protectors argue that since there is potential human life present, which, unlike "DNA" molecules *can* be protected, it must be preserved. But matters are not so simple. Obviously all potential life may not be protected. A legislative decision to cut appropriations for slum clearance, for medical facilities, for food subsidies; a declaration of war; a court's refusal to consider the habeas corpus petition of a condemned man—all in some way destroy life. And, to the extent that past experience shows that in the future "x" number of lives will be lost if the decisions are made, they are conscious decisions.

It is obvious that the legislative decision forbidding abortions also destroys potential life—that of the pregnant woman—just as a legislative decision to permit abortions destroys potential life. The question then becomes not one of destroying or preserving potential life, but one of who shall make the decision. Obviously some decisions are better left to a representative process since individual decisions on medical facilities, wars, or the release of a convict would tend toward the chaotic. It is our contention that the decision on abortion is exactly the opposite. A representative or majority decision making process has led to chaos. Indeed, in the face of two difficult, unresolvable choices—to destroy life potential in either a fetus or its host—the choice can only be left to one of the entities whose potential is threatened.

The above argument is perhaps only another way of stating that when fundamental rights are infringed upon, the State bears the burden of demonstrating a compelling interest for doing so. The question of the life of the fetus versus the woman's right to choose whether she will be the host for that life is incapable of answer through the legislative fact-finding process. Whether one considers the fetus a human being is a problem of definition rather than fact. Given a decision which cannot be reached on the basis of fact, the State must give way to the individual for it can never bear its burden of demonstrating that facts exist which set up a compelling state interest for denying individual rights. . . .

> Respectfully submitted,
> Roy Lucas
> Sarah Weddington
> James R. Weddington
> Linda N. Coffee

TEXAS'S BRIEF (1971)

[[1. The Right of Privacy.]] . . . Assuming arguendo that there are other marital rights the state must respect, may it then be urged that the right of marital privacy includes the freedom of a married couple to . . . commit infanticide, incest, engage in pandering and the like. Family privacy, like personal privacy, is highly valued, but not absolute. . . . The family may not practice polygamy, may not prohibit schooling for a child, . . . or expose the community or a child to communicable disease. . . .

Personal privacy is an exalted right but, as in marital privacy, it has never been regarded as absolute. A person may be subjected to a "stop and frisk" though it constitutes an intrusion upon his person, or a person may be required to submit to a vaccination, and a blood sample may forcibly be extracted from the body of an individual arrested for suspicion of driving while intoxicated. A woman has been required to submit to a blood transfusion necessary to preserve her life in order that her small child shall not be left without a mother. . . .

. . . [[T]]he New Jersey Supreme Court was asked to decide just such an issue—a conflict between the mother's privacy and the life of the unborn child. The issue was whether the rights of a child *in utero* were violated by the pregnant woman's refusal on religious grounds to submit to a blood transfusion necessary to preserve the lives of both the mother and the unborn child. The Court's finding favored the right to life of the unborn child over the pregnant woman's freedom of religion. . . .

[[2. The Interests of the State.]] Modern obstetrics has discarded the unscientific . . . concept that the child in the womb is but tissue of the mother. . . .

Yet the attack on the Texas statute assumes this discredited scientific concept and argues that abortions should be considered no differently than any medical measure taken to protect maternal health, thus completely ignoring the developing human being in the mothers' womb. . . .

It is our task . . . to show how clearly and conclusively modern science . . . establishes the humanity of the unborn child. We submit that the data not only shows the constitutionality of the Texas legislature's effort to save the unborn from indiscriminate extermination, *but in fact suggests a duty to do so*. We submit also that no physician who understands this will argue that the law is vague, uncertain or overbroad for he will understand that the law calls upon him to exercise his art for the benefit of his *two* patients: mother *and* child.

From conception the child is a complex, dynamic, rapidly growing organism. By a natural and continuous process the single fertilized ovum will, over approximately nine months, develop into the trillions of cells of the newborn. . . . At fertilization a new and unique being is created which, although receiving one-half of its chromosomes from each parent, is really unlike either.

About seven to nine days after conception, when there are already several hundred cells of the new individual formed, contact with the uterus is made and implantation begins. Blood cells begin at 17 days and a heart as early as 18 days. . . .

. . . By the end of the 20th day the foundation of the child's brain, spinal cord and entire nervous system will have been established. . . .

. . . The baby's eyes begin to form at 19 days. . . .

In the third month, the child becomes very active. By the end of the month he can kick his legs, turn his feet, curl and fan his toes, make a fist, move his thumb, bend his wrist, turn his head, squint, frown, open his mouth, press his lips tightly together. He can swallow and drinks the amniotic fluid that surrounds him. Thumb sucking is first noted at this age. . . .

In the fifth month, the baby gains two inches in height and ten ounces in weight. By the end of the month he will be about one foot tall and will weigh one pound. . . . The child's mother comes to recognize the movement and can feel the baby's head, arms and legs. She may even perceive a rhythmic jolting movement—fifteen to thirty per minute. This is due to the child hiccoughing. The doctor can now hear the heartbeat with his stethoscope.

The baby sleeps and wakes just as it will after birth. When he sleeps he invariably settles into his favorite position called his "lie". Each baby has a characteristic lie. . . . The child hears and recognizes his mother's voice before birth. . . .

In the sixth month, the child develops a strong muscular grip with his hands. He also starts to breathe regularly and can maintain respiratory response for twenty-four hours if born prematurely. He may even have a slim chance of surviving in an incubator. The youngest children known to survive were between twenty to twenty-five weeks old. The concept of *viability* is not a static one. . . . The concept of an artificial placenta may be a reality in the near future and will push the date of viability back even further, and perhaps to the earliest stages of gestation. After twenty-four to twenty-eight weeks the child's chances of survival are much greater. . . .

This review of the current medical status of the unborn serves us several purposes. Firstly, it shows conclusively the humanity of the fetus by showing that human life is a continuum which commences in the womb. There is no magic in birth. The child is as much a child in those several days before birth as he is those several days after. The maturation process, commenced in the womb, continues through the post-natal period, infancy, adolescence, maturity and old age. . . .

There seems little argument necessary if one can conclude [[that]] the unborn child is a human being, with birth but a convenient landmark in a continuing process—a bridge between two stages of life. The basic postulates from which the Appellees' arguments proceed are: (1) the pregnant woman has a right of control over her own body as a matter of privacy guaranteed to her by the Constitution of the United States; and (2) this right cannot be interfered with by the states since the state cannot demonstrate any compelling interest to justify its intrusion. The contrary position is the state's interest in preventing the arbitrary and unjustified destruction of an unborn child—a living human being in the very earliest stages of its development. Whatever personal right of privacy a pregnant woman may have with respect to the disposition and use of her body must be balanced against the personal right of the unborn child to life. . . .

Respectfully submitted,
CRAWFORD C. MARTIN,
Attorney General of Texas.

ORAL ARGUMENT (1971)

☙   ☙   ☙

JUSTICE STEWART: . . . Mrs. Weddington, so far on the merits, you've told us about the important impact of this law, . . . but we cannot here be involved simply with matters of policy, as you know. . . .

MRS. WEDDINGTON [[Roe's attorney]]: . . . I do feel that it is—that the Ninth Amendment is an appropriate place for the freedom to rest. I think the Fourteenth Amendment is equally an appropriate place, under the rights of persons to life, liberty, and the pursuit of happiness. I think that in as far as "liberty" is meaningful, that liberty to these women would mean liberty from being forced to continue the unwanted pregnancy.

STEWART: You're relying, in essence, in this branch of the argument simply on the due process clause of the Fourteenth Amendment?

WEDDINGTON: We had originally brought this suit alleging both the due process clause, equal protection clause, the Ninth Amendment, and a variety of others.

STEWART: And anything else that might obtain.

WEDDINGTON: Yeah, right. . . .

＊   ＊   ＊

JUSTICE WHITE: . . . And the statute doesn't make any distinctions based upon at what period of pregnancy the abortion is performed?

WEDDINGTON: No, Your Honor. There is no time limit or indication of time, whatsoever. So I think—

WHITE: Well, do you make any distinctions?

WEDDINGTON: No, sir. I do—I feel that the question of a time limit is not strictly before the Court, because of the nature of the situation in which the case is handled. Certainly I think, as a practical matter though, most of the states that do have some time limit indicated still permit abortions beyond the time limit for specified reasons, usually where the health of the mother is involved.

WHITE: What's your constitutional position here?

WEDDINGTON: As to a time limit—

WHITE: What about whatever clause of the Constitution you rest on—Ninth Amendment, due process, the general pattern penumbra—will that take you right up to the time of birth?

WEDDINGTON: It is our position that the freedom involved is that of a woman to determine whether or not to continue a pregnancy. Obviously I have a much more difficult time saying that a State has no interest in late pregnancy.

WHITE: Why? Why is that?

WEDDINGTON: I think that's more the emotional response to a late pregnancy, rather than it is any constitutional—

WHITE: Emotional response by whom?

WEDDINGTON: I guess by persons considering the issue outside the legal context. I think, as far as the State—

WHITE: Well, do you or don't you say that the constitutional . . . right you insist on reaches up to the time of birth, or—

WEDDINGTON: The Constitution, as I read it, . . . attaches protection to the person at the time of birth. Those persons born are citizens. . . . The Constitution, as I see it, gives protection to people after birth. . . .

＊   ＊   ＊

MR. FLOYD [[Attorney for Texas]]: Mr. Chief Justice, may it please the Court: It's an old joke, but when a man argues against two beautiful ladies like this, they are going to have the last word. . . .

✻   ✻   ✻

FLOYD: Your Honor, . . . [[a woman]] makes her choice prior to the time she becomes pregnant. That is the time of the choice. It's like, more or less, the first three or four years of our life we don't remember anything. But, once a child is born, a woman no longer has a choice, and I think pregnancy then terminates that choice. That's when.

THE COURT: Maybe she makes her choice when she decided to live in Texas. [Laughter]

FLOYD: . . . There is no restriction on moving. . . .

✻   ✻   ✻

JUSTICE MARSHALL: . . . What is Texas' interest? What is Texas' interest in the statute?

FLOYD: Mr. Justice, the *Thompson* case . . . held that the State had a compelling interest because of the protection of fetal life—of fetal life protection. They recognized the humanness of the embryo, or the fetus, and they said we have an interest in protecting fetal life.

Whether or not that was the original intent of the statute, I have no idea.

STEWART: Yet, Texas does not attempt to punish a woman who herself performs an abortion on herself.

FLOYD: That is correct, Your Honor. And the matter has been brought to my attention: Why not punish for murder, since you are destroying what you—or what has been said to be a human being? I don't know, except that I will say this. As medical science progresses, maybe the law will also progress along with it. Maybe at one time it could be possible, I suppose, statutes could be passed. Whether or not that would be constitutional or not, I don't know.

STEWART: But we're dealing with the statute as it is. There's no state, is there, that equates abortion with murder? Or is there?

FLOYD: There is none, Your Honor. . . .

✻   ✻   ✻

FLOYD: We say there is life from the moment of impregnation.

JUSTICE MARSHALL: And do you have any scientific data to support that?

FLOYD: Well we begin, Mr. Justice, in our brief, with the development of the human embryo, carrying it through the development of the fetus from about seven to nine days after conception.

MARSHALL: Well, what about six days?

FLOYD: We don't know.

MARSHALL: But the statute goes all the way back to one hour?

FLOYD: I don't—Mr. Justice, there are unanswerable questions in this field. I—
[Laughter]

MARSHALL: I appreciate it.

FLOYD: This is an artless statement on my part.

MARSHALL: I withdraw the question.

FLOYD: Thank you.
    When does the soul come into the unborn—if a person believes in a soul—I don't know. . . .

ORAL REARGUMENT (1972)

*   *   *

JUSTICE WHITE: Yes. But I'm just asking you, under the Federal Constitution, is the fetus a person, for the protection of due process?

MRS. WEDDINGTON: All of the cases—the prior history of this statute—the common law history would indicate that it is not. The State has shown no—

WHITE: Well, what about—would you lose your case if the fetus was a person?
. . .

WEDDINGTON: If the State could show that the fetus was a person under the Fourteenth Amendment, or under some other Amendment, or part of the Constitution, then you would have a situation of trying—you would have a State compelling interest which, in some instances, can outweigh a fundamental right. This is not the case in this particular situation.

CHIEF JUSTICE BURGER: Do you make any distinction between the first month, and the ninth month of gestation?

WEDDINGTON: Our statute does not.

BURGER: Do you, in your position in this case?

WEDDINGTON: We are asking, in this case, that the Court declare the statute unconstitutional; the State having proved no compelling interest at all. . . .

JUSTICE STEWART: Well, if—if it were established that an unborn fetus is a person, with the protection of the Fourteenth Amendment, you would have almost an impossible case here, would you not?

WEDDINGTON: I would have a very difficult case.

STEWART: I'm sure you would. So, if you had the same kind of thing, you'd have to say that this would be the equivalent—after the child was born, if the mother thought it bothered her health any having the child around, she could have it killed, isn't that correct?

WEDDINGTON: That's correct. . . .

✳   ✳   ✳

MR. FLOWERS [[Attorney for Texas]]: . . . [I]t is the position of the State of Texas that, upon conception, we have a human being; a person, within the concept of the Constitution of the United States, and that of Texas, also.

STEWART: Now how should that question be decided? Is it a legal question? A constitutional question? A medical question? A philosophical question? Or, a religious question? Or what is it?

FLOWERS: Your Honor, we feel that it could be best decided by a legislature, in view of the fact that they can bring before it the medical testimony—the actual people who do the research. But we do have—

STEWART: So then it's basically a medical question?

FLOWERS: From a constitutional standpoint, no, sir. I think it's fairly and squarely before this Court. We don't envy the Court for having to make this decision. . . .

WHITE: . . . Well, if you're correct that the fetus is a person, then . . . the State would have a great deal of trouble permitting an abortion, would it [[not]]?

FLOWERS: Yes, sir.

WHITE: In any circumstances?

FLOWERS: It would, yes, sir.

WHITE: To save the life of a mother, or her health, or anything else?

FLOWERS: Well, there would be the balancing of the two lives, and I think that—

WHITE: Well, what would you choose? Would you choose to kill the innocent one, or what?

FLOWERS: Well, in our statute, the State did choose that way, Your Honor. . . .

JUSTICE MARSHALL: Could Texas say, if it confronts the situation, for the benefit of the health of the wife, that the husband has to die? Could they kill him?

FLOWERS: I wouldn't think so, sir . . .

✳   ✳   ✳

FLOWERS: . . . I find no way that I know that any court or any legislature or any doctor anywhere can say that here is the dividing line. Here is not a life; and here is a life, after conception. Perhaps it would be better left to that legislature. There they have the facilities to have some type of medical testimony brought before them, and the opinion of the people who are being governed by it.

STEWART: Well, if you're right that an unborn fetus is a person, then you can't leave it to the legislature to play fast and loose dealing with that person. In other words, if you're correct, in your basic submission that an unborn fetus is a person, then abortion laws such as that which New York has are grossly unconstitutional, isn't it?

FLOWERS: That's right, yes.

STEWART: Allowing the killing of people.

FLOWERS: Yes, sir. . . .

STEWART: The basic constitutional question, initially, is whether or not an unborn fetus is a person, isn't it?

FLOWERS: Yes, sir, and entitled to the constitutional protection. . . .

THE OPINION (1973)

Mr. Justice Blackmun delivered the opinion of the Court. . . .

This right of privacy, whether it be founded in the Fourteenth Amendment's concept of personal liberty and restrictions upon state action, as we feel it is, or, as the District Court determined, in the Ninth Amendment's reservation of rights to the people, is broad enough to encompass a woman's decision whether or not to terminate her pregnancy. The detriment that the State would impose upon the pregnant woman by denying this choice altogether is apparent. Specific and direct harm medically diagnosable even in early pregnancy may be involved. Maternity, or additional offspring, may force upon the woman a distressful life and future. Psychological harm may be imminent. Mental and physical health may be taxed by child care. There is also the distress, for all concerned, associated with the unwanted child, and there is the problem of bringing a child into a family already unable, psychologically and otherwise, to care for it. In other cases, as in this one, the additional difficulties and continuing stigma of unwed motherhood may be involved. All these are factors the woman and her responsible physician necessarily will consider in consultation.

On the basis of elements such a these, appellant and some amici argue that the woman's right is absolute and that she is entitled to terminate her pregnancy at whatever time, in whatever way, and for whatever reason she alone chooses. With this we do not agree. Appellant's arguments that Texas either has no valid interest at all in regulating the abortion decision, or no interest strong enough to support any limitation upon the woman's sole determination, is unpersuasive. The Court's decisions recognizing a right of privacy also acknowledge that some state regulation in areas protected by that right is appropriate. . . .

We, therefore, conclude that the right of personal privacy includes the abortion decision, but that this right is not unqualified and must be considered against important state interests in regulation. . . .

The appellee and certain amici argue that the fetus is a "person" within the language and meaning of the Fourteenth Amendment. In support of this, they outline at length and in detail the well-known facts of fetal development. If this suggestion of personhood is established, the appellant's case, of course, collapses, for the fetus' right to life is then guaranteed specifically by the Amendment . . . .

All this, together with our observation that throughout the major portion of the 19th century prevailing legal abortion practices were far freer than they are today, persuades us that the word "person," as used in the Fourteenth Amendment, does not include the unborn. . . .

This conclusion, however, does not of itself fully answer the contentions raised by Texas. . . .

Texas urges that, apart from the Fourteenth Amendment, life begins at conception and is present throughout pregnancy, and that, therefore, the State has a compelling interest in protecting that life from and after conception. We need not resolve the difficult question of when life begins. When those trained in the respective disciplines of medicine, philosophy, and theology are unable to arrive at any consensus, the judiciary, at this point in the development of man's knowledge, is not in a position to speculate as to the answer.

It should be sufficient to note briefly the wide divergence of thinking on this most sensitive and difficult question. There has always been strong support for the view that life does not begin until live birth. This was the belief of the Stoics. It appears to be the predominant, though not the unanimous, attitude of the Jewish faith. . . .

As we have noted, the common law found greater significance in quickening. Physicians and their scientific colleagues have regarded that event with less interest and have tended to focus either upon conception, upon live birth, or upon the interim point at which the fetus becomes "viable," that is, potentially able to live outside the mother's womb, albeit with artificial aid. . . .

In view of all this, we do not agree that, by adopting one theory of life, Texas may override the rights of the pregnant woman that are at stake. We repeat, however, that the State does have an important and legitimate interest in preserving and protecting the health of the pregnant woman, whether she be a resident of the State or a nonresident who seeks medical consultation and treatment there, and that it has still *another* important and legitimate interest in protecting the potentiality of human life. These interests are separate and distinct. Each grows in substantiality as the woman approaches term and, at a point during pregnancy, each becomes "compelling."

With respect to the State's important and legitimate interest in the health of the mother, the "compelling" point, in the light of present medical knowledge, is at approximately the end of the first trimester. This is so because of the now-established medical fact . . . that until the end of the first trimester mortality in abortion may be less than mortality in normal childbirth. It follows that from and after this point, a State may regulate the abortion procedure to the extent that the regulation reasonably relates to the preservation and protection of maternal health. . . .

This means, on the other hand, that, for the period of pregnancy prior to this "compelling" point, the attending physician, in consultation with his patient, is free to determine, without regulation by the State, that, in his medical judgment, the patient's pregnancy should be terminated. If that decision is reached, the judgment may be effectuated by an abortion free of interference by the State.

With respect to the State's important and legitimate interest in potential life, the "compelling" point is at viability. This is so because the fetus then presumably has the capability of meaningful life outside the mother's womb. State regulation protective of fetal life after viability thus has both logical and biological justification. If the State is interested in protecting fetal life after viability, it may go so far as to proscribe abortion during that period, except when it is necessary to preserve the life or health of the mother. . . .

Mr. Justice White, dissenting . . .

With all due respect, I dissent. I find nothing in the language or history of the Constitution to support the Court's judgment. The Court simply fashions and announces a new constitutional right for pregnant mothers and, with scarcely any reason or authority for its action, invests that right with sufficient substance to override most existing state abortion statutes. The upshot is that the people and the legislatures of the 50 states are constitutionally disentitled to weigh the relative importance of the continued existence and development of the fetus, on the one hand, against a spectrum of possible impacts on the mother, on the other hand. As an exercise of raw judicial power, the Court perhaps has the authority to do what it does today; but in my view its judgment is an improvident and extravagant exercise of the power of judicial review that the Constitution extends to this Court. . . .

Mr. Justice Rehnquist, dissenting . . .

I have difficulty in concluding, as the Court does, that the right of "privacy" is involved in this case. Texas, by the statute here challenged, bars the performance of a medical abortion by a licensed physician on a plaintiff such as Roe. A transaction resulting in an operation such as this is not "private" in the ordinary usage of that word. Nor is the "privacy" that the Court finds here even a distant relative of the freedom from searches and seizures protected by the Fourth Amendment to the Constitution, which the Court has referred to as embodying a right to privacy. . . .

The fact that a majority of the States reflecting, after all, the majority sentiment in those States, have had restrictions on abortions for at least a century is a strong indication, it seems to me, that the asserted right to an abortion is not "so rooted in the traditions and conscience of our people as to be ranked as fundamental." . . . Even today, when society's views on abortion are changing, the very existence of the debate is evidence that the "right" to an abortion is not so universally accepted as the appellants would have us believe.

To reach its result the Court necessarily has had to find within the scope of the Fourteenth Amendment a right that was apparently completely unknown to the drafters of the Amendment. . . .

II. DEVELOPMENTS AFTER *ROE*

The pro-choice groups who had fought for the right to terminate unwanted pregnancies were largely satisfied with the results of *Roe v. Wade*. Though the decision did not recognize an unqualified right to have an abortion, the trimester framework gave women considerable control over their reproductive lives. In contrast, the emerging pro-life movement, centered at first around the Catholic Church, viewed *Roe* as an unmitigated disaster for the unborn. By 1978, the number of yearly legal abortions was approaching 1,400,000.[9] Ignoring the fact that a half million legal abortions and an unknown number of illegal abortions had taken place in 1972, the year before *Roe*, Catholic bishops condemned what the Court had done. It had opened the doors "to the greatest slaughter of innocent life in the history of mankind."[10] Convinced that abortion was equivalent to killing innocent human beings, the pro-life movement pursued several different tactics to circumvent or overturn *Roe*.

One option was a constitutional amendment, either a right-to-life amendment that would grant constitutional protection to the unborn or a "local-option" amendment that would reserve the power to regulate abortions to the states. Proposals for such amendments appeared in Congress during the mid-1970s. A subcommittee of the Senate Judiciary Committee held sixteen days of hearings in 1974 and 1975 that focused the nation's attention on abortion. In this great national debate, eighty-three witnesses representing all relevant groups and professions gave testimony. For the first time ever, four cardinals of the Catholic Church testified before a subcommittee of Congress. In his testimony, Cardinal John Krol of Philadelphia deplored the killing of defenseless human life and compared abortion to rape, suggesting that "the worst offense" was against the victim of an abortion. Bella Abzug, a representative from New York, argued that individual women should decide whether or not to have an abortion because they, not the state, were the ones who experienced pregnancy, childbearing, and childraising (see box 3.1). Though none of the proposed constitutional amendments made it to the Senate floor, the hearings revealed that compromise on abortion would be difficult, if not impossible, to achieve because the opposing groups were deeply committed to conflicting moral principles.

After 1975, there were several other futile attempts to enact pro-life constitutional amendments. The most successful effort was Orrin Hatch's Human Life Federalism Amendment in 1982. This Amendment, which transferred the issue of abortion to the states, was voted out of the Senate Judiciary Committee, but it failed to win a simple majority on the floor, falling far short of the two-thirds vote required. Frustrated by the amendment process, the pro-life movement made a concerted effort to narrow the effect of *Roe* at the state level. In the 1970s and 1980s, many states passed laws that restricted the right to an abortion without denying it entirely. Some states, for example, required a woman to have the consent of her spouse or, if an unmarried minor, of one of her parents before an abortion could take place. Others mandated that second trimester abortions be done only in hospitals or that they be done only after a doctor had "truly informed" the patient concerning the development of the fetus and the nature of the abortion procedure. A few even imposed criminal liability on doctors if they failed to follow guidelines when they had "sufficient reason" to believe that the fetus was viable. The Supreme Court invalidated all forms of the above regulations except those requiring parental consent.[11] Parental consent laws were constitutional if they gave the minor the opportunity to seek judicial approval without first notifying her parents. If such a minor could show a judge that she was competent to make the decision or that an abortion was in her best interest, then the judge had to permit the abortion without parental consent.[12]

In 1976, Representative Henry Hyde, a Republican from Illinois, led the fight to ban the use of any federal money for abortions. He felt that childbirth, but not abortions, should be funded. The Supreme Court upheld what became known as the "Hyde Amendment" in *Harris v. McCrae*.[13] The majority position in the 5–4 case was that the government could not "place obstacles in the path of a woman's exercise of her freedom of choice," but it did not have to "remove those not of its own creation."[14] A poor woman's indigency was not the result of anything the government had done. She had the same constitutional rights as a pregnant wealthy woman even though she did not have the money necessary to exercise them. The dissenters disagreed. In their view, the Hyde Amendment conflicted with *Roe* because it "burdened" a pregnant wom-

Box 3.1   DEBATE ON ABORTION

CARDINAL JOHN KROL:

... It has been estimated that there is 1 abortion every 20 seconds in the United States—3 every minute. Every week, since the Supreme Court's decision of January 22, 1973, there have been as many deaths from abortion as there were deaths at Nagasaki as a result of the atomic bomb. That is every week. Every 9 days there are as many deaths from abortions as there were American deaths in the 10 years of the Vietnam war. . . .

In order to grasp what is at stake in the issue before us, it is essential to understand the nature of the being whom an abortion kills. There is an impression in some quarters that the child before birth is simply a lump of tissue, an undifferentiated part of its mother's body, rather like an appendix. Nothing could be farther from the truth.

What comes into existence at the moment of conception is nothing less than a human being in the earliest stages of development. As our detailed statement shows, medical science has amply documented the humanity of the fetus. There would be no question about the humanity of the unborn except that some wish to kill them. . . .

. . . [[T]]he argument has been presented that there were 800,000 illegal abortions before and so the logical thing to do is to make it permissible. I am sure that [[if]] this kind of logic applies, let us say, to the whole area of rape, that it is being done outside the law, so, therefore let's remove the law and make it legal. . . . I don't think anybody could agree to that type of logic. . . .

There is a parallel . . . to rape. If you take the unborn child, no one gets its consent. The victim of a rape generally survives, the victim of abortion does not. So as I say, there is a parallel. It is not a perfect one, but if anything, the worst offense is against the victim of abortion. . . .

*   *   *

REPRESENTATIVE BELLA ABZUG:

. . . I find most difficult the comments of both Senators that appear to consign millions of women who have had abortions to the status of killers.

an's freedom of choice by utilizing financial incentives to encourage childbirth. Which argument is more persuasive? If a certain freedom is constitutionally protected, must the state distribute its financial benefits in a neutral fashion to those persons exercising the freedom? By encouraging one option, does the state "burden" the choice itself?

In its quest to reverse *Roe*, the pro-life movement tried to influence appointments to the Supreme Court. It was not, however, until the election of Ronald Reagan in 1980 that the antiabortion forces had a friend in the White House.

Not too long ago discussions concerning contraception and population control were also considered by many to be advocating killing. . . .

Man and woman are equal in the act of conception, but after that single act has occurred, it is the woman's body that carries and nurtures the embryo and the fetus.

It is the woman who experiences the physical and psychological changes of pregnancy.

It is the woman who has the discomforts and sometimes the medical complications that accompany pregnancy.

It is the woman who feels that pain of childbirth. It is the woman who may have the postpartum depression.

And in our society, it is still the woman who bears the major responsibility of caring for and raising the child and who often must leave school or her work to do so.

Childbearing and childraising is a great experience for most women. For some it is not. For some it is sometimes. The point is that it is a totally individual experience, the most highly personal process in a woman's life.

And yet the Buckley and Helms amendments might mobilize the full power and authority of the state and its legal apparatus to interfere in this private process, to dictate to the individual citizen who is a woman what she is to do with her body and with her life. . . .

. . . This Nation has already had the bitter experience of another kind of national prohibition as mandated by the 18th amendment to the Constitution. We know that not only did that Prohibition fail to accomplish its avowed highly moral purpose, but [[it]] was responsible for the lawless and violent era of the bootlegger and gangster, and the rise of organized crime which still plagues our society. . . .

Those who would overrule *Roe v. Wade* would ignore our experience with the practical consequences of attempting to prohibit abortion and the benefits we have seen in terms of improved maternal and infant health resulting from legalized abortion. . . .

None of these factors is taken into consideration in the proposed amendments, which assume a reverence for life that resolutely ignores the problems of the real world or the quality of life. . . .

Source: Hearings before the Subcommittee on Constitutional Amendments of the Committee on the Judiciary, Senate, 93rd Cong., 2nd Sess., March 6–7 and September 12, 1974, Part 1: 100–106, 153–56, 160–61, 175.

The same year saw the defeat of several prominent pro-choice Democratic senators—Birch Bayh of Iowa, Frank Church of Idaho, and George McGovern of South Dakota. The result was a Republican-led Senate—the house of Congress that has the constitutional responsibility of confirming Supreme Court nominees. The New Right, allied to some extent with the older Catholic-based opposition to abortion, had helped to produce this Republican victory. What they wanted in return was a Supreme Court more in sympathy with their concerns about school prayer and abortion. In 1981, Justice Sandra Day O'Connor was Reagan's first appointment. Though pro-life advocates at first opposed her nomination, her dissent in *Akron v. Akron Center for Reproductive Health* (1983)[15] indicated that there were now three justices who were uncomfortable with the *Roe* decision: O'Connor, William Rehnquist, and Byron White. Antonin Scalia's confirmation in 1986 left the Court with a bare majority clearly in favor of *Roe*. Then, in the summer of 1987, Justice Lewis Powell retired. The next appointee would, in all likelihood, be the decisive vote on the abortion question.

Ronald Reagan nominated Robert Bork, a federal appeals court judge whose earlier published views on the right to abortion and the more general right of privacy strengthened the impression that *Roe* was in the balance. If Bork was confirmed, the suspicion was that *Roe* would be directly or indirectly overturned. Behind the scenes the pro-choice and pro-life groups marshalled their forces as the Senate Judiciary Committee held public hearings on the Bork nomination. Democratic senators, who were once again in the majority of the Senate, "grilled" the nominee. Joseph Biden, Edward Kennedy, and Howard Metzenbaum charged that Bork's earlier academic writings and speeches proved that he had little respect for certain constitutional rights, especially those favoring minorities and women. His views were "outside the mainstream." Republican Senators Orin Hatch and Alan Simpson defended Bork's qualifications, describing the opposition to him as "political." Throughout the hearings, distortions competed with accusations and thinly disguised insults. In the end Bork was rejected by a vote of 58 to 42, the largest margin of defeat ever suffered by a Supreme Court nominee.

Even though the pro-choice movement was obviously pleased by the Senate's rejection of Bork, the eventual appointee, Anthony M. Kennedy, initially sided with those justices who were unsympathetic with *Roe*. In *Webster v. Reproductive Health Services* (1989), the Bush administration asked the Court to overturn *Roe*—the fifth time the federal government had made this request.[16] Though the Court did not explicitly overrule *Roe* in this case, its validity was seriously questioned. Kennedy joined Rehnquist, White, O'Connor, and Scalia in upholding a state law that proclaimed that life began at conception; that prohibited the use of any public facilities to perform abortions in cases in which the woman's life is not endangered or the use of any public funds to "counsel" a woman to have an abortion; and that required a physician to perform certain tests as to the fetus's viability if there were grounds to believe that the fetus was twenty or more weeks old. However, these justices diverged on the rationale for the decision. Scalia called for an explicit reversal of *Roe*. Rehnquist, Kennedy, and White abandoned the trimester framework of *Roe*, but said that the decision itself did not have to be, at this point, overruled. O'Connor disagreed. She argued that, though *Roe*'s trimester framework was "problematic," the above regulations could be upheld without abandoning it, much less overturning *Roe* itself.

In his dissent in *Webster*, Justice Blackmun observed that *Roe* and the right to an abortion "survive but are not secure." In his judgment, the plurality opinion was an invitation to the states to enact increasingly restrictive regulations that would, in time, give the Court the clear opportunity to overturn *Roe*: "the signs are evident and very ominous, and a chill wind blows."[17] Pennsylvania, acting upon the latitude that the Court recognized in *Webster*, amended its Abortion Control Act. The new provisions, among other things,[18] established a twenty-four-hour waiting period for abortions, required spousal notification, and mandated "informed" consent for all abortions. Arguably more restrictive than those upheld in *Webster*, these provisions were similar to ones that had already been declared unconstitutional by the Supreme Court during the 1970s and 1980s.[19] They were quickly challenged in federal court and the case, *Planned Parenthood v. Casey*, made its way to the Supreme Court. For the sixth time, the federal government asked the Court to overturn *Roe*.

Since the Supreme Court's commitment to *Roe* was clearly wavering, the case posed an interesting dilemma for the lawyers for both sides. Should they assume that *Roe* was defunct, even though it had not been explicitly overruled, or should they build their arguments around this central precedent? Legal and political factors had an impact upon how each side reacted to this question. Pennsylvania had an easier choice. It did not have to insist that *Roe* was dead and thereby risk offending justices who were crucial swing votes. It could take a moderate course in its brief and oral argument. *Roe* was still good law, but *Webster* had weakened it. Therefore, the standard that the Court should use to assess the constitutionality of abortion regulations should no longer be "strict scrutiny." Some less stringent standard was appropriate, and the brief endorsed the criterion that Justice O'Connor had suggested in previous cases: the standard of an "undue burden." Regulations of abortions were constitutional unless they were "unduly burdensome" upon a woman's right to an abortion.

Using this standard, Pennsylvania argued, all of the regulations—the twenty-four-hour waiting period, informed consent, and spousal notification—were constitutional because they served important state interests and did not severely limit access to abortions. For instance, requiring pregnant women to notify their husbands before having an abortion protected a husband's " 'deep and proper concern' in his wife's pregnancy and in the fetus she carries." The number of "battered women" who would not be able to get an abortion because of this provision was so small that the provision did not constitute an "undue burden." However, Pennsylvania concluded, if the Court did not accept this reasoning, if the Court could not reconcile these provisions with the "new" meaning of *Roe*, then *Roe* itself should be overruled. It was "an untenable" decision that "distorts" the Supreme Court's function and undermines "principles of self-governance."

In short, Pennsylvania had the luxury of arguing that the Court should affirm the regulations in question whether *Roe* was upheld or reversed. The lawyers for Planned Parenthood had a more difficult tactical situation. Not to acknowledge that *Webster* had weakened *Roe* risked building their legal arguments on quicksand. Perhaps better results could be obtained by recognizing that the Court was now operating with a standard of review that was somewhat lower than the one established in *Roe*. They would still oppose the constitutionality of the provisions of the Pennsylvania law, but their arguments would be in terms of this lower standard—perhaps the standard of "undue burden."

However, the long-term political costs of this option were enormous. It would appear as if those who had fought so hard for the principles endorsed in *Roe* had quickly abandoned them for short-term objectives. In a political sense, it was more important to affirm the full meaning of *Roe* than to convince the Court to invalidate the Pennsylvania provisions on the narrow ground that they constituted "undue burdens" on the right of abortion. After all, two new justices—David Souter and Clarence Thomas—had been appointed to the Supreme Court since *Webster*, replacing William Brennan and Thurgood Marshall, two of the Court's most consistent defenders of *Roe*. Though at the time their views on abortion were not definitely known, the best guess was that Souter and Thomas would support the trend to weaken or overturn *Roe*. There was therefore little to be gained by refining subtle arguments about "undue burdens" when it was likely that the Court would uphold the provisions in any case. It would be better to challenge the Court by demanding that *Roe* be upheld in its entirety, including its trimester framework.

Planned Parenthood took the long-term political and strategic course. The strategy was to use *Casey* to elevate the political temperature of the national debate. The brief and oral argument were therefore designed to appeal to the American people, especially American women, as much as they were designed to persuade individual justices now on the Supreme Court The relationship of the right of abortion to the right of privacy was highlighted. A reversal of *Roe* would be the first time that the Court ever "took back" a constitutional right. Such a reversal would endanger not only other rights of privacy, but also all the advances that women have made over the last several decades. Overwhelmingly male state legislatures could force women to return to the subservient position of homemaker and childbearer. The conclusion was that if the Court upheld any of the Pennsylvania provisions, then *Roe* was dead. Planned Parenthood had drawn a line in the sand and politically challenged the Court to step over it.

On June 29, 1992, the Supreme Court handed down its decision. In a 7–2 vote, the Court upheld the twenty-four-hour waiting period and the informed consent requirement, but rejected the spousal notification provision by a margin of 5–4. The three justices who constituted the crucial swing votes—Sandra Day O'Connor, Anthony Kennedy, and David Souter—took the unusual step of writing a joint opinion.[20] In it, they affirmed what they understood to be the "essential holding" of *Roe*. First, women still had the right to choose an abortion before viability. Second, the state could not impose "undue" burdens upon this right, but it could regulate abortions for the sake of the pregnant woman's health and the potential life of the fetus. Third, after viability, the state could prohibit all abortions that did not endanger the life of the woman.

The joint opinion therefore threw out the trimester framework of *Roe*. Viability was the key to whether the state could prohibit abortions, not the third trimester, and the state's interest in maternal health and potential life existed throughout pregnancy. These interests were not confined, as *Roe* had confined them, to separate trimesters. As long as regulations serving these interests did not constitute an "undue burden," the state could impose them even in the first trimester. According to this test, the three justices found that only the spousal notification requirement constituted an "undue" burden. It was a "substantial obstacle" because it would prevent "many" women who were physically or psychologically abused by their husbands from obtaining an abortion. In circumstances of this sort, it would permit "fear" to have an impact upon the choice of whether to have an abortion. Spousal notification therefore constituted an "undue burden." In contrast, the waiting-period and informed-consent provisions only made an abortion somewhat more expensive and difficult to obtain.

What is perhaps most interesting about the joint opinion written by O'Connor, Kennedy, and Souter is the role that precedent and the Court's legitimacy played in their decision to weaken, but not to overrule, *Roe*. In the view of these three justices, a judge has a general obligation to follow a precedent, even if he or she disagrees with it. This is especially so if the precedent is one that called "the contending sides of a national controversy to end their national division by accepting a common mandate rooted in the Constitution." Particularly in regard to such a precedent, a "decision to overrule should rest on some special reason over and above the belief that a prior case was wrongly decided." For instance, the Court legitimately overruled *Lochner v. New York* and *Plessy v. Ferguson* because society's understanding of the underlying factual situation had changed. Therefore, because it had a principled justification for the reversals apart from political pressure, the Court properly rejected, without any loss of legitimacy, the doctrines of "liberty of contract" and "separate but equal." Society had changed its mind about the factual relationship between "liberty of contract" and prosperity, and between segregation and equality. In the case of *Roe*, however, there has been no change in society's general understanding of the underlying facts about abortion. *Roe*'s central holding was a "workable" one that many people had relied upon for many years. The three justices therefore concluded that, since *Roe* was a decision that had this sort of "rare precedential force," there was no justification to override it.

If the Court reversed *Roe* without a principled justification, the perception would be that it was overruling *Roe* "under fire," thereby "subverting" the Court's legitimacy. *Roe* therefore had to be upheld, "with whatever degree of personal reluctance," so that the country would not lose confidence in the Supreme Court and, thereby, lose its ability to "see itself through its constitutional ideals." The conclusion of the joint opinion is that the "rule of law" is better served by upholding what might have originally been a "bad" constitutional decision, rather than by overruling it.

Justices Byron White and Clarence Thomas joined opinions written by Justice Antonin Scalia and Chief Justice Rehnquist that roundly condemned the joint opinion's concept of precedent and its general interpretation of the Court's role in the American political order. Rehnquist's and Scalia's opinions are similar in substance, but Scalia's is more personal and angry in tone, revealing the degree to which the issue of abortion has divided the Court as sharply as it has divided American society. Both opinions argue that the joint opinion is inconsistent, if not hypocritical. If a precedent like *Roe* must be respected, they ask, how can the plurality so "casually" discard *Roe*'s trimester framework and introduce an entirely new standard of analysis: the standard of an "undue burden"? Such an approach hardly respects precedent, since it treats *Roe* as a "storefront on a western movie set" or as "a sort of judicial Potemkin village." If the Court's legitimacy depends upon principled decision making, then the doctrine of precedent should be applied in a principled manner as well.

Rehnquist's and Scalia's more substantive charge is that the plurality's doctrine of precedent is wrong. Since Supreme Court decisions can only be politically reversed by way of the difficult process of amendment, they argue, the Court must be free to overturn precedents on the sole ground that they were mistakes. It does not have to wait until "opposition to the original decision had died away." Even when controversial landmarks like *Roe* are involved, no additional reason is required. The very cases that the plurality uses to illustrate its doctrine of constitutional precedent—*West Coast Hotel* overturning *Lochner*, and *Brown* overturning *Plessy*—show that the Court has overturned landmark precedents for no other reason than that they were mistaken interpretations of the Constitution. The New Deal Court did not overturn *Lochner* because it had discovered new "facts" about the requisites of a prosperous economy, nor did the Warren Court discover some new "fact" when it ruled that segregation was "inherently unequal." All that had changed was the Court's interpretation of the Constitution, and that sufficed to justify overturning the earlier landmarks.

In his opinion, Justice Scalia heaps scorn upon the idea, calling it "nothing less than Orwellian," that the "central holding" of *Roe* was a "statesmanlike 'settlement.'" Indeed, rather than contributing to resolving the issue, the Court exacerbated the situation. Acting in the spirit of an "imperial judiciary," it illegitimately took a nonconstitutional issue from the state legislatures by inventing a new constitutional right to an abortion. The plurality might think that the Court's legitimacy is preserved by resolutely defending this mistaken decision, despite its flawed character and the political opposition that has arisen against it, but Scalia argues that the exact opposite is more likely. In his view, the "American people love democracy and the American people are not fools." To the degree to which the Supreme Court no longer confines its function to interpreting the text and the traditions of the Constitution, but rather enlarges its role by making value judgments on divisive public-policy questions, it will lose its legitimacy, Scalia concluded, as a court of law.

Justice Harry Blackmun, the author of the majority opinion in *Roe*, criticizes the plurality for abandoning the trimester framework, but praises their endorsement of Roe's "central holding" and applauds their commitment to the principle of stare decisis. In contrast, he rejects Rehnquist's principles of individual liberty and precedent, calling the former "stunted" and the latter "narrow." He ends his opinion with the observation that *Roe* survives by the margin of a single vote and that he is eighty-three years old. Since he cannot remain on the Court forever, he predicts that the confirmation process for his successor "may well focus on the same issue before us today." Is Blackmun correct? Will the confirmation process focus on the next nominee's views on abortion? Is it inevitable? Is it appropriate? Does it indicate that the Court is abusing its power? Would it mean that all future nominees to the Court would undergo an examination similar to the one experienced by Robert Bork? Would that be so terrible? What sort of nomination process is compatible with the Court's role and legitimacy?

Casey did not satisfy either the pro-life side or the pro-choice side, which calls to mind the ultimate question of whether the Supreme Court has the institutional ability to resolve divisive public-policy questions. At the end of his dissent, Scalia addresses this theme by way of an analogy to Roger Taney's infamous opinion in the *Dred Scott* case. Just as Taney thought that he was resolving the question of slavery by asking each side to accept "a common mandate rooted in the Constitution," so also the authors of the joint opinion in *Casey*, in Scalia's view, think that they can solve the abortion controversy. In Scalia's judgment, a judicially imposed peace will never succeed. The three crucial swing justices will be as disappointed as Taney. In the United States, Scalia continues, controversial divisive issues cannot be settled outside of democratic political forums that give "all participants, even the losers, the satisfaction of a fair hearing and an honest fight." Is Scalia right? Are there limits to what the Supreme Court can do to resolve an issue like abortion?

BIBLIOGRAPHY

Condit, Celeste Michelle. *Decoding Abortion Rhetoric.* Urbana: University of Illinois, 1990.

Craig, Barbara Hinkson, and David M. O'Brien. *Abortion and American Politics.* Chatham, N.J.: Chatham House, 1993.

Jaffe, Frederick S., Barbara L. Lindheim, Philip R. Lee. *Abortion Politics.* New York: McGraw Hill, 1981.

Rodman, Hyman, Betty Sarvis, Joy Walker Bonar. *The Abortion Question.* New York: Columbia University Press, 1987.

Tribe, Laurence. *Abortion: The Clash of Absolutes.* New York: Norton Paperback, 1992.

BRIEFS

PLANNED PARENTHOOD'S BRIEF

[[1. The Meaning and Validity of *Roe*.]] . . . This Court has consistently applied *Roe*'s strict scrutiny standard to invalidate not only abortion bans but also laws that encumber the abortion choice with delay, administrative hurdles, or expense, or that disproportionately harm young, low-income, rural, or battered women. *Roe*'s central premise—that the right to choose abortion is a fundamental right protected by the most exacting scrutiny—thus forbids legislation that places roadblocks before women seeking abortion or that forecloses the abortion option for those women too vulnerable to overcome the state-imposed burdens. . . .

By overruling *Roe*, this Court would sanction an abrupt departure from 200 years of American constitutional history. Never before has this Court bestowed, then taken back, a fundamental right that has been a part of the settled rights and expectations of literally millions of Americans for nearly two decades. To regress by permitting states suddenly to impose burdensome regulations or criminalize conduct that a full generation of women has always known to be constitutionally protected would be anathema to any notion of principled constitutional decision-making . . . .

Given the certainty of disrupting the lives and settled expectations of countless women, overturning *Roe* would be "a rare and grave undertaking," which could be justified only by a strong showing by the Commonwealth that special circumstances demand that result. Only if the precedent is "unsound in principle," "unworkable in practice," or has led to inconsistent, unforeseen, or anomalous results would this radical step be warranted. None of these justifications is present here. . . .

State restrictions on abortion violate a woman's privacy in two ways. First, compelled continuation of a pregnancy infringes on a woman's right to bodily integrity by imposing substantial physical intrusions and significant risks of physical harm. . . .

In addition to violating principles of bodily integrity, abortion restrictions also deprive women of the right to make autonomous decisions about reproduction and family planning—critical life choices that this Court has long deemed central to the right of privacy. Because parenthood has a dramatic impact on a woman's educational prospects, employment opportunities, and self-determination, restrictive abortion laws deprive her of basic control of her life. For these reasons, "the decision whether or not to beget or bear a child" lies at "the very heart of this cluster of constitutionally protected choices." Indeed, the right to choose abortion partakes of those constitutional freedoms at the heart of a free society: the freedoms of spirit and self-determination. . . .

This Court must reject the view that the state's interest in potential life is compelling throughout pregnancy. That view would render meaningless this Court's recognition of the abortion choice as a protected liberty interest of fundamental importance. Any restriction, even criminalization of abortion in virtually all circumstances, might be justified by reference to the state's compelling interest in potential life. . . .

In addition to its soundness and workability as a constitutional doctrine, *Roe* has proven an enormously wise decision of immeasurable benefit to the lives, health, and equality of American women. First *Roe* has allowed millions of women to escape the dangers of illegal abortion and forced pregnancy. . . . In the 1950s and 1960s, an estimated 200,000 to 1.2 million illegal abortions occurred annually in the United States. As a result of these back-alley and self-induced abortions, as many as 5,000 to 10,000 women died each year, and many other women suffered severe physical and psychological injury. Still other women endured forced pregnancy and its attendant health risks. And history makes clear that, without constitutional protection, low-income women, who are disproportionately women of color, suffered the most. . . .

Experience throughout this country's history amply demonstrates that overturning *Roe* will not end abortion. Instead, permitting states to criminalize abortion or to impose burdensome restrictions, either singularly or cumulatively will tragically and undeniably return women to illegal, back-alley practitioners or self-abortions. As in the days before *Roe*, the number of abortion-related deaths and injuries will soar and women will be forced to continue unwanted pregnancies against their will.

Finally, by affording women greater control over their childbearing, *Roe* has permitted American women to participate more fully and equally in every societal undertaking. The option of safe, legal abortion has enabled great numbers of women to control the timing and size of their families and thus continue their education, enter the workforce, and otherwise make meaningful decisions consistent with their own moral choices. As a result, women have experienced significant economic and social gains since *Roe*. It is simply unconscionable for this Court to allow hostile state legislatures to force women back to the days when "the female [was] destined solely for the home and rearing of the family, and only the male for the marketplace and the world of ides." To do so would wreak havoc on a century of constitutional doctrine and "cast[ ] into darkness the hopes and visions of every woman in this country who had come to believe that the Constitution guaranteed her the right to exercise some control over her unique ability to bear children." . . .

[[2. Spousal Consent.]] . . . Ever since this Court established that a state may not empower a husband to veto a woman's abortion choice, no court has upheld as constitutional a husband notification requirement.

As this Court recognized, a notification statute may give the notified person a veto of the woman's decision, by given that person the opportunity to prevent the abortion or to penalize the woman severely for exercising her choice. . . .

The limited exceptions to the husband notification requirement do not relieve women of these severe burdens. . . .

. . . [[T]]he Act's exceptions for sexual assault and bodily injury will leave battered women vulnerable to a range of coercion and abuse. As the district court found and the court of appeals acknowledged, the pattern of random violence inflicted on them ensures that many "battered spouses are psychologically incapacitated from making the assertion required by the statute even when there is ample objective basis for the required fear." Survivors of marital rape will also be unable to make the exception's required report to law enforcement officials "[g]iven the devastating effect that a report . . . is likely to have on the marital relationship and the economic support provided the wife by marriage." . . .

In addition, even though "physical violence is *not* the only burden reasonably predictable," the harsh exceptions apply only to acts of *physical* violence against the married woman. As the district court found, the exceptions would not apply where a husband would if notified,

> threaten to (1) [sic] publicize her intent to have an abortion to family, friends or acquaintances; (b) retaliate against her in future child custody or divorce proceedings; (c) inflict psychological intimidation or emotional harm upon her, her children or other persons; (d) inflict bodily harm on other persons such as children, family members or other loved ones; or (e) use his control over finances to deprive [her] of necessary monies for herself or her children. . . .

Moreover, this burdensome provision serves no legitimate state interest whatsoever. . . . Where women choose not to notify their husbands, the state interests, to the extent they are legitimate at all, would actually be disserved by forced notification. As the district court found,

> The record clearly establishes that instead of fostering marital communication and bolstering the state's interest in marital integrity, the exact opposite effect would likely occur. . . . Not only could forced notice hasten the dissolution of a troubled marriage, but it could have potentially disastrous consequences, including subjecting the woman to physical abuse.

Nor can the Commonwealth's purported interest in protecting the husband's "interests in having children within marriage and in protecting the prenatal life of [his] child," justify the violation of the woman's right of privacy. Although both men and women have a constitutionally protected interest against state interference in their ability to procreate and in their children's welfare, neither interest is served by the husband notification requirement. Instead the statute protects only the husband's "interest" in compelling his wife to bear children for him. That decision, however, must remain with the pregnant woman, "who physically bears the child and who is the more directly and immediately affected by the pregnancy." . . .

[[3. Waiting Period.]] . . . In *Akron* this Court held that no

> legitimate state interest is furthered by an arbitrary and inflexible waiting period. There is no evidence suggesting that the abortion procedure will be performed more safely. Nor [is] . . . the state's legitimate concern that the woman's decision be informed . . . reasonably served by requiring a 24-hour delay as a matter of course.

Consistent with this holding, the district court confirmed the onerous burdens imposed by the Act's mandatory delay. In particular, the district court found that:

a. The 24-hour waiting period will force every woman seeking an abortion to make two separate trips to the physician.

b. Because of scheduling complications, the waiting period will "result in delays far in excess of 24 hours"; for most women, the delay will range from forty-eight hours to two weeks.

c. For many women, the 24-hour delay will significantly increase the cost of obtaining an abortion, including the costs of transportation, overnight lodging, and lost wages.

d. The requirement of two visits to the provider will subject "many women to the harassment and hostility of anti-abortion protestors. . . ."

e. The mandatory delay will be especially burdensome for low-income women, young women, women from rural areas, and women—such as battered women—who may have difficulty explaining their whereabouts. . . .

[[4. Informed Consent.]] . . . A state may require that a woman give her voluntary and informed consent to the abortion procedure. But precisely because the validity of an informed consent requirement rests on the state's interest in protecting the health of the pregnant woman, the state may not, under the guise of "informed consent," attempt to intimidate women into continuing their pregnancies by forcing physicians to deliver irrelevant, inaccurate, misleading, or inflammatory information. This is true under any standard of review. This Court has twice invalidated biased patient counseling requirements virtually identical to those at issue here. . . . Nothing in this record would compel a different result. . . .

Respectfully submitted,
KATHRYN KOLBERT

PENNSYLVANIA'S BRIEF

[[1. Undue Burden Standard.]] . . . [[T]]he Court should again reaffirm *Roe*'s holding that the right to abortion is not absolute or unlimited, but must accommodate legitimate and important state interests. In our view, that accommodation is best served, short of overruling *Roe*, by employing the "undue burden" standard for reviewing state regulation of abortion. . . .

"An undue burden will generally be found in situations involving absolute obstacles or severe limitations on the abortion decision. . . ." Thus, in *Roe* itself, the Court struck down a Texas law that prohibited all abortions except those necessary to save the life of the mother. In *Danforth*, the Court invalidated parental consent and spousal consent provisions which allowed third parties to interpose an absolute, and possibly arbitrary, veto on the right to seek an abortion. . . .

. . . "[[T]]he 'unduly burdensome' standard is particularly appropriate in the abortion context because of the *nature* and *scope* of the right that is involved. The privacy right in the abortion context 'cannot be said to be absolute.' " *Roe* is an attempt to establish a *limited* fundamental right, while at the same time recognizing and accommodating the important interests of the state; and unless the Court is prepared to overrule *Roe,* the Court should employ a judicial standard which reflects this attempt. . . .

[[2. Informed Consent.]] . . . [[P]]etitioners argue that these provisions do not further any legitimate state interest. As the Court of Appeals said, however, "this type of information 'clearly is related to maternal health and to the State's legitimate purpose in requiring informed consent.' " Petitioners do not contend that any of this information is inaccurate, unverifiable or inflammatory. Indeed, the worst that petitioners can find to say about any of the required information is that one item—the risks of carrying to term—may be irrelevant to those women who are forced to seek an abortion for medical reasons. But a law is not irrational merely because it is overinclusive or underinclusive; laws need not be perfect to be rational.

More broadly, the petitioners appear to be arguing for a *per se* rule that an informed consent law can *never* require the provision of *any* specific piece of information, on the ground that "the supply of specific information to all patients regardless of their specific circumstances . . . is contrary to the standard medical practice that informed consent be specifically tailored to the needs of the specific patient.' " There is no warrant for such a rule: even in *Akron,* the Court said that an informed consent law that required the disclosure of specific information including gestational age, was "certainly . . . not objectionable." . . .

[[3. Waiting Period.]] . . . Section 3205 requires that the information needed for an informed consent be provided to the woman at least 24 hours before the abortion is performed. . . .

Petitioners and the District court rely on the arguments that the 24-hour waiting period necessitates two trips to the abortion provider, which increases costs, especially for women who must travel; and that, because abortion clinics do not perform abortions every day the waiting period in practice will produce delays much longer than 24 hours, which in turn increases the risk of the abortion procedure. They ignore the facts that most women already make two trips—once for a pregnancy test and once for the abortion itself—and that there is typically a time lag between the two. None of the petitioners will even schedule an abortion without a positive pregnancy test, and the abortion is then typically scheduled within one to two weeks thereafter. . . .

As to the idea that a delay in performing an abortion increases the risk to the patient, this is true only in the most general sense, and provides no real support for the petitioners. The record is clear that there is no measurable increase in risk from a delay as short as a day, or even a week. . . .

Likewise, the Court of Appeals was correct that the waiting period rationally furthers the Commonwealth's interest "in ensuring that such a decision is *both* informed *and* well-considered [, which is] rationally related to the states' legitimate interest in the life and health of the mother as well as its interest in the potential life of the fetus." . . .

[[4. Spousal Notice.]] . . . [[T]]he number of women who even theoretically could be affected adversely by spousal notice is very small. . . . [[T]]he record shows that only about 20% of the women who obtain abortions are married; and of these, about 95% notify their husbands already. In other words, of all women who obtain abortions, only about 1% are married women who have not notified their husbands.

Of those women who did not notify their husbands and who offered a reason, none cited a fear of abuse. Moreover, . . . of these few women, surely some, if Section 3209 were to go into effect, would notify their husbands without adverse consequences, while still others would avail themselves of the statutory exceptions to spousal notice. The number of women who might actually be deterred from seeking an abortion by the spousal notice provision is thus unknown, and possibly nonexistent, but certainly, at less than one percent, very small. . . .

The petitioners and the majority in the Court of Appeals, however, rely heavily on the District Court's finding that "most battered women do not have the psychological ability to avail themselves" of this exception. . . .

The witness upon whom the District Court relied testified about women who are in a "battering relationship." According to this witness, women in such relationships are subjected not only to a recurring cycle of violence, but also to the constant monitoring of their activities and even their thoughts; "most batterers are so sensitive to what the women are behaving and thinking and feeling that he [sic] will pick up something [that] is different. . . ." Women in such relationships can suffer from a form of mental disorder called Post-Traumatic Stress Disorder, one manifestation of which is "learned helplessness," the perception by the woman that no action of hers will enable her to escape the violence. It is women manifesting this "learned helplessness" whom the District Court found would not be able to avail themselves of Section 3209's exception for physical abuse.

This finding, however, does not address the question of how many of these women would ever seek an abortion without their husband's knowledge in the first place. Battered women who perceive themselves as so helpless that they would never even try such a thing are indeed cruelly burdened, but by their batterers, not by the statute. In real life, the opportunity to invoke the fear-of-abuse exception will not be encountered by these battered women, but only by those battered women who have *already* mustered the psychological and physical resources necessary to verify their pregnancies, contact abortion providers, wait for their appointments, arrange for payment, and physically present themselves at the abortion sites—all without letting their husbands find out. Neither the District Court nor the witness—who had no actual experience with spousal notification provisions—said how many of *these* women would find themselves "psychologically incapable" of checking off a line on a form, which is all that Section 3209 requires.

The petitioners thus did not show that Section 3209 would have anything close to the "broad practical effect" of severely limiting access to abortions. Their challenge is more accurately characterized as an attempt to rely on a "worst-case analysis" which may never happen, and which is simply inadequate to support their facial challenge to the statute.

In the absence of any undue burden, the only remaining question is whether Section 3209 is reasonably related to any legitimate state interest. Despite what the petitioners say, there is no real question that a husband has a "deep and proper concern" in his wife's pregnancy and in the fetus she carries; that the abortion decision may profoundly affect the marriage, in which he also has an interest; and that the State legitimately may act to enable him to protect those interests. . . .

[[5. Overturning *Roe*.]] In the preceding sections, we have argued at length that *Roe v. Wade*, properly understood and applied, does not forbid the abortion regulations contained in Pennsylvania's statute, and that this case therefore does not confront the Court with the necessity of reconsidering *Roe*. Nevertheless, it remains true that *Roe* is a deeply flawed decision, and it may be that the time has come to reconsider it. . . .

First and most importantly, *Roe*'s holding that abortion is a fundamental constitutional right is untenable. The text of the Constitution obviously creates no such right; the text of the Constitution does not even mention abortion. Nor can such a right plausibly be located among the unenumerated, but still fundamental, rights protected by the Due Process Clause. . . .

Nor can *Roe* be defended as the logical extension of the Court's "privacy" decisions. The Court's decision in *Roe* underlined the difference between itself and these earlier privacy cases:

> The pregnant woman cannot be isolated in her privacy. She carries an embryo and later, a fetus. . . . The situation therefore is inherently different from marital intimacy, or bedroom possession of obscene material, or marriage, or procreation, or education, with which *Eisenstadt* and *Griswold, Stanley, Loving, Skinner,* and *Pierce* and *Meyer* were concerned.

The decision in *Roe* was thus in no way preordained by the decisions in *Eisenstadt, Griswold* and the rest of the cases cited. *Roe*'s creation of a "fundamental" right which has no sound basis in the Constitution, in history, in a societal consensus, or even in the Court's own precedents, is simply an illegitimate exercise of "raw judicial power," which the Court should disavow for this reason alone. . . .

. . . *Roe* stands as an anomaly among the Court's cases on fundamental constitutional rights, working "a major distortion in the Court's constitutional jurisprudence." Far from being a source of stability in the law, *Roe*'s arbitrariness has forced the Court to return to the issue of abortion time and time again, drawing ever finer lines to govern the states' attempts to regulate in this area. . . . In addition, by reinforcing the idea that the Court's proper function is to impose its own notions of sound public policy, *Roe* "continuously distorts the public perception of the role of this Court" in a way that in the long run is bound to damage the Court as an institution.

The damage is not to the Court alone, but also to the very "principles of self-governance" in a democracy. Abortion is "a field where [the Court] has little proper business since the answers to most of the cruel questions posed are political and not juridical." "Leaving the matter to the political process is not only legally correct, it is pragmatically so. That alone . . . can produce compromises satisfying a sufficient mass of the electorate that this deeply felt issue will cease distorting the remainder of our democratic process." For all these reasons, the Court should overrule *Roe*. . . .

Respectfully submitted,
ERNEST D. PREATE, JR.,
Attorney General

ORAL ARGUMENT

MS. KOLBERT [[Attorney for Planned Parenthood]]: . . . This Court must look generally to whether a right is reflected in our Nation's history and traditions rather than at whether the activity was illegal at the time of the adoption of the Fourteenth Amendment. Relying exclusively on what 50 States have legislated in determining the scope of liberty would imperil numerous freedoms such as rights recognized by this Court in *Brown, Bolling, Griswold* and *Loving*.

This Court has also recognized as—

JUSTICE SCALIA: Ms. Kolbert, on this last point, I am not sure what you suggest we look to. You say we should not look to what the practice was in 1868. Should we look to what the practice was at the time of *Roe* or what the practice is today? That is, what the States would do, left to their own devices?

KOLBERT: Your Honor, I believe that you have to look very generally at whether the Nation's history and tradition has respected the interests of bodily integrity and autonomy and whether there has been a tradition of respect for equality of women. Those are the central and core values—

SCALIA: But not to abortion in particular?

KOLBERT: Well, this Court is—if the Court was only to look at whether abortion was illegal in 1868, that is at the time of the adoption of the Fourteenth Amendment, it would be placed in a very difficult situation because at the time of the founding of the Nation, at the time the Constitution was adopted, abortion was legal.

SCALIA: Pick 1968, I gather you wouldn't accept 1968 either though.

KOLBERT: Well, we think that the Court ought to look generally at the principles that this decision protects. That while it is important to look—and I would not urge you to ignore the state of the law at different periods of our history, it is only one factor in a variety of factors that this Court has to look to in determining whether or not something is fundamental.

And fundamental status in this instance derives from a history of this Court's acknowledgment and acceptance that private, autonomous decisions made by women in the privacy of their families ought to be respected and accorded fundamental status. . . .

. . . [[I]]f we were only to look at whether State legislatures prohibited activity in determining whether or not an activity is fundamental, many of the most precious rights that we now have: rights to travel, rights to vote, rights to be free from racial segregation would not be accorded status because in fact, State legislators have acted to inhibit those rights at the time of the adoption of the Fourteenth Amendment.

SCALIA: Some of these are mentioned in the Constitution like racial segregation.

KOLBERT: Your Honor, this Court has recognized that the rights at issue here, that is, the rights of privacy, the rights of autonomy, flow from the liberty clause of the Fourteenth Amendment which is also mentioned in the Constitution.

The debate centers on what is the meaning of that term liberty, and we think that the precedents of this Court that began at the end of the 19th Century and have proceeded from this Court to the very present, would logically and necessarily include fundamental rights to decide whether to carry a pregnancy to term or to terminate that pregnancy.

JUSTICE KENNEDY: I don't question the importance of your arguing that there is a fundamental right, as you have done; however, . . . you have a number of specific provisions here that I think you should address.

KOLBERT: The critical factor is whether, as a result of its fundamental status, this Court will accord the standard of *Roe*, that is, strict scrutiny because under that standard there is no dispute among the parties. Under that standard, the bias counseling provisions, the 24-hour mandatory delay, have been found unconstitutional. . . .

KENNEDY: I am suggesting that our sustaining these statutory provisions does not necessarily undercut all of the holding of *Roe v. Wade.*

KOLBERT: It is our position, Your Honor that if this Court were to change the standard of strict scrutiny, which has been the central core of that holding, that in fact, that will undercut the holdings of this Court and effectively overrule *Roe v. Wade.*

To adopt a lesser standard, to abandon strict scrutiny for a less protective standard such as the undue burden test or the rational relationship test, which has been discussed by this Court on many occasions, would be the same as overruling *Roe.* . . .

Roe establishes and creates a burden on Government to come forward with a compelling purpose.

KENNEDY: Well, if you are going to argue that *Roe* can survive only in its most rigid formulation, that is an election you can make as counsel. I am suggesting to you that that is not the only logical possibility in this case. . . .

❊   ❊   ❊

MR. PREATE [[Pennsylvania's Attorney General]]: . . . It is the position of Pennsylvania that each of the five provisions is constitutional under the analysis that was applied by this Court in *Webster*; that, further, *Roe v. Wade* need not be revisited by this Court except to reaffirm that *Roe* did not establish an absolute right to abortion on demand, but rather a limited right subject to reasonable State regulations designed to serve important and legitimate State [[interests]]. . . .

In our view the accommodations of the woman's right and the State's legitimate interest in the unborn child is best served, short of overruling *Roe*, by employing the undue burden standard for reviewing State abortion regulations. However, as we argue in part 2 of our brief, if our statute cannot be upheld under the undue burden standard, *Roe*, being wrongly decided, should be overruled.

I will now address the specific provisions of our statute and start with the requirement of spousal notice which was the only aspect of our law that the court of appeals found unconstitutional . . .

JUSTICE O'CONNOR: Now, the provision does not require notification to a father who is not the husband, I take it—

PREATE: That's correct, Justice O'Connor.

O'CONNOR: Or notice if the woman is unmarried.

PREATE: It only applies to married women.

O'CONNOR: So what's the interest, to try to preserve the marriage?

PREATE: There are several interests. The interest, of course, in protecting the life of the unborn child.

O'CONNOR: Well then, why not require notice to all fathers? It's a curious sort of provision, isn't it?

PREATE: It is that, but the legislature has made the judgment that it wanted its statute to apply in this specific instance because it wanted to further the integrity of marriages. . . .

❊   ❊   ❊

PREATE: . . . We have a statute that provides exceptions where exceptions are appropriate, and there are five of them: medical emergency, where the husband is not the father of the child, where the husband cannot be found, where the pregnancy is the result of a reported sexual assault, or where the woman in her judgment believes it's likely that she will be physically abused. . . .

JUSTICE STEVENS: . . . Is it not true, therefore, that the only people affected by the statute, this very small group, are people who would not otherwise notify their husbands?

PREATE: I'm not sure I got all of the question, Justice Stevens.

STEVENS: Well, you've demonstrated that the public interest is in a very limited group of people, the few women who would not otherwise notify their husbands, and those are the only people affected by the statute.

PREATE: That is correct.

STEVENS: Everyone in that class, could we not assume, would not notify her husband but for the statute.

PREATE: That is correct. Now, in that 1 percent, not everyone would want to notify, and there are exceptions.

STEVENS: They would not without the statute.

PREATE: They would not without the statute, but there are exceptions, several of them—four.

STEVENS: No, they'd only—you've already taken the exceptions into account in narrowing the group very—to, you know, 1 percent, or whatever it is.

PREATE: Justice—

STEVENS: You aren't suggesting there's no one whose decision will be affected by the statute.

PREATE: Well, that's the point. On this record, which is what we have to go on, there is nothing established by the petitioners as to how many there are in that category.

STEVENS: Well, if there's no one affected by the statute, what is the State interest in upholding the statute?

PREATE: The State interest in upholding the statute is the protection of the life of the unborn and the protection of the marital integrity. . . .

THE OPINION

Justices O'Connor, Kennedy, and Souter announced the judgment of the Court. . . .

[[1. Right of Privacy.]] Liberty finds no refuge in a jurisprudence of doubt. Yet 19 years after our holding that the Constitution protects a woman's right to terminate her pregnancy in its early stages, that definition of liberty is still questioned. Joining the respondents as amicus curiae, the United States, as it has done in five other cases in the last decade, again asks us to overrule *Roe*. . . .

After considering the fundamental constitutional questions resolved by *Roe*, principles of institutional integrity, and the rule of stare decisis, we are led to conclude this: the essential holding of *Roe v. Wade* should be retained and once again reaffirmed.

It must be stated at the outset and with clarity that *Roe*'s essential holding, the holding we reaffirm, has three parts. First is a recognition of the right of the woman to choose to have an abortion before viability and to obtain it without undue interference from the State. Before viability, the State's interests are not strong enough to support a prohibition of abortion or the imposition of a substantial obstacle to the woman's effective right to elect the procedure. Second is a confirmation of the State's power to restrict abortions after fetal viability, if the law contains exceptions for pregnancies which endanger a woman's life or health. And third is the principle that the State has legitimate interests from the outset of the pregnancy in protecting the health of the woman and the life of the fetus that may become a child. . . .

Neither the Bill of Rights nor the specific practices of States at the time of the adoption of the Fourteenth Amendment marks the outer limits of the substantive sphere of liberty which the Fourteenth Amendment protects. . . .

The inescapable fact is that adjudication of substantive due process claims may call upon the Court in interpreting the Constitution to exercise that same capacity which by tradition courts always have exercised: reasoned judgment. . . .

. . . Some of us as individuals find abortion offensive to our most basic principles of morality, but that cannot control our decision. Our obligation is to define the liberty of all, not to mandate our own moral code. . . .

Our law affords constitutional protection to personal decisions relating to marriage, procreation, contraception, family relationships, child rearing, and education. Our cases recognize "the right of the individual, married or single, to be free from unwarranted governmental intrusion into matters so fundamentally affecting a person as the decision whether to bear or beget a child." Our precedents "have respected the private realm of family life which the state cannot enter." These matters, involving the most intimate and personal choices a person may make in a lifetime, choices central to personal dignity and autonomy, are central to the liberty protected by the Fourteenth Amendment. At the heart of liberty is the right to define one's own concept of existence, of meaning, of the universe, and of the mystery of human life. . . .

. . . Though abortion is conduct, it does not follow that the State is entitled to proscribe it in all instances. That is because the liberty of the woman is at stake in a sense unique to the human condition and so unique to the law. The mother who carries a child to full term is subject to anxieties, to physical constraints, to pain that only she must bear. That these sacrifices have from the beginning of the human race been endured by woman with a pride that ennobles her in the eyes of others and gives to the infant a bond of love cannot alone be grounds for the State to insist she make the sacrifice. Her suffering is too intimate and personal for the State to insist, without more, upon its own vision of the woman's role, however dominant that vision has been in the course of our history and our culture. The destiny of the woman must be shaped to a large extent on her own conception of her spiritual imperatives and her place in society. . . .

. . . [[T]]he inability to provide for the nurture and care of the infant is a cruelty to the child and an anguish to the parent. These are intimate views with infinite variations, and their deep, personal character underlay our decisions in *Griswold, Eisenstadt,* and *Carey.* The same concerns are present when the woman confronts the reality that, perhaps despite her attempts to avoid it, she has become pregnant. . . .

[[2. The Role of Precedent.]] . . . The sum of precedential inquiry to this point shows *Roe*'s underpinnings unweakened in any way affecting its central holding. While it has engendered disapproval, it has not been unworkable. An entire generation has come of age free to assume *Roe*'s concept of liberty in defining the capacity of women to act in society, and to make reproductive decisions; no erosion of principle going to liberty or personal autonomy has left *Roe*'s central holding a doctrinal remnant; *Roe* portends no developments at odds with other precedent for the analysis of personal liberty; and no changes of fact have rendered viability more or less appropriate as the point at which the balance of interest tips. Within the bounds of normal stare decisis analysis, then, and subject to the considerations on which it customarily turns, the stronger argument is for affirming *Roe*'s central holding, with whatever degree of personal reluctance any of us may have, not for overruling it.

In a less significant case, stare decisis analysis could, and would, stop at the point we have reached. But the sustained and widespread debate *Roe* has provoked calls for some comparison between that case and others of comparable dimension that have responded to national controversies and taken on the impress of the controversies addressed. Only two such decisional lines from the past century present themselves for examination, and in each instance the result reached by the Court accorded with the principles we apply today.

The first example is that line of cases identified with *Lochner v. New York,* which imposed substantive limitations on legislation limiting economic autonomy in favor of health and welfare regulation, adopting, in Justice Holmes' view, the theory of laissez-faire. . . . Fourteen years later, *West Coast Hotel Co. v. Parrish* signalled the demise of *Lochner.* . . . In the meantime, the Depression had come and, with it, the lesson that seemed unmistakable to most people by 1937, that the interpretation of contractual freedom protected by [[*Lochner*]] . . . rested on fundamentally false factual assumptions about the capacity of a relatively unregulated market to satisfy minimal levels of human welfare. . . .

The second comparison that 20th century history invites is with the cases employing the separate-but-equal rule for applying the Fourteenth Amendment's equal protection guarantee. . . .

The Court in *Brown* addressed these facts of life by observing that whatever may have been the understanding in *Plessy*'s time of the power of segregation to stigmatize those who were segregated with a "badge of inferiority," it was clear by 1954 that legally sanctioned segregation had just such an effect, to the point that racially separate public educational facilities were deemed inherently unequal. Society's understanding of the facts upon which a constitutional ruling was sought in 1954 was thus fundamentally different from the basis claimed for the decision in 1986. While we think *Plessy* was wrong the day it was decided, we must also recognize that the *Plessy* Court's explanation for its decision was so clearly at odds with the facts apparent to the Court in 1954 that the decision to reexamine *Plessy* was on this ground alone not only justified but required.

West Coast Hotel and *Brown* each rested on facts, or an understanding of facts, changed from those which furnished the claimed justifications for the earlier constitutional resolutions. . . . In constitutional adjudication as elsewhere in life, changed circumstances may impose new obligations, and the thoughtful part of the Nation could accept each decision to overrule a prior case as a response to the Court's constitutional duty.

Because the case before us presents no such occasion it could be seen as no such response. Because neither the factual underpinnings of *Roe*'s central holding nor our understanding of it has changed (and because no other indication of weakened precedent has been shown) the Court could not pretend to be reexamining the prior law with any justification beyond a present doctrinal disposition to come out differently from the Court of 1973. To overrule prior law for no other reason than that would run counter to the view repeated in our cases, that a decision to overrule should rest on some special reason over and above the belief that a prior case was wrongly decided. . . .

[[3. Legitimacy of the Supreme Court.]] . . . Where, in the performance of its judicial duties, the Court decides a case in such a way as to resolve the sort of intensely divisive controversy reflected in *Roe* and those rare, comparable cases, its decision has a dimension that the resolution of the normal case does not carry. It is the dimension present whenever the Court's interpretation of the Constitution calls the contending sides of a national controversy to end their national division by accepting a common mandate rooted in the Constitution.

The Court is not asked to do this very often, having thus addressed the Nation only twice in our lifetime, in the decisions of *Brown* and *Roe*. But when the Court does act in this way, its decision requires an equally rare precedential force to counter the inevitable efforts to overturn it and to thwart its implementation. Some of those efforts may be mere unprincipled emotional reactions; others may proceed from principles worthy of profound respect. But whatever the premises of opposition may be, only the most convincing justification under accepted standards of precedent could suffice to demonstrate that a later decision overruling the first was anything but a surrender to political pressure, and an unjustified repudiation of the principle on which the Court staked its authority in the first instance. So to overrule under fire in the absence of the most compelling reason to reexamine a watershed decision would subvert the Court's legitimacy beyond any serious question. . . .

The country's loss of confidence in the judiciary would be underscored by an equally certain and equally reasonable condemnation for another failing in overruling unnecessarily and under pressure. Some cost will be paid by anyone who approves or implements a constitutional decision where it is unpopular, or who refuses to work to undermine the decision or to force its reversal. The price may be criticism or ostracism, or it may be violence. An extra price will be paid by those who themselves disapprove of the decision's results when viewed outside of constitutional terms, but who nevertheless struggle to accept it, because they respect the rule of law. To all those who will be so tested by following, the Court implicitly undertakes to remain steadfast, lest in the end a price be paid for nothing. The promise of constancy, once given, binds its maker for as long as the power to stand by the decision survives and the understanding of the issue has not changed so fundamentally as to render the commitment obsolete. . . .

. . . Like the character of an individual, the legitimacy of the Court must be earned over time. So, indeed, must be the character of a Nation of people who aspire to live according to the rule of law. Their belief in themselves as such a people is not readily separable from their understanding of the Court invested with the authority to decide their constitutional cases and speak before all others for their constitutional ideals. If the Court's legitimacy should be undermined, then, so would the country be in its very ability to see itself through its constitutional ideals. The Court's concern with legitimacy is not for the sake of the Court but for the sake of the Nation to which it is responsible. . . .

[[4. *Roe* and the Undue Burden Standard.]] . . . A logical reading of the central holding in *Roe* itself, and a necessary reconciliation of the liberty of the woman and the interest of the State in promoting prenatal life, require, in our view, that we abandon the trimester framework as a rigid prohibition of all previability regulation aimed at the protection of fetal life. . . .

The very notion that the State has a substantial interest in potential life leads to the conclusion that not all regulations must be deemed unwarranted. Not all burdens on the right to decide whether to terminate a pregnancy will be undue. In our view, the undue burden standard is the appropriate means of reconciling the State's interest with the woman's constitutionally protected liberty. . . .

A finding of an undue burden is a shorthand for the conclusion that a state regulation has the purpose or effect of placing a substantial obstacle in the path of a woman seeking an abortion of a nonviable fetus. A statute with this purpose is invalid because the means chosen by the State to further the interest in potential life must be calculated to inform the woman's free choice, not to hinder it. And a statute which, while furthering the interest in potential life or some other valid state interest, has the effect of placing a substantial obstacle in the path of a woman's choice cannot be considered a permissible means of serving its legitimate ends. . . .

[[5. Pennsylvania's Provisions.]] To the extent *Akron I* and *Thornburgh* find a constitutional violation when the government requires, as it does here, the giving of truthful, nonmisleading information about the nature of the procedure, the attendant health risks and those of childbirth, and the "probable gestational age" of the fetus, those cases go too far, are inconsistent with *Roe's* acknowledgment of an important interest in potential life, and are overruled. . . .

. . . The idea that important decisions will be more informed and deliberate if they follow some period of reflection does not strike us as unreasonable, particularly where the statute directs that important information become part of the background of the decision. . . .

. . . For the great many women who are victims of abuse inflicted by their husbands, or whose children are the victims of such abuse, a spousal notice requirement enables the husband to wield an effective veto over his wife's decision. Whether the prospect of notification itself deters such women from seeking abortions, or whether the husband, through physical force or psychological pressure or economic coercion, prevents his wife from obtaining an abortion until it is too late, the notice requirement will often be tantamount to the veto found unconstitutional in *Danforth*. The women most affected by this law—those who most reasonably fear the consequences of notifying their husbands that they are pregnant—are in the gravest danger. . . .

Justice Blackmun, concurring in the judgment in part and dissenting in part . . .

. . . I do not underestimate the significance of today's joint opinion. Yet I remain steadfast in my belief that the right to reproductive choice is entitled to the full protection afforded by this Court before *Webster*. And I fear for the darkness as four Justices anxiously await the single vote necessary to extinguish the light. . . .

The Court's reaffirmation of *Roe's* central holding is also based on the force of stare decisis. . . . What has happened today should serve as a model for future Justices and a warning to all who have tried to turn this Court into yet another political branch. . . .

. . . [[However]], *Roe's* requirement of strict scrutiny as implemented through a trimester framework should not be disturbed. No other approach has gained a majority, and no other is more protective of the woman's fundamental right. Lastly, no other approach properly accommodates the woman's constitutional right with the State's legitimate interests. . . .

In one sense, the Court's approach is worlds apart from that of the Chief Justice and Justice Scalia. And yet, in another sense, the distance between the two approaches is short—the distance is but a single vote.

I am 83 years old. I cannot remain on this Court forever, and when I do step down, the confirmation process for my successor well may focus on the issue before us today. That, I regret, may be exactly where the choice between the two worlds will be made. . . .

*Chief Justice Rehnquist, concurring in the judgment in part
and dissenting in part . . .*

[[1. Role of Precedent.]] . . . Whatever the "central holding" of *Roe* that is
left after the joint opinion finishes dissecting it is surely not the result of that
principle. While purporting to adhere to precedent, the joint opinion instead
revises it. *Roe* continues to exist, but only in the way a storefront on a western
movie set exists: a mere facade to give the illusion of reality. . . .

In our view, authentic principles of stare decisis do not require that any portion of the reasoning in Roe be kept intact. . . . Erroneous decisions in such
constitutional cases are uniquely durable, because correction through legislative
action, save for constitutional amendment, is impossible. It is therefore our
duty to reconsider constitutional interpretations that "depart from a proper
understanding" of the Constitution. . . . Our constitutional watch does not
cease merely because we have spoken before on an issue; when it becomes clear
that a prior constitutional interpretation is unsound we are obliged to reexamine the question. . . .

. . . [T]he joint opinion's argument is based solely on generalized assertions
about the national psyche, on a belief that the people of this country have
grown accustomed to the Roe decision over the last 19 years and have "ordered
their thinking and living around" it. As an initial matter, one might inquire how
the joint opinion can view the "central holding" of Roe as so deeply rooted in
our constitutional culture, when it so casually uproots and disposes of that
same decision's trimester framework. Furthermore, at various points in the
past, the same could have been said about this Court's erroneous decisions that
the Constitution allowed 'separate but equal" treatment of minorities. The
"separate but equal" doctrine lasted 58 years after *Plessy*, and *Lochner*'s protection of contractual freedom lasted 32 years. However, the simple fact that a generation or more had grown used to these major decisions did not prevent the
Court from correcting its errors in those cases, nor should it prevent us from
correctly interpreting the Constitution here. . . .

But the joint opinion goes on to state that when the Court "resolves the sort
of intensely divisive controversy reflected in *Roe* and those rare, comparable
cases," its decision is exempt from reconsideration under established principles
of stare decisis in constitutional cases. . . . This is a truly novel principle, one
which is contrary to both the Court's historical practice and to the Court's
traditional willingness to tolerate criticism of its opinions. Under this principle,
when the Court has ruled on a divisive issue, it is apparently prevented from
overruling that decision for the sole reason that it was incorrect, unless opposition to the original decision has died away. . . .

The joint opinion picks out and discusses two prior Court rulings that it
believes are of the "intensely divisive" variety, and concludes that they are of
comparable dimension to *Roe*. It appears to us very odd indeed that the joint
opinion chooses as benchmarks two cases in which the Court chose not to
adhere to erroneous constitutional precedent, but instead enhanced its stature

by acknowledging and correcting its error, apparently in violation of the joint opinion's "legitimacy" principle. . . .

. . . [B]ut the opinion contends that the Court was entitled to overrule *Plessy* and *Lochner* . . . because both the Nation and the Court had learned new lessons in the interim. This is at best a feebly supported, post hoc rationalization for those decisions. . . .

When the Court finally recognized its error in *West Coast Hotel*, it did not engage in the post hoc rationalization that the joint opinion attributes to it today; it did not state that *Lochner* had been based on an economic view that had fallen into disfavor, and that it therefore should be overruled. Chief Justice Hughes in his opinion for the Court simply recognized what Justice Holmes had previously recognized in his *Lochner* dissent, that "the Constitution does not speak of freedom of contract." . . .

The joint opinion also agrees that the Court acted properly in rejecting the doctrine of "separate but equal" in *Brown*. . . . The joint opinion concludes that such repudiation was justified only because of newly discovered evidence that segregation had the effect of treating one race as inferior to another. But it can hardly be argued that this was not urged upon those who decided *Plessy*, as Justice Harlan observed in his dissent that the law at issue "puts the brand of servitude and degradation upon a large class of our fellow-citizens, our equals before the law." It is clear that the same arguments made before the Court in *Brown* were made in *Plessy* as well. The Court in *Brown* simply recognized, as Justice Harlan had recognized beforehand, that the Fourteenth Amendment does not permit racial segregation. . . .

[[2. Legitimacy of Court.]] There is also a suggestion in the joint opinion that the propriety of overruling a "divisive" decision depends in part on whether "most people" would now agree that it should be overruled. Either the demise of opposition or its progression to substantial popular agreement apparently is required to allow the Court to reconsider a divisive decision. How such agreement would be ascertained, short of a public opinion poll, the joint opinion does not say. But surely even the suggestion is totally at war with the idea of "legitimacy" in whose name it is invoked. The Judicial Branch derives its legitimacy not from following public opinion, but from deciding by its best lights whether legislative enactments of the popular branches of Government comport with the Constitution. The doctrine of stare decisis is an adjunct of this duty, and should be no more subject to the vagaries of public opinion than is the basic judicial task.

There are other reasons why the joint opinion's discussion of legitimacy is unconvincing as well. In assuming that the Court is perceived as "surrendering to political pressure" when it overrules a controversial decision, the joint opinion forgets that there are two sides to any controversy. The joint opinion asserts that, in order to protect its legitimacy, the Court must refrain from overruling a controversial decision lest it be viewed as favoring those who oppose the decision. But a decision to adhere to a prior precedent is subject to the same criticism, for in such a case one can easily argue that the Court is responding to those who have demonstrated in favor of the original decision. The decision in *Roe* has engendered large demonstrations, including repeated marches on this Court and on Congress, both in opposition to and in support of that opinion. A decision either way on *Roe* can therefore be perceived as favoring one group or the other. But this perceived dilemma arises only if one assumes, as the joint opinion does, that the Court should make its decisions with a view toward speculative public perceptions. If one assumes instead, as the Court surely did in both *Brown* and *West Coast Hotel*, that the Court's legitimacy is enhanced by faithful interpretation of the Constitution irrespective of public opposition, such self-engendered difficulties may be put to one side. . . .

[[3. Undue Burden Standard and Pennsylvania's Provisions.]] The end result of the joint opinion's paeans of praise for legitimacy is the enunciation of a brand new standard for evaluating state regulation of a woman's right to abortion—the "undue burden" standard. . . . It is a standard which even today does not command the support of a majority of this Court. And it will not, we believe, result in the sort of "simple limitation," easily applied, which the joint opinion anticipates. In sum, it is a standard which is not built to last. . . .

. . . Because the undue burden standard is plucked from nowhere, the question of what is a "substantial obstacle" to abortion will undoubtedly engender a variety of conflicting views. For example, in the very matter before us now, the authors of the joint opinion would uphold Pennsylvania's 24-hour waiting period, concluding that a "particular burden" on some women is not a substantial obstacle. But the authors would at the same time strike down Pennsylvania's spousal notice provision, after finding that in a "large fraction" of cases the provision will be a substantial obstacle. And, while the authors conclude that the informed consent provisions do not constitute an "undue burden," Justice Stevens would hold that they do. . . .

The sum of the joint opinion's labors in the name of stare decisis and "legitimacy" is this: *Roe v. Wade* stands as a sort of judicial Potemkin Village, which may be pointed out to passers by as a monument to the importance of adhering to precedent. But behind the facade, an entirely new method of analysis, without any roots in constitutional law, is imported to decide the constitutionality of state laws regulating abortion. Neither stare decisis nor "legitimacy" are truly served by such an effort. . . .

Justice Scalia, concurring in the judgment in part and dissenting in part . . .

. . . I have always thought . . . that the arbitrary trimester framework, which the Court today discards, was quite as central to *Roe* as the arbitrary viability test, which the Court today retains. It seems particularly ungrateful to carve the trimester framework out of the core of *Roe*, since its very rigidity (in sharp contrast to the utter indeterminability of the "undue burden" test) is probably the only reason the Court is able to say, in urging stare decisis, that *Roe* "has in no sense proven unworkable." . . .

The Court's description of the place of *Roe* in the social history of the United States is unrecognizable. Not only did *Roe* not, as the Court suggests, resolve the deeply divisive issue of abortion; it did more than anything else to nourish it, by elevating it to the national level where it is infinitely more difficult to resolve. National politics were not plagued by abortion protests, national abortion lobbying, or abortion marches on Congress, before *Roe v. Wade* was decided. Profound disagreement existed among our citizens over the issue—as it does over other issues, such as the death penalty—but that disagreement was being worked out at the state level. As with many other issues, the division of sentiment within each State was not as closely balanced as it was among the population of the Nation as a whole, meaning not only that more people would be satisfied with the results of state-by-state resolution, but also that those results would be more stable. Pre-*Roe*, moreover, political compromise was possible.

. . . [[T]]o portray *Roe* as the statesmanlike "settlement" of a divisive issue, a jurisprudential Peace of Westphalia that is worth preserving, is nothing less than Orwellian. *Roe* fanned into life an issue that has inflamed our national politics in general, and has obscured with its smoke the selection of Justices to this Court in particular, ever since. And by keeping us in the abortion-umpiring business, it is the perpetuation of that disruption, rather than of any pax Roeana, that the Court's new majority decrees. . . .

The Imperial Judiciary lives. It is instructive to compare this Nietzschean vision of us unelected, life-tenured judges—leading a Volk who will be "tested by following," and whose very "belief in themselves" is mystically bound up in their "understanding" of a Court that "speaks before all others for their constitutional ideals". . . .

The only principle the Court "adheres" to, it seems to me, is the principle that the Court must be seen as standing by *Roe*. That is not a principle of law (which is what I thought the Court was talking about), but a principle of Realpolitik—and a wrong one at that. . . .

. . . [[T]]he notion that the Court must adhere to a decision for as long as the decision faces "great opposition" and the Court is "under fire" acquires a character of almost czarist arrogance. We are offended by these marchers who descend upon us, every year on the anniversary of *Roe*, to protest our saying that the Constitution requires what our society has never thought the Constitution requires. These people who refuse to be "tested by following" must be taught a lesson. We have no Cossacks, but at least we can stubbornly refuse to abandon an erroneous opinion that we might otherwise change—to show how little they intimidate us. . . .

In truth, I am as distressed as the Court . . . is about the "political pressure" directed to the Court: the marches, the mail, the protests aimed at inducing us to change our opinions. How upsetting it is, that so many of our citizens (good people, not lawless ones, on both sides of this abortion issue, and on various sides of other issues as well) think that we Justices should properly take into account their views, as though we were engaged not in ascertaining an objective law but in determining some kind of social consensus. The Court would profit, I think, from giving less attention to the fact of this distressing phenomenon, and more attention to the cause of it. That cause permeates today's opinion: a new mode of constitutional adjudication that relies not upon text and traditional practice to determine the law, but upon what the Court calls "reasoned judgment," which turns out to be nothing but philosophical predilection and moral intuition. All manner of "liberties," the Court tells us, inhere in the Constitution and are enforceable by this Court—not just those mentioned in the text or established in the traditions of our society. . . .

What makes all this relevant to the bothersome application of "political pressure" against the Court are the twin facts that the American people love democracy and the American people are not fools. As long as this Court thought (and the people thought) that we Justices were doing essentially lawyers' work up here—reading text and discerning our society's traditional understanding of that text—the public pretty much left us alone. Texts and traditions are facts to study, not convictions to demonstrate about. But if in reality our process of constitutional adjudication consists primarily of making value judgments, . . . then a free and intelligent people's attitude towards us can be expected to be (ought to be) quite different. The people know that their value judgments are quite as good as those taught in any law school—maybe better. If, indeed, the "liberties" protected by the Constitution are, as the Court says, undefined and unbounded, then the people should demonstrate, to protest that we do not implement their values instead of ours. Not only that, but confirmation hearings for new Justices should deteriorate into question-and-answer sessions in which senators go through a list of their constituents' most favored and most disfavored alleged constitutional rights, and seek the nominee's commitment to support or oppose them. . . . Justice Blackmun not only regards this prospect with equanimity, he solicits it.

There is a poignant aspect to today's opinion. Its length, and what might be called its epic tone, suggest that its authors believe they are bringing to an end a troublesome era in the history of our Nation and of our Court. "It is the dimension" of authority they say, to "call the contending sides of national controversy to end their national division by accepting a common mandate rooted in the Constitution."

There comes vividly to mind a portrait by Emanuel Leutze that hangs in the Harvard Law School: Roger Brooke Taney, painted in 1859, the 82nd year of his life, the 24th of his Chief Justiceship, the second after his opinion in *Dred Scott*. He is all in black, sitting in a shadowed red armchair, left hand resting upon a pad of paper in his lap, right hand hanging limply, almost lifelessly, beside the inner arm of the chair. He sits facing the viewer, and staring straight out. There seems to be on his face, and in his deep-set eyes, an expression of profound sadness and disillusionment. Perhaps he always looked that way, even when dwelling upon the happiest of thoughts. But those of us who know how the lustre of his great Chief Justiceship came to be eclipsed by *Dred Scott* cannot help believing that he had that case—its already apparent consequences for the Court, and its soon-to-be-played-out consequences for the Nation—burning on his mind. I expect that two years earlier he, too, had thought himself "calling the contending sides of national controversy to end their national division by accepting a common mandate rooted in the Constitution."

It is no more realistic for us in this case, than it was for him in that, to think that an issue of the sort they both involved—an issue involving life and death, freedom and subjugation—can be "speedily and finally settled" by the Supreme Court. . . . Quite to the contrary, by foreclosing all democratic outlet for the deep passions this issue arouses, by banishing the issue from the political forum that gives all participants, even the losers, the satisfaction of a fair hearing and an honest fight, by continuing the imposition of a rigid national rule instead of allowing for regional differences, the Court merely prolongs and intensifies the anguish.

We should get out of this area, where we have no right to be, and where we do neither ourselves nor the country any good by remaining. . . .

POSTSCRIPT

Following the Supreme Court's decision in *Casey* in 1992, the Court has addressed only two state regulations of abortion under the new "undue burden" standard. In *Mazurek v. Armstrong* (1997), the Court upheld a Montana law that restricted the performance of abortions to licensed physicians. The authors of the joint opinion in *Casey* joined Chief Justice Rehnquist and Justices Scalia and Thomas in a per curiam opinion holding that there was no evidence in the record that the "purpose" or the "effect" of the law was to create a "substantial obstacle" to a woman's right to an abortion. Accordingly, even if Montana had allowed licensed nonphysicians to perform abortions for a period of time, the law in question did not constitute an "undue burden." Justice Stevens, along with two new justices appointed by President Bill Clinton, Justices Ruth Bader Ginsburg and Stephen G. Breyer, dissented. In *Stenberg v. Carhart* (2000), Justices Souter and O'Connor joined Justice Breyer's majority opinion that invalidated a ban on late-term "partial-birth abortions" because it contained no exception for the life or health of the woman and because the law was so vague it could be applied to other forms of second trimester abortions. Justice O'Connor wrote a separate concurrence in which she suggested that a ban of this type would be constitutional if it was narrowly drawn and if it included an exception that would permit "partial birth abortions" to preserve the life and health of the woman. Justice Kennedy, one of the authors of *Casey's* joint opinion, along with the Chief Justice and Justices Scalia and Thomas, dissented, claiming that the ban did not impose a "substantial obstacle" on a woman's right to an abortion and therefore it did not constitute an "undue burden."[21]

With only these two cases to consider, there is not a sufficient basis to determine whether the "undue burden" standard will undermine *Roe* as a workable precedent, as Chief Justice Rehnquist predicted in his *Casey* dissent. The fact that the authors of the joint opinion in *Casey* were not able to maintain their alliance in the face of the ban on "partial birth abortions" does suggest that the "undue burden" standard does not have the clarity and precision of *Roe's* trimester framework, but that hardly proves that it is too vague to be workable. Only time and future Supreme Court decisions will tell whether a relatively clear line can be drawn between those regulations which are and are not "undue burdens" of a woman's right to an abortion.

Despite Justice Blackmun's prediction in *Casey*, the confirmation hearings of Justices Ginsburg and Breyer neither resembled the Bork hearings nor revolved around the issue of abortion. They did not degenerate into heated partisan contests largely because both the Senate and the presidency were controlled by Democrats. Conservative Republicans had little incentive to oppose Ginsburg and Breyer since they were going to be confirmed anyway. In contrast, judicial appointments to the lower federal judiciary became more partisan after the Republicans regained control of the Senate in 1994 and initiated a strategy of holding up President Clinton's more liberal nominees by refusing to schedule confirmation hearings. This kind of partisan gridlock has continued in George W. Bush's presidency, especially after Vermont Senator James Jeffords quit the Republican Party in May 2001, giving the Democrats a majority of one in the Senate. Based on the November 2002 elections, the Republicans regained control of the Senate, but their majority was so narrow that the Democrats were yet able to block the confirmation of Miguel Estrada, a conservative Hispanic, and Janice Rogers Brown, a conservative African-American, both nominated for seats on the D.C. Circuit Court of Appeals.

In these confirmation battles of the last decade, the issue of abortion has occasionally surfaced,[22] but no more so than issues of civil rights, affirmative action, or judicial activism. Accordingly, though the judicial confirmation process of lower federal court judges may be more partisan today than it has ever been before, abortion is not the only issue driving this trend. In fact, it would appear that institutional implications of divided government and sharp differences in general ideologies are just as important. Nevertheless, abortion has undoubtedly been a factor in the slow but steady deterioration of the judicial confirmation process. Is this deterioration simply an inevitable effect of the partisan character of the contemporary political world, or is it an undesirable by-product of the Court's unwise attempt to resolve hotly contested, emotionally charged issues like abortion, or is it both? In any case, is the Supreme Court institutionally capable of resolving such issues?

Notes

1. See Mary Ann Glendon, *Abortion and Divorce in Western Law* (Cambridge, Mass.: Harvard Univ. Press, 1987). For the counterargument, see Laurence Tribe, *Abortion: The Clash of Absolutes* (New York; Norton, 1990), pp. 49–51.

2. See *NAACP v. Alabama*, 357 U.S. 449 (1958); *Meyer v. Nebraska*, 262 U.S. 390 (1923); and *Pierce v. Society of Sisters*, 268 U.S. 510 (1925).

3. 198 U.S. 45 (1905). *Lochner* was overruled in *West Coast Hotel Co. v. Parrish*, 300 U.S. 379 (1937). For more of a discussion of the New Deal's impact on constitutional adjudication, see H. L. Pohlman, *Constitutional Debate in Action: Governmental Powers* (Boulder, Colo.: Rowman & Littlefield, 2004), Chap. 2.

4. In *Eisenstadt v. Baird*, 405 U.S. 438 (1972), the Court ruled that the right of privacy included an unmarried person's right to purchase contraceptives. This case extended the principle of *Griswold* in two respects: First, the right of privacy was not confined to the associational relationship of married persons, but was individual in character; second, the right protected the purchase of contraceptives as well as the use of them.

5. Walter F. Murphy and C. Herman Pritchett, *Courts, Judges, and Politics*, 4th ed. (New York: Random House, 1986), p. 191.

6. For the above historical sketch of the "internal dynamics" on the Court during the 1972 abortion litigation, I rely upon David M. O'Brien, *Constitutional Law and Politics: Volume II: Civil Rights and Liberties* (New York: Norton, 1991), pp. 1161–62.

7. For the suggestion that Burger deliberately used his vote to manipulate opinion assignment, see Bob Woodward and Scott Armstrong, *The Brethren* (New York: Avon, 1979), pp. 200–204.

8. In *Roe*, Chief Justice Burger and Justices Douglas and Stewart wrote concurring opinions. At the same time as *Roe*, the Court also declared Georgia's abortion law unconstitutional in a companion case, *Doe v. Bolton*, 410 U.S. 179 (1973).

9. Frederick S. Jaffe, Barbara L. Lindheim, and Philip R. Lee, *Abortion Politics* (New York: McGraw-Hill, 1982), p. 7.

10. A claim made by Cardinal John Krol, president of the National Catholic Conference, reported by Marion K. Sanders, "Enemies of Abortion," *Harpers*, March 1974, p. 26, cited in Robin, *Abortion, Politics, and the Courts*, p. 88.

11. See *Planned Parenthood v. Danforth*, 428 U.S. 52 (1976); *Colautti v. Franklin*, 439 U.S. 379 (1979); *Akron v. Akron Center for Reproductive Health*, 462 U.S. 416 (1983).

12. See *Belltiotti v Baird*, 443 U.S. 622 (1979). The Court has also upheld certain laws requiring parental notification. See *H. L. v. Matheson*, 450 U.S. 398 (1981); *Hodgson v. Minnesota*, 497 U.S. 417 (1990); *Ohio v. Akron Center for Reproductive Health*, 497 U.S. 502 (1990).

13. 448 U.S. 297 (1980). Three years earlier, in *Maher v. Roe*, 432 U.S. 464 (1977), the Court upheld a state rule that denied Medicaid funding for nontherapeutic, medically unnecessary abortions.

14. *Id*. at 316.

15. 462 U.S. 416 (1983).

16. 492 U.S. 490 (1989).

17. *Id*., at 537 and 560.

18. Other provisions of the Pennsylvania statute required parental consent for unmarried minors (though a judicial bypass was permitted), mandated that abortion providers keep detailed records, and defined the kind of "medical emergency" that would exempt an abortion from the above regulations. Though the Supreme Court upheld these provisions in *Casey*, they are not discussed in this chapter.

19. See *Planned Parenthood of Missouri v. Danforth*, 428 U.S. 52 (1976); *Akron v. Akron Center for Reproductive Health*, 462 U.S. 416 (1983).

20. Harry Blackmun and John Paul Stevens were the two justices who voted to invali-

date all the Pennsylvania provisions. Stevens wrote an opinion, but no excerpt from it is included below.

21. President George W. Bush signed the federal Partial Birth Abortion Ban Act that included an exception for the life of a woman, but not for her health, on November 5, 2003. In this ban, Congress officially found that "a partial-birth abortion is never necessary to preserve the health of a woman, poses significant health risks to a woman upon whom the procedure is performed and is outside the standard of medical care." At this writing, three federal district courts in Nebraska, New York, and California have declared the law unconstitutional because the ban does not include an exception for the mother's health. See *Carhart v. Ashcroft*, 300 F. Supp. 2d 921 (Neb. 2004); *National Abortion Federation*, 03 Civ. 8695 (RCC), 2004 U.S. Dist. LEXIS 17084 (S.D.N.Y 2004); *Planned Parenthood Fed'n of America v. Ashcroft*, 320 F. Supp. 2d 957 (N.D. Cal. 2004). Without an exception for the mother's health, it is unclear whether the Supreme Court will eventually uphold or invalidate this new ban on partial birth abortions.

22. For example, in 2002 Democrats opposed Priscilla Owen's appointment to the Fifth Circuit Court of Appeals in part because, as a Texas Supreme Court justice, she had ruled against pregnant teens who did not want to notify their parents that they were going to have abortions.

CHAPTER 4

Hate Speech and Cross Burning

R.A.V. v. City of St. Paul
505 U.S. 377 (1992)

Virginia v. Black
538 U.S. 343 (2003)

I. BACKGROUND TO *R.A.V.*

Is freedom of speech primarily a limited right of individuals to say what they want or a near absolute command to the government not to take sides in any ideological debate, or is it both? If it is both, which concept is more fundamental? Laws punishing "hate speech" (*R.A.V. v. City of St. Paul*) and cross burning (*Virginia v. Black*) provide an excellent opportunity to reflect upon this question concerning the ultimate meaning of free speech. The more traditional view is that free speech is a limited individual right. Over sixty years ago, in *Chaplinsky v. New Hampshire* (1942), the Supreme Court identified certain categories of speech that were placed completely outside the guarantee of free speech.

> There are certain well-defined and narrowly limited classes of speech the prevention and punishment of which have never been thought to raise any Constitutional problem. These include the lewd and obscene, the profane, the libelous, and the insulting or "fighting" words—those which by their very utterance inflict injury or tend to incite an immediate breach of the peace. It has been well observed that such utterances are no essential part of any exposition of ideas, and are of such slight social value as a step to truth that any benefit that may be derived from them is clearly outweighed by the social interest in order and morality.[1]

Over the years the Supreme Court has narrowed the categories of unprotected speech identified in *Chaplinsky*. For example, it limited the category of "fight-

ing words" to situations involving face-to-face insults.[2] In the landmark case of
New York Times v. Sullivan (1964), the Court held that a statement concerning
a public official could be libel only if it was false, defamatory (injurious to reputation), and made with actual malice—"that is, with knowledge that it was false
or with reckless disregard of whether it was false or not."[3] In *Miller v. California* (1973), the Court limited obscenity to material depicting sexual conduct
that (1) appeals to "prurient interest" according to "contemporary community
standards"; (2) is "patently offensive"; and (3) "lacks serious literary, artistic,
political, or scientific value."[4] Lastly, in *Watts v. United States* (1969), the Court
limited the category of threats placed outside the First Amendment to "true
threats."[5]

Any speech activity that did not fit into one of these categories of unprotected speech (fighting words, libel, obscenity, and true threats) was presumed
to be within the First Amendment, but inclusion did not mean that the speech
activity in question was absolutely protected. The Court instead applied a
"compelling interest" standard that balanced the individual right of free speech
against the state's purported interest. If and when the state's interest was "compelling" and if there was no other way for the state to obtain its goal, then the
right of free speech had to give way. For example, advocacy of illegal action was
not excluded from the Constitution, but was rather protected conditionally.
Free speech protected the speaker unless a "clear and present danger" of serious
harm to the state existed.[6] In this conditional sense, though it could be punished
in certain circumstances, advocacy of illegal action was within the right of free
speech.[7]

It was within the area of conditionally protected speech that the idea first
arose that the principle of free speech, besides constituting a limited individual
right, also barred the state from using its coercive power to favor one side of an
ideological debate over another. For example, in *Police Dept. v. Mosley* (1972),
the Supreme Court considered whether a city could bar picketing within 150
feet of a school, but exempt peaceful labor picketing from the ordinance. The
Court ruled that the ordinance was unconstitutional because the state was preferring one form of political protest over others. Such "favoritism" was incompatible with free speech because "the First Amendment means that government
has no power to restrict expression because of its message, its ideas, its subject
matter, or its content."[8] As Justice Robert Jackson had said in an earlier case, if
"there is any fixed star in our constitutional constellation, it is that no official,
high or petty, can prescribe what shall be orthodox in politics, nationalism, religion, or other matters of opinion. . . ."[9] Relying upon the spirit of this passage,
the Court concluded in *Mosley* that the government was obliged to "afford all
points of view an equal opportunity to be heard."[10]

The Supreme Court buttressed the principle that free speech prohibited any
content-based restrictions of speech in cases dealing with "expressive" or
"symbolic" conduct. The landmark decision was *United States v. O'Brien*
(1968).[11] In this case, the Court ruled that it was constitutional to punish those
who burned their draft cards to protest the Vietnam War. The Court did not

doubt that the activity in question was "expressive," but nonetheless ruled that when "speech" and "non-speech" elements are combined in the same course of conduct,

> a sufficiently important governmental interest in regulating the non-speech element can justify incidental limitations on First Amendment freedoms. . . . [[W]]e think it clear that a government regulation is sufficiently justified if it is within the constitutional power of the Government; if it furthers an important or substantial governmental interest; *if the governmental interest is unrelated to the suppression of free expression*; and if the incidental restriction on alleged First Amendment freedoms *is no greater than is essential to the furtherance of that interest*. [[Emphasis mine.]]

O'Brien buttressed the idea that free speech barred the state from censoring ideas. Though the state only needed an "important" interest, not a "compelling" one, to justify regulations of "expressive conduct," the interest in question had to be "unrelated to the suppression of free expression" and it justified only those restrictions that were "essential to the furtherance of that interest."

In *Texas v. Johnson* (1989), the Court relied on the "no-censorship" branch of the *O'Brien* test to invalidate laws punishing flag burning. Did the state's interest in preserving the flag as a national symbol justify the prohibition of this form of political expression? In a 5–4 decision, the Court held that free speech forbade government from using its coercive power to favor the values symbolized by the flag.

> If we were to hold that a State may forbid flag-burning wherever it is likely to endanger the flag's symbolic role, but allow it wherever burning a flag promotes that role—as where, for example, a person ceremoniously burns a dirty flag—we would be saying that when it comes to impairing the flag's physical integrity, the flag itself may be used as a symbol—as a substitute for the written or spoken word or a "short cut from mind to mind"—in only one direction. We would be permitting a State to "prescribe what shall be orthodox."[12]

In terms of the *O'Brien* test, the state's interest justifying the ban on flag burning was not "unrelated to the suppression of ideas." That fact alone was sufficient to invalidate all such statutes. It did not matter that such statutes only prohibited "conduct" (not speech or writing *per se*) or that the state had an important governmental interest. Laws punishing flag burning were content-based restrictions involving governmental censorship of expressive conduct. They were unconstitutional for that reason.[13]

Prior to *R.A.V.*, courts often invalidated laws punishing "hate speech" by invoking the doctrine of overbreadth, a free speech doctrine which reverses the normal rule that a litigant can only claim that those portions of a law are invalid that were unconstitutionally applied to him or her. In other words, in a free speech case, someone whose speech activity may be punishable could demand a dismissal of an indictment and the invalidation of a criminal statute on the ground that it might be applied to someone whose speech activity was constitutionally protected. Relying on this doctrine, the Seventh Circuit Court of Appeals in *Collin v. Smith* (1978) invalidated an ordinance that prohibited any dissemination of materials that intentionally "promotes and incites hatred against persons by reason of their race, national origin, or religion." Skokie, Illinois, a suburb of Chicago whose 70,000 inhabitants included 30,000 Jews, 5,000 of whom were survivors of the Holocaust and their families, had enacted this ordinance to prevent a demonstration by the National Socialist Party of America (NSPA).[14] In a related development, many public and private universities and colleges, to insure an equal opportunity for an education to all racial minority and other victimized groups, enacted "speech codes" during the 1980s that prohibited various forms of hate speech on campus. For example, the University of Michigan's "speech code" prohibited any behavior that

> stigmatizes or victimizes an individual on the basis of race, ethnicity, religion, sex, sexual orientation, creed, national origin, ancestry, age, marital status, handicap or Vietnam-era veteran status, and that . . . has the purpose or reasonably foreseeable effect of interfering with an individual's academic efforts, employment, participation in University sponsored extra-curricular activities or personal safety.

Professors Charles Lawrence and Gerald Gunther, both of Stanford Law School, debated whether such codes were required by the Equal Protection Clause or were prohibited by freedom of speech. Lawrence argued that the spirit of *Brown v. Board of Education* would never be fully realized as long as students were subjected to "denigrating verbal harassment and assault." In response, Gunther insisted that "curbing speech" was the wrong way for a university to foster diversity and tolerance (see box 4.1 on p. 152). Which law professor has the better argument? Should public universities be allowed to punish hate speech on campus? What about private universities? Should different rules apply to them? Does it bother you that lower federal and state courts have invalidated these speech codes, including the University of Michigan's, on the ground that they are overbroad?[15]

The Supreme Court finally addressed the constitutionality of a law that punished "hate speech" in *R.A.V. v. City of St. Paul* (1992). The central facts of the case were uncontested. Sometime between 1:00 and 3:00 a.m., June 21, 1990, a seventeen-year-old white male in St. Paul, Minnesota (R.A.V.), along with several friends, burned a few wooden crosses within the fenced yard of an African-American family that had recently moved into the neighborhood. Local authorities charged him, among other things, with violating the St. Paul Bias-Motivated Crime Ordinance (Section 292.02), which provided the following:

> Whoever places on public or private property a symbol, object, appellation, characterization or graffiti, including but not limited to, a burning cross or Nazi swastika, which one knows or has reasonable grounds to know arouses anger, alarm, or resentment in others on the basis of race, color, creed, religion or gender commits disorderly conduct and shall be guilty of a misdemeanor.[16]

The Juvenile District Court dismissed this particular charge, but the Minnesota Supreme Court reversed, remanding the case for trial. The state high court said that if the ordinance was properly limited to "fighting words" and to "direct incitements," it was constitutional since it only punished unprotected speech. R.A.V. appealed to the Supreme Court.

R.A.V.'s attorney, Edward J. Cleary, argued that the ordinance was unconstitutional because it discriminated between fighting words on the basis of content and because it was overbroad. Accordingly, in his view, it was unconstitutional whether free speech was understood as a prohibition of governmental censorship or as a limited individual right. According to Cleary, the state high court's attempt to narrow the scope of the law was ineffective because the broad language of the ordinance would "chill" protected speech. The content-based character of the ordinance resided in the fact that it imposed liability only on certain fighting words, only those that aroused "anger, alarm, or resentment in others on the basis of race, color, creed, religion or gender." Other types of fighting words were free of liability. Since the ordinance punished speech in this content-based fashion, it was constitutional, Cleary argued, only if it was a "necessary" means to a "compelling" state interest. But public safety and order did not require special "hate speech" crimes. Ordinary penal statutes (e.g., trespass and assault) sufficed to protect the community and the city had no authority to enact such a statute for the purpose of encouraging social tolerance. The law was therefore unconstitutional because it was overbroad and because it was a form of governmental censorship.

St. Paul's defense of the ordinance relied heavily upon the state high court's narrow interpretation of the law. According to Tom Foley, the attorney representing St. Paul, there was no overbreadth problem with the ordinance because R.A.V. could only be convicted if the state proved that he had acted with the requisite *scienter*: that is, with the required "intent" or "knowledge." Though the ordinance had said that liability could be imposed if the speaker either knew or had reason to know that his speech aroused anger, alarm, or resentment in others, the state's highest court had ruled that punishment was constitutional only if R.A.V. had used a "bias-related symbol to threaten, cause fear in, or intimidate a particular targeted person or persons." Foley also insisted that the ordinance was not a content-based restriction of free speech. The purpose of the law was not to suppress any idea or message, but to prevent certain harms by protecting minority members who were vulnerable to victimization because of the country's history of past discrimination. However, the brief continued, if the Court disagreed, if the Court decided that the ordinance was a content-based regulation, it was nonetheless constitutional because the state had a compelling interest in fostering equality and social harmony and because cross burning has little or no expressive value.

The Supreme Court unanimously invalidated St. Paul's Bias-Motivated Crime Ordinance, but the justices divided over the rationale for the decision, revealing sharp differences concerning the ultimate meaning of free speech, and disagreed about the degree to which "hate speech" was protected by the Con-

Box 4.1   A DEBATE ON COLLEGE CAMPUS SPEECH CODES

PROFESSOR CHARLES LAWRENCE: . . .

. . . I would also argue that the university's responsibility for ensuring that these students receive an equal educational opportunity provides a compelling justification for regulations that ensure them safe passage in all common areas. A minority student should not have to risk becoming the target of racially assaulting speech every time he or she chooses to walk across campus. . . .

The *Brown* case . . . speaks directly to the psychic injury inflicted by racist speech by noting that the symbolic message of segregation affected "the hearts and minds" of Negro children "in a way unlikely ever to be undone." Racial epithets and harassment often cause deep emotional scarring and feelings of anxiety and fear that pervade every aspect of a victim's life.

Brown also recognized that black children did not have an equal opportunity to learn and participate in the school community when they bore the additional burden of being subjected to the humiliation and psychic assault contained in the message of segregation. University students bear an analogous burden when they are forced to live and work in an environment where at any moment they may be subjected to denigrating verbal harassment and assault. . . .

Whenever we decide that racist speech must be tolerated because of the importance of maintaining societal tolerance for all unpopular speech, we are asking blacks and other subordinated groups to bear the burden for the good of all. We must be careful that the ease with which we strike the balance against the regulation of racist speech is in no way influenced by the fact that the cost will be borne by others. We must be certain that those who will pay that price are fairly represented in our deliberations and that they are heard. . . .

stitution. Justice Byron White's concurring opinion took the more traditional approach.[17] He argued that the ordinance should be invalidated on the simple ground that it was overbroad, implying that a properly worded ban on a subset of "fighting words" would be constitutional because the subset only included speech that was "by definition worthless and undeserving of constitutional protection." In his concurring opinion, Justice John Paul Stevens rejected White's premise that "fighting words" were wholly unprotected. Stevens wanted to abandon entirely the tradition that certain categories of speech were completely outside free speech. For him, all speech was within the Amendment, but certain kinds of speech, like "fighting words," had "low value." Hence the interests served by punishing an incident of hate speech that constituted a

PROFESSOR GERALD GUNTHER:

. . . My deep belief in the principles of the First Amendment arises in part from my own experiences.

I received my elementary education in a public school in a very small town in Nazi Germany. There I was subjected to vehement anti-Semitic remarks from my teacher, classmates and others—"Judensau" (Jew pig) was far from the harshest. I can assure you that they hurt. More generally, I lived in a country where ideological orthodoxy reigned and where the opportunity for dissent was severely limited.

The lesson I have drawn from my childhood in Nazi Germany and my happier adult life in this country is the need to walk the sometimes difficult path of denouncing the bigots' hateful ideas with all my power, yet at the same time challenging any community's attempt to suppress hateful ideas by force of law. . . .

The phenomenon of racist and other offensive speech that Stanford now faces is not a new one in the history of the First Amendment. In recent decades, for example, well-meaning but in my view misguided majorities have sought to suppress not only racist speech but also antiwar and antidraft speech, civil rights demonstrators, the Nazis and the Ku Klu Klan, and left-wing groups. . . .

Those in power in a community recurrently seek to repress speech they find abhorrent; and their efforts are understandable human impulses. Yet freedom of expression—and especially the protection of dissident speech, the most important function of the First Amendment—is an anti-majoritarian principle. Is it too much to hope that, especially on a university campus, a majority can be persuaded of the value of freedom of expression and of the resultant need to curb our impulses to repress dissident views? . . .

Source: Stanford Lawyer 24 (Spring, 1990), pp. 6–8; 40–41. Reprinted with permission of Stanford University and *Chronicle of Higher Education.*

"fighting word" could justify the constitutionality of such a law. It was not important that such a law made a content-based distinction.

In contrast to the two concurring opinions, Justice Antonin Scalia's majority opinion extended the principle that free speech barred governmental censorship. Scalia agreed with Stevens that no type of speech was "entirely invisible" to the Constitution, but he denied that government could make content-based regulations of speech. Such regulations, according to Scalia, were "presumptively invalid." Even in regard to those types of speech historically excluded from constitutional protection, the free speech clause meant that the government could not make content-based distinctions. It could not pick and choose, as St. Paul had done, which fighting words to prohibit. Government had to remain neutral. It must not "play favorites" by punishing fighting words involving denigration of a person's "race, color, creed, religion, or gender," while ignoring insults directed at a person's political affiliation or outlook. Such "favoritism" sends a signal of government disapproval that the First Amendment condemns. The city's only option was to prohibit all fighting words or none at all.

Scalia recognized three exceptions to his rule that government cannot engage in content discrimination. First, when "the basis for the content discrimination consists entirely of the very reason the entire class of speech at issue is proscribable," then the discrimination in question is valid. The state could, for example, punish the "worst" types of fighting words or the "most obscene" forms of obscenity, without punishing all fighting words or all types of obscenity, so long as the definition of "worst" or "most obscene" was derived from why the entire class was excluded from constitutional protection in the first place. Also, government can impose differential treatment on a subclass of proscribable speech if "the subclass happens to be associated with particular 'secondary effects' of the speech, so that the regulation is 'justified without reference to the content of the . . . speech." For example, "sexually derogatory fighting words" may "produce a violation of Title VII's general prohibition against sexual discrimination in employment practices." The state can prohibit the discrimination, the "secondary effect," even though the evidence for the violation consists entirely of "sexually derogatory fighting words." Lastly, it may not be necessary for the government to identify a "neutral basis" for its action if "the nature of the content discrimination is such that there is no realistic possibility that official suppression of ideas is afoot." The state could, for example, prohibit "obscene motion pictures with blue-eyed actresses" because there is no reason to believe that the policy involves censorship.

Both White and Stevens underlined the implicit irony in Scalia's argument. According to his no-censorship interpretation of the First Amendment, it would be more compatible with free speech if the government punished more speech (if it punished all "fighting words") than if the government punished less speech (if it punished only those "fighting words" that expressed hatred of victimized groups). Does Scalia's position make sense? Can free speech be a reason for punishing more speech rather than less? White and Stevens say no because, at bottom, they are committed to a concept of free speech as a *limited* individual right. In contrast, Scalia believes that the more fundamental free speech principle is that the government should be neutral. It can retain its neutrality, of course, by not punishing any "fighting words," but if the state insists upon punishing some "fighting words," such as provocative racial epithets, then it must punish *all* "fighting words." Accordingly, free speech can be a reason why government must punish more speech, not less.

How certain of the justices voted in *R.A.V.* and *Texas v. Johnson* raises interesting questions. In the flag-burning case, Scalia voted in favor of the free speech rights of the flag burner, Stevens acknowledged that flag burning was speech but that it could be regulated because its value was low, and White voted to uphold laws punishing flag burning. How these justices voted in *Johnson* more or less coincided with what they said in *R.A.V.* Scalia believed that the state would be engaged in censorship if it punished the flag burner or if it only punished the racist cross burner. In contrast, Stevens and White believed that narrowly drawn statutes could prohibit both flag burning and cross burning because both forms of expressive conduct were of "low value" or outside the limited right of free speech. However, Chief Justice William Rehnquist voted to uphold flag-burning statutes, but then joined Scalia's majority opinion in *R.A.V.* Is it fair to say that his position is that flag burners, but not racist cross burners, can be punished. Is such a position consistent? Is it morally and constitutionally defensible? In contrast, Justice Harry Blackmun voted to invalidate flag-burning statutes, but insisted in a concurring opinion (not excerpted below) that a narrowly drawn statute punishing racist cross burners would be constitutional. Is he more or less consistent than Rehnquist? Is a flag burner engaging in protected political expression, while a racist cross burner is not? The following excerpts from *R.A.V.* indirectly address these questions.

BIBLIOGRAPHY

Cleary, Edward J. *Beyond the Burning Cross.* New York: Random House, 1994.
Downs, Donald A. *Nazis in Skokie.* Notre Dame, Ind.: University of Notre Dame Press, 1985.
Greenawalt, Kent. *Fighting Words.* Princeton, N.J.: Princeton University Press, 1995.
Matsuda, Mari, et al. *Words That Wound: Critical Race Theory, Assaultive Speech, and the First Amendment.* Boulder, Colo.: Westview Press, 1993.
Shiell, Timothy C. *Campus Hate Speech on Trial.* Lawrence: University Press of Kansas, 1998.
Strum, Philippa. *When the Nazis Came to Skokie.* Lawrence: University Press of Kansas, 1999.

BRIEFS

R.A.V.'s BRIEF

[[1. Content-Neutrality.]] . . . "Above all else, the First Amendment means that government has no power to restrict expression because of its message, its ideas, its subject matter, or its content." . . .

By its terms, section 292.02 regulates both symbolic conduct ("symbol, object, appellation") and written expression ("characterization or graffiti"). More significantly, this ordinance addresses the communicative impact of that expressive conduct. By including specific symbols (Nazi swastika, burning cross) the ordinance not only regulates the content of the message but is a "censorial statute" directed at particular groups and viewpoints. The ordinance compounds its impermissible reach not only by addressing the content of the expression but by censoring expression associated with unpopular minorities. "[T]he First Amendment forbids the government to regulate speech in ways that favor some viewpoints or ideas at the expense of others." By focusing on the content and viewpoint of the offensive expression, the ordinance attempts impermissibly to protect and shield its audience. . . .

When, as here, a government regulation is directed at and infringes upon constitutionally protected areas, including content-based expression, the government must demonstrate that a compelling state interest is furthered by the regulation. In this case, the government has failed to satisfy this burden. . . .

. . . Since existing general criminal laws satisfy the state's interest in maintaining order, this ordinance is unnecessary to further this interest. . . .

It would appear that the real interest advanced by the ordinance is that of increasing social tolerance by prohibiting intolerant expressions regarding race, color, creed, religion, and gender. While the government may have an interest in increasing understanding among its citizens, it may not promote this interest by regulating individual opinion and expression. Government may not seek to control individual expression as a means of encouraging certain viewpoints, including racial and religious tolerance, even if such viewpoints are widely held. The notion of a "consensus" is irrelevant to the protections of the First Amendment or to any government regulation of expression. "[T]he Government may not prohibit the expression of an idea simply because society finds the idea itself offensive or disagreeable." . . .

The number of groups designated for protection by the ordinance is indicative of the government's approach. By specifying two hate symbols, the ordinance appears to be aimed primarily at protecting African Americans and Jewish Americans from intolerance. . . .

The government amended this ordinance in 1990 to add "gender" to the list of protected groups who may be offended by the display of symbols of expressions. This amendment reflects an inherent problem with this type of law: it is always subject to the changing political climate of the community and the consensus of the majority regarding acceptable expressive conduct. Left unchecked, law-making bodies will continue to court political support by enlarging the list of protected groups while precluding unpopular minority expressions. . . .

[[2. Overbreadth.]] Neither the "fighting words" exception nor the "imminent lawless action" exception clarify the permissible reach of section 292.02. By its very nature, symbolic and written expression may stir some to anger by reason of its content. Yet, narrowing the ordinance to reach "fighting words" or "imminent lawless action" is ineffective due to the breadth of the language used in drafting the ordinance. Thus, narrowing the "arouses anger, alarm or resentment in others" clause leaves intact the overbreadth of the remaining terms. To the degree the narrowing construction attempts to limit the impact of the ordinance on protected expression, it fails in its objective. Those expressions which rise to the level of "fighting words" or "imminent lawless action" as narrowly interpreted by the decisions of this Court constitute only a small portion of expression addressed by this ordinance. Any reduction in the chilling effect of the ordinance is equally negligible. . . .

To construe this ordinance narrowly, as applying to only those areas unprotected by the First Amendment, results in an additional problem of constitutional dimension, for persons "of common intelligence must necessarily guess at its meaning." The ordinance fails to provide any certainty in guiding citizens in their conduct or police in their enforcement of the law. . . .

[[3. Speech Codes.]] Laws similar to section 292.02 have been enacted throughout the nation in an attempt to counter "hate speech." Consequently, the ordinance mirrors many speech and conduct codes in both public and private universities across the nation. Such codes and conduct regulations are proliferating. According to a survey by the Carnegie Foundation for the Advancement of Teaching, over sixty percent of the responding colleges and universities had developed or were developing written policies on bigotry, racial harassment or sexual harassment on campus. Of the remaining schools, eleven percent were working to establish similar restrictions on written, spoken, and symbolic speech. Contrary to this trend, a bill was recently introduced in Congress that seeks to extend First Amendment guarantees of freedom of speech to private schools and universities.

A university campus is a virtual microcosm of a community such as the City of St. Paul. Just as St. Paul has both public and private forums, the university campus contains within its boundaries a mall, classrooms, and areas of residence. Whether it be within the limits of the City of St. Paul or on a campus elsewhere in the nation, substantially overbroad laws or regulations which suppress expressive conduct on the basis of viewpoint obscure our goal of a tolerant pluralistic society.

Any expansion of narrowly recognized exceptions to the First Amendment would further diffuse the nearly indistinguishable line between permissible and proscribable expression. Further restrictions might curtail some offensive expression but only at the cost of chilling a great deal of protected speech. The result may well be the silencing of political debate, the encouraging of orthodoxy, and the endangering of the individual's right to dissent. To enforce a notion of civility to the point of forbidding unpopular minority expression is to underestimate the citizens of this country at the cost of our basic right of self-expression. This Court should not ignore the guidance of established First Amendment analysis and create a new category of expressive communication subject to regulation. . . .

> Respectfully submitted,
> EDWARD J. CLEARY

ST. PAUL'S BRIEF

[[1. Overbreadth.]] . . . To save the Ordinance from the challenge of substantial overbreadth, the Minnesota Supreme Court . . . limited it to:

(a) "fighting words," "those which by their very utterance inflict injury or tend to incite an immediate breach of the peace;" and (b) conduct that is "directed to inciting or producing imminent lawless action and is likely to incite or produce such action."

The existence of *scienter*, as defined by the Minnesota Supreme Court, that the State must prove, must be inferred from the words and acts of the accused. That is, the context in which the symbol is used. It is for the trier of fact to decide whether the State in a particular case has shouldered its burden of persuasion. . . .

Substantial overbreadth is absent unless there is an objective basis for predicting that the right of expression of others will materially be chilled. Clearly, no such basis exists in the instant case.

However the substantial overbreadth test is articulated it seems speculative at best, absurd at worst, to postulate that there will be significant amounts of expressive conduct chilled by the mere existence of this bias-related Ordinance on the books and by Petitioner's pending prosecution for violation of it. Only where one uses a bias-motivated symbol with the requisite *scienter* is the Ordinance applicable. . . .

A part of the rationale of the Minnesota Supreme Court's decision upholding the ordinance here at issue involved the state's undoubted authority to prohibit conduct or words "that by their very utterance inflict injury." That is, threaten harm to others. The Minnesota Supreme Court relied on the fact that the use of a burning cross is "an unmistakable symbol of violence and hatred based on virulent notions of racial supremacy."

It is settled that a statute forbidding threats of physical violence to another is constitutional on its face. Nevertheless, in its application, what is a genuine threat must be distinguished from what is constitutionally protected speech. The context is important in determining whether an apparent threat is indeed a true threat. . . .

Cross-burning, by nature and history, is intimidating to anyone targeted. The only issue is thus whether the threat is clear and present.

To an African American family, the meaning of a burning cross in one's lawn is not remotely ambiguous.

Cross-burning, at least directly, carries no message other than to its targeted victim, who is both captive and vulnerable. The reasonable, even inevitable belief of the victim is that he is to be further targeted with physical injury or death unless he, as coerced, departs from the neighborhood. . . .

[[2. Content-Neutrality.]] . . . Under the *O'Brien* test, the conduct of the accused which is criminalized must further a legitimate governmental purpose unrelated to the suppression of free expression. To decide this issue, the Court analyzes the enactment in terms of its purpose of justification, which is the controlling consideration.

In the instant case, the Ordinance is intended not to impact on the right of free expression of the accused but rather to protect against the victimization of a person or persons who are particularly vulnerable because of their membership in a group that historically has been discriminated against. The governmental purpose evaluation looks particularly to the effects, primary and secondary, on the victims. . . .

The minimal expressive conduct of the accused here stands in stark contrast to the important and vital personal rights of victims that are vitiated by violation of the Ordinance. . . . Victims are targeted not, essentially, because of their individual attributes but simply because they are members of a particular race, religion, or gender that has historically suffered discriminatory treatment. Moreover, experts understand that by attacking a persons' community, one interferes with that person's concept of self and individual growth and development.

In the instant case, the victims' right to live in peace where they wish, and where they have a constitutional right to reside, is seriously compromised. The message of the cross burner is that the targeted victim should move out of the neighborhood; the only—and brutal—message conveyed. . . .

Burning of crosses, or the use of symbols of like racial, religious, or gender-related meaning, is intended to further the goal of isolating or stigmatizing persons because of the group of which they are a part. Such symbols serve their purposes not in creating, but in suppressing dialogue that could lead to reconciliation among communities. . . .

From reading Petitioner's Brief . . . , one would think that violation of the St. Paul Ordinance is a victimless crime. That is not the case.

There are rights to liberty at least as basic on the side of the victim as on the side of the perpetrator of this offense. Where rights are in conflict, they must be balanced. It is Respondent's position that the minimal interest in free expression on the part of the Petitioner is far outweighed by the freedom of the victim to live where he wishes and by the right to equal treatment in the society of which he is a member.

In summation, even were the St. Paul Ordinance found to be content-biased, the vital interests of the victim constitute that compelling state interest which justifies limiting the perpetrator's conduct. . . .

Respectfully submitted,
Tom Foley

ORAL ARGUMENT

JUSTICE SCALIA: . . . Mr. Cleary, isn't one of your complaints that the Minnesota statute as construed by the supreme court of Minnesota punishes only some fighting words and not others?

MR. CLEARY [[Attorney for R.A.V.]]: It is, Your Honor. That is one of my positions, that in doing so, even though it is a subcategory, technically, of unprotected conduct, it still is picking out an opinion, a disfavored message, and making that clear through the State. It's a paternalistic idea, and the problem that we have is that the Government must not betray neutrality, and I believe it does, even when it picks out a subcategory.

With the First Amendment, it does not necessarily follow that if you punish the greater you can punish the lesser. If we had a law that banned the posting of signs, for instance, somewhat akin to *Vincent*, and if we had in there including but not limited to signs regarding the Democratic Party symbols, now that might be a mere example, and it might be a subcategory, but I believe this Court would be offended by that.

I believe the Court would feel that that was betraying sympathy or hostility to a political viewpoint, and I believe the same principle is in course here, because I think the problem we have is that we have—regardless of whether those symbols are mere examples, we have the possibility, the real possibility, that we have a Government signaling its disagreement with the particular type of opinion. . . .

SCALIA: . . . [[I]]sn't it the case that the ordinance only considers disorderly conduct the placing on public or private property of a symbol, object, et cetera, which one knows or has reasonable grounds to know arouses anger, alarm, or resentment in others, on the basis of race, color, creed, religion, or gender? Now, that's selective, isn't it? Aren't there a lot of other reasons why anger might be aroused?

CLEARY: Yes, there are, Your Honor.

SCALIA: . . . [[T]]he ordinance is limited to causing alarm or resentment for only certain reasons, and if you cause alarm or resentment for other reasons, that is not unlawful under the ordinance, isn't that right?

CLEARY: That is right. . . .

✻   ✻   ✻

CLEARY: The debate in this case is not about the wisdom of eradicating intolerance, the debate is about the method of reaching that goal. I believe that the city council officials in this case and in other communities are very well-meaning, and that's usually the case, but the problem is that I believe these type of laws cross the line from the Fourteenth Amendment duty of the State to not participate in any racist State action or any intolerant State action, in that sense, with the First Amendment right of self-expression, even if it be intolerant, provided it does not cross the line of illegal conduct itself.

I believe the danger in a law like this is that it does pick out viewpoints, that it is viewpoint-discriminatory. . . .

JUSTICE KENNEDY: All right. Could this conduct be punished by a narrowly drawn statute that proscribes threats that cause violence? Could that state a cause of action against your client?

CLEARY: I believe it could.

KENNEDY: On these facts?

CLEARY: I believe it could. . . . I have never argued that . . . the conduct alleged in this case could not be addressed by viewpoint-neutral laws, but this type of a law leaves open the possibility for viewpoint discrimination, and it opens up, again, the selective enforcement idea.

JUSTICE O'CONNOR: Well, you say its underinclusive.

CLEARY: I do, Your Honor, in the sense . . . that it definitely picks and betrays government neutrality. I think the government must be neutral when they go about compiling laws or construing laws that may affect First Amendment rights. . . .

    I believe that this is the hour of danger for the First Amendment in that there are many groups that would like to encroach upon its principles with well-meaning intentions, but doing so, they are still punishing the content of the communication and they are doing so in a discriminatory manner, and the government is betraying a neutral principle in the sense that they are allowing that to happen and they are partaking in that. . . .

✻   ✻   ✻

SCALIA: Well, Mr. Foley, would you address the concern expressed by your opponent that the ordinance is limited to only fighting words that arouse anger, alarm, or resentment on the basis of race, color, creed, or religion or gender and not other fighting words that could cause the same reaction in people?
    The argument is that the statute is underinclusive.

MR. FOLEY [[Attorney for St. Paul]]: Your Honor, it's our position that the statute is not underinclusive, that this is a fighting words case, that this is unprotected conduct under the First Amendment, and that the City of St. Paul has the right to determine which harms it can proscribe within the limits of its jurisdiction.

SCALIA: Well, certainly it is limited by subject matter or content of the fighting words that are spoken, is it not? In that sense it is a content-based ordinance.

FOLEY: Your Honor, it's our position that it is not a content-based ordinance, that it certainly could be used to be a content-neutral ordinance.

SCALIA: Well, but it doesn't cover fighting words that are not limited to words on the basis of race, color, creed, religion, or gender.

FOLEY: That's correct, Your Honor.

SCALIA: So why, I mean, how can you possibly say it isn't content-based to that extent?

FOLEY: Your Honor, we have alternative theories that it is content-based, but it is unprotected conduct because it is fighting words, but we also believe that the main purpose of the ordinance is not to limit freedom of expression in that the harm that it's attempting to regulate is neutral and it could be considered content-neutral under the Renton-Barnes analysis that this Court has engaged in, but even if the Court feels that it is content-based, . . . there is a compelling State purpose in public safety and order to pass such an ordinance. . . .

*   *   *

FOLEY: I think the city has an absolute right and purpose to try to regulate the harm that goes onto its citizens. And certainly this bias-motivated conduct and violence is much more harmful and has more harmful impacts to its citizens—

SCALIA: That's a political judgment. I mean, you may feel strongest about race, color, creed, religion, or gender. Somebody else may feel strong as to about philosophy, about economic philosophy, about whatever. You picked out five reasons for causing somebody to breach the peace. But there are a lot of other ones. What's your basis for making that subjective discrimination?

FOLEY: Your Honor, the City of St. Paul is attempting to fashion responses to violence that it deems necessary to prohibit and will add additional harms to be regulated as it finds them.

Under this particular ordinance, it seemed that this is a particular harm going on that is necessary within the City of St. Paul to prohibit and regulate.

SCALIA: It doesn't have to add anything. You could just drop the words and, you know, just say that [[a speaker who]] arouses anger, alarm, or resentment in others . . . shall be guilty of a misdemeanor. It didn't have to say arouses anger, alarm, or resentment on the basis of race, color, creed, religion, or gender. You don't need that for *Chaplinsky*. If it's a fighting word, it's a fighting word. They could get the cross burning, they could get all sorts of activities.

FOLEY: Your Honor, I think it's the city's position that this is a fighting words case, that the ordinance has been sufficiently narrowed by the Minnesota supreme court. And you could reread that ordinance under these facts to say that whoever based on race, places an object or symbol with the intent to inflict injury, incite immediate violence, or provoke imminent lawless action is guilty of a crime. And I think that the Minnesota supreme court's narrowing of that ordinance is sufficient to uphold its constitutionality under the *Chaplinsky* and *Brandenburg* holdings of this Court.

SCALIA: Well, are you saying that because they can prevent or punish all fighting words, they can select any category within the broad scope of fighting words for it to be singled out?

FOLEY: Yes, Your Honor. . . .

THE OPINION

Justice Scalia delivered the opinion of the Court. . . .

. . . Assuming, arguendo, that all of the expression reached by the ordinance is proscribable under the "fighting words" doctrine, we nonetheless conclude that the ordinance is facially unconstitutional in that it prohibits otherwise permitted speech solely on the basis of the subjects the speech addresses.

The First Amendment generally prevents government from proscribing speech, or even expressive conduct, because of disapproval of the ideas expressed. Content-based regulations are presumptively invalid. From 1791 to the present, however, our society, like other free but civilized societies, has permitted restrictions upon the content of speech in a few limited areas, which are "of such slight social value as a step to truth that any benefit that may be derived from them is clearly outweighed by the social interest in order and morality." We have recognized that "the freedom of speech" referred to by the First Amendment does not include a freedom to disregard these traditional limitations. Our decisions since the 1960's have narrowed the scope of the traditional categorical exceptions for defamation, and for obscenity, but a limited categorical approach has remained an important part of our First Amendment jurisprudence.

We have sometimes said that these categories of expression are "not within the area of constitutionally protected speech," or that the "protection of the First Amendment does not extend" to them. Such statements must be taken in context, however, and are no more literally true than is the occasionally repeated shorthand characterizing obscenity "as not being speech at all." What they mean is that these areas of speech can, consistently with the First Amendment, be regulated because of their constitutionally proscribable content (obscenity, defamation, etc.)—not that they are categories of speech entirely invisible to the Constitution, so that they may be made the vehicles for content discrimination unrelated to their distinctively proscribable content. Thus, the government may proscribe libel; but it may not make the further content discrimination of proscribing only libel critical of the government. We recently acknowledged this distinction in *Ferber*, where, in upholding New York's child pornography law, we expressly recognized that there was no "question here of censoring a particular literary theme. . . ."

Our cases surely do not establish the proposition that the First Amendment imposes no obstacle whatsoever to regulation of particular instances of such proscribable expression, so that the government "may regulate [them] freely." That would mean that a city council could enact an ordinance prohibiting only those legally obscene works that contain criticism of the city government or, indeed, that do not include endorsement of the city government. Such a simplistic, all-or-nothing-at-all approach to First Amendment protection is at odds with common sense and with our jurisprudence as well. It is not true that "fighting words" have at most a "de minimis" expressive content, or that their content is in all respect "worthless and undeserving of constitutional protection;" sometimes they are quite expressive indeed. We have not said that they constitute "no part of the expression of ideas," but only that they constitute "no essential part of any exposition of ideas." . . .

. . . [[T]]he prohibition against content discrimination that we assert the First Amendment requires is not absolute. It applies differently in the context of proscribable speech than in the area of fully protected speech. The rationale of the general prohibition, after all, is that content discrimination "raises the specter that the Government may effectively drive certain ideas or viewpoints from the marketplace." But content discrimination among various instances of a class of proscribable speech often does not pose this threat.

When the basis for the content discrimination consists entirely of the very reason the entire class of speech at issue is proscribable, no significant danger of idea or viewpoint discrimination exists. Such a reason, having been adjudged neutral enough to support exclusion of the entire class of speech from First Amendment protection, is also neutral enough to form the basis of distinction within the class. To illustrate: A State might choose to prohibit only that obscenity which is the most patently offensive in its prurience—i.e., that which involves the most lascivious displays of sexual activity. But it may not prohibit, for example, only that obscenity which includes offensive political messages. And the Federal Government can criminalize only those threats of violence that are directed against the President—since the reasons why threats of violence are outside the First Amendment (protecting individuals from the fear of violence, from the disruption that fear engenders, and from the possibility that the threatened violence will occur) have special force when applied to the person of the President. But the Federal Government may not criminalize only those threats against the President that mention his policy on aid to inner cities. And to take a final example (one mentioned by Justice Stevens), a State may choose to regulate price advertising in one industry but not in others, because the risk of fraud (one of the characteristics of commercial speech that justifies depriving it of full First Amendment protection) is in its view greater there.

Another valid basis for according differential treatment to even a content-defined subclass of proscribable speech is that the subclass happens to be associated with particular "secondary effects" of the speech, so that the regulation is "justified without reference to the content of the . . . speech." A State could, for example, permit all obscene live performances except those involving minors. Moreover, since words can in some circumstances violate laws directed not against speech but against conduct (a law against treason, for example, is violated by telling the enemy the nation's defense secrets), a particular content-based subcategory of a proscribable class of speech can be swept up incidentally within the reach of a statute directed at conduct rather than speech. Thus, for example, sexually derogatory "fighting words," among other words, may produce a violation of Title VII's general prohibition against sexual discrimination in employment practices. Where the government does not target conduct on the basis of its expressive content, acts are not shielded from regulation merely because they express a discriminatory idea or philosophy. . . .

. . . [T]o validate such selectivity (where totally proscribable speech is at issue) it may not even be necessary to identify any particular "neutral" basis, so long as the nature of the content discrimination is such that there is no realistic possibility that official suppression of ideas is afoot. (We cannot think of any First Amendment interest that would stand in the way of a State's prohibiting only those obscene motion pictures with blue-eyed actresses.) Save for that limitation, the regulation of "fighting words," like the regulation of noisy speech, may address some offensive instances and leave other, equally offensive, instances alone.

Applying these principles to the St. Paul ordinance, we conclude that, even as narrowly construed by the Minnesota Supreme Court, the ordinance is facially unconstitutional. Although the phrase in the ordinance, "arouses anger, alarm or resentment in others," has been limited by the Minnesota Supreme Court's construction to reach only those symbols or displays that amount to "fighting words," the remaining, unmodified terms make clear that the ordinance applies only to "fighting words" that insult, or provoke violence, "on the basis of race, color, creed, religion or gender." Displays containing abusive invective, no matter how vicious or severe, are permissible unless they are addressed to one of the specified disfavored topics. Those who wish to use "fighting words" in connection with other ideas—to express hostility, for example, on the basis of political affiliation, union membership, or homosexuality—are not covered. The First Amendment does not permit St. Paul to impose special prohibitions on those speakers who express views on disfavored subjects.

In its practical operations, moreover, the ordinance goes even beyond mere content discrimination, to actual viewpoint discrimination. Displays containing some words—odious racial epithets, for example—would be prohibited to proponents of all views. But "fighting words" that do not themselves invoke race, color, creed, religion, or gender—aspersions upon a person's mother, for example—would seemingly be usable ad libitum in the placards of those arguing in favor of racial, color, etc. tolerance and equality, but could not be used by that speaker's opponents. One could hold up a sign saying, for example, that all "anti-Catholic bigots" are misbegotten; but not that all "papists" are, for that would insult and provoke violence "on the basis of religion." St. Paul has no such authority to license one side of a debate to fight freestyle, while requiring the other to follow Marquis of Queensbury Rules. . . .

The content-based discrimination reflected in the St. Paul ordinance comes within neither any of the specific exceptions to the First Amendment prohibition we discussed earlier, nor within a more general exception for content discrimination that does not threaten censorship of ideas. . . .

. . . St. Paul and its amici defend the conclusion of the Minnesota Supreme Court that, even if the ordinance regulates expression based on hostility towards its protected ideological content, this discrimination is nonetheless justified because it is narrowly tailored to serve compelling state interests. Specifically, they assert that the ordinance helps to ensure the basic human rights of members of groups that have historically been subjected to discrimination, including the right of such group members to live in peace where they wish. We do not doubt that these interests are compelling, and that the ordinance can be said to promote them. . . . The dispositive question in this case, therefore, is whether content discrimination is reasonably necessary to achieve St. Paul's compelling interests; it plainly is not. An ordinance not limited to the favored topics for example, would have precisely the same beneficial effect. In fact the only interest distinctively served by the content limitation is that of displaying the city council's special hostility towards the particular biases thus singled out. That is precisely what the First Amendment forbids. The politicians of St. Paul are entitled to express that hostility—but not through the means of imposing unique limitations upon speakers who (however benightedly) disagree.

Let there be no mistake about our belief that burning a cross in someone's front yard is reprehensible. But St. Paul has sufficient means at its disposal to prevent such behavior without adding the First Amendment to the fire. . . .

Justice White, concurring in the judgment. . . .

I agree with the majority that the judgment of the Minnesota Supreme Court should be reversed. However, our agreement ends there. . . .

[[T]]he majority casts aside long-established First Amendment doctrine without the benefit of briefing and adopts an untried theory. This is hardly a judicious way of proceeding, and the Court's reasoning in reaching its result is transparently wrong.

This Court's decisions have plainly stated that expression falling within certain limited categories so lacks the values the First Amendment was designed to protect that the Constitution affords no protection to that expression. . . .

All of these categories are content based. But the Court has held that the First Amendment does not apply to them because their expressive content is worthless or of de minimis value to society. We have not departed from this principle, emphasizing repeatedly that, "within the confines of [these] given classifications, the evil to be restricted so overwhelmingly outweighs the expressive interests, if any, at stake, that no process of case-by-case adjudication is required." This categorical approach has provided a principled and narrowly focused means for distinguishing between expression that the government may regulate freely and that which it may regulate on the basis of content only upon a showing of compelling need. . . .

In its decision today, the Court points to "nothing . . . in this Court's precedents warranting disregard of this longstanding tradition." Nevertheless, the majority holds that the First Amendment protects those narrow categories of expression long held to be undeserving of First Amendment protection—at least to the extent that lawmakers may not regulate some fighting words more strictly than others because of their content. The Court announces that such content-based distinctions violate the First Amendment because the "government may not regulate use based on hostility—or favoritism—towards the underlying message expressed." Should the government want to criminalize certain fighting words, the Court now requires it to criminalize all fighting words.

To borrow a phrase, "Such a simplistic, all-or-nothing-at-all approach to First Amendment protection is at odds with common sense and with our jurisprudence as well." It is inconsistent to hold that the government may proscribe an entire category of speech because the content of that speech is evil, but that the government may not treat a subset of that category differently without violating the First Amendment; the content of the subset is by definition worthless and undeserving of constitutional protection. . . .

In a second break with precedent, the court refuses to sustain the ordinance even though it would survive under the strict scrutiny applicable to other protected expression. Assuming, arguendo, that the St. Paul ordinance is a content-based regulation of protected expression, it nevertheless would pass First Amendment review under settled law upon a showing that the regulation "is necessary to serve a compelling state interest and is narrowly drawn to achieve that end." St. Paul has urged that its ordinance, in the words of the majority, "helps to ensure the basic human right of members of groups that have historically been subjected to discrimination. . . ." The Court expressly concedes that this interest is compelling and is promoted by the ordinance. Nevertheless, the Court treats strict scrutiny analysis as irrelevant to the constitutionality of the legislation. . . .

Under the majority's view, a narrowly drawn, content-based ordinance could never pass constitutional muster if the object of that legislation could be accomplished by banning a wider category of speech. This appears to be a general renunciation of strict scrutiny review, a fundamental tool of First Amendment analysis. . . .

[[T]]he majority has engrafted the following exception onto its newly announced First Amendment rule: "Content-based distinctions may be drawn within an unprotected category of speech if the basis for the distinctions is the very reason the entire class of speech at issue is proscribable." Thus, the argument goes, the statute making it illegal to threaten the life of the President is constitutional, "since the reasons why threats of violence are outside the First Amendment (protecting individuals from the fear of violence, from the disruption that fear engenders, and from the possibility that the threatened violence will occur) have special force when applied to the person of the President."

The exception swallows the majority's rule. Certainly, it should apply to the St. Paul ordinance, since the reasons why [[fighting words]] are outside the First

Amendment . . . "have special force when applied to [groups that have historically been subjected to discrimination]." . . .

As its second exception, the Court posits that certain content-based regulations will survive under the new regime if the regulated "subclass happens to be associated with particular 'secondary effects' of the speech," which the majority treats as encompassing instances in which words can "violate laws directed not against speech but against conduct." Again, there is a simple explanation for the Court's eagerness to craft an exception to its new First Amendment rule: Under the general rule the Court applies in this case, Title VII hostile work environment claims would suddenly be unconstitutional.

Title VII makes it unlawful to discriminate "because of [an] individuals' race, color, religion, sex, or national origin," and the regulations covering hostile workplace claims forbid "sexual harassment," which includes "unwelcome sexual advances, requests for sexual favors, and other verbal or physical conduct of a sexual nature" which creates "an intimidating hostile or offensive working environment." The regulation does not prohibit workplace harassment generally: it focuses on what the majority would characterize as the "disfavored topic" of sexual harassment. In this way, Title VII is similar to the St. Paul ordinance that the majority condemns because it "imposes special prohibitions on those speakers who express views on disfavored subjects." Under the broad principle the Court uses to decide the present case, hostile work environment claims based on sexual harassment should fail First Amendment review; because a general ban on harassment in the workplace would cover the problem of sexual harassment, any attempt to proscribe the subcategory of sexually harassing expression would violate the First Amendment. . . .

As the third exception to the Court's theory for deciding this case, the majority concocts a catchall exclusion to protect against unforeseen problems, a concern that is heightened here given the lack of briefing on the majority's decisional theory. This final exception would apply in cases in which there is "no realistic possibility that official suppression of ideas is afoot." As I have demonstrated, this case does not concern the official suppression of ideas. The majority discards this notion out-of-hand.

As I see it, the Court's theory does not work and will do nothing more than confuse the law. Its selection of this case to rewrite First Amendment law is particularly inexplicable, because the whole problem could have been avoided by deciding this case under settled First Amendment principles. . . .

. . . Although the ordinance reaches conduct that is unprotected, it also makes criminal expressive conduct that causes only hurt feelings, offense, or resentment, and is protected by the First Amendment. The ordinance is therefore fatally overbroad and invalid on its face. . . .

Justice Stevens, concurring on the judgment . . .

. . . [[M]]y colleagues today wrestle with two broad principles: first, that certain "categories of expression [including 'fighting words'] are not within the area of 'constitutionally protected speech;'" and second, that "content-based regulations [of expression] are presumptively invalid." Although in past opinions the Court has repeated both of these maxims, it has—quite rightly—adhered to neither with the absolutism suggested by my colleagues. Thus, while I agree that the St. Paul ordinance is unconstitutionally overbroad for the reasons stated in part II of Justice White's opinion, I write separately to suggest how the allure of absolute principles has skewed the analysis of both the majority and concurring opinions. . . .

. . . Contrary to the broad dicta in *Mosley* and elsewhere, our decisions demonstrate that content-based distinctions, far from being presumptively invalid, are an inevitable and indispensable aspect of a coherent understanding of the First Amendment. . . .

Our First Amendment decisions have created a rough hierarchy in the constitutional protection of speech. Core political speech occupies the highest, most protected position; commercial speech and nonobscene, sexually explicit speech are regarded as a sort of second-class expression; obscenity and fighting words receive the least protection of all. Assuming that the Court is correct that this last class of speech is not wholly "unprotected," it certainly does not follow that fighting words and obscenity receive the same sort of protection afforded core political speech. Yet in ruling that proscribable speech cannot be regulated based on subject matter, the Court does just that. Perversely, this gives fighting words greater protection than is afforded commercial speech. If Congress can prohibit false advertising directed at airline passengers without also prohibiting false advertising directed at bus passengers and if a city can prohibit political advertisements in its buses while allowing other advertisements, it is ironic to hold that a city cannot regulate fighting words based on "race, color, creed, religion or gender" while leaving unregulated fighting words based on "union membership or homosexuality." The Court today turns First Amendment law on its head: Communication that was once entirely unprotected (and that still can be wholly proscribed) is now entitled to greater protection than commercial speech—and possibly greater protection than core political speech. . . .

In sum, the central premise of the Court's ruling—that "content-based regulations are presumptively invalid"—has simplistic appeal, but lacks support in our First Amendment jurisprudence. To make matters worse, the Court today extends this overstated claim to reach categories of hitherto unprotected speech and, in doing so, wreaks havoc in an area of settled law. Finally, although the Court recognizes exceptions to its new principle, those exceptions undermine its very conclusion that the St. Paul ordinance is unconstitutional. Stated directly, the majority's position cannot withstand scrutiny.

Although I agree with much of Justice White's analysis, I do not join part I-A of his opinion because I have reservations about the "categorical approach" to the First Amendment. . . .

Admittedly, the categorical approach to the First Amendment has some appeal: either expression is protected or it is not—the categories create safe harbors for governments and speakers alike. But this approach sacrifices subtlety for clarity and is, I am convinced, ultimately unsound. As an initial matter, the concept of "categories" fits poorly with the complex reality of expression. Few dividing lines in First Amendment law are straight and unwavering, and efforts at categorization inevitably give rise only to fuzzy boundaries. Our definitions of obscenity "and public forum" illustrate this all too well. The quest for doctrinal certainty through the definition of categories and subcategories is, in my opinion, destined to fail. . . .

In sum, the St. Paul ordinance (as construed by the Court) regulates expressive activity that is wholly proscribable and does so not on the basis of viewpoint, but rather in recognition of the different harms caused by such activity. Taken together, these several considerations persuade me that the St. Paul ordinance is not an unconstitutionally content-based regulation of speech. Thus, were the ordinance not overbroad, I would vote to uphold it. . . .

II. POST–*R.A.V.* DEVELOPMENTS

The Supreme Court invalidated St. Paul's Bias-Motivated Crime Ordinance because it contained content-based distinctions and was not narrowly tailored to serve a compelling state interest. Since the focus of the decision was on the unconstitutional character of the ordinance, not the act of cross burning itself, *R.A.V.* left open the possibility that cross burning could be prosecuted under content-neutral statutes. During the twentieth century, cross burning in the United States has been inextricably linked to the Ku Klux Klan. The Klan used the symbol to send threats of violence and to affirm the group's shared ideology of white Protestant supremacy. The first recorded case of a cross burning was in 1915, when a Georgia mob burned a large cross on Stone Mountain to celebrate the lynching of Leo Frank, a Jew unjustly convicted of killing a thirteen-year-old girl. In reaction to these events, the Klan was reborn, having largely died out during Reconstruction in the 1870s. A few months after the Frank lynching, the Klan burned a forty-foot cross on Stone Mountain at its first initiation ceremony. In the years that followed, the Klan engaged in many acts of violence that were often prefaced by cross burnings. In this way, the burning cross became a tool of intimidation and an implicit threat of impending violence. The Klan's record of intimidation and violence prompted Virginia to enact its first cross-burning statute in 1952. A couple of years later, the Supreme Court's decision in *Brown v. Board of Education* and the evolving civil rights movement sparked a resurgence of Klan violence in much of the South. Throughout this time period, the burning cross was also a symbol of Klan identity and ideology. At rallies and initiations, Klan members would light a cross on fire, raise their left arms toward the burning cross, and sing "The Old Rugged Cross."

Four months after the Supreme Court handed down *R.A.V.*, the federal government filed charges against R.A.V. and his fellow defendants under federal laws that neutrally prohibited acts and conspiracies of intimidation.[18] A district judge found all the defendants guilty in a bench trial and the Eighth Circuit Court of Appeals upheld the convictions in *United States v. J.H.H.* (1994), ruling that the federal statutes were qualitatively different from the ordinance invalidated in *R.A.V.* While St. Paul's ordinance punished only those defendants who aroused "anger, alarm, or resentment" on the basis of "race, color, creed, religion or gender," the federal statutes were "directed only at intentional threats, intimidation, and interference with federally guaranteed rights." Moreover, the statutes in question prohibited *any* threat or act of intimidation or *any* conspiracy to threaten or to intimidate, "regardless of the viewpoint guiding the action." Accordingly, the Eighth Circuit held that the federal statutes did not violate the *R.A.V.* principle that content-based regulations were presumptively invalid.[19]

In contrast to prohibitions of "hate speech," such as the one invalidated in *R.A.V.*, a number of states during the 1980s adopted "hate crime" statutes that authorized enhanced prison sentences for offenders who selected their victims "because of" their race, religion, color, disability, sexual orientation, national origin, or ancestry. One year after *R.A.V.* the Supreme Court considered the constitutionality of these statutes in *Wisconsin v. Mitchell* (1993), a case involving a racially motivated assault. After discussing a scene from the motion picture *Mississippi Burning*, a group of young African-Americans left an apartment. Once on the street, Todd Mitchell asked, "Do you feel hyped up to move on some white people?" Then, seeing a young white boy walking up the street, Mitchell asked, "You all want to fuck somebody up? There goes a white boy; go get him." The group beat the boy severely. Though Mitchell did not participate in the beating, he was convicted of aggravated battery. The sentencing judge, relying on a "hate crime" statute that authorized a maximum five-year enhancement, increased Mitchell's sentence from two to four years. The Wisconsin Supreme Court, however, overturned the conviction, reasoning that, since "the statute punishes the 'because of' aspect of the defendant's selection, the *reason* the defendant selected the victim, the *motive* behind the selection," it violated *R.A.V.* because "the Wisconsin legislature cannot criminalize bigoted thought with which it disagrees."[20] According to the Wisconsin Supreme Court, the statute violated free speech because it discriminated on the basis of ideology.

The Supreme Court unanimously reversed the Wisconsin decision. In an opinion written by Chief Justice William Rehnquist, the Court noted that sentencing judges traditionally "have considered a wide variety of factors in addition to evidence bearing on guilt in determining what sentence to impose on a convicted defendant." Accordingly, though "a defendant's abstract beliefs, however obnoxious to most people, may not be taken into consideration by a sentencing judge," there was no *per se* First Amendment barrier to the admission of evidence concerning a convicted defendant's beliefs and associations at sentencing. Rehnquist pointed to federal and state antidiscrimination laws to bolster his position that a racial motive can elevate an offender's culpability. If the state can make it unlawful for an employer to discriminate against an employee "because of such individual's race, color, religion, sex, or national origin," the state can enhance the penalties for offenders who select their victims "because of" the same characteristics. Nothing in *R.A.V.* compelled a different result, Rehnquist insisted. Whereas "the ordinance struck down in *R.A.V.* was explicitly directed at expression (i.e., 'speech' or 'messages'), the statute in this case is aimed at conduct unprotected by the First Amendment." Moreover, Rehnquist added, the state has singled out "bias-inspired conduct" for sentence enhancement because "this conduct is thought to inflict greater individual and societal harm" than ordinary crime. It is more likely "to provoke retaliatory crimes, inflict distinct emotional harms on their victims, and incite community unrest." The legislature, which has "the primary responsibility for fixing criminal penalties," has elevated the punishment for such crimes to prevent these harms, not to punish the offender's beliefs or biases. Accordingly, Wisconsin was not engaged in unconstitutional content or viewpoint discrimination. [21]

Despite the Supreme Court's unanimous opinion upholding their constitutionality, "hate crime" statutes remain controversial, at least in certain academic circles. Critics charge that enhancing criminal sentences based on, for example, an offender's racist or sexist motive is at times indistinguishable from punishing the offender for his thoughts and beliefs because the motive and the underlying ideology are so inextricably linked together that the state cannot punish one without punishing the other.[22] Whatever the merits of this criticism, the political trend in favor of "hate crime" legislation has continued unabated since the *Mitchell* decision. In 1994, Congress mandated that the federal sentencing guidelines authorize additional punishment for offenders motivated by race, color, religion, national origin, ethnicity, gender, disability, or sexual orientation.[23] By 1995, thirty-seven states and the District of Columbia had enacted various types of "hate crime" statutes. Later in the decade, two tragic incidents mobilized political support for additional "hate crimes" legislation. In October of 1998, two men beat Mathew Shepard, a twenty-one-year-old gay student at the University of Wyoming, unconscious and lashed him to a fence post to die in near-freezing conditions. In the same year, three white men in Texas chained James Byrd Jr., an African-American, to the back of a pickup truck and dragged him to his death. Two of the three defendants were members of white supremacy organizations. In response, the Texas state legislature passed a "hate crimes" statute (the James Byrd Jr. Hate Crimes Act of 2001) that was stronger and broader than its predecessor. By 2003, forty-six states had enacted "hate crime" statutes, a trend that has to some extent marginalized the above free speech objection.

By the mid-1990s, it was fairly well settled that cross burning could be prosecuted under general statutes that prohibited "fighting words," "true threats," or "acts and conspiracies of intimidation" and that states could enhance the penalties of criminals who selected their victims "because of" their race, religion, color, disability, sexual orientation, national origin, or ancestry. What was not clear was the constitutionality of statutes that focused exclusively on cross burning. Were these statutes obviously constitutional since they only prohibited conduct? Or, by prohibiting the use of only one symbol, did these statutes constitute viewpoint discrimination and run afoul of *R.A.V.*'s ban on governmental censorship? The St. Paul ordinance invalidated in *R.A.V.* had mentioned a "burning cross," along with a Nazi swastika, as a possible symbol or object that could arouse "anger, alarm, or resentment" in others on the basis of "race, color, creed, religion or gender." Since the ordinance only banned cross burnings that aroused the above feelings in terms of the above characteristics, it constituted content discrimination and was therefore unconstitutional. Did *R.A.V.* require the same result if a statute banned only cross burning or only cross burnings that were intended to threaten or intimidate? Following *R.A.V.*, courts in Maryland and South Carolina invalidated laws prohibiting cross burning because they unconstitutionally discriminated on the basis of content, while courts in California and Florida upheld them because they neutrally punished an act that was a threat and/or a fighting word.[24]

On May 2, 1998, Richard Elliott and Jonathan O'Mara, who were not in any way affiliated with the Klan, attempted to burn a cross in the yard of James Jubillee, an African-American who lived next door to Elliott in Virginia Beach, Virginia. Their motive was to "get back" at Jubillee for complaining about Elliott firing a gun in his backyard. On August 22, 1998, Barry Black organized a Ku Klux Klan rally of twenty-five to thirty people on private property in Carroll County, Virginia. A 25 to 30-foot cross, which was located between 300 and 350 yards from a state highway, was burned at the event. Local authorities prosecuted Elliott, O'Mara, and Black for violating Virginia's cross-burning statute, which made it "unlawful for any person or persons, with the intent of intimidating any person or group of persons, to burn, or cause to be burned, a cross on the property of another, a highway or other public place." Private cross burnings and cross burnings without the intent to intimidate were legal, but the statute added that burning a cross "shall be prima facie evidence of an intent to intimidate a person or group of persons." A jury could convict on the basis of the cross burning itself, so long as the defendant did not rebut the initial presumption. Pursuant to a plea agreement, O'Mara pleaded guilty to attempted cross burning and conspiracy to commit cross burning, but retained his right to challenge the constitutionality of the cross-burning statute. Following their convictions in separate jury trials, Elliott and Black appealed. The Virginia Supreme Court reversed all three convictions on the ground that the statute was "analytically indistinguishable from the ordinance found unconstitutional in *R.A.V.*" The law discriminated on the basis of content because it "selectively chooses only cross burning because of its distinctive message." In addition, the prima facie evidence provision rendered the statute overbroad because it chilled protected speech.[25] Virginia appealed to the Supreme Court.

In the brief he filed to the Supreme Court on Virginia's behalf, William H. Hurd, State Solicitor and Counsel of Record, claimed that the statute, unlike the municipal ordinance invalidated in *R.A.V.*, was content-neutral. Since the statute was first enacted in 1952, when racial segregation was commonplace in Virginia, it was ludicrous to think that the statute's purpose was to suppress the ideology of Protestant white supremacy. Though it is true that the law in question only banned burning a cross, not a circle or square, it nonetheless only reached proscribable speech and it did so in a content-neutral way. However, if the Supreme Court found that the statute did constitute content or viewpoint discrimination, it was yet constitutional, Hurd argued, because it fit all three exceptions established in *R.A.V.* The cross-burning statute prohibited an egregious type of intimidation; reduced the undesirable secondary effects of cross burnings; and was not in any way related to the suppression of ideas. Lastly, the statute was not unconstitutionally overbroad. The statute only covered cross burners who intended to intimidate. If, however, the Court found that the prima facie evidence provision rendered the statute overbroad, it should invalidate this provision without invalidating the entire statute.

Rodney Smolla, a professor of law at the University of Richmond School of Law, authored the brief filed on behalf of Barry Black, Richard Elliott, and Jonathan O'Mara. In his brief, Smolla described "viewpoint-neutrality" as a "dynamic requirement that cuts across all other First Amendment doctrines." Accordingly, he argued, it did not matter that intentional threats and intimidation were outside of free speech. Virginia nonetheless could not single out cross burning and prohibit it without engaging in unconstitutional viewpoint discrimination. No doubt a burning cross was frequently a "tool" of intimidation, but it was also a symbol "with a variety of connotations relating to race, religion, politics, and prejudice." By prohibiting cross burning, Virginia was suppressing a symbol "laden with many communicative emanations and meanings." According to Smolla, the state could not engage in the suppression of such a symbol without engaging in viewpoint discrimination. For the same reason, Virginia's statute did not fit any of the three *R.A.V.* exceptions to the rule that viewpoint or content discrimination was unconstitutional. By suppressing a single symbol that "conjures up" a set of messages and meanings, Virginia cannot claim that it is merely punishing a subclass of unprotected speech, preventing certain secondary effects of expressive conduct, or not engaging in "official suppression of ideas." Lastly, Smolla insisted that the prima face evidence provision both exacerbated the problem of content and viewpoint discrimination and rendered the entire statute overbroad.

In a reply brief, Virginia emphasized certain analogies that later resurfaced during oral argument on December 11, 2002, presided over by Justice John Paul Stevens because Chief Justice William Rehnquist was recovering from knee surgery. Was cross burning more like flag burning, which was constitutionally protected, or was it more like brandishing a gun, which everyone agreed was outside constitutional protection? Hurd claimed cross burning was fundamentally different from flag burning because a flag burner stands in opposition "to the government or to some idea that the unburned flag is viewed as representing." In contrast, a cross burner does not burn a cross to express opposition to Christianity, but rather to instill fear, just as a thug instills fear by brandishing a gun. Smolla struggled during oral argument to advance the contrary positions. He conceded that the government had a "functional purpose" for punishing anyone who brandished a gun because a gun was not just a symbol. It was a weapon and the government can regulate its use for that reason: a reason that was totally unrelated to the content of any message that a brandished gun may convey. A burning cross, on the other hand, was not a weapon of any sort. It was merely a symbol. The government could not prohibit it without engaging in unconstitutional censorship.

Justice Clarence Thomas, the second African-American ever appointed to the Supreme Court, played an unusually active and forceful role during oral argument in *Virginia v. Black*. Ever since his appointment to the Supreme Court in 1991, he has said little or nothing at oral arguments, including the oral argument that took place in *R.A.V.* on December 4, 1991, several weeks after his confirmation on October 15. In the cross-burning case argued eleven years later, however, Thomas, in a booming voice, interrupted Deputy Solicitor General Michael R. Dreeben, who was defending the federal government's position that Virginia's statute was constitutional. Thomas warned Dreeben that he was understating the effects of cross burning by comparing it to simple cases of intimidation. According to Thomas, the burning cross was a symbol of a "reign of terror" and that it was intended "to terrorize a population." In the new post-9/11 era, Thomas's chilling references to terrorism changed the atmosphere in the courtroom and perhaps marked a turning point in the case. Many of those present appeared to be deeply affected by what Thomas had said, including the other justices, a number of whom referred back to his comments later in the oral argument.[26]

Is it possible that the lone African-American justice on the Court, one who had faced discrimination himself during his youth in Pin Point, Georgia, had special insight into the evils of cross burning? Do you think Thomas knows more about the negative effects of a burning cross than his white colleagues or does his personal experience and knowledge actually disable him from appreciating the free speech implications of the Virginia statute? Do you think his white colleagues should defer to Thomas's perception of what a burning cross means? Was the Court better able to come to a correct decision in this case because Justice Thomas was on the Court? If so, should future justices be selected to some extent on the basis of their racial identity? Is racial diversity on the Supreme Court a good thing? A necessary thing?

In its decision in *Virginia v. Black*, handed down on April 7, 2003, the Supreme Court splintered over the issue of the constitutionality of cross burning. On one side, in dissent, Justice Thomas claimed that cross burning done for the purpose of intimidation was conduct, not expression, and therefore the free speech tests used in *O'Brien* (draft card burning) or *Texas v. Johnson* (flag burning) were simply not applicable to the Virginia statute. In Thomas's view, all three convictions should be upheld. On the other side, Justice Souter wrote an opinion, joined by Justices Kennedy and Ginsburg, that favored overturning all three convictions on the ground that the Virginia statute was unconstitutional because it contained content-based distinctions in violation of *R.A.V.* Justice O'Connor's opinion, joined by Justices Stevens, Scalia, and Breyer and the Chief Justice, held that the Virginia's statute, though content-based, was constitutional since it met the "special virulence" exception established in *R.A.V.* These five justices supported the constitutionality of statutes prohibiting cross burning done with the intent to intimidate, but they could not agree on whether the prima facie evidence provision contained in Virginia's statute rendered the statute overbroad. Justice Scalia had no problem with the provision, though he thought the jury instruction given in the case of Barry Black was unconstitutional. Accordingly, he voted to affirm the convictions of Elliott and O'Mara, but vacate Black's, with the understanding that Virginia could retry the case if it wanted to. The other four justices vacated all the convictions and dismissed the indictment against Black (presumably on the ground that the statute could not constitutionally be applied to a cross burning at a Klan rally), but granted Virginia the option of retrying both Elliott and O'Mara. Excerpts from the opinions written by Justices Thomas, Souter, and O'Connor are included below.

Though the decision was a splintered one, it clearly upheld the constitutionality of statutes prohibiting cross burning done with the intent to intimidate, so long as they did not contain prima facie evidence provisions like the one found in the Virginia statute. The Court defined "intimidation" as a type of "true threat" in which a "speaker directs a threat to a person or group of persons with the intent of placing the victim in fear of bodily harm or death." The decision leaves unanswered the question whether states can prohibit the intentional use of other symbols "to intimidate" others in the above sense of that term. Throughout this litigation, Virginia claimed that a burning cross was a "unique" symbol, but never conceded that the state could not prohibit the intentional use of other symbols for the purpose of intimidation. In fact, since 1983 Virginia has prohibited placing "a swastika on any church, synagogue or other building or place used for religious worship, or on any school, educational facility or community center owned or operated by a church or religious body" with the "intent of intimidating another person or group of persons."[27]

Whether Virginia's swastika law fits into *R.A.V.*'s "special virulence" exception is an interesting question, especially since it prohibits placing swastikas only on buildings owned by religious organizations. Is such a law content-neutral? Does it violate free speech because it constitutes governmental censorship? What about other symbols that are historically associated with violence: the skull and crossbones, the hammer and sickle, gang colors and symbols? Are these symbols constitutionally subject to state regulation if used for the purpose of placing someone in fear of bodily harm? And what about symbols that constitute, not threats, but fighting words? Could a state punish someone who displays a Confederate flag, not for the purpose of intimidation, but for the purpose of inflicting a "psychic injury" or provoking a violent reaction? Could burning the American flag be prohibited if done with the intent to provoke violence? Does *Virginia v. Black* require at least a partial reconsideration of *Texas v. Johnson*? Do questions of this sort ultimately depend on whether free speech is, first and foremost, a limited individual right or a command to the government not to engage in censorship?

BRIEFS

VIRGINIA'S BRIEF

[[1. Content-Neutrality.]] . . . [[T]]he St. Paul ordinance was invalid not because it banned fighting words, but because it banned *only* those fighting words which were addressed to *specific disfavored subjects*.

The Virginia statute is markedly different. First, the focus of the Virginia statute is intimidation. Fighting words and the intimidation are alike in that they can both be constitutionally proscribed. . . . But intimidation is a far more insidious evil. Hurling an epithet may sometimes provoke a breach of the peace in the heat of the moment, but the danger is likely soon to pass. It is different with intimidation. A threat to do bodily harm to an individual or his family is likely to sink deep into the psyche of its victim, acquiring more force over time. . . . "The value of a sword of Damocles is that it hangs—not that it drops."

Second, and more importantly, unlike the St. Paul ordinance, the Virginia law is not limited to any set of disfavored subjects. It applies whenever *anyone* burns a cross to intimidate *anyone* for *any* reason. Political affiliation, union membership *vel non*, sexual orientation, age, gender, personal grievance: it makes no difference what may prompt the intimidation. So long as there is an intent to intimidate, *all* acts of cross burning are banned. All are subject to the same punishment. Thus, the statute is content-neutral. . . .

Although the lower court conceded that the Virginia statute contains no content-based categories, it was not satisfied with this level of inquiry. Instead, it looked to what it thought was the legislature's "motivating purpose" and found it problematic. . . .

There is nothing here to show any purpose other than a wholly legitimate one. Indeed, there is very little to show legislative purpose at all. There is no legislative preamble, no committee report and no official record of floor debates. Instead, there are several old newspaper articles, cited by the Virginia Supreme Court, showing a rash of cross burnings in the years leading up to passage of the original statute in 1952. These incidents were, in the words of the time, "un-American act[s], designed to intimidate Negroes from seeking their rights as citizens." The articles also report the stated purpose of the measure. The bill was presented to the House of Delegates by a former FBI agent, Delegate Mills E. Godwin, Jr., who later became twice Governor of Virginia. According to the article: "Godwin said law and order in the State were impossible if organized groups could create fear by intimidation." This is the best available statement of the motivating purpose, and it is wholly legitimate.

The decision below seems to imply that the statute may have been enacted as a gesture of modern day political correctness. History belies the suggestion. In 1952, when the statute was enacted, racial segregation was still the prevailing practice— and often the law—in Virginia. Indeed, the General Assembly that originally banned cross burning in 1952 was substantially the same legislature as the one that soon initiated a campaign of "massive resistance" in response to this Court's decision in *Brown v. Board of Education*. Clearly, the legislature's purpose was *not* to usher in a new era of racial equality, or to disfavor ideas of white supremacy. The purpose was to prevent a particularly virulent form of intimidation and thus to preserve law and order. It is a purpose still legitimate today. . . .

The court below did not find that cross burning is limited to the Klan, or that the tactic can only be used by persons espousing ideas of racial or religious bigotry. Nor have respondents made such a suggestion. Indeed, this case would refute any such claim. Two respondents—Elliot and O'Mara—burned a cross to frighten a neighbor in Virginia Beach. Yet, they are not Klansmen, nor do they have any discernible ideas on race, religion or any other topic. They burned a cross on the neighbor's lawn because he asked questions about gunfire in Elliot's backyard. Elliot and O'Mara did not have a political agenda, they had a personal grievance. People of *any* race can be frightened by cross burnings. So intimidating was the incident in Carroll County that one witness—who is Caucasian—was brought to tears, fearing for the safety of her children and home.

A burning cross—standing alone and without explanation—is understood in our society as a message of intimidation. . . . A white, conservative, middle-class Protestant, waking up at night to find a burning cross outside his home, will reasonably understand that someone is threatening him. His reaction is likely to be very different than if he were to find, say, a burning circle or square. In the latter case, he may call the fire department. In the former, he will probably call the police. . . .

The Virginia Supreme Court also suggested that the Virginia statute is impermissibly content-based because, while it bans the burning of crosses with intent to intimidate, it does not ban the burning of "other geometric shapes," such as "circles and squares." Yet there is a good reason for focusing on crosses. There is a history and practice of intimidation by cross burning that has no counterpart with other geometric shapes. The record contains no evidence of anyone ever burning a circle or square for any expressive purpose, much less a purpose of intimidation. Indeed, the Commonwealth is unaware of a single reported American case concerning a burning circle or a burning square used to intimidate. In our society, a burning cross *means* intimidation. By contrast, burning a circle or a square expresses nothing. As the Virginia Supreme Court recognized, "no animating message is contained in such an act." Given this concession, it is difficult to understand why the Virginia Supreme Court thought content discrimination was afoot. Indeed, it is not.

Perhaps someday, somewhere, somebody in Virginia may intimidate someone—and simultaneously express an idea—by burning some geometric shape other than a cross. But such speculation does not make the current law invalid. "States adopt laws to address the problems that confront them. The First Amendment does not require states to regulate problems that do not exist." The Virginia statute seeks to deal with a tactic of intimidation that has been a source of trouble in the past, without speculating about future developments, and without trivializing cross burning by equating it, say, with a burning Jack O'Lantern impishly left on a neighbor's porch at Halloween. . . .

[[2. The *R.A.V.* Exceptions.]] [[*R.A.V.*]] . . . recognized three broad exceptions to the general rule against content-based distinctions. Assuming *arguendo* that the Virginia cross burning statute constitutes "content discrimination," it nevertheless qualifies as constitutional under all three exceptions.

In laying out its first exception, *R.A.V.* said that a subclass of proscribable speech may be signaled out when it manifests, in some extreme form, the concerns that allow the whole class to be proscribed. . . . Just as a state may choose to prohibit only that obscenity which is *most lascivious*, it may also choose to enact a statute focusing on acts of intimidation that are *most virulent* —that is to say, acts that demonstrate with "special force" the reasons why "threats of violence are outside the First Amendment." The court has given three such reasons: "protecting individuals [1] from the fear of violence, [2] from the disruption that fear engenders, and [3] from the possibility that the threatened violence will occur.". . .

It is no accident that the Ku Klux Klan—grand masters of intimidation—chose a burning cross to do their work. Such a structure instills fear in a way that mere words can rarely equal. As this Court has recognized, use of a symbol bypasses the need for the victim to read and decipher the message, so as to make the effect penetrating and immediate. It is a "short cut from mind to mind." The symbol of a burning cross is especially powerful. It takes fire—an archetype of destruction—and marries it with a deeply evocative icon of Christianity, transmogrifying a sign of heavenly assurance into a hellish threat. The impact is underscored when the cross is burned at night—as is usually the case—when the cover of darkness hides the identity of the perpetrators and taps into the basic human fears of the unknown.

Moreover, the business of constructing, transporting, erecting and igniting a cross suggests more than the effort of a single individual. It suggests the presence of a group, whose size and membership are unknown, but whose malevolence—and whose resolve to *act* on that malevolence—is plain enough. The flames are not only a *metaphor* for destruction, they demonstrate a *means* of destruction. By burning a cross in public view, the perpetrators step beyond words, even beyond conventional symbolism, and provide a physical example of what may come. By an act of destruction, they assert their ability—and their will—to engage in further acts of destruction. This is especially so when the victim's own property has been invaded. The message of a cross burning is this:

> We may kill you, or hurt you badly. Believe it. We have already come to your home, and we have done this hateful and dangerous thing in front of you. So, we don't just talk. We act. Next time we may torch your home. Or bomb your car. Or shoot into your windows. No one stopped us when we burned the cross. No one will stop us next time either: Fear us.

These considerations make cross burning an especially fearsome weapon, thus implicating with "special force" the first reason why threats are constitutionally proscribable—i.e. "fear of violence.". . .

For the second *R.A.V.* exception, this Court turned to the "secondary effects" doctrine. . . .

. . . In *Renton [[v. Playtime Theatres, Inc.* (1986)]], the Court approved the challenged ordinance [[that prohibited an adult theatre within 1000 feet of a residential zone, single- or multiple-family dwelling, church, park, or school]] because it was designed to "prevent crime, protect the city's retail trade, maintain property values, and generally [protect] and [preserve] the quality of [the city's] neighborhoods, commercial district, and the quality of urban life." Similarly, the Virginia cross burning statute is intended not just to prevent intimidation of the victim, but to preserve law and order in the surrounding community. Cross burnings are historically associated not with threatened fisticuffs or other minor assault, but with threats to burn, lynch, behead or otherwise murder innocent victims. It is not hard to imagine how unchecked spates of intimidation by cross burning could spark retaliation, retard commerce, depress property values and generally transform our society into one reminiscent of Northern Ireland or the Balkans. It was to preserve law and order—and thereby "insure domestic tranquility"—that the General Assembly saw fit to ban cross-burning fifty years ago. There is no reason to question its judgment now. . . .

For its third exception, *R.A.V.* describes a broad "catch-all" category of content-based distinctions, saying "it may be not even be necessary to identify any particular 'neutral' basis, so long as the nature of the content discrimination is such that there is no realistic possibility that official suppression of ideas is afoot." Here, no such possibility exists.

Assuming *arguendo* that the Virginia statute contains some form of content-based distinction, it nevertheless qualifies for this third exception as shown by an array of pertinent facts. First, the statute contains no content-based categories. It bans *all* cross burning with intent to intimidate not just cross burning that conveys racial and religious bigotry. Second, the law was originally enacted by a legislature that embraced a policy of racial inequality. Suppressing such ideas could not have been its purpose. Third, while the Commonwealth no longer adheres to a policy of segregation, Virginia law still leaves ample opportunity for such ideas to be expressed—as the First Amendment requires—so long as they are not intertwined with intimidation. Simply causing "resentment" or "ill-feeling" is not enough to run afoul the Virginia statute. Fourth, the plausibility of the asserted purpose—to preserve law and order—is confirmed by the spate of cross burnings that preceded the law. Fifth, no comparable form of intimidation was being practiced—not in 1952, and not now. . . . In sum, there is no "realistic possibility" that official suppression of ideas is afoot. Cross burning with the intent to intimidate "[a]t its core, is an act of terrorism that inflicts pain on its victim, not the expression of an idea." . . .

[[3. Overbreadth.]] The Virginia Supreme Court also ruled that the cross burning statute is void under the overbreadth doctrine. . . .

. . . [[The Virginia court]] looked at the statutory inference, which allows—but does not require—a jury to infer an intent to intimidate based on the act of cross burning alone. The court did not doubt that the prosecutor still must prove every element of the offense—including intent—beyond a reasonable doubt. Nor did the court otherwise suggest that the statute fails to meet the constitutional requirements that ordinarily govern statutory presumptions. Instead, the court focused on the mere *possibility* of arrest and prosecution. . . . In other words, what concerned the court was the possibility that an *innocent* cross-burner—i.e., one who burns a cross *without* an intent to intimidate—might still be arrested and prosecuted. The conduct of such a person is not barred by the statute; yet, the court thought the prospect of a trial might chill innocent expression, and that the mere possibility of such an occurrence was sufficient to make the Virginia statute overbroad. This is error. . . .

. . . [[T]]he mere possibility that someone might be mistakenly charged does not render a statute overbroad. Indeed, if the lower court were correct in its approach, it would be difficult for *any* regulation of expressive conduct to withstand scrutiny. There will always be cases where conduct [[that]] is lawful initially appears culpable and result[[s]] in charges that are ultimately dismissed. For example, this Court has held that government may constitutionally prohibit possession of child pornography, even where the same images would not be proscribable as obscene if their subjects were adults. Yet, when confronted with the printed image of a youthful individual engaged in sex, law enforcement officers necessarily must evaluate whether the individual appears to be a minor before deciding whether to make an arrest. Sometimes the evaluation may be difficult. Sometimes the evaluation may be mistaken. Yet, the possibility that law enforcement might err does not make these important statutes "overbroad." Pornographers who prefer "barely legal" models—those who recently turned 18 and who look even younger—may be deterred in some instances, or they may find it advisable to surround their work with assurances of their subjects' adult status. Yet, so long as the statute's *prohibitory* terms do not reach too far, these collateral effects are not the sort of "chill" the overbreadth doctrine is designed to prevent. . . .

[[If, however,]] . . . the Court agrees that the statute's prohibitory terms are constitutional—but concludes that the statutory presumption is not—the statute should not be stricken on its face. Instead, the presumption should be severed and the rest of the statute allowed to stand. . . .

Respectfully submitted,

JERRY W. KILGORE,
Attorney General of Virginia

WILLIAM H. HURD,
State Solicitor & Counsel of Record

RESPONDENT'S BRIEF

[[1. Content Discrimination.]] . . . Certain symbols—the American Flag, the Star of David, the Cross, the swastika—exude powerful magnetic charges, positive and negative, and are often invoked to express beliefs and emotions high and low, sublime and base, from patriotism, faith, or love to dissent, bigotry, or hate. Symbolic expression is often combined with group expression, such as sit-ins, meetings, marches, or rallies. Symbolic expression may be relatively simple and passive, such as the wearing of a black armband to protest the war in Vietnam. Quite often, however, symbolic expression is far more incendiary and graphic. Symbolic expression may involve either the consecration or the desecration of a symbol. A flag may be proudly waved or angrily defiled, a cross may be reverently worshiped or wrathfully burned. The destruction or defilement of a symbol is often the method through which a speaker communicates the intensity of the message, which may frequently be a message defiant of authority or disrespectful of mainstream values and sensibilities.

If this Court were to draw a distinction between the St. Paul ordinance struck down in *R.A.V.* and the Virginia cross-burning statute, a dramatic and dangerous rift would suddenly be created in First Amendment law, a rift treating articulated verbal content discrimination (such as that in *R.A.V.*) as different *in kind* from symbolic content discrimination. Symbolic expression would thereby be rendered a second-class First Amendment citizen. Decades of First Amendment cases are aligned against any such move.

Cross-burning is a shorthand, as all symbolic speech is a shorthand, speaking heart-to-heart and mind-to-mind. The central principle animating the First Amendment is that the government may not censor speech on the basis of viewpoint, and this principle is as important in the context of symbols as it is in the context of language. Cross-burning, like flag-burning, is undoubtedly offensive and disturbing to most citizens. Yet . . . [[the]] Constitution protects not only the analytic vocabulary of the mind but the inarticulate speech of the heart. . . .

Virginia seems to believe that it may browse the universe of symbols, passing laws targeting those it does not like. In the same section of its statutory code that contains the cross-burning law, for example, Virginia has enacted a provision, worded identically, targeting swastikas. Yet a burning cross cannot be made a form of expressive contraband. The state cannot by fiat brand this one symbol as taboo, eliminating its use in social discourse. The government may no more single out a burning cross for especially disfavorable legal treatment than it may single out a burned or mutilated American flag, or the likeness of Osama bin Laden, or a swastika.

To go down the road suggested by Virginia would be perilous business, for if the government is permitted to select one symbol for banishment from public discourse there are few limiting principles to prevent it from selecting others. And it is but a short step from the banning of offending symbols such as burning crosses or flags to the banning of offending words. A word is, after all, but a symbol itself, "the skin of a living thought."

Virginia and its supporting *amici* incessantly repeat the mantra that the Virginia law requires an intent to intimidate. But the point of *R.A.V.* is that it does not matter. A law banning "fighting words" is permissible, but not a law banning "racist fighting words." A law banning intimidation is permissible if the concept of "intimidation" is sufficiently confined, but not a law banning "intimidation-through-cross-burning." *R.A.V.* teaches that viewpoint-neutrality is a First Amendment prime, a dynamic requirement that cuts across all other First Amendment doctrines. The content and viewpoint discrimination in Virginia's cross-burning law inheres in the prohibition of cross-burning alone. Virginia's labored effort to convince this Court that the statute's exclusive focus on burning crosses is *not* content-based ultimately collapses on itself and dissolves into incoherence, for the statute only makes logical sense if it is construed as driven by Virginia's concern with *what is communicated* when a cross is burned. . . .

Try as it might, Virginia cannot read the burning cross out of its cross-burning law. Even cross-burning laws that are otherwise constitutional violate the First Amendment simply and completely because they *are* cross-burning laws. Any suggestion that cross-burning is *intrinsically* intimidating is wordplay. . . .

. . . Virginia's insistence that cross-burning and intimidation are essentially equivalent, so that cross-burning is deemed either inherently intimidating, or at least usually intimidating, is based entirely on Virginia's invocation of our societal experience with cross-burning, and principally with cross-burning as a ritual practice of the Ku Klux Klan. The Supreme Court of Virginia cogently observed that the State "cannot have it both ways," ignoring the history of cross-burning in one part of its argument and invoking it in the next.

Virginia's history, of course, is far from unique. Cross-burning has long been a well-recognized ritual of the Ku Klux Klan, a symbol with intense political and religious resonance, often communicating hatred. . . . [[And it is true that]] the burning cross is often a *tool* for intimidation and harassment. No one disputes that. But it is not a tool in the same sense that a gun or a knife is a tool. The burning cross is a *symbol* . . . with a variety of connotations relating to race, religion, politics, and prejudice.

Again it should be emphasized that neither Barry Elton Black, who is a Klan leader, nor Richard J. Elliott and Jonathan O'Mara, who have no affiliation with the Klan, claim that the constitutional infirmity of the Virginia cross-burning law resides in any deliberate intent by the Virginia legislature to suppress the Klan or its ideological agenda. Nor was this the holding of the Supreme Court of Virginia below. Rather, as the Supreme Court of Virginia correctly reasoned, the difficulty with the Virginia cross-burning statute is not that it is calculated to suppress the Ku Klux Klan or a message of white supremacy, but that it seeks to suppress one symbol laden with many communicative emanations and meanings. As the Supreme Court of Virginia understood, the cross is not just any geometric shape, a vertical pole traversed by a horizontal bar. The cross is a symbol steeped in meaning, and cross-burning is a ritual steeped in expression.

The Supreme Court of Virginia thus correctly emphasized that the cross-burning law focused on one form of symbolic speech, a burning cross, leaving other geometric configurations, such as circles and squares, untouched. Somewhat derisively, the State chides the Supreme Court of Virginia on this issue, reasoning that the legislature cannot be faulted for failing to include all symbols.

Respectfully, it is the State of Virginia, not the Supreme Court of Virginia, that misses the point. Of course Virginia did not make it a crime to burn a circle or square. And why not? Because such a law would have targeted mere impotent gibberish. In our societal experience burning circles and squares have acquired no meanings; to burn them would be fury signifying nothing, to ban such burning would be a silly and meaningless legislative act. So too, Virginia's ban on cross-burning is an act of legislative nonsense *unless* it is interpreted as grounded in what is communicated when the cross is ignited. In noting the law's failure to include benign symbols such as squares and circles the Supreme Court of Virginia thus persuasively underscored the verisimilitude of its judgment that the law was content-based. . . .

Virginia pushes a red-herring in its many ingenious attempts to explain its law as resting on something other than "political correctness." Whether Virginia's legislature in 1952 was or was not racist, or whether Virginia's legislature in 1952 did or did not single-mindedly seek to suppress the Ku Klux Klan, are simply issues that do not matter, if the *means* chosen by the legislators to accomplish their mix of objectives and motivations, whatever they may have been, was geared to the content of speech. . . .

There are no valid governmental interests underlying cross-burning statutes that cannot be vindicated through content-neutral criminal laws. Laws of general applicability, proscribing palpable conduct that incites or threatens physical harm do not violate the First Amendment. Beyond that, under this Court's ruling in *Wisconsin v. Mitchell* (1993), hate *crime* laws, singling out for special punishment conduct undertaken out of biased motivation, are also constitutional. . . .

[[2. *R.A.V.* Exceptions.]] Virginia argues that even if its cross-burning law is construed as content- or viewpoint-based, the statute remains valid under three "exceptions" purportedly established in *R.A.V.* . . . [[However,]] Virginia . . . interpret[[s]] the three alleged exceptions so expansively that the net effect is to entirely marginalize the central and vital First Amendment principles *R.A.V.* embraced.

. . . Virginia's claim . . . that its cross-burning law reaches only "secondary effects" is an attempt to extend the secondary effects doctrine in a manner this Court has clearly rejected. Once again Virginia confuses ulterior motive with surface means. The secondary effects doctrine of *Renton v. Playtime Theatres, Inc.* (1986) and its progeny is grounded in the supposition that regulation of sexually-oriented adult establishments may be justified because such businesses often attract other social ills such as crime or prostitution. The secondary effects doctrine therefore posits that the social harm at which the government regulation at issue is aimed flows not from the communicative impact of the speaker's message, but from harms extraneous to that communicative impact, harms that tend to correlate with certain types of speech activity.

When the communicative impact of the expressive activity is what causes the alleged harm, however, the secondary effects doctrine may not be invoked. Plainly, it is the communicative impact of a burning cross that allegedly engenders intimidation. Virginia's entire case is otherwise incoherent. The secondary effects doctrine simply has no place here.

In a remarkable passage, Virginia in its Brief actually places in bold typeface the "message" that it claims is communicated by cross-burning. Virginia then argues that because this message, apparently endemic to cross-burning, is "especially virulent," the State is entitled to ban it under an "exception" in *R.A.V.* supposedly approving of content or viewpoint discrimination for such especially dangerous messages. . . .

The cross, however, is a communicative symbol, highly charged with religious, historical, social, and political meanings. The burning of a cross, like the burning of the flag, or the effigy of a political leader, intentionally plays on those religious, historical, social, and political meanings to add emotional and psychological intensity to the message, a message likely to be seen by many onlookers as perversion, blaspheme, or sacrilege. Admittedly, it may also be seen, in a given time and place, as a true threat. But it cannot plausibly be maintained . . . that *every* act of cross-burning is a threat. Virginia's law thus does not merely define a subclass partaking of elements generic to all threats, but rather instead introduces a further content distinction, the burning of one symbol heavily laden with expressive connotations and meanings.

To put the point another way, compare a law targeting threats against the President with a law targeting threats accomplished through cross-burning. The two are not equivalent. The law targeting threats against the President creates a subclass within the broad category of threats geared to the *identity* of the intended victim—the President—and grounded in the policy judgment that such a threat is especially dangerous and damaging to the polity. The presidential threat law contains no additional and gratuitous reference to any particular symbol or message; it bans all threats directed [[at]] one identified victim. Indeed, the law does not target expression *as such*, but merely targets the conduct of threatening a specific target, the President. That speech might be used to establish a violation of the law is merely an application of the principle that the mere evidentiary use of speech to establish illegal intent does not violate the

First Amendment. A cross-burning law, in contrast, does not focus exclusively on intent, or on victim-identity, but on the invocation of a specific symbol. In a final catch-all argument, Virginia claims that under *R.A.V.* content and viewpoint discrimination are excusable when, in the words of *R.A.V.*, "there is no realistic possibility that official suppression of ideas is afoot." Virginia's understanding of this isolated passage in *R.A.V.* is that as long as its *underlying* motivations were the altruistic goals of sheltering citizens from fear and maintaining law and order, the law is constitutional. If this is all that *R.A.V.* means, it means nothing. . . .

. . . [[U]]nder our First Amendment traditions to single out for special treatment one symbol in this manner *does* pose a danger that suppression of ideas is afoot. When a legislative body uses *language* to define its expressive target, it is relatively simple to locate and identify with precision the nature of the offending viewpoint discrimination. When a legislative body uses a *symbol* to define its expressive target, the nature of the viewpoint discrimination is often less determinate, as symbols themselves are often less determinate, conjuring up a wider range of meanings. Yet the First Amendment reaches both forms of discrimination. Virginia's cross-burning law stands in no better constitutional position than would a law prohibiting intimidation through flag-burning. . . .

[[3. Overbreadth.]] A central distinction in modern First Amendment law is the line that divides mere "abstract advocacy" from actual lawless action. In dealing with the relationship between violent speech and violent action, modern First Amendment jurisprudence employs a variety of legal doctrines that work in essentially parallel ways to separate mere violent rhetoric from speech closely intertwined with violence. . . .

The core flaw of the prima facie evidence provision is that it short-circuits this central First Amendment distinction, compounding the content and viewpoint discrimination by extracting the teeth from the required element of intentional intimidation, rendering it a "now you see it now you don't" requirement. The provision instructs law enforcement officers, prosecutors, trial judges, and juries that nothing beyond the mere burning of the cross is *required* to sustain an arrest, prosecution, or conviction. . . .

. . . Virginia cannot simply label a symbol a presumptive threat and be done with it. A change of terminology is not a change in principle. Virginia insists that cross-burning is a shorthand for intimidation. Yet cross-burning is not intimidation, any more than flag-burning is sedition, or an erotic movie is sex. Cross-burning is symbolic expression. At a given time and place a burning cross may be an instrument of intimidation, as an almost infinite variety of expression and conduct may, in context, be such an instrument. But Virginia cannot simply declare, through fiat, a presumptive equation between intimidation and one expressive ritual. Virginia's claimed shorthand is an unconstitutional shortcut. . . .

Respectfully submitted,
RODNEY A. SMOLLA,
Counsel of Record

VIRGINIA'S REPLY BRIEF

. . . Respondents repeatedly assert that cross burning is analogous to flag burning, an act that is constitutionally protected. Superficially, the analogy might seem appealing; but, in this regard, "a page of history is worth a volume of logic." Given our history, flag burning and cross burning are fundamentally different. Those who burn a flag—any flag—typically do so in order to express ardent—and disrespectful—opposition to the government or to some idea that the unburned flag is viewed as representing. By contrast, cross burning is typically not intended to express opposition to Christianity or to any other idea that an unburned cross might conceivably represent. Crosses are burned to instill fear. Thus, when a legislature prohibits burning the American flag, it is targeting a protected message: dissent from the values or policies the flag represents. In contrast, when a legislature bans cross burning with the intent to intimidate, the only message it targets is intimidation—and intimidation is not protected. . . .

The position advocated by respondents would lead to extreme results. Virtually any symbol used to intimidate has the potential to convey a message that is protected. For example, brandishing or discharging a firearm in the presence of another is often intended—and understood—as an act of intimidation. Yet, the display of such a weapon might also be used symbolically to convey a constitutionally protected message, such as expressing support for the right to keep and bear arms, or emphasizing the intensity of the speaker's views about war and peace or some other issue of public policy. The discharge of such a weapon might also be used to celebrate some victory or to honor a fallen hero, as is done at military funerals. Yet, surely the capacity of weapons to convey protected messages does not preclude government from enacting laws that prohibit brandishing or discharging firearms with the intent to intimidate. So it is with cross burning. The fact that a burning cross might conceivably be used to convey some constitutionally protected message does not preclude Virginia from making the act unlawful when it is intended to intimidate. . . .

Respectfully submitted,
JERRY W. KILGORE,
Attorney General of Virginia

WILLIAM H. HURD,
State Solicitor & Counsel of Record

ORAL ARGUMENT

❊   ❊   ❊

JUSTICE SCALIA: I thought the key here is that this is not just speech. It is not just speech. It's action that—that is intended to convey a message.

MR. HURD [[Virginia's Attorney]]: It is—

SCALIA: Surely—surely your State could make it unlawful to brandish—brandish an automatic weapon with the intent of—of intimidating somebody, couldn't it?

HURD: Justice Scalia, we—we have statutes that prohibit brandishing of firearms. In fact, a—a burning cross is very much like a brandishing of a firearm.

SCALIA: That's your point.

HURD: It is virtually . . . a present offer of force. That makes it an especially virulent form of—of intimidation. . . .

*   *   *

JUSTICE STEVENS: So that in—in a case in which there was a cross burned out in the middle of a desert somewhere, and that's all that's proved, that would be enough to sustain the conviction.

HURD: That would be enough to—to get you past a motion to strike. Of course, sustaining a—

STEVENS: Let's say . . . the defendant puts in no evidence, just . . . remains mute. He could be convicted on it in that case, I think.

HURD: If the instruction were given, he could be convicted. Of course, in this case, we have more than a burning cross. . . .

STEVENS: I understand that. But then my next question is—I'm asking about whether there's content discrimination. Supposing he burned a—a circle, he could not be convicted on the same evidence.

HURD: He could not. A burning circle, unlike a burning cross, carries no particular message. . . .

*   *   *

JUSTICE GINSBURG: . . . You have said that the . . . burning cross is a symbol like no other. . . . What about other things that are associated with the Klan? For example, the white robes and the mask? Are they also symbols that the State can ban, or is there something about the burning cross that makes it unique?

HURD: Justice Ginsburg, there—there are several things about the burning cross that make it unique. First, it is the symbol that the Klan has used to—to threaten bodily harm. . . . It says—it says, we're close at hand. We don't just talk. We act. And it deliberately invokes the precedent of 87 years of cross-burning as a tool of intimidation.

Burn anything else. Burn the flag. Burn a sheet. The message is opposition to the thing that the symbol unburned represents. Burning a cross is not opposition to Christianity. The message is a threat of bodily harm, and it—it is unique. And it's not simply a message of bigotry. It's a message that—that whoever has it in their hands, a message of bodily harm is coming. That is the primary message. . . .

*   *   *

JUSTICE KENNEDY: Is there—is there an immediacy component . . . [[required for threats]]?

MR. DREEBEN [[Attorney for the United States]]: No, there is not, Justice Kennedy, and it's crucial to underscore why that is. The harms that can be brought about by threat statutes are not only putting somebody in fear of bodily harm and thereby disrupting their movements, but providing a signal that the violence may actually occur. It may not occur tomorrow, the next day, or next week, but it's like a sword of Damocles hanging over the person whose head—who has been threatened. And in that sense it creates a pervasive fear that can be ongoing for a considerable amount of time.

JUSTICE THOMAS: Mr. Dreeben, aren't you understating the—the effects of—of the burning cross? This statute was passed in what year?

DREEBEN: 1952 originally.

THOMAS: Now, it's my understanding that we had almost 100 years of lynching and activity in the South by the Knights of Camellia and—and the Ku Klux Klan, and this was a reign of terror and the cross was a symbol of that reign of terror. Was—isn't that significantly greater than intimidation or a threat?

DREEBEN: Well, I think they're coextensive, Justice Thomas, because it is—

THOMAS: Well, my fear is, Mr. Dreeben, that you're actually understating the . . . the effect of the cross, the burning cross. I—I indicated, I think, in the Ohio case that the cross was not a religious symbol and that it has—it was intended to have a virulent effect. And I—I think that what you're attempting to do is to fit this into our jurisprudence rather than stating more clearly what the cross was intended to accomplish and, indeed, that it is unlike any symbol in our society.

DREEBEN: Well, I don't mean to understate it, and I entirely agree with Your Honor's description of how the cross has been used as an instrument of intimidation against minorities in this country. That has justified 14 States in treating it as a distinctive—

THOMAS: Well, it's—it's actually more than minorities. There's certain groups. And I—I just—my fear is that the—there was no other purpose to the cross. There was no communication of a particular message. It was intended to cause fear—

DREEBEN: It—

THOMAS:—and to terrorize a population.

DREEBEN: It absolutely was, and for that reason can be legitimately proscribed without fear that the focusing on a cross—burning of a cross with the intent to intimidate would chill protected expression. . . .

In the Virginia statute, and in the other statutes that the States have, the focus is not on any particular message. It is on the effect of intimidation, and the intent to create a climate of fear and, as Justice Thomas has said, a climate of terror.

JUSTICE SOUTER: So your argument would be the same even if we assumed that the capacity of the cross to convey this message was limited to certain groups, blacks, Catholics, or whatnot.

DREEBEN: It would, Justice Souter. . . .

STEVENS: But it seems to me from this argument, if the message is as powerful as Justice Thomas suggests it is—and I'm sure he's—he's right about that—why is it necessary to go beyond the message itself? Why—why wouldn't it still be proscribable even if the person burning it didn't realize all of this history, just did it innocently, but it nevertheless had that effect?

DREEBEN: Well, that would—

STEVENS: Why do you need the intent?

DREEBEN: I think that would raise a much more difficult question because notwithstanding the fact that there is a very powerful linkage in our society such that the State is justified in singling out the cross, it may be that under certain contexts, a particular individual is attempting to express a message rather than attempting to intimidate.

And it—it is important to note that merely expressing a message of race-based hatred is not something that the State can proscribe—. . .

✳   ✳   ✳

SCALIA: What—what about the symbol of brandishing an automatic weapon in—in somebody's face?

MR. SMOLLA [[Attorney for the Respondents]]: Justice Scalia, I think . . . that a core element of our argument is that there is a fundamental First Amendment difference between brandishing a cross, and brandishing a gun. The physical properties of the gun as a weapon add potency to the threat, and so if the State makes a threat committed with a firearm an especially heinous type of threat, it is acting within the confines of what is permissible under *R.A.V.* because it is creating a subclass of threat and defining that subclass of threat for the same reasons that allow it to define the outer perimeter of threat law, things going to the danger posed by that threat.

But the properties of the cross are not physical properties, and the burning element of a burning cross are not what communicate the threat.

SOUTER: But is—isn't the—isn't your argument an argument that would have been sound before the cross, in effect, acquired the history that it has? If we were in the year 1820, and you had a choice between somebody brandishing the loaded gun, and somebody brandishing a cross and nobody knew how the cross had been used because it had not been used, your argument, it seems to me, would be—would be a winning one.

How does your argument account for that fact that the cross has acquired a potency which I would suppose is at least as equal to that of the gun?

SMOLLA: Justice Souter, I think that our argument is that in fact it works the reverse way, that what the cross and the burning cross have acquired as a kind of secondary meaning, somewhat akin to the way that trademarks acquire secondary meaning in intellectual property law, are a multiplicity of messages. Undoubtedly a burning cross identified as—as effectively the trademark of the Ku Klux Klan carries horrible connotations of terrorism of the kind—. . .

SOUTER: How about a cross—how about a cross . . . on your lawn?

SCALIA: Yes. I dare say that you would rather see a man with a—with a rifle on your front lawn—If you were a black man at night, you'd rather see a man with a rifle than see a burning cross on your front lawn.

SMOLLA: Your Honor, I concede that. However—however—

SCALIA: The whole purpose of that is—is to terrorize.

SMOLLA:—as—as powerful as that point is—and I totally accept it, and totally accept the history that Justice Thomas has—has recounted. . . .

        *   *   *

GINSBURG: Mr. Smolla . . . there's a huge difference between a flag and a burning cross, and it's been pointed out in the briefs. The flag is a symbol of our government, and one of the things about free speech is we can criticize the President, the Supreme Court, anybody, and feel totally free about doing that. It's the symbol of government.

But the cross is not attacking the government. It's attacking people, threatening their lives and limbs. And so I don't—I think you have to separate the symbol that is the burning cross from other symbols that are critical of government, but that don't—that aren't a threat to personal safety.

SMOLLA: Justice Ginsburg, I only partially accept that—that dichotomy. In fact, when the Klan engages in cross-burning, as it did in *Brandenburg versus*

Ohio, and as it did here, it is—it is a melange of messages. Yes, to some degree, it is a horizontal message of hate speech, the Klan members attacking Jews and Catholics and African-Americans and all of the various people that have been the—the point of its hatred over the years.

But it's also engaged in dissent and in a political message. If you remember in *Brandenburg versus Ohio*, Brandenburg says if the Congress doesn't change things, some revenges will have to be taken. In this case, President Clinton was talked about by the Klan members. Hillary Clinton was talked about by the Klan members. Racial preferences and the idea that the—where they're using taxes to support minority groups. There is a jumble of political anger. . . .

✳   ✳   ✳

SMOLLA: Your Honor . . . the First Amendment requires that we flip the question. It is not why can't the government single out this particular form of expression. It is why do you need to. And if you have no need to—

SCALIA: Wait, wait, wait. I think—I don't think our cases say you have to use the least restrictive alternative. I'm sure there are other ways of getting at the person who brandishes an automatic weapon, but surely you can make brandishing an automatic weapon a crime—

SMOLLA: Your Honor—

SCALIA:—even though there are other ways you could get at it.

SMOLLA: Justice Scalia, you do not need to use the least restrictive alternative when you are not regulating a fundamental right, or engaged in a suspect classification.

SCALIA: A symbol—I mean, that's a symbol too. Brandishing a weapon is a symbol just as burning a cross is a symbol.

SMOLLA: Except, Your Honor, under—under the *Brandenburg* test—excuse me—under the *O'Brien* test, the government has functional elements of—of— that relate to the weapon that allow it to cite things utterly unrelated to the content of expression that empower it to say you may not—you may not brandish a weapon.

SCALIA: I don't know what you're talking about.

SMOLLA: That—that it's—it's like the difference, Justice Scalia, between burning a draft card and burning a cross or burning a flag, that—that the reason *O'Brien*—the draft card case—allowed the government to punish burning the draft card was that the draft card had a functional purpose—the administration of the Selective Service System—that had nothing to do with what was being expressed when one burned the draft card.

The gun is like that. When the government says you may not threaten someone by brandishing a gun, there is a functional element to the gun. It's a weapon that the government can cite as its basis.

But a symbol only has symbolic meaning. . . .

*   *   *

SOUTER: . . . [[If the Pavlovian quality of cross burning]] is giving us difficulty in deciding whether we should classify this in the *O'Brien* direction, or the flag direction, what's the—what's the—in effect, the tie-breaker?

SMOLLA: Your Honor, I think the tie-breaker is what I've kept coming back to a number of times, which is really would there be any fall-off through content-neutral alternatives, and if there would not be any fall-off through content-neutral alternatives, then err on the side of freedom of speech. . . .

*   *   *

STEVENS: Thank you, Mr. Smolla.

Mr. Hurd, you have 2 minutes . .

HURD: Very briefly. Justice Souter, the tie-breaker is the intent to intimidate which is in our statute. If there's no intent to intimidate, there's no violation here. . . .

OPINIONS

Justice O'Connor, announcing the judgment of the Court. . . .

. . . Intimidation in the constitutionally proscribable sense of the word is a type of true threat, where a speaker directs a threat to a person or group of persons with the intent of placing the victim in fear of bodily harm or death. Respondents do not contest that some cross burnings fit within this meaning of intimidating speech. . . .

. . . It is true, as the Supreme Court of Virginia held, that the burning of a cross is symbolic expression. The reason why the Klan burns a cross at its rallies, or individuals place a burning cross on someone else's lawn, is that the burning cross represents the message that the speaker wishes to communicate. Individuals burn crosses as opposed to other means of communication because cross burning carries a message in an effective and dramatic manner. . . .

[[1. *R.A.V.*'s "Special Virulence" Exception.]] We did not hold in *R.A.V.*[[, however,]] that the First Amendment prohibits *all* forms of content-based discrimination within a proscribable area of speech. Rather, we specifically stated that some types of content discrimination did not violate the First Amendment. . . .

[[For example, in *R.A.V.*]] . . . we noted that it would be constitutional to ban only a particular type of threat: "[T]he Federal Government can criminalize only those threats of violence that are directed against the President . . . since the reasons why threats of violence are outside the First Amendment . . . have special force when applied to the person of the President." And a State may "choose to prohibit only that obscenity which is the most patently offensive *in its prurience*—*i.e.,* that which involves the most lascivious displays of sexual activity." Consequently, while the holding of *R.A.V.* does not permit a State to ban only obscenity based on "offensive *political* messages," or "only those threats against the President that mention his policy on aid to inner cities," the First Amendment permits content discrimination "based on the very reasons why the particular class of speech at issue . . . is proscribable."

Similarly, Virginia's statute does not run afoul of the First Amendment insofar as it bans cross burning with intent to intimidate. Unlike the statute at issue in *R.A.V.,* the Virginia statute does not single out for opprobrium only that speech directed toward "one of the specified disfavored topics." It does not matter whether an individual burns a cross with intent to intimidate because of the victim's race, gender, or religion, or because of the victim's "political affiliation, union membership, or homosexuality." Moreover, as a factual matter it is not true that cross burners direct their intimidating conduct solely to racial or religious minorities. Indeed, in the case of Elliott and O'Mara, it is at least unclear whether the respondents burned a cross due to racial animus.

The First Amendment permits Virginia to outlaw cross burnings done with the intent to intimidate because burning a cross is a particularly virulent form of intimidation. Instead of prohibiting all intimidating messages, Virginia may choose to regulate this subset of intimidating messages in light of cross burning's long and pernicious history as a signal of impending violence. Thus, just as a State may regulate only that obscenity which is the most obscene due to its prurient content, so too may a State choose to prohibit only those forms of intimidation that are most likely to inspire fear of bodily harm. A ban on cross burning carried out with the intent to intimidate is fully consistent with our holding in *R.A.V.* and is proscribable under the First Amendment. . . .

[[2. Prima Facie Evidence Provision.]] . . . As construed by the jury instruction, the prima facie provision strips away the very reason why a State may ban cross burning with the intent to intimidate. The prima facie evidence provision permits a jury to convict in every cross-burning case in which defendants exercise their constitutional right not to put on a defense. And even where a defendant like Black presents a defense, the prima facie evidence provision makes it more likely that the jury will find an intent to intimidate regardless of the particular facts of the case. The provision permits the Commonwealth to arrest, prosecute, and convict a person based solely on the fact of cross burning itself.

It is apparent that the provision as so interpreted " 'would create an unacceptable risk of the suppression of ideas.' " The act of burning a cross may mean that a person is engaging in constitutionally proscribable intimidation. But that same act may mean only that the person is engaged in core political speech. The prima facie evidence provision in this statute blurs the line between these two meanings of a burning cross. As interpreted by the jury instruction, the provision chills constitutionally protected political speech because of the possibility that a State will prosecute—and potentially convict—somebody engaging only in lawful political speech at the core of what the First Amendment is designed to protect. . . .

Justice Thomas, dissenting.

[[1. Only Conduct Prohibited.]] Although I agree with the majority's conclusion that it is constitutionally permissible to "ban . . . cross burning carried out with intent to intimidate," I believe that the majority errs in imputing an expressive component to the activity in question. In my view, whatever expressive value cross burning has, the legislature simply wrote it out by banning only intimidating conduct undertaken by a particular means. A conclusion that the statute prohibiting cross burning with intent to intimidate sweeps beyond a prohibition on certain conduct into the zone of expression overlooks not only the words of the statute but also reality. . . .

. . . Even for segregationists, violent and terroristic conduct, the Siamese twin of cross burning, was intolerable. The ban on cross burning with intent to intimidate demonstrates that even segregationists understood the difference between intimidating and terroristic conduct and racist expression. It is simply beyond belief that, in passing the statute now under review, the Virginia legislature was concerned with anything but penalizing conduct it must have viewed as particularly vicious.

Accordingly, this statute prohibits only conduct, not expression. And, just as one cannot burn down someone's house to make a political point and then seek refuge in the First Amendment, those who hate cannot terrorize and intimidate to make their point. In light of my conclusion that the statute here addresses only conduct, there is no need to analyze it under any of our First Amendment tests. . . .

[[2. Prima Facie Evidence Provision.]] . . . Given that this Court's definitions of a "permissive inference" and a "mandatory presumption" track Virginia's definitions of "inference" and "presumption," the Court should judge the Virginia statute based on the constitutional analysis applicable to "inferences": they raise no constitutional flags unless "no rational trier could make a connection permitted by the inference." As explained [[above, however,]] . . . not making a connection between cross burning and intimidation would be irrational.

But even with respect to statutes containing a mandatory irrebuttable presumption as to intent, the Court has not shown much concern. For instance, there is no scienter requirement for statutory rape. That is, a person can be arrested, prosecuted, and convicted for having sex with a minor, without the government ever producing any evidence, let alone proving beyond a reasonable doubt, that a minor did not consent. . . .

Statutes prohibiting possession of drugs with intent to distribute operate much the same way as statutory rape laws. Under these statutes, the intent to distribute is effectively satisfied by possession of some threshold amount of drugs. . . .

The plurality, however, is troubled by the presumption because this is a First Amendment case. The plurality laments the fate of an innocent cross-burner who burns a cross, but does so without an intent to intimidate. The plurality fears the chill on expression because, according to the plurality, the inference permits "the Commonwealth to arrest, prosecute and convict a person based solely on the fact of cross burning itself." First, it is, at the very least, unclear that the inference comes into play during arrest and initiation of a prosecution, that is, prior to the instructions stage of an actual trial. Second, as I explained above, the inference is rebuttable and, as the jury instructions given in this case demonstrate, Virginia law still requires the jury to find the existence of each element, including intent to intimidate, beyond a reasonable doubt.

Moreover, even in the First Amendment context, the Court has upheld such regulations where conduct that initially appears culpable, ultimately results in dismissed charges. A regulation of pornography is one such example. While possession of child pornography is illegal, possession of adult pornography, as long as it is not obscene, is allowed. As a result, those pornographers trafficking in images of adults who look like minors, may be not only deterred but also arrested and prosecuted for possessing what a jury might find to be legal materials. This "chilling" effect has not, however, been a cause for grave concern with respect to overbreadth of such statutes among the members of this Court. . . .

Justice Souter, concurring in the judgment in part and dissenting in part.

I agree with the majority that the Virginia statute makes a content-based distinction within the category of punishable intimidating or threatening expression, the very type of distinction we considered in *R.A.V.* v. *St. Paul* (1992). I disagree that any exception should save Virginia's law from unconstitutionality under the holding in *R.A.V.* or any acceptable variation of it.

[[1. *R.A.V.*'s "Special Virulence" Exception.]] . . . [[T]]he *R.A.V.* exception most likely to cover the statute is the first of the three mentioned there, which the *R.A.V.* opinion called an exception for content discrimination on a basis that "consists entirely of the very reason the entire class of speech at issue is proscribable." This is the exception the majority speaks of here as covering statutes prohibiting "particularly virulent" proscribable expression. . . .

. . . [[T]]his case [[does not]] present any analogy to the statute prohibiting threats against the President, . . . the one the majority relies upon. The content discrimination in that statute relates to the addressee of the threat and reflects the special risks and costs associated with threatening the President. Again, however, threats against the President are not generally identified by reference to the content of any message that may accompany the threat, let alone any viewpoint, and there is no obvious correlation in fact between victim and message. Millions of statements are made about the President every day on every subject and from every standpoint; threats of violence are not an integral feature of any one subject or viewpoint as distinct from others. Differential treatment of threats against the President, then, selects nothing but special risks, not special messages. A content-based proscription of cross burning, on the other hand, may be a subtle effort to ban not only the intensity of the intimidation cross burning causes when done to threaten, but also the particular message of white supremacy that is broadcast even by nonthreatening cross burning.

I thus read *R.A.V.*'s examples of the particular virulence exception as covering prohibitions that are not clearly associated with a particular viewpoint, and that are consequently different from the Virginia statute. On that understanding of things, I necessarily read the majority opinion as treating *R.A.V.*'s virulence exception in a more flexible, pragmatic manner than the original illustrations would suggest. . . .

[[2. Prima Facie Evidence Provision.]] . . . [[W]]hether or not the Court should conceive of exceptions to *R.A.V.*'s general rule in a more practical way, no content-based statute should survive even under a pragmatic recasting of *R.A.V.* without a high probability that no "official suppression of ideas is afoot." I believe the prima facie evidence provision stands in the way of any finding of such a high probability here. . . .

As I see the likely significance of the evidence provision, its primary effect is to skew jury deliberations toward conviction in cases where the evidence of intent to intimidate is relatively weak and arguably consistent with a solely ideological reason for burning. . . . [[T]]he provision will have the practical effect of tilting the jury's thinking in favor of the prosecution. What is significant is not that the provision permits a factfinder's conclusion that the defendant acted with proscribable and punishable intent without any further indication, because some such indication will almost always be presented. What is significant is that the provision will encourage a factfinder to err on the side of a finding of intent to intimidate when the evidence of circumstances fails to point with any clarity either to the criminal intent or to the permissible one. . . .

To the extent the prima facie evidence provision skews prosecutions, then, it skews the statute toward suppressing ideas. . . . The question here is not the permissible scope of an arguably overbroad statute, but the claim of a clearly content-based statute to an exception from the general prohibition of content-based proscriptions, an exception that is not warranted if the statute's terms show that suppression of ideas may be afoot. Accordingly, the way to look at the prima facie evidence provision is to consider it for any indication of what is afoot. And if we look at the provision for this purpose, it has a very obvious significance as a mechanism for bringing within the statute's prohibition some expression that is doubtfully threatening though certainly distasteful.

It is difficult to conceive of an intimidation case that could be easier to prove than one with cross burning, assuming any circumstances suggesting intimidation are present. The provision, apparently so unnecessary to legitimate prosecution of intimidation, is therefore quite enough to raise the question whether Virginia's content-based statute seeks more than mere protection against a virulent form of intimidation. It consequently bars any conclusion that an exception to the general rule of *R.A.V.* is warranted on the ground "that there is no realistic [or little realistic] possibility that official suppression of ideas is afoot." Since no *R.A.V.* exception can save the statute as content based, it can only survive if narrowly tailored to serve a compelling state interest, a stringent test the statute cannot pass; a content-neutral statute banning intimidation would achieve the same object without singling out particular content.

NOTES

1. 315 U.S. 568, 571-72 (1942).
2. See *Terminiello v. Chicago*, 337 U.S. 1 (1949); *Edward v. South Carolina*, 372 U.S. 229 (1963); *Gregory v. Chicago*, 394 U.S. 111 (1969); *Cohen v. California*, 403 U.S. 15 (1971); and *Gooding v. Wilson*, 405 U.S. 518 (1972).
3. *New York Times v. Sullivan*, 376 U.S. 254, 280 (1964).
4. 413 U.S. 15 (1973).
5. 395 U.S. 444, 447 (1969). Also see *Madsen v. Women's Health Center, Inc.*, 512 U.S. 753, 774 (1994) and *Schenck v. Pro-Choice Network of Western New York*, 519 U.S. 357, 373 (1997).
6. The Court's interpretation of the "clear and present danger" doctrine has varied over time. See *Schenck v. United States*, 249 U.S. 47 (1919); *Debs v. United States*, 249 U.S. 211 (1919); *Abrams v. United States*, 250 U.S. 616 (1919); *Gitlow v. New York*, 268 U.S. 652 (1925); *Whitney v. California*, 274 U.S. 357 (1927); *Dennis v. United States*, 341 U.S. 494 (1951); *Yates v. United States*, 354 U.S. 298 (1957); *Brandenburg v. Ohio*, 395 U.S. 444 (1969); *Hess v. Indiana*, 414 U.S. 105 (1973).
7. In contrast to how the Court conditionally protected illegal advocacy, it has determined that the state's interest in decency never justifies a prohibition of "offensive" speech. The central precedent is *Cohen v. California*, 403 U.S. 15 (1971).
8. 408 U.S. 92, 96 (1972).
9. *Board of Ed. v. Barnette*, 310 U.S. 586, 642 (1943).
10. *Police Dept. v. Mosley*, 408 U.S. 92, 96 (1972).
11. 391 U.S. 367 (1968). See also *Tinker v. Des Moines School District*, 393 U.S. 503 (1969) and *Clark v. Community for Creative Non-Violence*, 468 U.S. 288 (1984).
12. *Texas v. Johnson*, 491 U.S. 397, 416 (1989). One year later, in another flag-burning case, the Court affirmed the reasoning of *Johnson*. See *United States v. Eichman*, 496 U.S. 310 (1990).
13. Other Supreme Court decisions that discuss the constitutionality of content-based regulations include *Boos v. Barry*, 485 U.S. (1988) (invalidating a provision that prohibited a display within 550 feet of a foreign embassy any sign tending to bring that foreign government into "public odium" or "public dispute"); *Barnes v. Glen Theatre, Inc.*, 501 U.S. 560 (1991) and *City of Erie v. Pap's A.M.*, 529 U.S. 277 (2000) (upholding bans of public nudity).
14. *Collin v. Smith*, 578 F. 2d 1197, 1207 (1978).
15. Lower federal court decisions invalidating campus "speech codes" include *Doe v. University of Michigan*, 721 F. Supp 852, 856 (E.D. Michigan 1989); *UWM Post v. Board*

of Regents of the University of Wisconsin, 774 F. Supp. 1163 (E.D. Wis. 1991); *Dambrot v. Central Michigan University*, 839 F. Supp. 477 (E.D. Mich. 1993). Stanford University eventually adopted a speech code, but a state court invalidated it because California law applied federal standards of free speech to private colleges and universities. See *Corry v. Stanford*, No. 74039 (Cal. Super. Ct. Santa Clara Co. Feb., 27, 1995).

16. St. Paul, Minn. Legis. Code Section 292.02.

17. Justices Blackmun and O'Connor joined Justice White's concurring opinion, and Justice Stevens partly joined it. Justices White and Blackmun partly joined Justice Stevens's concurring opinion. Chief Justice Rehnquist and Justices Kennedy, Souter, and Thomas joined Justice Scalia's majority opinion.

18. See 18 U.S.C. Section 241 and 42 U.S.C. Section 3631.

19. 22 F.3d 821 (8th Cir. 1994).

20. *Wisconsin v. Mitchell*, 169 Wis. 2d 153, 164, 171; 485 N.W. 2d 807, 812, 815 (1992).

21. *Wisconsin v. Mitchell*, 508 U.S. 476, 485-90.

22. For a review of the literature, see Joe Deshotel and Richard Clarkson, "Crimes of Hate Deserve Special Penalties, 64 *Texas Bar Journal* 70 (2001); Frederick M. Lawrence, *Punishing Hate: Bias Crimes under American Law* (Cambridge, Mass.: Harvard University Press, 1999); James B. Jacobs and Kimberly Potter, *Hate Crime: Criminal Law and Identity Politics* (New York: Oxford University Press, 1998), especially chap. 8; Martin Redish, "Freedom of Thought as Freedom of Expression: Hate Crime Sentencing Enhancement and First Amendment Theory," 11 *Criminal Justice Ethics* 29 (1992); and James Weinstein, "First Amendment Challenges to Hate Crime Legislation: Where's the Speech," 11 *Criminal Justice Ethics* 6 (1992).

23. See the Violent Crime and Law Enforcement Act of 1994, discussed in Jacobs and Potter, *Hate Crime*, pp. 30, 76-77.

24. See *Maryland v. Sheldon*, 332 Md. 45; 629 A. 2d 753 (1993); *State v. Ramsey*, 311 S.C. 555; 430 S.E. 2d 511 (1993); *In re Steven S.*, 25 Cal. App. 4th 598; 31 Cal. Rptr. 2d 644 (1994); and *Florida v. T.B.D.*, 656 So. 2d 479 (1995).

25. *Black v. Virginia*, 262 Va. 764, 772, 774, 777; 553 S.E. 2d 738, 742, 744, 746 (2001).

26. Tony Mauro, "Thomas Transforms Debate in Cross-Burning Case," *American Lawyer Media*, December 12, 2002, available on LexisNexis Academic.

27. Va. Code Ann., Section 18.2-423.1 (1996).

CHAPTER 5

Campaign Finance Regulation and Freedom of Speech

McConnell v. Federal Election Commission
540 U.S. 93 (2003)

Most political campaigns in the United States are financed by contributions from private individuals and groups. Citizens, alone or in groups of likeminded individuals, contribute to the candidate of their choice or spend their own money directly or indirectly on the candidate's behalf. Since such contributions and expenditures are intimately related to political speech and are integral to a functioning democracy, they are arguably at the core of what is protected by freedom of speech. Just as the government cannot regulate the substance of political advocacy, so also it cannot regulate how a citizen contributes and spends money for the purpose of electing someone who supports that ideology. However, it is also true that large contributions of money to a particular candidate or expenditures on his or her behalf pose the possibility of corruption or at least the risk of its appearance. In addition, candidates who are able to raise relatively large sums of money from a small group of rich backers perhaps have an "unfair" advantage over their opponents. It leads to the perception that money can buy an election, which erodes public confidence in the electoral process and mocks the principle of one-person, one-vote. The issue of campaign finance regulation is therefore a very difficult one that balances the democratic value of freedom of speech against the integrity and fairness of democratic elections. These two principles of democracy are in tension with one another, constituting a dilemma of the first magnitude, one the Supreme Court has grappled with for decades. In *McConnell v. FEC* (2003), a sharply divided Court established a new balance of these principles by allowing Congress to impose new limits on the role of money in federal political campaigns.

The first step in the direction of imposing some control over the role of money in federal campaigns came early in the twentieth century. In 1907, Congress banned corporations from contributing money "in connection with" any federal election. In 1925, Congress extended the prohibition on corporate contributions to "anything of value" and also made it a crime to "accept" such a donation. In several pieces of legislation during the 1940s, Congress limited the amount political committees could receive and spend and gradually subjected union contributions to the same prohibitions already imposed on corporations. By 1947, unions could not contribute to candidates or pay for "election-related expenditures" in either primary or general elections.[1] In 1971, Congress enacted the Federal Election Campaign Act (FECA), which required disclosure of contributions above $100 and of expenditures above $1,000 per year. In an important step, this law also permitted corporations and unions to create segregated funds (political action committees or PACs) that could be used for campaign contributions and expenditures. Soon thereafter the investigation of the Watergate scandal revealed that highly controversial fund-raising and campaign practices had occurred during the 1972 presidential election. For example, the American Milk Producers, a trade association that had contributed $2 million to Richard Nixon's 1972 reelection effort, circumvented mandatory disclosure rules by breaking down the money into numerous small contributions. In a 1973 congressional hearing, the milk producers admitted that the purpose of the contribution was to set up a meeting with White House officials to discuss price supports.[2]

Congress responded by amending FECA in 1974. At the time, these amendments constituted Congress's most ambitious attempt to regulate federal elections by rebalancing the free speech right to contribute and spend money for political causes and candidates against the perceived need to restore integrity and fairness to the federal electoral process. The 1974 amendments limited the amount an individual could contribute to a candidate to $1,000 per election and set an overall annual limit of $25,000 on what an individual could contribute to candidates, political parties, or PACs. In addition, the amendments imposed a ceiling on what candidates, political parties, and interest groups could spend on campaigns; required disclosure of contributions and expenditures exceeding certain limits; instituted a system of public financing of presidential elections; and established the Federal Election Commission, which would administer and enforce the legislation. A diverse coalition, including conservative Senator James Buckley (R-NY), a former presidential candidate, liberal Senator Eugene McCarthy, (D-MN), also a former presidential candidate, and the American Civil Liberties Union filed a lawsuit claiming that the amended FECA unconstitutionally abridged the free speech rights of citizens, candidates, political parties, and interest groups. In *Buckley v. Valeo* (1975), the Court of Appeals for the District of Columbia generally upheld the constitutionality of the 1974 amendments on the ground that large campaign donations contributed to the appearance of corruption.

The Supreme Court's decision in *Buckley v. Valeo* (1976) was the most important decision on the constitutionality of campaign finance regulation until the Court decided *McConnell v. FEC* in 2003. A majority of the justices sustained the law's system of public financing of presidential elections, the disclosure and reporting provisions, and the individual contribution limits, but rejected all limitations on campaign expenditures, whether those expenditures were made by a campaign committee, by an individual or group independent of a campaign, or by a candidate from his or her personal funds. The Court reasoned that both contribution and expenditure limitations implicated fundamental free speech interests, but that the latter were more burdensome since they necessarily reduced "the quantity of expression by restricting the number of issues discussed, the depth of their exploration, and the size of the audience reached." In contrast, a limitation on contributions was "only a marginal restriction upon the contributor's ability to engage in free communication." A contribution served as a "general expression of support" for a candidate and his views and provided a "very rough index of the intensity of the contributor's support for the candidate," but it did not "communicate the underlying basis for the support" or prevent the contributor from discussing "candidates and issues." The Court concluded that the "overall effect of the Act's contribution ceilings is merely to require candidates and political committees to raise funds from a greater number of persons and to compel people who would otherwise contribute amounts greater than the statutory limits to expend such funds on direct political expression, rather than to reduce the total amount of money potentially available to promote political expression." On the basis of this reasoning, contribution limits, though they implicated free speech interests, were held to a lower constitutional standard than limits on expenditures.[3]

Limits on contributions would be sustained, the Court explained, if they served a "sufficiently important interest" and were "closely drawn" to avoid "unnecessary abridgment of the freedom of political expression and the right of association." The primary purpose of FECA's contribution limits was to reduce "the actuality and appearance of corruption resulting from large individual financial contributions." This goal, according to the Court, qualified as a sufficiently important interest because political quid pro quos and "the appearance of corruption stemming from . . . large individual financial contributions" undermined "the integrity of our system of representative democracy." And though bribery and disclosure laws helped to reduce both the reality and appearance of corruption, Congress was entitled to conclude that limits on contributions were also necessary. In contrast, expenditure limits, even if narrowly defined as limits on communications that "include explicit words of advocacy of election or defeat of a candidate," had to satisfy "exacting scrutiny applicable to limitations on core First Amendment rights of political expression." The governmental interest in preventing corruption and the appearance of corruption did not justify limits of this type for two reasons. First, the limits would not be very effective since individuals could easily devise expenditures "that skirted the restriction on express advocacy of election or defeat but nevertheless benefited the candidate's campaign." Second, expenditures for express advocacy of candidates that are made "totally independent"

of the candidate "may well provide little assistance to the candidate's campaign
and indeed may prove counterproductive." The law was therefore overinclusive
and underinclusive. It failed to limit expenditures that could be the basis for
corruption or its appearance, while it limited other expenditures that arguably
would not have this effect.[4]

Other interests that the government relied upon to justify expenditure limits
were the goal of reducing campaign cost and "equalizing the relative ability of
individuals and groups to influence the outcome of elections." The Court,
however, rejected these goals as "wholly foreign to the First Amendment." The
state could not "restrict the speech of some elements of our society in order
to enhance the relative voice of others" because the very purpose of the First
Amendment was to secure "the widest possible dissemination of information
from diverse and antagonistic sources" and assure "unfettered interchange of
ideas." For very similar reasons, the goal of reducing the cost of political campaigns could not justify limiting either the amount of personal funds a candidate could spend during his or her campaign or the overall amount of money
spent during the campaign. The First Amendment denied government the
power to determine that political expenditures, including those of a campaign,
were "wasteful, excessive, or unwise." It was not government, "but the people—individually as citizens and candidates and collectively as associations and
political committees—who must retain control over the quantity and range of
debate on public issues in a political campaign." Accordingly, since none of
the purported interests justified any form of expenditure limits, they were all
unconstitutional.[5]

Two justices sharply criticized the Court's central distinction between contribution and expenditure limits. On the one side, Chief Justice Burger claimed
that the Court, in upholding the contribution limits, was ignoring "the reasons
it finds so persuasive in the context of expenditures." If the First Amendment
did not permit the government to limit the overall amount of political advocacy
and debate, then it also barred government from limiting contributions since
they too "will put an effective ceiling on the amount of political activity." It
did not matter, according to Burger, that in the case of contributions someone
other than the contributor uttered the words. Since the very purpose of the
contribution was to support whatever the speaker advocated, it was core political speech that could only be restricted on the basis of the most compelling
state interests. As no such interests were served by either contribution or
expenditures limits, both were unconstitutional.[6]

Justice White argued in the opposite direction, insisting that "limiting independent expenditures is essential to prevent transparent and widespread evasion
of the contribution limits." In White's opinion, it simply made no sense "to
limit the amounts an individual may give to a candidate or spend with his
approval but fail to limit the amounts that could be spent on his behalf." Moreover, since expenditure limits reinforced the contribution limits in this way,
they served the same important governmental purpose of controlling corruption and dispelling "the impression that federal elections are purely and simply

a function of money." A large independent expenditure on behalf of a candidate could foster the appearance of corruption to the same degree as a large contribution. If the latter could be limited, so could the former. Lastly, White defended the overall campaign expenditures limit and the limit on the amount a candidate could spend of his personal funds. Controlling campaign costs, maintaining public confidence in federal elections, equalizing access to the political arena by encouraging the less wealthy to run for office—all of these, according to White, were important governmental interests that justified both contribution and expenditure limits.[7]

From 1976 until *McConnell*, the Court in a variety of contexts preserved the basic regulatory framework of *Buckley*, upholding limits on contributions to candidates and campaign entities but invalidating what were perceived to be limits on independent political expenditures. In *First National Bank of Boston v. Bellotti* (1978), the Court rejected a state law prohibiting corporations from making contributions or expenditures for the purpose of influencing how citizens voted in a referendum. Since there was no election of a candidate, corruption was not a relevant governmental interest. In such a context, a corporation had a First Amendment right to engage in any amount of political advocacy.[8] In contrast, in *California Medical Association v. FEC* (1981) the Court upheld a $5,000 limit on how much an individual could contribute to a multicandidate political committee. The government could not limit how much such an association or an individual contributor could spend independently on behalf of a candidate, but it could regulate how much that association or individual could contribute to a political committee.[9]

In *FEC v. National Right to Work Committee* (1982), the Court upheld a regulation prohibiting a nonprofit corporation from soliciting funds from nonmembers to raise funds for contributions to candidates.[10] Four years later, however, in *FEC v. Massachusetts Citizens for Life, Inc.* (MCLF) (1986), the Court ruled that nonprofit corporations that were more akin to "voluntary political associations than business firms" could make independent expenditures on behalf of candidates from their general funds. Such MCLF-organizations had to be "formed for the express purpose of promoting political ideas," have no shareholders, and must not be established by a business corporation or labor union. In the Court's view, requiring such entities to establish special segregated funds for independent expenditures violated freedom of speech and association. So long as such expenditures were made independently of the federal candidate, they could not be limited by the government.[11] However, in *FEC v. Beaumont* (2003), the Court held that a MCFL-type corporation did not have a right to contribute from general funds to candidate campaigns. It was consistent with freedom of speech if such nonprofit advocacy corporations were required to make contributions of this type through a PAC.[12]

Corporations and labor unions, of course, could set up PACs funded, not by general funds, but by contributions from executives, members, and/or their families (so-called "segregated funds"). Though the contributions to these PACs were limited by FECA, the PACs themselves had the right to spend an unlimited amount of money so long as the expenditures were not coordinated with the candidate's campaign. In *FEC v. National Conservative PAC* (1985), the Court invalidated a provision of federal law that prohibited PACs from spending more than $1,000 on behalf of a presidential candidate who participated in the public financing program. If such expenditures were coordinated with the candidate, then they were in effect contributions and limits could be imposed. However, so long as the expenditures were made independently of the candidate, they were constitutionally protected. The Court came to the same conclusion in regard to political parties in *Colorado Republican Federal Campaign Committee v. FEC* ("Colorado I") (1996).[13] The Court held that political parties had the same status as individuals and political action committees. They had a right to make unlimited independent (not coordinated) expenditures on behalf of a particular candidate. However, five years later, in *FEC v. Colorado Republican Federal Campaign Committee* ("Colorado II") (2001), the Court concluded that expenditures by a political party that were coordinated with a candidate were nothing more than contributions.[14] Accordingly, political parties did not have additional First Amendment rights because of their special role in the American electoral process. Coordinated expenditures by them were subject to the normal contribution limits, which were constitutional so long as the limits were not so low as to render political association "ineffective."[15]

During the 1980s and 1990s, while the Supreme Court maintained and extended the regulatory structure established in *Buckley*, money continued to flow in and out of the American electoral system. Most of this money was "hard" or "federal" money, terms used to describe the money subject to the federal contribution limits established by FECA. For example, as figure 5.1 indicates, in the 1993–1994 election cycle, the Democratic Party raised $133 million in hard money and the Republicans raised $244 million, but in 1995–1996 the corresponding figures were $222 and $417 million and in 1999–2000 they were $275 and $466 million. Political parties could contribute hard money to individual candidates up to a contribution limit or spend it independently of the candidate's campaign organization, even if the money was used to engage in express advocacy of a particular candidate's election or defeat.

In the years following *Buckley*, the federal system of campaign regulation operated alongside state systems of campaign regulation, which varied significantly from state to state. Some states imposed no limits on contributions to state candidates or state political parties; others imposed limits that were lower than what federal law required. Given the dual systems of regulation, it was unclear which system should regulate party activities that affected both federal and state elections but were not equivalent to campaigns, activities such as voter registration, voter identification, and get-out-the-vote efforts. In 1978, the FEC decided that state and local party committees could use a combination of hard money and money only subject to state regulation (called "state" or "soft" money) to finance party activities that effected both federal and state elections. Later the FEC permitted national party committees to do the same thing, which encouraged these committees to set up hard and soft money accounts.

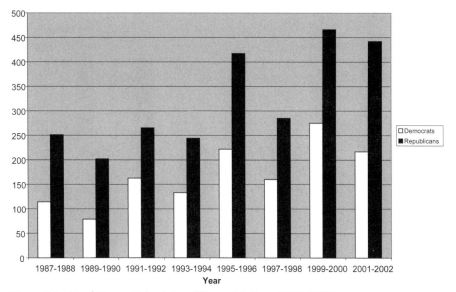

Figure 5.1   Hard Money Raised, in millions of dollars (1987–2002)
Source: Center for Responsive Politics

Since the soft money accounts were not subject to FECA contribution limits, donors could contribute to these funds in unlimited amounts and the national parties could transfer these funds to the state parties, which could then use them to finance local party activities or the permitted soft money component of activities that affected both state and federal elections.

During the 1980s and 1990s, the FEC expanded the types of party activities that could be financed with soft money to include administrative expenses, party-building initiatives, and, most importantly, issue advocacy. The latter was so important because TV and radio "issue ads" could be designed to benefit a particular candidate, but could be financed with soft money, so long as the party avoided "magic words" that expressly advocated the election or defeat of any candidate. Accordingly, parties could use donations well over the $1,000 limit on hard money to finance "issue ads" as long as they did not explicitly urge voters to "vote for" or "vote against" a particular candidate. The trend in the direction of issue ads, soft money, and unlimited contributions was unmistakable during the 1990s. As figure 5.2 indicates, the Democrats in 1993–1994 raised $101 million of soft money, while the Republicans raised $114 million. Four years later, the respective figures were $245 million and $250 million.

As more and more large contributions flowed into the soft-money coffers of political parties and as more and more of the soft money of political parties, along with unregulated money of various political action committees and advocacy groups, was used to finance TV and radio issue ads that benefited specific candidates running for federal office, the more the impression grew that federal

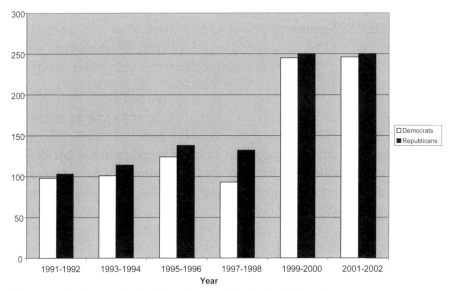

Figure 5.2   Soft Money Raised, in millions of dollars (1991–2002)
Source: Center for Responsive Politics

candidates were largely circumventing the FECA system of campaign regulation that had been upheld in *Buckley*. Members of Congress, in particular Senators John McCain (R-AZ) and Russell Feingold (D-WI) and Congressmen
Christopher Shays (R-CT) and Marty Meehan (D-MA), began to call for over-
hauling the campaign finance system. In a 2002 Senate debate, Senator McCain,
a sponsor of the Bipartisan Campaign Reform Act (BCRA), defended it vigor-
ously, while Senator Mitch McConnell (R-KY), the bill's foremost critic,
attacked it on constitutional and policy grounds (see box 5.1). The arguments
of both senators reflected differing perspectives on the influence of money in
politics and the possibility of its connection to political corruption or the
appearance of political corruption. Soon after the Senate debate, Congress
passed the BCRA and President George W. Bush, despite reservations about its
constitutionality, signed it into law on March 27, 2002.

   As it finally emerged after years of debate and compromise, the BCRA was
a very lengthy and complex piece of legislation.[16] It regulated fund-raising on
federal property and campaign activities of foreign nationals; banned minors
from contributing any money to federal candidates or political parties; required
candidates who wanted the lowest rate for broadcast advertising to either cer-
tify that he or she would never refer to any other candidate in any of his or her
advertising or include a statement in the ad that he or she had authorized it;
compelled broadcasters to disclose who filed requests for the purchase of
broadcast time relating to political matters of national importance; raised hard
money contribution limits for candidates to $2,000; increased further contribu-

tion limits of candidates facing self-financing opponents; and, finally, set more severe penalties for violations of campaign finance laws. At the law's core, however, were two controversial provisions: Title I, which banned national, state, and local political parties from raising, transferring, or spending any soft money for any "federal election activity," a category that included voter registration drives, get-out-the-vote efforts, and party-building initiatives during federal elections; and Title II, which banned corporations (both profit and non-profit)[17] and unions from spending soft money on any "federal election communication," which the law defined as any television or radio broadcast targeted to the relevant electorate that referred to a clearly identified candidate for federal office within sixty days of a general election or thirty days of a primary. Such communications were often called issue ads because, though they were designed to benefit a candidate, they did not explicitly advocate the election or defeat of any candidate.

Titles I and II of BCRA called into question the meaning and the validity of *Buckley's* distinction between campaign contributions and expenditures. It appeared that BCRA banned a political party from engaging in any form of soft money expenditures and corporations and unions from using soft money expenditures to pay for issue ads within the time limits provided by the statute. A number of groups, political action committees, and individuals, led by Senator Mitch McConnell, immediately challenged the BCRA in federal court. These cases were quickly consolidated under the name *McConnell v. Federal Election Commission* and came before a special three-judge district court in Washington, D.C., with a direct appeal to the Supreme Court. The district court heard oral argument on December 4 and 5, 2002, and handed down its decision upholding most of Title I and invalidating most of Title II on May 2, 2003, along with four opinions that numbered 1,638 pages of typescript pages. Each judge wrote his or her own opinion and two judges collaborated on a separate per curiam opinion. One judge ruled Title I constitutional; another that it was mostly unconstitutional; and the third partly agreed and partly disagreed with the other two. Perhaps in part because of the ruling's confusing nature, the district court stayed its enforcement on May 19, 2003, which meant that the BCRA was legally in effect as the case was appealed to the Supreme Court.[18]

In his brief to the Supreme Court, Senator McConnell argued that both Titles I and II violated freedom of speech. Title I (referred to in the briefs as BCRA, Section 101 or the new FECA, Section 323) was unconstitutional because it barred individuals from giving "soft" money to political parties; prohibited national political parties from receiving, transferring, soliciting, or spending "soft" money; forbade state and local political parties from spending "soft" money for any "federal election activity"; and "impermissibly interfered with the associational rights of political parties and their members."[19] Because the law regulated the *"uses"* for which money was raised and spent, it was not simply a "limit," whether of contributions or expenditures. It therefore had to satisfy strict scrutiny, which it could not do because it was not a "narrowly tailored" means of serving the compelling interest of preventing *quid pro quo*

Box 5.1   SENATE DEBATE OVER BCRA

SENATOR JOHN MCCAIN (R-Arizona):
. . . The sad truth is that most Americans do believe that we conspire to hold onto every single political advantage, lest we jeopardize our incumbency. . . . Most Americans believe that we would let this Nation pay any price, bear any burden for the sake of securing our own ambitions, no matter how injurious the effect might be to the national interest. And who can blame them? As long as the wealthiest Americans and richest organized interests can make the six and seven figure donations to political parties and gain the special access to power that such generosity confers on the donor, most Americans will dismiss the most virtuous politician's claim of patriotism. . . .

Why can't we all agree to this very simple, very obvious truth: that campaign contributions from a single source that run into the hundreds of thousands or millions of dollars are not healthy to a democracy? Is that not self-evident? . . . It is to the people. . . .

Real campaign finance reform will not cure all public cynicism about modern politics. Nor will it completely free politics from influence peddling or the appearance of it. But I believe it will cause many Americans who are at present quite disaffected from the machinations of politics to begin to see that their elected officials value their reputations more than their incumbency. And maybe that recognition will even encourage more of them to seek public office, not for the privileges bestowed upon election winners, but for the honor of serving a great Nation. . . .

Source: Congressional Record, 107th Congress, 1st Session, March 19, 2001.

corruption or the appearance of such corruption. Title II's prohibition of issue ads abridged the right of corporations and unions to speak out on issues and candidates. So long as such an ad avoided the express advocacy of the election or the defeat of particular federal candidates, government could not regulate them without violating the principles enshrined in *Buckley*.

The brief filed by the FEC insisted that Title I did not have to satisfy strict scrutiny since it functioned solely as a "source-and-amount" limit. Though the limit on the amount of soft money that any individual or group could donate to the national political party was set at zero, it was still a contribution limit, if only because it did not limit in any way the amount of hard money that a political party could spend during an election year. It simply required the party to raise the money it spent through a greater number of hard money donations, rather than a smaller number of large soft money donations. Congress could prohibit soft money donations because they created a substantial risk of actual or apparent corruption. The FEC's brief highlighted the fact that "well over

SENATOR MITCH MCCONNELL *(R-Kentucky)*:
. . . Although the facts about the provisions of this bill are almost always misrepresented, the driving mantra behind the entire movement is that we are all corrupt or that we appear to be corrupt.

We have explored corruption and the appearance of corruption before in this Chamber. You cannot have corruption unless someone is corrupt. At no time has any Member of either body offered evidence of even the slightest hint of corruption by any Member of either body. As for the appearance of corruption, our friends in the media who are part and parcel of the reform industry continue to make broad and baseless accusations. . . .

With no basis in fact or reality, the media constantly and repeatedly alleges that our every decision can be traced back to money given to support a political party. I trust that every Member in the Chamber recognizes how completely absurd, false, and insulting these charges are. . . .

Each Member is elected to represent our constituents. We act in what we believe is the best interest of the country and, obviously, of our home States. Does representing the interests of our State and our constituents lead to corruption or the appearance of corruption? These allegations are not an attack on us, they are an attack on representative democracy.

What we are talking about today is speech: the Government telling people how, when, and how much speech they are allowed. This wholesale regulation of every action of every American anytime there is a Federal election is truly unprecedented. . . .

Source: Congressional Record, 107th Congress, 2nd Session, March 20, 2002.

half the 50 largest 'soft' money donors gave money to *both* of the major political parties," which arguably confirmed that the gifts were to obtain access and influence inside the legislative process, not to express some ideological sympathy or compatibility. Title II's ban on so-called issue ads by corporations and unions during specified periods of a federal campaign were also justifiable according to the FEC. Such ads referred to a federal candidate and were designed to influence federal elections. The fact that they did not include express advocacy of the candidate's defeat or election was irrelevant because the "overwhelming majority of modern campaign advertisements do not use words of express advocacy, whether they are financed by candidates, political parties, or other organizations." Accordingly, the FEC's brief concluded, the distinction between express advocacy and issue ads was essentially meaningless and therefore could not mark the boundary of Congress's power to regulate federal political campaigns.

In a very unusual session held on September 8, 2003, the Supreme Court heard oral argument in *McConnell* for four and one-half hours. Not only was the session unusual because it occurred outside the Court's normal term, but its length and the number of attorneys who participated in the argument made it a truly exceptional event. Eight lawyers appeared before the Court that day, including Kenneth W. Starr, the former Independent Counsel who investigated whether President William Clinton committed perjury in the Paula Jones case; Theodore B. Olson, Solicitor General of the United States; Seth P. Waxman, former Solicitor General under the Clinton administration; and Floyd Abrams, a prominent free speech attorney. In the brief excerpts that follow, Starr and Olson square off on whether Title I's ban on soft money is constitutional, while Abrams, and Paul Clement, Deputy Solicitor General debate Title II's prohibition of so-called issue ads sponsored by corporations and unions during federal elections. In particular, Abrams explained why corporations like the NRA did not want to pay for issue ads through PACs, while Clement defended the exemption in BCRA which freed media corporations from the rule banning issue ads.

The Supreme Court handed down its decision in the *McConnell* case on December 10, 2003, just prior to the Democratic presidential primary season that was about to get underway in early 2004. Joined by Justices Souter, Ginsburg, and Breyer, Justice John Paul Stevens and Justice Sandra Day O'Connor wrote a joint opinion that upheld the key provisions of Titles I and II. In assessing the constitutionality of Title I's soft money ban, the Court's majority did not apply strict scrutiny. Even though Title I included spending and solicitation restrictions, the Court applied the lower standard that had been applied to contribution limits in *Buckley* and found that Congress's interest in preventing corruption and the appearance of corruption was more than sufficient to justify the ban. In coming to this conclusion, the Court underlined the fact that Congress's interest in this area extended beyond *quid pro quo* exchanges of contributions for votes. It also included instances of what the Court called "undue influence" on a candidate's or officeholder's "judgment" or the "appearance" of such influence. In contrast, the Court applied strict scrutiny to Title II's regulation of issue ads, yet nevertheless upheld the regulation since there was no question Congress could regulate advertisements that expressly advocated the election or defeat of a candidate for federal office. Since there was no meaningful distinction between ads containing express advocacy and issue ads that are "intended to influence the voters' decisions and have that effect," Congress could regulate both. Title II was not a complete ban since corporation and unions could still run issue ads by "avoiding any specific reference to federal candidates or in doubtful cases by paying for the ad from a segregated fund."

All four dissenting justices wrote opinions in *McConnell* and each dissent explored a somewhat different theme. Justice Scalia argued that the BCRA reflected the interests of the incumbents who enacted it and that it cut "to the heart of what the First Amendment is meant to protect: the right to criticize government." Justice Thomas emphasized that the government's "anticircumvention" rationale was a "never-ending and self-justifying process." Justice Kennedy attacked the majority's assumption that access to a federal candidate or officeholder was sufficient to establish corruption or the appearance of corruption. In his opinion, a *quid pro quo* exchange or at least a *"quid pro quo* danger" had to be established before Congress could regulate political speech. In addition, according to Justice Kennedy, Title II's ban on so called "sham issue ads" was a flagrant attempt by the government to regulate a "mass communication technique." It was unconstitutional because the government's purpose was to suppress a potent and effective form of speech and because "hostility toward corporations and unions" was "inconsistent with the viewpoint neutrality" demanded by the First Amendment. Lastly, Chief Justice Rehnquist claimed that the government and the Court's majority were all too willing to "impute corruption" on the basis of a "close relationship" between federal officeholders and national and state parties. Such an imputation greatly infringed associational rights and unduly expanded Congress's power to regulate political speech.

McConnell proved beyond doubt that the Supreme Court today is as deeply fractured over the issue of campaign finance regulation as it was when it decided *Buckley* over twenty-seven years ago. Justices Scalia and Thomas are suspicious of most forms of campaign regulation; reject *Buckley*'s distinction between contribution and expenditures; and generally favor a wide open system in which citizens and groups would be able to contribute and spend their money for political purposes in any way they wished. Chief Justice Rehnquist and Justice Kennedy are more moderate in tone, balancing the government's interest in regulating *quid pro quo* corruption against the value of free speech. However, in *McConnell* five justices have supported the extension of federal regulations considerably beyond what *Buckley* would have tolerated. Whether this majority is solid in character and whether the BCRA system of campaign regulation will form an enduring structure are unanswerable questions at this point. Multibillionaire financier George Soros has pledged millions of dollars to partisan groups (so-called "527 committees" based on the section of the Internal Revenue Code that created them) that are in sympathy with the Democratic Party. These committees plan to finance issue ads and get-out-the-vote-drives during the 2004 presidential election with soft money. Campaign finance watchdog groups and the Republican National Committee asked the FEC to block these efforts to "circumvent" the restrictions established by BCRA.[20] In an Advisory Opinion issued on February 19, 2003, the FEC ruled that "527 committees," unlike political parties in the post-*McConnell* period, can finance broadcast and other types of communications with a combination of hard and soft money. Given this ruling, it is expected that individuals in sympathy with the Republican Party will soon establish "527 committees" of their own and that soft money will continue to have a significant impact on the American electoral process. What the FEC will do, can do, or should do in this situation is a highly controversial question. Just as money and politics in the United States are irresistibly attracted to each other, so also freedom of speech and the integrity of the electoral system are in a dynamic tension.

BIBLIOGRAPHY

Baxter, W. Parker. "Note: Recent Developments in Campaign Finance Law: Implementing the Bipartisan Campaign Finance Act of 2002." 6 *New York University School of Law Journal of Legislation and Public Policy* (2003): 589–601.

Corrado, Anthony. *Paying for Presidents: Public Financing in National Elections.* New York: The Twentieth Century Fund Press, 1993.

Hasen, Richard L. "Buckley Is Dead, Long Live Buckley: The New Campaign Finance Incoherence of McConnell v. Federal Election Commission." *University of Pennsylvania Law Review* (2004).

Krasno, Jonathan S., and Frank J. Sorauf. "Report: Evaluating the Bipartisan Campaign Finance Reform Act (BCRA)." 28 *New York University School of Law Review of Law and Social Change* (2003): 121–81.

Malbin, Michael J., ed. *Life after Reform: When the Bipartisan Campaign Reform Act Meets Politics.* New York: Rowman & Littlefield, 2003.

Sullivan, Kathleen M. "Political Money and Freedom of Speech," 30 *U.C. Davis Law Review* (1997): 663–90.

BRIEFS

SENATOR MCCONNELL'S BRIEF

[[1. Free Speech, the Right of Association and Soft Money.]] Like the contribution and expenditure limits at issue in *Buckley*, section 101 [[of BCRA's Title I]] burdens the speech and associational rights of donors, who will no longer be able to give donations previously permitted by state law to national party committees, and of the parties themselves, which will no longer be able to spend state-regulated funds either at all (in the case of national party committees) or except for certain limited activities that do not qualify as "federal election activity" (in the case of state and local party committees). In *Buckley*, the Court noted (as to expenditures) that "[a] restriction on the amount of money a person or group can spend on political communication during a campaign necessarily reduces the quantity of expression by restricting the number of issues discussed, the depth of their exploration, and the size of the audience reached." . . .

Section 101 burdens speech rights in additional ways not at issue in *Buckley*. For instance, it imposes restrictions not just on contributions and expenditures, but also on *solicitations*. This Court has repeatedly affirmed that a restriction on solicitations is the most direct form of restriction on speech. That is unsurprising, for "solicitation is characteristically intertwined with informative and perhaps persuasive speech seeking support for particular causes or for particular views on economic, political, or social issues," and "without solicitation the flow of such information and advocacy would likely cease." . . .

In addition to speech rights, section 101 burdens associational rights in ways not implicated in *Buckley*. Specifically, by pervasively regulating the relationships among party committees, and between party committees and others, section 101 impermissibly interferes with the associational rights of political parties and their members. It is beyond question that "[t]he right to associate with the political party of one's choice is an integral part" of the First Amendment freedom of association. It is also well established that the right of association inheres not only in the members of a political party, but also in the party itself. So too, when the government attempts to regulate the internal structure of political parties, it infringes on the parties' associational rights. . . .

Most significantly, [[Section 101]] . . . bans national committees from transferring state-regulated funds to state and local committees. . . . As numerous witnesses testified below, the net effect of these provisions is to strip from political parties much of their traditional power both to engage in coordinated fundraising and to allocate funds on the national, state, and local levels. The provisions will also force political parties to shift their fundraising activities from the national committees, which have developed comparative expertise in fundraising, to state and local committees. . . .

[[2. Strict Scrutiny and Corruption.]] It is well established that "exacting" or strict scrutiny is applied to limitations on independent expenditures; limitations on solicitations; and any other limitations that impose a severe burden on associational rights. Strict scrutiny therefore unquestionably applies to all of the provisions of section 101 that were upheld (as modified) by the district court. . . .

First, unlike the provisions of FECA at issue in *Buckley*, section 101 does not impose any new limits on the *amounts* of contributions to national committees: instead, it merely subjects funds used by national committees for a variety of previously unregulated purposes to the preexisting source-and-amount limitations of FECA, and requires that national committees raise and spend federally regulated, rather than state-regulated, funds for those activities. Because section 101 thereby effectively regulates the *uses* for which money is raised and spent, rather than imposing any new limits on the *amounts* of contributions or expenditures, *Buckley*'s dichotomy between contributions and expenditures is inapposite, and strict scrutiny is warranted. . . .

This Court held in *Buckley*, and has since reaffirmed, that "preventing corruption or the appearance of corruption are the only legitimate and compelling government interests thus far identified for restricting campaign finances." "The hallmark of corruption," in turn, "is the financial *quid pro quo*: dollars for political favors."

Section 101 cannot implicate the governmental interest in preventing actual or apparent corruption in the classic, *quid pro quo* sense, since a *political party* (unlike a current or future officeholder) cannot respond to a donation by taking some legislative action, but instead can act only through its officeholders. Unsurprisingly, defendants have failed, despite voluminous discovery, to identify a single instance of *quid pro quo* corruption attributable to the donation of state-regulated funds. Consequently, defendants contend that the donation of

state-regulated funds can be corrupting because it allows donors to buy not
some particular legislative action, but rather "access" to officeholders through
their political parties. Defendants have suggested that this alleged purchasing of
"access" gives rise not to actual corruption or the appearance of corruption,
but rather to the "*possibility* of the appearance of corruption."

We recognize that language in some of this Court's most recent campaign
finance opinions suggests that the government's interest in preventing corruption sweeps beyond preventing classic, *quid pro quo* corruption, to stemming
the "broader threat from politicians too compliant with the wishes of large contributors," and barring "undue influence on an officeholder's judgment, and
the appearance of such influence." However broad these formulations may be,
they do not reach as far as defendants' "access"-based interest. Defendants'
"unexamined, anecdotal accounts" aside, there are no legislative findings, and
certainly no valid statistical evidence, that money secures access to officeholders. Even if there were sufficient evidence of such a link, however, defendants'
"access"-based interest proves too much. Assuming that officeholders naturally
provide greater access to their supporters, and specifically to their financial supporters (whether or not that includes the financial supporters of their political
parties), than to their opponents, the only solution would be to take all money
(whether federally regulated and state-regulated) out of politics altogether—
which BCRA does not purport to do. In any event, this Court has squarely
rejected such a broad equality-based rationale as a justification for campaign
finance regulation.

[[3. Circumvention of Contribution Limits.]] In the alternative, BCRA's
defenders have contended that the government has an interest in imposing additional limits that, while themselves not justified by the anti-corruption rationale, are necessary to prevent circumvention of existing limits that *are* justified
by the anti-corruption rationale.

To the extent this Court has invoked such a rationale, it has done so only in
a limited context: namely, to uphold limits on contributions that could be used
for the same purposes as direct contributions to federal candidates themselves.
Thus, in *Buckley*, the Court upheld the $25,000 federal limit on aggregate con-
tributions by an individual in a calendar year, on the ground that otherwise an
individual could circumvent the $1,000 limit on contributions to a single candi-
date simply by contributing to that candidate's political party or sympathetic
PACs. . . . [[I]]n *Colorado II*, the Court, while frequently referring to "circumvention," upheld limits on coordinated expenditures by political parties on the
basis of the longstanding rule, dating from *Buckley*, that expenditures coordinated with federal candidates are the functional equivalent of contributions to
the candidates themselves. Pivotally, however, the Court has never embraced
an anti-circumvention rationale to justify limitations on donations that are not
interchangeable with direct contributions to *candidates*, much less limitations
on independent expenditures (which, of course, are entitled to the fullest First
Amendment protection). . . .

In reality, defendants' anti-circumvention rationale is no rationale at all. *Any* currently lawful use of money to affect the political process could be character-ized as an attempt to "circumvent" currently existing prohibitions on other uses. If this Court were to uphold BCRA on the basis of the anti-circumvention rationale, defendants would likely justify future restrictions as necessary to pre-vent circumvention of BCRA, much as they have justified BCRA as necessary to prevent circumvention of existing law (and, indeed, have justified certain pro-visions of BCRA as necessary to prevent circumvention of *other* provisions of BCRA). This house of cards cannot stand. The Court should reject defendants' perverse attempt to fashion a limitless "prophylactic" rationale for *suppressing*, rather than *protecting*, core constitutional rights.

[[4. Narrowly Tailored Means.]] At the outset, it is questionable whether sec-tion 101 is tailored to the government's interest in preventing corruption *at all*. To conclude that it is, the Court would have to indulge two critical assumptions.

First, the Court would have to assume that the donation of state-regulated funds to, or the spending of state-regulated funds by, a political party is just as corrupting of a candidate as a contribution directly to the candidate. To make such an assumption would work a major departure from existing law. In *Colo-rado Republican Fed. Campaign Comm. v. FEC*, (*Colorado I*), this Court held that Congress could not constitutionally limit independent expenditures of fed-erally regulated funds by political parties. The plurality expressly rejected the argument that there are "any special dangers of corruption associated with political parties that tip the constitutional balance in a different direction." Indeed, the Court noted that expenditures by political parties were designed not only to get the party's candidates elected, but to promote the views of the party's members. Defendants advance no justification for treating the disburse-ment of state-regulated funds by political parties (or the donation of state-regu-lated funds to political parties for use in such disbursements) differently from expenditures of federally regulated funds by the same parties for purposes of First Amendment analysis.

Second, the Court would have to assume that a donation of state-regulated funds to be used for activities that do not exclusively serve to get a candidate elected, but instead benefit candidates up and down the party ticket (such as party-promoting campaign activity), or the spending of state-regulated funds for such activities, is just as corrupting of a candidate as a contribution to be used for activities that exclusively do so (such as express advocacy). Again, this Court's decisions counsel against such an assumption. In *Colorado I*, the plu-rality expressly recognized that "FECA permits unregulated 'soft money' con-tributions to a party for certain activities." Nevertheless, the plurality stated outright that "the opportunity for corruption posed by these greater opportu-nities for contributions is, *at best, attenuated*." As a matter of common sense, because state-regulated funds by definition can be used only for activities that influence state elections (or in combination with federally regulated funds, for activities that influence *both* state and federal elections), a candidate will feel less indebted, *ceteris paribus*, to a donor for contributing state-regulated funds, which will affect his own election only indirectly and partially (if at all), than to another donor who contributes federally regulated funds, which can be used directly and entirely to support his election. . . .

. . . [[T]]o the extent "large" donations of state-regulated funds are seen to be corrupting, Congress could have imposed a cap on the amount of such donations. Indeed, the Hagel Amendment, which Congress considered and rejected, would have done just that. Specifically, it would have imposed a $60,000 aggregate limit on donations of federally regulated funds and state-regulated funds from any one donor to a national party committee. Instead, section 101 bans *any* donations of state-regulated funds to national committees, no matter how small, and further bans *disbursements* of state-regulated funds by national committees for any purpose (and by state and local committees for "federal election activity"). . . .

Likewise, to the extent particular *uses* of state-regulated funds are seen as corrupting, Congress could have imposed narrower limits on the uses to which such funds could be put. Specifically, Congress could have limited the use of state-regulated funds only for those activities that arguably have a more direct effect on a federal candidate's election (such as advertising that refers to a federal candidate, assuming for the moment that such disbursements could constitutionally be regulated), and not for those activities whose effect on a federal candidate's election is concededly more attenuated (such as party-promoting campaign activity). Instead, section 101 bans *all* uses of state-regulated funds by national committees, and restricts a number of uses of state-regulated funds by state and local committees which primarily or only affect state elections. And section 101 imposes a variety of restrictions on the transfer and solicitation of funds, which cannot be justified by any concern about the use of state-regulated funds for certain activities. This is overkill in the extreme. Given the availability of more narrowly tailored alternatives, section 101 violates the First Amendment. . . .

[[5. Discrimination against Political Parties.]] Section 101 also fails constitutional muster because it limits speech by political parties but not identical speech by other entities. As this Court has observed, "[i]n the realm of protected speech, the legislature is constitutionally disqualified from dictating the subjects about which persons may speak and *the speakers who may address a public issue.*" This requirement of neutrality among speakers is drawn not only from the equal protection component of the Fifth Amendment, but from the First Amendment itself. Discrimination among speakers is a species of impermissible underinclusiveness, insofar as the government is prohibiting regulable speech by some speakers but not others. . . .

It is indisputable that section 101 will place political party committees at a severe disadvantage compared to interest groups. Whereas national party committees are barred outright from raising state-regulated funds—or spending them on contributions to state or local candidates, voter registration, voter identification, get-out-the-vote efforts, party-promoting campaign activity, or even administrative expenses—interest groups will be able to continue to raise and spend non-federally regulated funds for all of these purposes. . . .

By effectively diverting funds from the political parties to interest groups, section 101 will empower narrowly focused interest groups at the expense of the political parties, and thereby detract from the central and unifying role that parties have played in our political process from the earliest days of the Republic. "The preservation and health of our political institutions, state and federal, depends to no small extent on the continued vitality of our two-party system, which permits both stability and measured change." By impermissibly disadvantaging political parties, section 101 violates fundamental principles of free speech and equal protection.

[[6. Title II: Issue Advocacy.]] We begin with first principles. Speech about politics, issues, and elections is entitled to the most solicitous protection of the First Amendment. Just last year, this Court observed:

> [T]he notion that the special context of electioneering justifies an *abridgment* of the right to speak out on disputed issues sets our First Amendment jurisprudence on its head. [D]ebate on the qualifications of candidates is at the core of our electoral process and of the First Amendment freedoms, not at the edges.

But abridging the right to speak out on issues and candidates is precisely what BCRA's "electioneering communications" provisions do, and that is precisely why they cannot withstand scrutiny under the First Amendment. . . .

In the nearly three decades since this Court's decision in *Buckley*, courts and commentators alike have consistently concluded that *Buckley*, and then *MCFL* [[*FEC v. Massachusetts Citizens for Life* (1986)]], drew a constitutionally mandated line between speech that expressly advocates the election or defeat of a candidate and speech that does not. In a number of post-*Buckley* opinions rejecting the FEC's persistent efforts to expand the definition of express advocacy articulated by this Court, and therefore to do by regulation what BCRA now attempts to do by statute, the lower courts have consistently concluded that only express advocacy can constitutionally be regulated. . . .

In and of itself, the *Buckley* "bottom line" dooms BCRA's "electioneering communications" provisions. The primary definition of "electioneering communications" in section 201, which covers advertising that merely "refers" to a clearly identified candidate for federal office, sweeps well beyond express advocacy, as it fails to require that the advertising contain "express words of advocacy of election or defeat." . . .

In addition to contending that *Buckley* and *MCFL* did not draw a constitutional distinction between express advocacy and all other speech about issues and candidates, defendants have urged in the alternative that such a distinction does not apply to corporations and unions. The argument is unavailing. . . .

In *MCFL*, the Court drew the same constitutional line in the specific context of speech by a corporation. The Court construed . . . the provision of FECA banning all expenditures by corporations and unions "in connection with" federal elections, to reach only express advocacy. The Court did not limit its statutory construction to expenditures by qualified non-profit corporations, but instead held categorically, with respect to *all* corporations, that "an expenditure must constitute 'express advocacy' in order to be subject to the prohibition of §441*b*." In fact, it was only after the Court proffered its narrowing construction of section 441*b*, and concluded that the speech at issue *was* express advocacy, that the Court even drew a distinction between qualified non-profit corporations and other corporations, in resolving the ultimate issue of whether expenditures for express advocacy by the defendant non-profit corporation could be regulated. . . .

Austin v. Michigan Chamber of Commerce is not, as the government suggests to the contrary. In *Austin*, the Court held that a State could constitutionally restrict corporate independent expenditures for express advocacy. Nothing in *Austin*, however, even remotely hints that the Court intended to overrule *Buckley*, *MCFL*, and *Bellotti* so as to allow the government to regulate expenditures by corporations and unions for speech other than express advocacy. *Austin* itself involved a state statute modeled on the federal provision at issue in *MCFL*, and an ad that urged voters, in large bold type, to "Elect Richard Bandstra"—an ad that plainly constituted express advocacy. *Austin* held only that Michigan could regulate the Michigan Chamber of Commerce's expenditure for the express advocacy at issue, since the Chamber was not a qualified non-profit corporation under *MCFL*. . . .

In a related vein, defendants have urged that corporations and unions may be required to engage in "electioneering communications" through PACs (or "segregated funds"), as BCRA permits. Leaving aside the fact that many corporations and unions may have no desire to establish PACs . . . [[,]] requiring a corporation to speak exclusively through a PAC substantially burdens its right to speak. It is simply no answer to say that these entities can "speak" by having a PAC speak for them. PACs provide neither a constitutionally sufficient nor practically workable alternative to speech by plaintiffs themselves. If the speech at issue is fully protected by the First Amendment—and it is nothing less—plaintiffs are permitted to utter it in their own name, and to pay for it with their own funds, without fear of governmental interference.

Defendants' theory is that only speech that is "genuinely" about "issues" is constitutionally protected, while all other speech is subject to government regulation. This is, of course, precisely the opposite of what this Court concluded in *Buckley* and reaffirmed in *MCFL*: that only speech expressly advocating the election or defeat of a candidate is regulable, while all other speech about issues and candidates is not. Defendants' theory then proceeds to the dubious proposition that "most" speech that is "genuinely" about "issues" is not broadcast in close proximity to elections. Therefore, the syllogism marches on, by banning any reference to a federal candidate in any communication aired within 30 days of a primary or 60 days of a general election, BCRA will eliminate disfavored speech about issues and candidates—pejoratively referred to by defendants as "sham" issue ads—but not most "genuine" speech about issues. Defendants' theory is both legally and factually indefensible.

A review of actual advertisements aired in the 30- and 60-day periods before the 1998 and 2000 primary and general elections powerfully illustrates the sort of protected speech that would be criminalized by BCRA's regulation of "electioneering communications." As would be expected (and as *Buckley* predicted), a vast majority of the ads covered by BCRA refer to incumbent officeholders who are running for re-election. One such ad, broadcast within 60 days of the 1998 general election in the district of Oregon Congressman David Wu, urged him as follows:

> The people of America should be running our government. That's the way it was set up in the first place. The problem is the special interests and the paid lobbyists who control the Washington politicians. The answer is term limits. Term limits replace Washington insiders with new people who reflect community interests, not politics as usual. Molly Bordonaro has signed the pledge to limit her terms in Congress. David Wu refused. Call David Wu and tell him to sign the US Term Limits Pledge.

The ad thus informed the viewers that Congressman Wu had failed to sign a term-limits pledge, and attempted to pressure him to do so. Though it may seem unthinkable that such core political speech could be the subject of criminal sanctions, Americans for Term Limits (the group that sponsored the ad) would be subject to such sanctions for airing the same ad today. . . .

Finally, the federal defendants have identified the following ad, aired in Michigan within 60 days of the 2000 general election, as an example of a so-called "sham" issue ad:

WOMAN: My mom started this business and my brother and I worked hard to make it grow. One day we hope to own it but because of the law, we can never be sure.

ANNOUNCER: Because of the death tax, people like Melanie are always at risk of losing family businesses. Debbie Stabenow voted twice against getting rid of the death tax.

WOMAN: Everything we have worked for can be taken away in an instant and that's not fair.

ANNOUNCER: Call Debbie Stabenow. Tell her our working families need a break. Paid for by the Michigan Chamber of Commerce.

Remarkably, far from acknowledging that this ad is speech fully protected by the First Amendment, defendants have viewed it as a perfect example of speech that should be criminalized.

These ads—sometimes using pointed, critical, and antagonistic speech—all sought to lobby and pressure federal officeholders on issues of unquestioned importance to the groups that sponsor them. They are fully protected by *Buckley*, to say nothing of the core principle of *New York Times Co. v. Sullivan* that "uninhibited, robust, and wide-open speech" is protected by the First Amendment.

To counter these and the many other examples of BCRA's overbreadth, defendants relied almost exclusively on two reports by the Brennan Center for Justice . . . entitled *Buying Time 1998: Television Advertising in the 1998 Congressional Elections* and *Buying Time 2000: Television Advertisements in the 2000 Federal Elections*.

The *Buying Time* reports surveyed ads aired during the 1998 and 2000 election cycles and concluded that the vast majority of ads that would have been banned by BCRA were "sham" issue ads, and thus speech that, in the authors' view, should not be entitled to First Amendment protection. The reports concluded that only a tiny fraction of so-called "genuine" issue ads—speech that defendants admit is entitled to full First Amendment protection—would have been covered by BCRA's primary definition of "electioneering communications." . . .

The very premise of the *Buying Time* reports (and indeed, defendants' entire argument about BCRA's "electioneering communication" provisions) is itself fundamentally flawed. In insisting that BCRA will have only a modest effect on "genuine" issue advocacy, defendants and the *Buying Time* authors have sought to seize for themselves the role of determining—in a way wholly inconsistent with *Buckley*—what advocacy is "genuine." They have embraced the notion that only speech about a bill or an issue is "genuine" and is protected by the First Amendment, while speech about candidates is rarely, if ever, protected. This view, as we have observed, is flatly at odds both with this Court's decisions and with fundamental First Amendment principles. . . .

. . . As Craig Holman, chief author of *Buying Time 2000*, acknowledged in his deposition, any effort to determine the "purpose" of a political advertisement is by its nature not a "black and white issue," but is instead a "subjective judgment" that can be reasonably debated. Indeed, defendants' own expert Professor Goldstein noted that the students involved in coding ads for the *Buying Time* studies disagreed 25% of the time as to whether a particular ad was intended to "generate support or opposition for a particular candidate" or not. . . .

Respectfully submitted,
Kenneth W. Starr,
Counsel of Record

BRIEF FOR THE FEDERAL ELECTION COMMISSION

[[1. Contribution Limits Not Subject to Strict Scrutiny.]] New FECA §323(a)(1) (added by BCRA §101(a)) prohibits any national committee of a political party from receiving funds that are not subject to the FECA contribution limits. The effect of that provision is to close loopholes in the regulation of donations to political parties by barring national party committees from receiving any donations whatever of corporate and union general treasury funds, and by limiting individual donations to the national committees to an annual maximum of $25,000. Those restrictions easily satisfy the relatively relaxed standard of review applicable to contribution limits.

New FECA §323(a)(1) places no restrictions either on the total amount of money that a national committee may spend, or on the uses to which lawfully-acquired funds may be put. It functions solely as a source-and-amount limit analogous to (though much larger than) the limits that FECA imposes on contributions to federal candidates and to non-party political committees. Since this Court's decision in *Buckley*, "restrictions on political contributions have been treated as merely 'marginal' speech restrictions subject to relatively complaisant review under the First Amendment, because contributions lie closer to the edges than to the core of political expression.". . .

In *Buckley* itself, this Court upheld FECA's $25,000 annual limit on an individual's aggregate contributions to all federal candidates and political committees, including national parties, characterizing that provision as a "quite modest restraint upon protected political activity" and as "no more than a corollary of the basic individual contribution limitation." The Court did not suggest that limits on contributions to parties or other political committees are subject to more searching review than limits on contributions to candidates. . . .

Similarly, the Court in *Buckley*, in distinguishing between contribution and expenditure limits for purposes of First Amendment analysis, referred repeatedly to limits on contributions to candidates *or* political associations. And unlike the expenditure caps struck down in *Buckley*,—which limited the total amounts that candidates and others could spend on electoral activity, without regard to the size of the increments in which the relevant funds were raised—the effect of the national party soft-money ban "is merely to require [national party committees] to raise funds from a greater number of persons." There is consequently no basis for plaintiffs' suggestions that new FECA §323(a)(1)'s ban on soft-money donations to national party committees is subject to strict scrutiny.

. . . In upholding FECA's $25,000 annual ceiling on an individual's aggregate contributions, the *Buckley* Court observed that, absent such a limit, a donor could circumvent the $1,000 cap on contributions to a federal candidate by making "huge contributions to the candidate's political party." And, in light of the close connections between federal office-holders and the parties with which they are affiliated, and the degree to which the candidate's fortunes are intertwined with those of the larger party organization, the concern that some federal officeholders may be unduly protective of the interests of their parties' large-scale donors is an entirely plausible one.

Presumably for these reasons, plaintiffs do not take issue with the basic pre-existing $20,000 limit on contributions to national parties (increased to $25,000 by BCRA), but only challenge its extension to all donations made to national parties, regardless of their ostensible purpose. The premise of the underlying contribution limit, however, is that large contributions to the parties may ultimately influence the official conduct of party members within the government. Once the validity of that premise is conceded, Congress is entitled to considerable deference in deciding whether donations ostensibly made for non-federal purposes should be exempted from the limits, or whether those donations also create an unacceptable risk of actual or apparent corruption of office-holders.

The reasonableness of Congress's judgment regarding the potential corruptive effects of soft-money donations to the national parties is confirmed by the record in this case. . . . Former Senator Warren Rudman testified that "[l]arge soft money contributions in fact distort the legislative process" because "[t]hey affect whom Senators and House members see, whom they spend their time with, what input they get, and—make no mistake about it—this money affects outcomes as well." One lobbyist testified that "[t]he amount of influence that a lobbyist has is often directly correlated to the amount of money that he or she and his or her clients infuse into the political system." . . .

[[2. Corruption.]] Perhaps the most telling evidence that donors view large soft-money donations as a means to affect the legislative process is the fact that in both 1996 and 2000, well over half of the 50 largest soft-money donors gave money to *both* of the major political parties. That pattern of giving belies an ideological motivation and is explicable instead as an effort to obtain influence within the legislative process. As former Senator Dale Bumpers testified, "[g]iving soft money to both parties, the Republicans and the Democrats, makes no sense at all unless the donor feels that he or she is buying access." . . .

The record makes clear not only that donors and federal office-holders perceive a connection between large soft-money donations and influence upon the legislative process, but that the national party committees actively seek to foster that perception. The RNC's own documents "show that the RNC's donor programs offer greater access to federal office holders as the donations grow larger, with the highest level and most personal access offered to the largest soft money donors." . . .

In crafting new FECA §323(a), Congress chose to close the loophole that allowed unlimited soft-money donations to national party committees for the financing of activities ostensibly intended solely to influence state elections. The decision to regulate all donations to the national parties reflects Congress's judgment that "[b]ecause the national parties operate at the national level, and are inextricably intertwined with federal officeholders and candidates, who raise the money for the national party committees, there is a close connection between the funding of the national parties and the corrupting dangers of soft money on the federal political process." Congress concluded that "[t]he only effective way to address this problem of corruption is to ban entirely all raising and spending of soft money by the national parties." In light of Congress's greater familiarity with the nature of party fundraising and its effects on the legislative process, that determination is entitled to substantial judicial deference. It is also supported by extensive record evidence demonstrating that large soft-money donors to the national party committees have been promised and granted access to the parties' federal office-holders, notwithstanding the fact that soft money is (by definition) not permitted to be used in order to influence federal elections. . . .

It is wholly understandable, moreover, that an elected federal official will tend to look favorably on his party's large donors, even when a particular dona-tion is earmarked for activities directed solely at state elections. Because money is fungible, a donation that defrays the costs of state electoral advocacy will free up funds for other activities that may directly and tangibly affect federal elections. . . .

Thus, whether or not a particular donation earmarked for state elections has a foreseeable spillover effect on any federal race, a federal office-holder's close identification with his political party may cause him to regard a large-scale party benefactor as an ally of his own. That potential is magnified when the soft-money donor has already made hard-money contributions to the candi-date and party up to the legal limit. Although soft-money donations may have less tangible benefits to a federal candidate or office-holder because of legal restrictions on how the money may be spent, soft money nevertheless benefits such persons by assisting the organization of which they are integral members. And, in any event, the process by which the funds are raised, in which access to federal office-holders has been systematically exchanged for large soft-money donations, creates a substantial risk of actual or apparent corruption, regardless of how the funds are ultimately spent. . . .

[[3. Regulation of State Parties.]] With respect to state political party com-mittees, Congress employed a somewhat different approach. Congress did not place a federal limit on all donations to the state parties. Rather, BCRA applies the federal source-and-amount restrictions and disclosure requirements . . . only to the funds used for four specified categories of "Federal election activ-ity." That term is defined to include (i) "voter registration activity" within the 120 days before a federal election; (ii) "voter identification, get-out-the-vote activity, or generic campaign activity conducted in connection with an election in which a candidate for Federal office appears on the ballot"; (iii) any "public communication that refers to a clearly identified candidate for Federal office . . . and that promotes or supports a candidate for that office, or attacks or opposes a candidate for that office"; and (iv) all services provided by any employee who devotes more than 25% of his compensated time in any month to activities in connection with federal elections. The requirement that such activities be financed entirely with money raised in compliance with the FECA/BCRA con-tribution limits is consistent with the First Amendment.

Contrary to the RNC plaintiffs' contention, the restrictions imposed by new FECA §323(b) are properly treated as limits on contributions rather than on expenditures, even though the applicability of those restrictions turns on the use to which the relevant funds are ultimately put. Unlike the expenditure caps that were struck down in *Buckley*, new FECA §323(b) does not limit the total amount of money that either the donor or the party may spend, either on polit-ical advocacy generally or on "Federal election activity" in particular. Rather, like the contribution limits that the *Buckley* Court sustained, the effect of new

FECA §323(b) "is merely to require . . . [party] committees to raise funds from a greater number of persons and to compel people who would otherwise contribute amounts greater than the statutory limits to expend such funds on direct political expression, rather than to reduce the total amount of money potentially available to promote political expression." Indeed, Congress placed distinct restrictions on disbursements for "Federal election activity" not in order to impose some overall limit on state party spending, but solely to allow spending for non-federal purposes to remain free from federal regulation. The RNC plaintiffs' argument would have the perverse effect of subjecting Congress's limited regulation of contributions used for defined activities to more demanding constitutional scrutiny than an absolute cap on donations for any purpose.

Each category of "Federal election activity" as defined in the Act involves conduct that by its nature will influence federal elections. Disbursements for such activities . . . will often influence state elections as well. But the potential impact on state elections does not diminish the federal interest in preventing actual or apparent corruption of federal office-holders. If a state party's voter-registration and get-out-the-vote activities in connection with an even-year election are successful, the party's federal candidate(s) will inevitably benefit; and the extent of that benefit does not depend on the number of state offices that are contested at the same election. Because federal candidates are likely to regard large donations used to finance "Federal election activity" within their States or districts as substantially assisting their own campaigns, such donations directly implicate the concern that the donor may exercise "undue influence on an officeholder's judgment, and the appearance of such influence." . . .

. . . And once the propriety of *some* restriction on the funding of "Federal election activity" is accepted, "a court has no scalpel to probe" whether 100% or some lesser portion of the costs of such activities should be required to be financed with hard money. Based on its Members' extensive experience under the Commission's former allocation rules, Congress determined that greater constraints on state parties' use of soft money were needed to preserve the integrity of federal elections and federal office-holders. The Constitution does not prevent Congress from acting upon that judgment. . . .

[[4. Solicitations of Soft Money.]] Plaintiffs also challenge . . . restrictions imposed by BCRA §101(a) on the solicitation of funds by political party officials and by federal office-holders and candidates. . . .

New FECA §323(a)'s ban on soft-money solicitations by national political party committees is based on the reasonable premise that, if a large donation to the national party has sufficient corruptive potential to justify a ban, a similar donation to an associated entity (*e.g.*, a state party committee or candidate for state office) designated by the national party may create a comparable threat of corruption. That risk is particularly acute in light of the close connections between national and state party committees and candidates within the party, which increase the danger that a large soft-money donation solicited by a national party committee will be perceived—by the donor, the national party, and federal office-holders—as the functional equivalent of a donation to the national party committee itself. Congress properly acted to prevent the use of such solicitations as a means of circumventing the statutory ban on donations of soft money directly to the national parties. . . .

New FECA §323(e)'s restrictions on soft-money solicitations by federal candidates and office-holders are also constitutional. New FECA §323(e) reflects Congress's reasonable concern that large donations made to other candidates or political committees at the behest of a federal candidate or office-holder may create the same kind of risks of actual or apparent corruption as are posed by large donations to a federal candidate's own campaign. . . .

[[5. Express Advocacy vs. Issue Advocacy.]] The electioneering-communications provisions of Title II of BCRA are addressed to the second major problem that has developed in connection with federal elections over the past decade: the "spectacular rise" in candidate-centered issue advertisements that are paid for with general treasury funds amassed by corporations and unions and that are designed to influence federal candidate elections or likely to have that effect. The direct funding of such advertisements has escaped regulation under [[the]] longstanding prohibition on the use of a corporation's or union's treasury funds in connection with federal elections simply because the advertisements do not contain express advocacy (*e.g.*, Vote for Jones), even though the advertisements are just as likely to influence federal candidate elections as advertisements that contain express advocacy. . . .

For example, the evidence shows an escalating cycle of activity. During the 1995–1996 election cycle, about $135 to $150 million was spent by organizations on multiple broadcasts of about 100 separate issue advertisements; during the 1997–1998 election cycle, about $250 to $340 million was spent by 77 organizations on broadcasts of 423 separate issue advertisements; and during the 1999–2000 cycle, more than $500 million was spent by 130 groups on 1100 separate issue advertisements. Plaintiffs' "own expert readily concede[d] that the number of organizations sponsoring issue advertisements has 'exploded' over the past three election cycles." . . .

A side by side comparison of two advertisements that were broadcast in 2000 by the NRA—whose Executive Vice President acknowledged that the NRA "spent what it took to defeat Al Gore" in 2000—illustrates the ease with which Section 441b was circumvented by corporations and unions. One advertisement was paid for by the NRA's PAC and the other by the NRA's general treasury. Both advertisements clearly identify Al Gore, are nearly identical in their content, and would in all likelihood have the same influence on the Presidential election in the districts in which the advertisements were run. The only significant difference between the advertisements is that the tag line at the end of the advertisement paid for by the PAC says "Vote George W. Bush for President."

The express-advocacy test is not only easy to circumvent, but it does not accurately identify communications designed to affect candidate elections. Even when they are overtly designed for electioneering, "the overwhelming majority of modern campaign advertisements do not use words of express advocacy, whether they are financed by candidates, political parties, or other organizations." Indeed, "[t]he uncontroverted testimony of political consultants demonstrates that it is neither common nor effective to use the 'magic words' of express advocacy in campaign advertisements." . . .

[[6. Strict Scrutiny and Compelling Purpose.]] This Court has held that "independent campaign expenditures constitute 'political expression'" entitled to the highest constitutional protection. In reviewing plaintiffs' challenge to the constitutionality of BCRA's electioneering-communications provisions, the Court must therefore decide whether those provisions are narrowly tailored to advance a compelling government interest. This Court's prior precedents bear strongly on that determination. . . .

BCRA's source-of-funding limitation on electioneering communications protects against . . . "the corrosive and distorting effects of immense aggregations of wealth that are accumulated with the help of the corporate form and that have little or no correlation to the public's support for the corporation's political ideas." In addition, the government has a related but equally important interest in "protect[ing] the individuals who have paid money into a corporation or union for purposes other than the support of candidates from having that money used to support political candidates to whom they may be opposed."

. . . BCRA's source limitation on the financing of electioneering communications directly advances the same "compelling" interest identified in *Austin* by requiring corporations and unions to finance electioneering communications through a separate segregated fund that consists of contributions from individuals who choose to fund such political activity, as opposed to general treasury funds that are accumulated as a result of the benefits of the corporate form and may or may not correlate with public support for the corporation's or union's political activity. . . .

Although the Court did not need to reach the issue in *Austin*, and it need not do so here in light of the fact that Title II of BCRA directly advances the government's compelling interest in eliminating the specific type of corruption identified and relied on in *Austin*, the record in this case nonetheless demonstrates a sufficient risk of real or apparent quid pro quo corruption to justify Congress's judgment that corporations and unions should be prevented from using general treasury funds to finance "electioneering communications."

NRA states that "gratitude for political support is not corruption." But gratitude for political support in the form of *contributions* directly from a corporate or union treasury has long been viewed as corruption, as has gratitude for political support in other forms. . . . Even the appearance of such corruption is sufficient to justify Congress's enactment of Title II, regardless of whether federal officeholders who have benefited from those advertisements in fact have responded with political favors.

[[Lastly,]] Congress's compelling interest in preventing the evasion of existing limits is all the more compelling when, as here, the record demonstrates that those limits are practically illusory and other political actors have demonstrated that the preexisting limits no longer accurately delimit core electioneering expenditures. In light of the hundreds of millions of dollars spent by corporations and unions on advertisements virtually indistinguishable from electioneering advertisements funded by *candidates themselves*, Congress clearly needed to update the limits on corporate and union expenditures to prevent the evasion of the longstanding policy embodied in Section 441b.

[[7. Strict Scrutiny and Narrowly Tailored Means.]] BCRA's primary definition of "electioneering communications" (§201) is clear and objective. An advertisement falls within the definition only if it satisfies four criteria. First, it must be distributed by broadcast, cable, or satellite—*i.e.*, television or radio. Second, it must refer to "a clearly identified candidate for Federal office." Third, it must be distributed within 60 days before a general election or 30 days before a primary election. Fourth, it must be "targeted" to the identified candidate's electorate, *i.e.*, the advertisement must reach at least 50,000 voters in the relevant district or State in an election for the House of Representatives or the Senate. . . .

. . . [[I]]t is significant to note that because of the exceptional clarity of the lines drawn by BCRA's primary definition, any entity truly not interested in airing electioneering communications may easily avoid the source limitation on such communications by simply not referring to a candidate for federal office, running the advertisement outside the 30- or 60-day window, or running the advertisement outside the candidate's district. The clarity with which Congress defined "electioneering communications" therefore itself has considerable constitutional virtue from the standpoint of entities interested in communicating only about genuine issues, and not in influencing the election of particular candidates. . . .

Zeroing in on advertisements that meet BCRA §201's criteria directly advances each of the compelling government interests discussed above. First, it prevents corporations from deploying funds amassed with the benefit of the corporate form to broadcast advertisements that are designed to or will influence candidate elections, but yet do not necessarily correlate with public support for the corporation's political ideas. Second, it eliminates the danger—demonstrated by the record in this case—that candidates who benefit from advertisements that clearly identify them or their opponents and that are run at the most critical junctures of their campaigns will become indebted to the corporations and unions that pay for those advertisements, or that the public will perceive such indebtedness. Third, it prevents corporations and unions from circumventing the federal policy embodied in Section 441b by funding advertisements that do not contain express advocacy but yet are virtually indistinguishable from most *candidate*-funded advertisements and thus presumably are designed to have the same influence on the election of candidates. . . .

Plaintiffs suggest that *Buckley* and *MCFL* erected an inalterable First Amendment rule "that the government may constitutionally regulate only independent expenditures for speech expressly advocating the election or defeat of a candidate, known as express advocacy."

Certainly nothing in *Buckley* imposes such a categorical constitutional restraint on Congress's "well-established" authority to regulate federal elections. In adopting an express-advocacy requirement, the Court in *Buckley* was not expounding on such first principles; it was resolving plaintiffs' argument that the use . . . of the phrase "relative to [[a candidate]]" was "unconstitutionally vague."

When the Court adopts a saving construction of a statute that is amenable to such a construction, the Court by no means forecloses Congress from devising a different or more carefully targeted legislative solution to a problem. . . . If Congress later clarifies its intent, then, and only then, is the constitutional issue ripe for adjudication. That is particularly true when, as here, Congress revisits an area to devise a solution to a problem that has developed in the decades since this Court adopted a saving construction of a different statutory provision in a prior case.

. . . [[I]]t is clear that even the most favorable examples that plaintiffs' lawyers could locate fail to advance their overbreadth claim. Even if plaintiffs' account of the advertisements' alleged *purpose* were taken at face value, it would not alter the fact that—based on the presence of the objective factors identified in BCRA §201—the advertisements were just as likely to influence the outcome of the candidate elections in connection with which they were run as advertisements containing express advocacy.

For example, "Stabenow Death Tax," sponsored by the Michigan Chamber of Commerce, criticized then-Senate candidate Debbie Stabenow for her past votes against repeal of the estate tax. The advertisement ran from September 20, 2000, until a week before election day, in one of the most closely contested Senate races of the year. It is implausible to suggest that the advertisement was not likely or designed to influence the election. . . .

Lastly, it is significant that, although plaintiffs go to extraordinary lengths in attempting to show that BCRA's definition of "electioneering communications" is imperfect at its margins, they have never proposed a better test for identifying such communications other than claiming that it is necessary to adhere to the express-advocacy test. As discussed, the uncontroverted evidence shows that the express advocacy test is a grossly inaccurate proxy for identifying electioneering communications. Indeed, nearly 90% of the advertisements that federal candidates themselves aired in 2000 did not contain express advocacy, though presumably *all* of them were designed to influence their own election. The overbreadth doctrine provides no basis for invalidating Congress's definition of "electioneering communications" in BCRA and limiting federal regulation of the source-of-funding for electioneering advertisements to the blunt proxy of the express-advocacy test. . . .

Respectfully submitted,
Theodore B. Olson,
Solicitor General

ORAL ARGUMENT

JUSTICE GINSBURG: But to the extent that . . . your challenge is based on the First Amendment, then state laws that are similar or even more stringent than the Federal law would also . . . [[fall]]? . . .

MR. STARR [[Counsel for Senator McConnell]]: Well, I don't think so, Your Honor, because what Congress has seen fit to do is regulate activity throughout the system, including then a Federal committee's or national committee's relationship with a state and local committee that ends up affecting what the national committee can do in mayoral elections. . . .

JUSTICE SCALIA: Of course, some states might choose to make no law abridging the freedom of speech. . . .

STARR: And the Commonwealth of Virginia has that, and it is a very good system of total transparency and it's a very vibrant system that is not infected with corruption or the appearance of corruption in the view of its Governor and others. . . .

✻   ✻   ✻

MR. OLSON [[Solicitor General]]: The issues the Court considers today, every single one of them in connection with Title I, are not new. For a century, with the overwhelming support of the public, Congress has struggled to curb the corrupting influence of corporate, union and large, unregulated contributions in Federal elections. . . .

SCALIA: General Olson, is every problem soluble?

OLSON: Well, this Court hasn't found every problem to be solvable.

SCALIA: If for example, the executive should make a compelling case that it is really impossible to eradicate crime if we continue with this silly procedure of having warrants for searches of houses? We wouldn't entertain the argument that, you know, this is the only way to achieve this result.

OLSON: Of course not.

SCALIA: There are certain absolutes, aren't there, even if problems subsist? There are just some things that government can't do?

OLSON: Of course, Justice Scalia, . . . but this Court has said over and over again, not only is it a critical problem that's fundamental to the integrity of our election system, but that the solutions that the legislature has enacted before, the central principles of which are embodied in BCRA, are constitutional solutions to that problem. . . .

*   *   *

SCALIA: . . . But what do you do about expenditures? This law regulates a lot of expenditures.

OLSON: This law, referring to Title I, makes certain contributions illegal to the Federal—to the national parties and to their conduits and surrogates. . . . Of course . . . once it said that the contribution is illegal, the solicitation of the contribution is comparably illegal. And the expenditure of that contribution, . . . the use of that money from that source in excess of those limits [[, is also illegal]]. . . .

*   *   *

SCALIA: Excuse me. You keep calling them abuses. People were taking advantage of those gaps in the law that existed. Is that an abuse, every time—we do it with the tax code all the time. We don't say oh, it's an abuse. He took advantage of—

OLSON: It is—the evidence—

SCALIA: And there will be abuses under this law, too.

OLSON: Of course, of course—

SCALIA: Water will run downhill, and if you cannot make your voices heard in this fashion, they'll find another fashion. . . .

*   *   *

MR. ABRAMS [[Counsel for Senator McConnell]]: As we turn from Title I to Title II, we turn to efforts by Congress to limit, to regulate, and ultimately to punish what are only expenditures, expenditures not made in coordination with parties or candidates which would result in them being treated as contributions, but independently, and so we deal here this afternoon in an area which as this Court observed in Colorado II, it has routinely struck down expend—any limitations in this area. We are all agreed here that strict scrutiny applies. . . .

JUSTICE SOUTER: Beyond express advocacy, do you concede that anything can be regulated?

ABRAMS: I thought very hard about that, Justice Souter, to see if there was something I could give you in that respect. No, I do not concede that there is anything beyond express advocacy.

*   *   *

ABRAMS: The NRA—let me give you an example. The NRA raised an enormous amount of money in the last campaign. They were mentioned a lot on the floor of Congress with great unhappiness by a lot of people. They appealed to 80 million gun owners in America. They have 4 million members. Under the standard rules that apply with respect to a PAC, they could only get money from the 4 million people, not from the 80 million. . . .

SOUTER: Basically that—I didn't mean to interrupt you. Go ahead.

ABRAMS: Sorry. I'm finishing it. They raised $300 million from their ads on television and spent it on more ads to get out their views. . . . [[T]]hat they must, as a matter of law, abandon their general efforts to raise money from the public, is a very significant burden. . . .

JUSTICE BREYER: In other words, you can't go and ask—if I start a PAC or anybody here starts a PAC, you can't go and just ask the general public to belong? . . .

ABRAMS: No. The general public may not belong to the PAC.

SOUTER: But can the NRA go out and say, look, we want you to join the NRA, X dollars. We also want you to give the PAC some money, Y dollars. Can they do that?

ABRAMS: Yes, they can get people to join the NR—. . .

JUSTICE STEVENS: But the appeal to the public is not just to make this ad. It's to join the NRA and get all the benefits of membership, which include a magazine and all sorts of other things.

ABRAMS: But people were free, until this statute, to send contributions to the NRA. They were free to send money, not just to join.

STEVENS: So what the interest at stake here is the nonmembers of the NRA who want to support the policies of the NRA?

ABRAMS: Yes, the difference is between the 80 million people who have guns and the 4 million who are now members.

SCALIA: I assume that there is a membership fee that goes along with joining most organizations. So if you want to contribute $25 to the campaign, you would have to contribute 50, in effect, to join the NRA, plus the 25.

ABRAMS: Yes. . . .

                  *   *   *

SOUTER: . . . Is it plain that in these discussions, the term genuine issue ad meant an ad that dealt with issues to the exclusion of any reasonable interpretation that it also dealt with advocacy for candidates? . . .

ABRAMS: Let me say the word genuine comes from the study conducted by the Brennan Center, in which they asked students from a particular university to opine as to the . . . state of the mind of the people that did the ads.

SOUTER: And it was out of context, too.

ABRAMS: That's all it was.

SOUTER: You just saw the ad.

ABRAMS: . . . Tell us, now, is that a genuine ad—an ad genuinely directed at an issue or is its purpose electoral? They . . . did not permit for a moment an answer of both.

BREYER: It was a false dichotomy.

ABRAMS: Absolutely. . . .

*   *   *

MR. CLEMENT [[Deputy Solicitor General]]: . . . The students were asked whether or not the issue in the particular ad had a tendency to support or go against a candidate, or if it addressed an issue. There was no mixed motive box, and I think the net effect of that is that whatever overbreadth is estimated by the studies, it actually overstates the overbreadth because it didn't account for the mixed motive case.

And as I say, I think the mixed motive case does reflect the reality in a number of situations. But I do think that the point that a corporation makes that conscious decision to link some controversial issue to a candidate election, at that point, the interest[[s]] that this Court found sufficient in Austin are fully implicated.

CHIEF JUSTICE REHNQUIST: One of the briefs argues that frequently these issues are before Congress almost at the same time the election comes up, because the Congress is catching up perhaps on things that it didn't do earlier in the session. And so it's not the corporation's voluntary choice to put it up there. That's the time it has to do it, if it's going to do any good.

CLEMENT: Again, . . . the safe harbors that we talked about earlier are still available in that situation. And they are, as Justice Breyer pointed out, twofold. One, if all the corporation is really concerned about is a pending legislative issue, it doesn't need to make a reference to the candidate and it can run the issue through treasury funds. On the other hand, if they want to make a specific reference to the candidate, tie that legislative issue to the broader context of the campaign, then they're free to do so as long as they do so through their separate segregated fund.

SCALIA: Mr. Clement, why do you make an exception for these corporations, these aggregations of vast wealth that happen to own television stations? . . .

CLEMENT: . . . [[M]]edia corporations are exempted for the same reason they've always been exempted from the law, which is that they do pose a different situation, a difference of kind. And this court—

SCALIA: And why is that? Why is that? I don't understand that.

CLEMENT: I mean, I think the traditional role of media companies has been quite different than the traditional role of other companies.

JUSTICE KENNEDY: What case do you have that we can distinguish speech based on the identity of the speaker? Outside of this area?

CLEMENT: Well, I don't know. . . .

KENNEDY: Well, but this, this is a serious question. A large part of—of the necessity, or at least the perceived necessity for these ads is to counter the influence of the press. This—this is a very serious First Amendment issue.

CLEMENT: I know it is, Justice—. . .

REHNQUIST: Well, what, what about say the National Rifle Association? It's against gun laws. A media corporation is very much in favor of gun laws, it prints editorials, perhaps it even slants, God forbid, its coverage of the subject. There is a substantial difference, substantial similarity there, isn't there?

CLEMENT: Well, there certainly is the similarity in the sense that they're both addressing the same issue, but I do think that again this Court has drawn that distinction in the Austin case and Congress has drawn that distinction throughout its campaign finance reform. This is not some new provision.

KENNEDY: But what do you think should be the underlying valid principle that allows that distinction to be drawn? . . . Why is it that a group of citizens concerned about what they consider to be slanted press cannot get together, have a corporation and take out issue ads on the other side of that issue?

CLEMENT: Oh, absolutely they can, and I think if what you're talking about is running an issue about the slanted press, I can't imagine how that has to refer to a candidate, so I think you come within both safe harbors that are available to corporations. . . .

SCALIA: Mr. Clement, Austin aside, do you know of any case of ours that says that the press, quote, has greater First Amendment rights than Joe Mimeograph Machine?

CLEMENT: I don't. . . .

SCALIA: There are none.

CLEMENT: Right. . . .

THE OPINION

Justice Stevens and Justice O'Connor delivered the opinion of the Court with respect to Title I and II. . . .

[[1. Political Parties and Soft Money.]] Like the contribution limits we upheld in *Buckley*, §323's restrictions have only a marginal impact on the ability of contributors, candidates, officeholders, and parties to engage in effective political speech. Complex as its provisions may be, §323, in the main, does little more than regulate the ability of wealthy individuals, corporations, and unions to contribute large sums of money to influence federal elections, federal candidates, and federal officeholders.

Plaintiffs contend that we must apply strict scrutiny to §323 because many of its provisions restrict not only contributions but also the spending and solicitation of funds raised outside of FECA's contribution limits. But for purposes of determining the level of scrutiny, it is irrelevant that Congress chose in §323 to regulate contributions on the demand rather than the supply side. The relevant inquiry is whether the mechanism adopted to implement the contribution limit, or to prevent circumvention of that limit, burdens speech in a way that a direct restriction on the contribution itself would not. That is not the case here.

For example, while §323(a) prohibits national parties from receiving or spending nonfederal money, and §323(b) prohibits state party committees from spending nonfederal money on federal election activities, neither provision in any way limits the total amount of money parties can spend. Rather, they simply limit the source and individual amount of donations. That they do so by prohibiting the spending of soft money does not render them expenditure limitations.

Similarly, the solicitation provisions of §323(a) and §323(e), which restrict the ability of national party committees, federal candidates, and federal officeholders to solicit nonfederal funds, leave open ample opportunities for soliciting federal funds on behalf of entities subject to FECA's source and amount restrictions. . . .

. . . The fact that party committees and federal candidates and officeholders must now ask only for limited dollar amounts or request that a corporation or union contribute money through its PAC in no way alters or impairs the political message "intertwined" with the solicitation. [[Moreover,]] . . . the restriction here tends to increase the dissemination of information by forcing parties, candidates, and officeholders to solicit from a wider array of potential donors. As with direct limits on contributions, therefore, §323's spending and solicitation restrictions have only a marginal impact on political speech.

The modest impact that §323 has on the ability of committees within a party to associate with each other does not independently occasion strict scrutiny. None of this is to suggest that the alleged associational burdens imposed on parties by §323 have no place in the First Amendment analysis; it is only that we account for them in the application, rather than the choice, of the appropriate level of scrutiny.

With these principles in mind, we apply the less rigorous scrutiny applicable to contribution limits to evaluate the constitutionality of new FECA §323. Because the five challenged provisions of §323 implicate different First Amendment concerns, we discuss them separately. We are mindful, however, that Congress enacted §323 as an integrated whole to vindicate the Government's important interest in preventing corruption and the appearance of corruption. . . .

The Government defends §323(a)'s ban on national parties' involvement with soft money as necessary to prevent the actual and apparent corruption of federal candidates and officeholders. . . .

The question for present purposes is whether large *soft-money* contributions to national party committees have a corrupting influence or give rise to the appearance of corruption. Both common sense and the ample record in these cases confirm Congress' belief that they do. . . . [[T]]he FEC's allocation regime has invited widespread circumvention of FECA's limits on contributions to parties for the purpose of influencing federal elections. Under this system, corporate, union, and wealthy individual donors have been free to contribute substantial sums of soft money to the national parties, which the parties can spend for the specific purpose of influencing a particular candidate's federal election. It is not only plausible, but likely, that candidates would feel grateful for such donations and that donors would seek to exploit that gratitude. . . .

Plaintiffs argue that without concrete evidence of an instance in which a federal officeholder has actually switched a vote (or, presumably, evidence of a specific instance where the public believes a vote was switched), Congress has not shown that there exists real or apparent corruption. But the record is to the contrary. The evidence connects soft money to manipulations of the legislative calendar, leading to Congress' failure to enact, among other things, generic drug legislation, tort reform, and tobacco legislation. To claim that such actions do not change legislative outcomes surely misunderstands the legislative process.

More importantly, plaintiffs conceive of corruption too narrowly. Our cases have firmly established that Congress' legitimate interest extends beyond preventing simple cash-for-votes corruption to curbing "undue influence on an officeholder's judgment, and the appearance of such influence." . . . Justice Kennedy would limit Congress' regulatory interest *only* to the prevention of the actual or apparent *quid pro quo* corruption "inherent in" contributions made directly to, contributions made at the express behest of, and expenditures made in coordination with, a federal officeholder or candidate. Regulation of any other donation or expenditure—regardless of its size, the recipient's relationship to the candidate or officeholder, its potential impact on a candidate's election, its value to the candidate, or its unabashed and explicit intent to purchase influence—would, according to Justice Kennedy, simply be out of bounds. This crabbed view of corruption, and particularly of the appearance of corruption, ignores precedent, common sense, and the realities of political fundraising exposed by the record in this litigation. . . .

Plaintiffs also contend that §323(a)'s prohibition on national parties' soliciting or directing soft-money contributions is substantially overbroad. . . .

[[However, the validity of this]] . . . limited restriction on solicitation follows sensibly from the prohibition on national committees' receiving soft money.

The same observations that led us to approve the latter compel us to reach the same conclusion regarding the former. . . .

We begin by noting that, in addressing the problem of soft-money contributions to state committees, Congress both drew a conclusion and made a prediction. Its conclusion, based on the evidence before it, was that the corrupting influence of soft money does not insinuate itself into the political process solely through national party committees. Rather, state committees function as an alternate avenue for precisely the same corrupting forces. . . .

Congress also made a prediction. Having been taught the hard lesson of circumvention by the entire history of campaign finance regulation, Congress knew that soft-money donors would react to §323(a) [[the ban on soft-money donations to national parties]] by scrambling to find another way to purchase influence. It was "neither novel nor implausible," for Congress to conclude that political parties would react to §323(a) by directing soft-money contributors to the state committees, and that federal candidates would be just as indebted to these contributors as they had been to those who had formerly contributed to the national parties. We "must accord substantial deference to the predictive judgments of Congress," particularly when, as here, those predictions are so firmly rooted in relevant history and common sense. Preventing corrupting activity from shifting wholesale to state committees and thereby eviscerating FECA clearly qualifies as an important governmental interest. . . .

Finally, plaintiffs argue that Title I violates the equal protection component of the Due Process Clause of the Fifth Amendment because it discriminates against political parties in favor of special interest groups such as the National Rifle Association (NRA), American Civil Liberties Union (ACLU), and Sierra Club. As explained earlier, BCRA imposes numerous restrictions on the fundraising abilities of political parties, of which the soft-money ban is only the most prominent. Interest groups, however, remain free to raise soft money to fund voter registration, GOTV activities, mailings, and broadcast advertising (other than electioneering communications). We conclude that this disparate treatment does not offend the Constitution. . . .

. . . Congress is fully entitled to consider the real-world differences between political parties and interest groups when crafting a system of campaign finance regulation. Interest groups do not select slates of candidates for elections. Interest groups do not determine who will serve on legislative committees, elect congressional leadership, or organize legislative caucuses. Political parties have influence and power in the legislature that vastly exceeds that of any interest group. As a result, it is hardly surprising that party affiliation is the primary way by which voters identify candidates, or that parties in turn have special access to and relationships with federal officeholders. Congress' efforts at campaign finance regulation may account for these salient differences. . . .

[[2. Corporations, Unions, and Issue Ads.]] . . . [[A]] plain reading of *Buckley* makes clear that the express advocacy limitation, in both the expenditure and the disclosure contexts, was the product of statutory interpretation rather than a constitutional command. In narrowly reading the FECA provisions in *Buck-*

ley to avoid problems of vagueness and overbreadth, we nowhere suggested that a statute that was neither vague nor overbroad would be required to toe the same express advocacy line. Nor did we suggest as much in *MCFL*, in which we addressed the scope of another FECA expenditure limitation and confirmed the understanding that *Buckley*'s express advocacy category was a product of statutory construction. . . .

Nor are we persuaded, independent of our precedents, that the First Amendment erects a rigid barrier between express advocacy and so-called issue advocacy. That notion cannot be squared with our longstanding recognition that the presence or absence of magic words cannot meaningfully distinguish electioneering speech from a true issue ad. Indeed, the unmistakable lesson from the record in this litigation . . . is that *Buckley*'s magic-words requirement is functionally meaningless. Not only can advertisers easily evade the line by eschewing the use of magic words, but they would seldom choose to use such words even if permitted. And although the resulting advertisements do not urge the viewer to vote for or against a candidate in so many words, they are no less clearly intended to influence the election. *Buckley*'s express advocacy line, in short, has not aided the legislative effort to combat real or apparent corruption, and Congress enacted BCRA to correct the flaws it found in the existing system.

Finally we observe that new FECA §304(f)(3)'s definition of "electioneering communication" raises none of the vagueness concerns that drove our analysis in *Buckley*. The term "electioneering communication" applies only (1) to a broadcast (2) clearly identifying a candidate for federal office, (3) aired within a specific time period, and (4) targeted to an identified audience of at least 50,000 viewers or listeners. These components are both easily understood and objectively determinable. Thus, the constitutional objection that persuaded the Court in *Buckley* to limit FECA's reach to express advocacy is simply inapposite here.

. . . [[U]]nder BCRA, corporations and unions may not use their general treasury funds to finance electioneering communications, but they remain free to organize and administer segregated funds, or PACs, for that purpose. Because corporations can still fund electioneering communications with PAC money, it is "simply wrong" to view the provision as a "complete ban" on expression rather than a regulation. . . .

In light of our precedents, plaintiffs do not contest that the Government has a compelling interest in regulating advertisements that expressly advocate the election or defeat of a candidate for federal office. Nor do they contend that the speech involved in so-called issue advocacy is any more core political speech than are words of express advocacy. After all, "the constitutional guarantee has its fullest and most urgent application precisely to the conduct of campaigns for political office," and "[a]dvocacy of the election or defeat of candidates for federal office is no less entitled to protection under the First Amendment than the discussion of political policy generally or advocacy of the passage or defeat of legislation." Rather, plaintiffs argue that the justifications that adequately support the regulation of express advocacy do not apply to significant quantities of speech encompassed by the definition of electioneering communications. This argument fails to the extent that the issue ads broadcast during the 30- and 60-day periods preceding federal primary and general elections are the functional equivalent of express advocacy. The justifications for the regulation of express advocacy apply equally to ads aired during those periods if the ads are intended to influence the voters' decisions and have that effect. The precise percentage of issue ads that clearly identified a candidate and were aired during those relatively brief preelection time spans but had no electioneering purpose is a matter of dispute between the parties . . . [[but]] the vast majority of ads clearly had such a purpose. Moreover, whatever the precise percentage may have been in the past, in the future corporations and unions may finance genuine issue ads during those time frames by simply avoiding any specific reference to federal candidates, or in doubtful cases by paying for the ad from a segregated fund. . . .

. . . [[Lastly,]] FECA §304(f)(3)(B)(i) excludes from the definition of electioneering communications any "communication appearing in a news story, commentary, or editorial distributed through the facilities of any broadcasting station, unless such facilities are owned or controlled by any political party, political committee, or candidate." Plaintiffs argue this provision gives free rein to media companies to engage in speech without resort to PAC money. Section 304(f)(3)(B)(i)'s effect, however, is much narrower than plaintiffs suggest. The provision excepts news items and commentary only; it does not afford *carte blanche* to media companies generally to ignore FECA's provisions. The statute's narrow exception is wholly consistent with First Amendment principles. "A valid distinction . . . exists between corporations that are part of the media industry and other corporations that are not involved in the regular business of imparting news to the public." Numerous federal statutes have drawn this distinction to ensure that the law "does not hinder or prevent the institutional press from reporting on, and publishing editorials about, newsworthy events."

Many years ago we observed that "[t]o say that Congress is without power to pass appropriate legislation to safeguard . . . an election from the improper use of money to influence the result is to deny to the nation in a vital particular the power of self protection." We abide by that conviction in considering Congress' most recent effort to confine the ill effects of aggregated wealth on our political system. We are under no illusion that BCRA will be the last congressional statement on the matter. Money, like water, will always find an outlet. What problems will arise, and how Congress will respond, are concerns for another day. In the main we uphold BCRA's two principal, complementary features: the control of soft money and the regulation of electioneering communications. . . .

Justice Scalia, . . . dissenting with respect to BCRA Titles I and V, and concurring in the judgment in part and dissenting in part with respect to BCRA Title II. . . .

This is a sad day for the freedom of speech. Who could have imagined that the same Court which, within the past four years, has sternly disapproved of restrictions upon such inconsequential forms of expression as virtual child pornography, tobacco advertising, dissemination of illegally intercepted communications, and sexually explicit cable programming would smile with favor upon a law that cuts to the heart of what the First Amendment is meant to protect: the right to criticize the government. For that is what the most offensive provisions of this legislation are all about. We are governed by Congress, and this legislation prohibits the criticism of Members of Congress by those entities most capable of giving such criticism loud voice: national political parties and corporations, both of the commercial and the not-for-profit sort. It forbids pre-election criticism of incumbents by corporations, even not-for-profit corporations, by use of their general funds; and forbids national-party use of "soft" money to fund "issue ads" that incumbents find so offensive.

To be sure, the legislation is evenhanded: It similarly prohibits criticism of the candidates who oppose Members of Congress in their reelection bids. But as everyone knows, this is an area in which evenhandedness is not fairness. If *all* electioneering were evenhandedly prohibited, incumbents would have an enormous advantage. Likewise, if incumbents and challengers are limited to the same quantity of electioneering, incumbents are favored. In other words, *any* restriction upon a type of campaign speech that is equally available to challengers and incumbents tends to favor incumbents.

Beyond that, however, the present legislation *targets* for prohibition certain categories of campaign speech that are particularly harmful to incumbents. Is it accidental, do you think, that incumbents raise about three times as much "hard money"—the sort of funding generally *not* restricted by this legislation—as do their challengers? Or that lobbyists (who seek the favor of incumbents) give 92 percent of their money in "hard" contributions? Is it an oversight, do you suppose, that the so-called "millionaire provisions" raise the contribution limit for a candidate running against an individual who devotes to the campaign (as challengers often do) great personal wealth, but do not raise the limit for a candidate running against an individual who devotes to the campaign (as incumbents often do) a massive election "war chest"? And is it mere happenstance, do you estimate, that national-party funding, which is severely limited by the Act, is more likely to assist cash-strapped challengers than flush-with-hard-money incumbents? Was it unintended, by any chance, that incumbents are free personally to receive some soft money and even to solicit it for other organizations, while national parties are not? . . .

And what exactly are these outrageous sums frittered away in determining who will govern us? A report prepared for Congress concluded that the total amount, in hard and soft money, spent on the 2000 federal elections was between $2.4 and $2.5 billion. *All* campaign spending in the United States, including state elections, ballot initiatives, and judicial elections, has been estimated at $3.9 billion for 2000, which was a year that "shattered spending and contribution records." Even taking this last, larger figure as the benchmark, it means that Americans spent about half as much electing all their Nation's officials, state and federal, as they spent on movie tickets ($7.8 billion); about a fifth as much as they spent on cosmetics and perfume ($18.8 billion); and about a sixth as much as they spent on pork (the nongovernmental sort) ($22.8 billion). If our democracy is drowning from this much spending, it cannot swim.

Justice Thomas, . . . concurring in the judgment in part and dissenting in part with respect to BCRA Title II, and dissenting with respect to BCRA Titles I, V and §311. . . .

. . . [[T]]he *Buckley* Court was concerned that bribery laws could not be effectively enforced to prevent *quid pro quos* between donors and officeholders, and the only rational reading of *Buckley* is that it approved the $1,000 contribution ceiling on this ground. The Court then, however, having at least in part concluded that individual contribution ceilings were necessary to prevent easy evasion of bribery laws, proceeded to uphold a separate contribution limitation, using, as the only justification, the "prevent[ion] [of] evasion of the $1,000 contribution limitation." The need to prevent circumvention of a limitation that was itself an anti-circumvention measure led to the upholding of another significant restriction on individuals' freedom of speech.

The joint opinion now repeats this process. . . . [[It]] upholds §323(a), in part, on the grounds that it had become too easy to circumvent the $2,000 cap by using the national parties as go-betweens.

. . . The joint opinion's handling of §323(f) is perhaps most telling, as it upholds §323(f) only because of "Congress' eminently reasonable *prediction* that . . . state and local candidates and officeholders will become the next conduits for the soft-money funding of sham issue advertising." That is, this Court upholds a third-order anticircumvention measure based on Congress' anticipation of circumvention of these second-order anticircumvention measures that might possibly, at some point in the future, pose some problem.

It is not difficult to see where this leads. Every law has limits, and there will always be behavior not covered by the law but at its edges; behavior easily characterized as "circumventing" the law's prohibition. Hence, speech regulation will again expand to cover new forms of "circumvention," only to spur supposed circumvention of the new regulations, and so forth. Rather than permit this never-ending and self-justifying process, I would require that the Government explain why proposed speech restrictions are needed in light of actual Government interests, and, in particular, why the bribery laws are not sufficient. . . .

I have long maintained that *Buckley* was incorrectly decided and should be overturned. But, most of Title II should still be held unconstitutional even under the *Buckley* framework. Under *Buckley* and *Federal Election Comm'n* v. *Massachusetts Citizens for Life, Inc.* (1986) *(MCFL)*, it is, or at least was, clear that any regulation of political speech beyond communications using words of express advocacy is unconstitutional. . . .

. . . The express-advocacy line was drawn to ensure the protection of the "discussion of issues and candidates," not out of some strange obsession of the Court to create meaningless lines. And the joint opinion misses the point when it notes that "*Buckley*'s express advocacy line, in short, has not aided the legislative effort to combat real or apparent corruption." *Buckley* did not draw this line solely to aid in combating real or apparent corruption, but rather also to ensure the protection of speech unrelated to election campaigns. . . .

Justice Kennedy, concurring in the judgment in part and dissenting in part with respect to BCRA Titles I and II. . . .

[[1. "Soft" Money.]] *Buckley* made clear, by its express language and its context, that the corruption interest only justifies regulating candidates' and officeholders' receipt of what we can call the "*quids*" in the *quid pro quo* formulation. The Court rested its decision on the principle that campaign finance regulation that restricts speech without requiring proof of particular corrupt action withstands constitutional challenge only if it regulates conduct posing a demonstrable *quid pro quo* danger . . . :

The Court [[today]] ignores these constitutional bounds and in effect interprets the anticorruption rationale to allow regulation not just of "actual or apparent *quid pro quo* arrangements," but of any conduct that wins goodwill from or influences a Member of Congress. It is not that there is any quarrel between this opinion and the majority that the inquiry since *Buckley* has been whether certain conduct creates "undue influence." On that we agree. The very aim of *Buckley*'s standard, however, was to define undue influence by reference to the presence of *quid pro quo* involving the officeholder. The Court, in contrast, concludes that access, without more, proves influence is undue. Access, in the Court's view, has the same legal ramifications as actual or apparent corruption of officeholders. This new definition of corruption sweeps away all protections for speech that lie in its path. . . .

Access in itself, however, shows only that in a general sense an officeholder favors someone or that someone has influence on the officeholder. There is no basis, in law or in fact, to say favoritism or influence in general is the same as corrupt favoritism or influence in particular. By equating vague and generic claims of favoritism or influence with actual or apparent corruption, the Court adopts a definition of corruption that dismantles basic First Amendment rules, permits Congress to suppress speech in the absence of a *quid pro quo* threat, and moves beyond the rationale that is *Buckley*'s very foundation. . . .

Though the majority cites common sense as the foundation for its definition of corruption, in the context of the real world only a single definition of corruption has been found to identify political corruption successfully and to distinguish good political responsiveness from bad—that is *quid pro quo*. Favoritism and influence are not, as the Government's theory suggests, avoidable in representative politics. It is in the nature of an elected representative to favor certain policies, and, by necessary corollary, to favor the voters and contributors who support those policies. It is well understood that a substantial and legitimate reason, if not the only reason, to cast a vote for, or to make a contribution to, one candidate over another is that the candidate will respond by producing those political outcomes the supporter favors. Democracy is premised on responsiveness. *Quid pro quo* corruption has been, until now, the only agreed upon conduct that represents the bad form of responsiveness and presents a justiciable standard with a relatively clear limiting principle: Bad responsiveness may be demonstrated by pointing to a relationship between an official and a *quid*. . . .

. . . [[T]]he Court today should not ask, as it does, whether some persons, even Members of Congress, conclusorily assert that the regulated conduct appears corrupt to them. Following *Buckley*, it should instead inquire whether the conduct now prohibited inherently poses a real or substantive *quid pro quo* danger, so that its regulation will stem the appearance of *quid pro quo* corruption. . . .

. . . The record confirms that soft money party contributions, without more, do not create *quid pro quo* corruption potential. . . .

[[2. Issue Ads.]] The Government and the majority are right about one thing: The express-advocacy requirement, with its list of magic words, is easy to circumvent. The Government seizes on this observation to defend BCRA §203, arguing it will prevent what it calls "sham issue ads" that are really to the same effect as their more express counterparts. What the Court and the Government call sham, however, are the ads speakers find most effective. Unlike express ads that leave nothing to the imagination, the record shows that issues ads are preferred by almost all candidates, even though politicians, unlike corporations, can lawfully broadcast express ads if they so choose. It is a measure of the Government's disdain for protected speech that it would label as a sham the mode of communication sophisticated speakers choose because it is the most powerful.

The Government's use of the pejorative label should not obscure §203's practical effect: It prohibits a mass communication technique favored in the modern political process for the very reason that it is the most potent. That the Government would regulate it for this reason goes only to prove the illegitimacy of the Government's purpose. The majority's validation of it is not sustainable under accepted First Amendment principles. The problem is that the majority uses *Austin*, a decision itself unfaithful to our First Amendment precedents, to justify banning a far greater range of speech. This has it all backwards. If protected speech is being suppressed, that must be the end of the inquiry. . . .

Austin was the first and, until now, the only time our Court had allowed the Government to exercise the power to censor political speech based on the speaker's corporate identity. The majority's contrary contention is simply incorrect. I dissented in *Austin*, and continue to believe that the case represents an indefensible departure from our tradition of free and robust debate. Two of my colleagues joined the dissent, including a member of today's majority [[Justice O'Connor]]. . . .

Even under *Austin*, BCRA §203 could not stand. All parties agree strict scrutiny applies; §203, however, is far from narrowly tailored.

The Government is unwilling to characterize §203 as a ban, citing the possibility of funding electioneering communications out of a separate segregated fund. This option, though, does not alter the categorical nature of the prohibition on the corporation. "[T]he corporation *as a corporation* is prohibited from speaking." What the law allows—permitting the corporation "to serve as the founder and treasurer of a different association of individuals that can endorse or oppose political candidates"—"is not speech by the corporation." . . .

The hostility toward corporations and unions that infuses the majority opinion is inconsistent with the viewpoint neutrality the First Amendment demands of all Government actors, including the members of this Court. Corporations, after all, are the engines of our modern economy. They facilitate complex operations on which the Nation's prosperity depends. To say these entities cannot alert the public to pending political issues that may threaten the country's economic interests is unprecedented. Unions are also an established part of the national economic system. They, too, have their own unique insights to contribute to the political debate, but the law's impact on them is just as severe. The costs of the majority's misplaced concerns about the "corrosive and distorting effects of immense aggregations of wealth," moreover, will weigh most heavily on budget-strapped nonprofit entities upon which many of our citizens rely for political commentary and advocacy. These groups must now choose between staying on the sidelines in the next election or establishing a PAC against their institutional identities. PACs are a legal construct sanctioned by Congress. They are not necessarily the means of communication chosen and preferred by the citizenry. . . .

Chief Justice Rehnquist, dissenting with respect to BCRA Titles I and V. . . .

The Court attempts to sidestep the unprecedented breadth of this regulation by stating that the "close relationship between federal officeholders and the national parties" makes all donations to the national parties "suspect." But a close association with others, especially in the realm of political speech, is not a surrogate for corruption; it is one of our most treasured First Amendment rights. The Court's willingness to impute corruption on the basis of a relationship greatly infringes associational rights and expands Congress' ability to regulate political speech. And there is nothing in the Court's analysis that limits congressional regulation to national political parties. In fact, the Court relies in part on this closeness rationale to regulate *nonprofit organizations*. Who knows what association will be deemed too close to federal officeholders next. When a donation to an organization has no potential to corrupt a federal officeholder, the relationship between the officeholder and the organization is simply irrelevant.

. . . Notwithstanding the Court's citation to the numerous abuses of FECA, under any definition of "exacting scrutiny," the means chosen by Congress, restricting all donations to national parties no matter the purpose for which they are given or are used, are not "closely drawn to avoid unnecessary abridgment of associational freedoms."

[[For example,]] . . . Newspaper editorials and political talk shows *benefit* federal candidates and officeholders every bit as much as a generic voter registration drive conducted by a state party; there is little doubt that the endorsement of a major newspaper *affects* federal elections, and federal candidates and officeholders are surely "grateful," for positive media coverage. I doubt, however, the Court would seriously contend that we must defer to Congress' judgment if it chose to reduce the influence of political endorsements in federal elections. . . .

NOTES

1. See *Burroughs v. United States*, 290 U.S. 534 (1934); *United States v. Automobile Workers*, 352 U.S. 567 (1940); and *Federal Election Commission v. National Right to Work Comm.*, 459 U.S. 197 (1982).

2. See the reference to this example in the district judge's opinion in *Buckley v. Valeo*, 519 F.2d 821, 839 (1975).

3. *Buckley v. Valeo*, 424 U.S. 1, 19, 20, 21–22 (1976).

4. *Id.* at 25, 26–27, 43, 44, 45, 46.

5. *Id.* at 48–49, 57.

6. *Id.* at 241–42.

7. *Id.* at 261, 265.

8. 435 U.S. 765 (1978). In *Citizens Against Rent Control v. Berkeley*, 454 U.S. 290 (1981), the Court threw out a municipal ordinance that set a $250 limit on individual contributions to committees that were formed to support or oppose ballot measures. As in *Bellotti*, the basis for the Court's decision was that corruption was not implicated in ballot measures as it was in elections.

9. 453 U.S. 182 (1981).

10. 459 U.S. 197 (1982).

11. 479 U.S. 238 (1986). Four years after *FEC v. Massachusetts Citizens for Life*, however, the Court upheld a state regulation that prohibited the Chamber of Commerce from using its general funds to engage in independent political expenditures on behalf of a candidate. The Court reasoned that the Chamber of Commerce was not "more akin to voluntary political associations than business firms." See *Austin v. Michigan Chamber of Commerce*, 494 U.S. 652 (1990).

12. 539 U.S. 146 (2003).

13. 518 U.S. 604 (1996).

14. 533 U.S. 431 (2001).

15. In *Nixon v. Shrink Missouri Government PAC*, 528 U.S. 377 (2000), the Court upheld a state contribution limit against the objection that inflation had rendered it too low to be constitutional.

16. The text of BCRA is available at *http://www.law.stanford.edu/library/campaign finance/107.155.pdf*.

17. It is not clear whether nonprofit corporations that qualified for the MCLF exception defined above would be exempt from Title II's prohibition of issue advocacy.

18. The parties to the *McConnell* case and various *amici* filed numerous briefs and reply briefs to the Supreme Court. When these are added to the voluminous appendices attached to the briefs and to the lengthy district court opinion, the record of the case

approaches staggering proportions that can only be scratched in a chapter case study. Accordingly, this chapter will consider only those provisions of Title I that prohibited national, state, and local political parties from having anything to do with soft money and only the provision of Title II that prohibited corporations and unions from engaging in "federal election communications."

19. Title I completely banned the national party from receiving, transferring, or spending any soft money. In contrast, state parties were banned from receiving and spending soft money for "federal election activity," a term defined to include (i) voter registration activity within 120 days before a federal election; (ii) voter identification, get-out-the-vote activity, or generic campaign activity at a time in which a candidate for federal office appears on the ballot; (iii) any public communication that refers to a federal candidate; and (iv) all services provided by an employee who devotes more than 25 percent of his compensated time in any month to activities related to a federal election. However, the BCRA, under the "Levin Amendment," allowed state and local party committees to use soft money to finance a share of the above expenses if (i) the permitted activities did not refer to a clearly identified federal candidate; (ii) activities did not involve any broadcast communications other than those that referred only to state or local candidates; (ii) no donor donated more that $10,000 to the state or local party annually for these activities; and (iv) all money (both hard and soft) spent on such activities had to be raised by the local or state party entity. These provisions illuminate the complex character of the BCRA.

20. Sharon Theimer, "RNC Wants Ban on 'Soft Money' Spending," January 12, 2004; "Groups Target New 'Soft Money' Groups, January 15, 2004, *Associated Press*, available on FINDLAW.COM, Legal News and Commentary.

CHAPTER 6

Peyote Use and Religious Freedom

*Employment Div., Dept. of Human
Resources of Oregon v. Smith
494 U.S. 872 (1990)*

Religious freedom in the United States is based upon two constitutional principles that pose difficult problems of interpretation because they are in tension with one another. The First Amendment prohibits the federal government from enhancing any law "respecting an establishment of religion" or "prohibiting the free exercise thereof."[1] Is a tax on church property an illegitimate burden upon religion prohibited by the "free exercise" clause or is a religious exemption from the tax an illegitimate "establishment" of religion? Clearly, the government cannot be acting unconstitutionally whether it grants the exemption or not, but how any particular issue should be resolved is not at all self-evident. On the one side of the spectrum, certain types of accommodations of religion are "required" by the Free Exercise Clause. In these instances, courts will compel the state to grant exemptions for the particular religions that are burdened. On the other side, certain kinds of accommodations are "prohibited" by the Establishment Clause and courts will invalidate them. But in the middle of the spectrum there exists another category of accommodations: those that are neither "forbidden" nor "required," but are rather "permissible." In regard to these forms of accommodations, legislatures have discretion to accommodate religion as they wish.[2]

The Supreme Court balances the Establishment Clause and the Free Exercise Clause by defining these three different categories of accommodation. The process, of course, has direct political implications. If the categories of "forbidden" and "required" accommodations are small, taking up only a small amount of space on the extreme sides of the spectrum, then the legislature will have a large amount of power over public policy that bears upon religious freedom. Such a situation clearly favors mainstream religions that have prominent voices in the legislative body. In contrast, if "forbidden" and "required" accommodations are defined in such a way that the resulting categories are large, then legislative discretion shrinks while judicial control over issues of religious freedom increases. The legislature would be sharply limited in what it could do without triggering the Establishment Clause. The Free Exercise Clause, on the other hand, would exempt those with little political power—members of small non-mainstream religions—from a wide number of legal restrictions. The general point is that how the categories of "forbidden," "required," and "permissible" accommodations are defined has a direct bearing upon the relative institutional role of courts versus legislatures and upon the interests of mainstream versus nonmainstream religions. Accordingly the issue of how to define the different types of accommodation is quite a political one, having a large impact upon the relative institutional functions of legislatures and courts and upon the religious interests of all Americans.[3]

Starting in the 1960s, the Supreme Court generally defined "forbidden" and "required" accommodations in a way that allowed for considerable judicial control over religious freedom. With respect to forbidden accommodations, Court rulings on prayer in public schools were the clearest indications of a broad reading of the Establishment Clause.[4] In 1962, the Court first invalidated all laws that provided for nonsectarian prayer conducted as a regular classroom activity.[5] Similarly in 1963, it struck down laws that sanctioned Bible readings in class.[6] In *Lemon v. Kurtzman* (1971), the Court formulated a specific set of criteria to evaluate Establishment Clause issues. The so-called *Lemon* test invalidated state-related religious practices if they (1) had no secular purpose; (2) had the "primary effect" of promoting or inhibiting religion; or (3) "excessively entangled" government with religion.[7] Despite public opposition to the Court's school prayer decisions, the Court relied on the *Lemon* test in 1985 to reject a law requiring moments of silence in public school classrooms.[8]

The Court also applied the *Lemon* test to governmental aid to parochial schools, another important category of Establishment Clause issues. The Court generally allowed more accommodation of religion in the area of parochial school aid than in the area of school prayer, though it nonetheless established a significant range of forbidden accommodations. For instance, during the 1960s and 1970s, the Court upheld aid for religious schools to provide transportation and books to parochial students,[9] but invalidated direct governmental subsidies for teacher salaries, tuition, and maps and other instructional materials.[10] During the 1980s, the Court became somewhat more tolerant of public aid to students of religiously affiliated schools. For example, the Court allowed tax deductions for parents to pay for educational expenses that included private and religious school tuition.[11] It also permitted a state government to subsidize the education of a blind student studying at a Christian college to become a pastor, missionary, or youth director.[12] Both types of aid were part of neutral programs that offered benefits to both public and private school students, and they only offered aid to parochial schools as a result of choices by private individuals.

In light of these cases, certain justices became critical of how the *Lemon* test was being used to adjudicate Establishment Clause claims and suggested various alternatives. In *Lynch v. Donnelly* (1984), the Court held that a city's display of a nativity scene in the context of a general, partly secular, holiday display was constitutional. Chief Justice Burger's majority opinion declined to apply the *Lemon* test in determining if the crèche display ran afoul of the Establishment Clause. He and the other conservative justices in the majority instead cited the lack of "direct coercion" involved in the public religious display. This criterion permitted more public practices that "acknowledged" religion than a literal application of the *Lemon* test would have allowed. Justice O'Conner's concurring opinion set forth the "endorsement" test as an alternative to both the *Lemon* test and Burger's new "direct coercion" test. In her view, a governmental program or practice should be invalidated if it endorsed religion in a manner that made religious beliefs "relevant in any way to a person's standing in the political community." Although several justices have applied both the "direct coercion" and "endorsement" tests in later cases, a clear majority of justices have never completely abandoned the *Lemon* test. Accordingly, the Court has not decisively determined the contours of its Establishment Clause jurisprudence. In general, governmental policies are classified as either "forbidden" or "permissible" accommodations based on a searching review of the overall context of the policies themselves.

With respect to the Free Exercise Clause, the Warren Court in the 1960s formulated the definition of "required" accommodations that gave it a prominent role defending nonmainstream religions from burdensome legislation. A state had to grant a religious exemption from a law burdening a religion unless it was "the least restrictive means" to obtain "a compelling state purpose.[13] For twenty-five years, the religious practices of Americans were protected by this high standard.[14] But in *Employment Division, Department of Human Resources of Oregon v. Smith* (1990), a case addressing the issue whether Oregon had to grant a peyote-use exemption from its criminal laws to the Native American Church, the Court radically changed course by sharply narrowing the category of "required" accommodations. If generally applicable criminal laws, like the drug laws, were religiously neutral, the majority of the Court said that they were not in violation of the Free Exercise Clause, even if they incidentally burdened a particular religion. Enforcement of the drug laws against peyote-use by the Native American Church no longer had to be "the least restrictive means" for the state to obtain "a compelling state purpose." Since *Smith* constitutes a radical departure from precedent, it serves as a useful context not only to assess the proper balance between the Establishment Clause and the Free Exercise Clause, but also to consider the respective roles that legislatures and courts should play in the area of religious liberty and the proper definitions of "required," "prohibited," and "permissible" accommodations.

A couple of earlier Supreme Court precedents played an important role in the *Smith* litigation. In November of 1935, the school district of Minersville, Pennsylvania, adopted a regulation requiring all teachers and students to salute the flag daily. No exceptions were acknowledged. Lillian (aged twelve) and William Gobitis (aged ten), children of Walter Gobitis, objected on religious grounds. They were Jehovah's Witnesses who understood the Bible as the literal Word of God. Its literal commands had to be absolutely obeyed to avoid eternal damnation. The flag salute, in their view, conflicted with the biblical command not to "bow down" or "serve" any "graven image."[15] The children therefore refused to give the salute and were expelled. Their father sued in federal court, arguing that the flag-salute requirement unconstitutionally violated their religious freedom.

The Gobitis family won in the district court and in the court of appeals, but in a decision handed down on June 3, 1940, the Supreme Court rejected their argument of conscience. The political context may have had something to do with the way the case was resolved. At the time, Germany was bombing Paris, Britain was evacuating Dunkerque, and the United States was readying itself, both militarily and emotionally, for war. In any case, the Court ruled in the 8-1 decision that Pennsylvania was not "required" to accommodate the religious beliefs of the Witnesses. Justice Felix Frankfurter's majority opinion articulated a view of the relationship between religious freedom and the respective roles of courts and legislatures. He sympathized with the plight of the Gobitis children, but he insisted that there would be no liberty, "civil or religious," unless the "binding tie of cohesive sentiment" that united all Americans of whatever religious background into one people was preserved. Of course, it was unclear whether requiring all schoolchildren to engage in a daily flag-salute ceremony was an efficacious means of instilling or maintaining this "cohesive sentiment." Nonetheless, the compelled salute, in Frankfurter's judgment, was not "beyond the pale of legislative power." It must always be remembered, he said, that "to the legislature no less than to courts is committed the guardianship of deeply cherished liberties" and that "personal freedom is best maintained . . . when it is ingrained in a people's habits and not enforced against popular policy by the coercion of adjudicated law."[16]

Gobitis did not remain the law of the land for long. In 1943, the Court overturned the earlier decision in *West Virginia State Board of Education v. Barnette*, a 6-3 decision.[17] What explains this unusually quick reversal? One explanation was that Justice Jackson's majority opinion in *Barnette* did not rely upon the Free Exercise Clause. The "issue as we see it," Jackson announced, does not "turn on one's possession of particular religious views or the sincerity with which they are held."[18] Instead, the reason why compulsory flag-salute statutes were unconstitutional was because they violated free speech. All citizens, not just those of particular religions, had the right to refuse to salute the flag. It was a "fixed star of our constitutional constellation," Jackson insisted, that "no official, high or petty, can prescribe what shall be orthodox in politics, nationalism, religion, or other matters of opinion or force citizens to confess by word or act their faith therein."[19] Any such prescription was a violation of the individual's right of free speech. The government cannot force anyone to say something they do no believe in. The right of the individual to freely exercise his or her religion had little to do with the matter.

Since Jackson's majority opinion relied exclusively upon free speech, *Barnette* left unresolved the issue of whether the Free Exercise Clause alone was a sufficient basis for requiring the state to exempt the Jehovah's Witnesses from saluting the flag. In other words, after *Barnette*, it was still unclear whether states had to exempt students who raised religious objections to criminal laws that did *not* implicate free speech. This question was not decisively answered until the Supreme Court considered, in *Wisconsin v. Yoder* (1972), whether a state could force Amish students to attend school until the age of 16.[20] The Amish argued that the law violated their religious freedom, but they could not rely on their right of free speech, since the children were not required to say anything contrary to their religion, but only to attend school, whether a public school or a private one licensed by the state.

The Supreme Court ultimately agreed with the Amish. The contrast to the flag-salute cases was striking. While the Free Exercise Clause, by itself, was not a sufficient basis for requiring the state to accommodate religiously motivated refusals to salute the flag in 1943, it was, twenty-nine years later, sufficient to compel the state to accommodate religiously motivated refusals to go to school after the eighth grade.

Justice Warren Burger's majority opinion invoked the test that the Court had established in *Sherbert v. Verner* (1963), a case that prohibited states from refusing unemployment compensation to a person who declined, on religious grounds, to work on Saturday.[21] In the earlier case, the Court had decided that if the state was going to override the free exercise claim, it had to pursue the "least restrictive" means to "a compelling state interest." Applying this test in *Yoder*, Burger noted that Wisconsin's compulsory attendance law had two basic purposes: "to prepare citizens to participate effectively and intelligently in our open political system: and to produce "self-reliant and self-sufficient participants in society."[22] Though Burger admitted that education generally was "at the very apex of the function of the State,"[23] he did not find it necessary to evaluate whether these purposes were "of the highest order." Why? Because in his judgment, forcing the Amish children to go to school until they were sixteen was unnecessary, if not counterproductive.

According to Burger, the Amish did not need any lessons in self-reliance. Not only were they "productive and very law-abiding members of society," but they also "reject[ed] public welfare in any of its usual forms."[24] Moreover, Amish political skills were keen enough for them to survive "as a separate, sharply identifiable and highly self-sufficient community for more than 200 yeas in this country."[25] American democracy would therefore not suffer if their children left school after the eighth grade. "Indeed, the Amish communities singularly parallel and reflect many of the virtues of Jefferson's ideal of the 'sturdy yeoman' who would form the basis of what he considered as the ideal of a democratic society."[26] Accordingly, despite the "neutral" character of the compulsory attendance law, the state legislature did not have the discretion to decide whether to accommodate the Amish religion or not. The exemption was a "required" accommodation, not a "permissible" one.

While *Sherbert* dealt with excluding persons from governmental benefits on the ground of religiously motivated conduct, *Yoder* involved something that was arguably more serious: an exemption from a criminal law. As a general precedent, it suggested that the state was presumptively obliged to exempt religiously motivated conduct from its criminal laws. "A regulation neutral on its face may, in its application, nonetheless offend the constitutional requirement for governmental neutrality if it unduly burdened the free exercise of religion."[27] The question of whether a "neutral" criminal law violated "neutrality" therefore depended on whether it was the "least restrictive means" to a "compelling purpose."

Burger's majority opinion only briefly discussed the notion that an exemption from a general criminal law might entangle the state in an illicit establishment of religion. "The Court must not ignore the danger," he said,

> that an exception from a general obligation of citizenship on religious grounds may run afoul of the Establishment Clause, but that danger cannot be allowed to prevent any exception no matter how vital it may be to the protection of values promoted by the right of free exercise. By preserving doctrinal flexibility and recognizing the need for a sensible and realistic application of the Religion Clauses, "we have been able to chart a course that preserved the autonomy and freedom of religious bodies while avoiding any semblance of established religion. This is a 'tightrope' and one we have successfully traversed."[28]

Whether Burger's approach in *Yoder* successfully "traversed" the "tightrope" stretching from the Free Exercise Clause to the Establishment Clause is an interesting question. But in any case, the Court in *Employment Div., Dept. of Human Resources v. Smith* reopened issues that many thought *Yoder* had settled. If, as *Smith* decided, the sacramental use of peyote by the Native American Church could be prohibited, the basic question was whether *Yoder* was still a valid precedent.

Peyote, which grows mainly in northern Mexico and southern Texas, is a small cactus having psychedelic properties. For centuries, the native Indians of Mexico had used it in their religion. Not until 1880, however, did peyote find its way north to the Indian reservations of western Oklahoma. From there the practice quickly spread among the Native American tribes throughout the western United States. It became a crucial element of a religion that combined various aspects of traditional Indian religion and Christianity. According to the various legends that arose concerning how Indians discovered peyote, it was thought to embody the Holy Spirit because it brought those who ingested it into direct contact with God. In 1918, the peyotists formalized the religion by incorporating the Native American Church. Article II of the church identified the purpose of the corporation as the promotion of the Christian religion "with the practice of the Peyote Sacrament as commonly understood and used among the adherents of this religion."[29] A hallucinatory drug had become a crucial part of a religious ritual whose popularity grew among Native Americans throughout the twentieth century.

The modern peyote ceremony is an all-night session consisting of prayer, singing, peyote use, and meditation. A "road chief" leads the rite, which takes place around a fire inside a tepee. He places a peyote "button"—the top of the peyote cactus that is ingested—on a crescent-shaped altar. This "button" is called "Father Peyote" and all prayers and songs are directed to it. After a few initial rituals, everyone is given the opportunity to eat four "buttons," but anyone can ask for more peyote throughout the service. All the participants take turns singing and praying. At dawn a ritual breakfast marks the end of the ceremony. Everyone files out of the tepee, the fire is put out, the altar is removed, and the tepee is dismantled. The religious service is then followed by a large feast.

Alfred Smith and Galen Black, both members of the Native American Church, were not criminally prosecuted for their sacramental use of peyote. Instead, the state refused to pay them unemployment compensation because their employer, a drug rehabilitation clinic, had fired them for use of a Schedule 1 drug—peyote. Years of litigation followed at the state and federal levels, ending with the result that, if the state could punish sacramental peyote use, it could deny Smith and Black unemployment compensation. The fact that their conduct was religiously motivated would make no difference. On the other hand, if the state could not constitutionally punish their activities, then it could not deny them unemployment compensation. Therefore, even though neither Smith nor Black was criminally prosecuted under Oregon's drug laws, the issue of whether they could be prosecuted became the crucial question in regard to whether the state could deny them unemployment compensation.

In its brief to the Supreme Court and in oral argument, Oregon utilized two basic arguments. First, the state insisted that Oregon's refusal to grant an exemption for sacramental peyote use satisfied the compelling interest standard of *Yoder*. Controlling the use of dangerous drugs as a "compelling" interest and criminal prohibitions on drug use were effective only if they were generally applicable and comprehensive. Any sort of exemptions for particular religions undermined the program's effectiveness. Moreover, the state added, such exemptions implicated the state in an establishment of religion by preferring one religion's use of a drug over another religion's use of the same drug or some other one. The state would have either to refuse all exemptions or give the exemptions to all religions for all drugs. The "door to religious drug use must be opened fully if it is opened at all." The state concluded that since the "door" cannot be opened "fully" without compromising the war against drugs, it must remain tightly closed.

Craig J. Dorsay, the attorney for Smith and Black, disputed both of these contentions. First, the state's refusal to grant an exemption to the Native American Church failed to satisfy the compelling interest standard. The state had not shown that the use of dangerous drugs could not be controlled if an exemption was made for the sacramental use of peyote. Just as Wisconsin could achieve its objectives and, at the same time, grant the Amish an exemption from the compulsory school attendance law, so Oregon could limit the use of dangerous drugs and, at the same time, grant the Native American Church an exemption from its drug laws. Second, such a denominational exemption would not constitute an establishment of religion. Accommodations that are "required" by the Free Exercise Clause cannot be "prohibited" by the Establishment Clause. It was, therefore, legitimate for the government to open the "door" of religious drug use part way, confining the exemption to the Native American Church. Such a limited exemption would not undermine the effectiveness of the drug laws.

Both sides of the *Smith* litigation had assumed that the tension between the Free Exercise Clause and the Establishment Clause would be resolved by some sort of interpretation of the compelling interest test applied in *Yoder*. However, Justice Antonin Scalia, who wrote the majority opinion in *Smith*, took a different course. In his opinion (joined by Chief Justice Rehnquist and Justices White, Stevens, and Kennedy), he argued that the state, if it decided for legitimate reasons not to exempt religiously motivated conduct from generally applicable criminal laws, did not have to satisfy the criteria of the compelling interest test. Relying in part upon Justice Frankfurter's opinion in *Gobitis*, Scalia concluded that religious scruples do not override an individual's obligation to obey a general law, at least if the purpose of the law was not to promote or suppress a particular religion. A private religious right to violate valid criminal laws contradicted "common sense" and produced a "constitutional anomaly." Of course, legislatures could, if they wished, exempt certain types of religiously motivated conduct. Such accommodations were not violations of the Establishment Clause. They were "permissible," but not constitutionally "required," accommodations. The fact that nonmainsteam religions might have little success in the legislature was an "unavoidable consequence of democratic government."

Scalia distinguished the facts of *Smith* from the earlier cases in which the Court had applied the compelling interest test. In the field of unemployment compensation, Scalia admitted, the Court had used the compelling interest test to invalidate state laws that "conditioned the availability of benefits upon an applicant's willingness to work under conditions forbidden by his religion." However, in his judgment, this test should not be extended beyond the field of unemployment compensation. The *Barnette* and *Yoder* cases were also not direct precedents for requiring the state to exempt the Native American Church from Oregon's drug laws. Both of these cases had involved rights in addition to the right to freely exercise one's religion. Compelling children to salute the flag implicated the right of free speech in *Barnette*, while forcing the Amish children to attend school beyond the eighth grade impinged upon the right of parents to control the education of their children. In neither case, according to Scalia, was the Free Exercise Clause a sufficient constitutional basis for compelling the state to grant an exemption to a generally applicable law, especially not a criminal law.

By interpreting the Court's precedents in this fashion, Scalia (and the four justices who joined his opinion) radically changed constitutional doctrine in regard to religious freedom when neither party to the litigation had specifically argued for such a result. Should the Court ever decide a case in such a fashion? Is it wise for the Court to give one of the parties more than it was asking? Justice Sandra Day O'Connor, who concurred in the result but not in Scalia's opinion, regretted what the Court had done. She called the decision "unnecessary" and "incompatible with our Nation's fundamental commitment to individual religious liberty." It was unnecessary, in her judgment, because Oregon's refusal to exempt the Native American Church from its drug laws did satisfy the compelling interest standard. The Court did not have to change free-exercise doctrine to deny the Native American Church an exemption from the state's drug laws. Any such exemption would endanger Oregon's program of controlling the use of dangerous drugs. Hence, refusing the exemption to the Native American Church was a "necessary" means to a "compelling" state purpose.

But what really troubled Justice O'Connor was the majority's "insensitivity" to the constitutional value of religious freedom. The free exercise of religion was "a preferred constitutional activity." It was therefore not an "anomaly," but a "constitutional norm." Judges in the past and in the future have had the duty and the capacity to balance religious liberty and competing state interests. In the context of the Bill of Rights, the very purpose of the Free Exercise Clause was to "require" the government to accommodate, if possible, those minority religions that were politically powerless. That is what the Court did in *Yoder*. In that case, the Court understood the Free Exercise Clause to be a sufficient constitutional basis for an exemption from a generally applicable criminal law. An exemption for the sacramental use of peyote may not be possible, but the judiciary should not abandon its role of protecting the freedom of nonmainstream religions.

The dissenting opinion written by Justice Harry Blackmun (and joined by Justices William Brennan and Thurgood Marshall) also lamented the Court's "wholesale overturning of settled law concerning the Religion Clauses of our Constitution." Blackmun called for the continued adherence to the compelling interest standard and affirmed the judiciary's role in protecting religious freedom. His major disagreement with O'Connor concerned how she applied the test to the facts of *Smith*. Since Oregon had not prosecuted anyone for the sacramental use of peyote, the state's interest was only "to the symbolic preservation of an unenforced prohibition." Moreover, the potential harm of granting the exemption was based on "mere speculation." Indeed, Blackmun argues, granting an exemption for the sacramental use of peyote would, as the exemption from the compulsory attendance laws did in *Yoder*, aid the state's interests. The Native American Church "advocates self-reliance, familial responsibility, and abstinence from alcohol" and therefore an exemption would promote the values that "Oregon's drug laws are presumably intended to foster." Lastly, Blackmun added, granting exemptions for religious drug use will not result in an establishment of religion, even if only a few religious sects would qualify for them. Any accommodation "required" by the Free Exercise Clause cannot be an accommodation "prohibited" by the Establishment Clause.

In *Smith*, the Court has taken a new direction in the area of religious freedom. Therefore, the facts and arguments of this litigation, as well as the Supreme Court's opinion, provide a useful context to reconsider the tensions between the Free Exercise Clause and the Establishment Clause and the respective functions that courts and legislatures should play in regard to religious liberty. Justice Scalia represents one end of the spectrum on these issues. He believes that the categories of "required" and "prohibited" accommodations should be kept rather small. In a democracy, the legislature should make the decisions. Courts should neither compel legislatures to make exemptions to generally applicable laws nor prevent them from accommodating religion. If the legislatures use their powers to enact stupid or silly laws, courts should not intervene. In contrast, Justices Blackmun and O'Connor, like Chief Justice Burger before them, have a wider category of "required" accommodations. States must, if it is possible, exempt religiously motivated conduct from generally applicable laws. If legislatures refuse to do so, courts must step in. Courts have an obligation to protect, to some unclear degree, nonmainstream religions from indifferent or insensitive legislatures. Justice Stevens represents another position on the spectrum. Though he agrees with Scalia that the number of "required" accommodations should be kept small, he also supports an expansive view of "prohibited" accommodations and a relatively narrow category of "permissible" accommodations. In his view, neither mainstream nor nonmainstream religion should benefit from governmental action. The general question as to the respective role of courts and legislatures in the area of religious liberty has a direct bearing upon any assessment of what the Supreme Court did in *Gobitis*, *Yoder*, and *Smith*. Of course, the reverse is also true. A thoughtful consideration of these cases contributes to a better understanding of the proper balance between the Establishment Clause and the Free Exercise Clause.

BIBLIOGRAPHY

Kurland, Philip, "Of Church and State and the Supreme Court." *University of Chicago Law Review* 29 (1961), pp. 1–96.

Kurland, Philip. "The Irrelevance of the Constitution: The Religion Clauses of the First Amendment and the Supreme Court." *Villanova Law Review* 24 (1978), pp. 3–27.

Marshall, William. "The Case against the Constitutionally Compelled Free Exercise Exemption." *Case Western Reserve Law Review* 40 (1989–90), pp. 357–412.

McConnell, Michael W. "Free Exercise Revisionism and the *Smith* Decision." *University of Chicago Law Review* 57 (1990), pp. 1109–53.

Stone, Geoffrey R. "Constitutionally Compelled Exemptions and the Free Exercise Clause." *William & Mary Law Review* 27 (1986), pp. 985–96.

Tushnet, Mark. "The Emerging Principle of Accommodation of Religion (dubitante)." *Georgetown Law Journal* 76 (1988), pp. 1691–1714.

BRIEFS

OREGON'S BRIEF

[[1. Compelling Interest in Drug Enforcement.]] . . . Few problems confronting society today are as devastating in their consequences, as unmanageable in their proportions, and as immediate in their danger as that of drug use and abuse. The nation's drug crisis pervades every facet of our citizens' lives. It is present in our cities, our streets, our work places, our schools and our homes. Illicit drug use also crosses all social boundaries: age, economic class, gender, profession, national origin, religious and political affiliation, [[and]] geographic location. The federal and state governments, together with the local authorities, are engaged in a battle against dangerous drugs that in real terms, not just euphemistically, is a "war." . . .

Peyote (*Lophophora williamsii*), a Schedule I drug in Oregon is a powerful and dangerous hallucinogen derived from a species of cactus which grows in the southwestern United States and in Mexico. When ingested in a quantity sufficient to produce a psychotropic effect, the drug alters certain basic physiological functions and the way in which the user sees and perceives reality. In high doses, the drug can permanently damage health and be life-threatening. . . .

The inquiry does not necessarily end with the recognition that government has a compelling interest in controlling dangerous drug use. The question remains whether government can "accommodate" religious drug use by exempting it from the reach of criminal prohibition. If government can allow a religion-based exemption without compromising its interest, the Free Exercise Clause requires it to do so.

In actual practice, this Court has found no room for "accommodating" religion-by-religion exemptions from neutral laws of general applicability when those laws directly serve health, safety or public order interest. The decisions recognize that regulations of that kind depend on uniformity and comprehensiveness to be effective. Thus, for example, there may be some "exceptional" polygamists who conceivably could engage in multiple marriages without disturbing the social order. The constitution, however, does not require government to exempt them from laws making polygamy criminal. Similarly, although certain precautions may be taken by adults to avoid the hazards of child labor, the government constitutionally may eliminate all risk of harm through an absolute prohibition And when a regulatory scheme would become difficult to administer and diluted in effectiveness by "myriad exceptions flowing from a wide variety of religious beliefs," government is not constitutionally obligated to grant exemptions based on religious beliefs. Government must be able to regulate the conduct of all citizens if it is to serve effectively the society's common needs. . . .

[[2. The Establishment Problem.]] A second, equally significant concern flows through the decisions. This Court has recognized that granting religion-by-religion exemptions from facially neutral laws raises the potential for government to discriminate among religions and to suggest preference for some sects over others. A fundamental Establishment Clause principle holds that government cannot abandon secular purposes in order to put "an imprimatur on one religion, or on religion as such, or to favor the adherents of any sect or religious organization." That principle is difficult to reconcile with a government-sanctioned exemption which permits religious adherents only to escape the reach of a neutral law of general applicability. The prospect, for example, that "those who do not make polygamy a part of their religious belief may be found guilty and punished, while those who do must be acquitted and go free" certainly suggests Establishment Clause problems, as the Court intimated in *Reynolds v. United States.* . . .

As a constitutional matter, any protection extended to Smith and Black for their religious peyote use should honor not only their claim to religious freedom, but it should honor all others on like terms. Government cannot, however, "accommodate" their religious drug use without disserving its interest in religious neutrality and its compelling interest in comprehensive drug control.

Religious motivated drug use is not a phenomenon unique to one church, one religious belief system, or one narrow group of religious adherents. Hallucinogenic drugs have religious significance in several cultures. Some of these religions have deep roots. Others may have been borne of more contemporary revelation. Without question, however, the number of organizations and individuals proclaiming religious motivations for drug use is far from small.

Reported appellate cases from across the country provide a sampling that reveals both the range of these religious claims and the persistence of those who assert them. Like members of the Native American Church, Peyote Way Church members have claimed a free exercise right to peyote for religious reasons. The Native American Church of New York has judicially pursued exemptions for several psychedelic drugs. Members of the Aquarian Brotherhood Church have claimed a free exercise right to use marijuana, LSD and hashish for religious purposes. Moslems have asserted a free exercise entitlement to use and possess heroin and marijuana. The Ethiopian Zion Coptic Church, Hindus, Hindu Tantrists, the Twelve Tribes of Israel (Rastafarians), Tantric Buddhists and others have sought constitutional exemptions from laws prohibiting marijuana use. In addition, individuals without any particular church or organizational affiliation also sought constitutional protection for their religious use of otherwise unlawful drugs.

This list is far from exhaustive. But it accurately illustrates the diversity and volume of claims for religious drug use protection that have confronted both state and federal courts. It also realistically demonstrates that if the Free Exercise Clause protects religiously motivated drug use from the reach of comprehensive drug control schemes, government must attempt to craft religion-by-religion, drug-by-drug, and individual-by-individual exemptions from those laws. That result would wreak havoc with government's efforts to control dangerous drug use in this country. . . .

[[3. Role of Courts and Legislatures.]] Courts and legislatures alike have uniformly recognized that a neutral rule granting drug use exemptions to all religions on the same terms would spell disaster for comprehensive drug regulations. No legislative body or regulatory agency in the country has created an exemption for all sincere drug use in the course of religious worship. . . .

Granted, some courts and some legislative bodies have "accommodated" religious drug use in a limited way. But they have done so only by creating what is largely a denomination-specific exemption, available only to the adherents of one set of religious beliefs (the Native American Church and sometimes related churches), for the use of one drug (peyote). The apparent theory underlying a narrowly drawn exemption is that the interference with comprehensive drug regulation is "de minimis" if only a small number of people may invoke the Constitution's protections. The desire of lower courts to find some means to accommodate Native American Church members' peyote use may be understandable. As a matter of constitutional jurisprudence, however, these denomination-specific exemptions are neither tenable nor sound. . . .

The 1970's and 1980's brought with them an unprecedented number of claims for religious exemptions from . . . uniform regulatory enactments. Judges have sometimes struggled with the analysis, unsure of their ability to quantify the weight of a citizen's needs as a whole, and then to gauge how the scales balance. . . .

Many courts have attempted to scrutinize the importance or centrality of religious drug use to a particular religion or religious practice. Where drug use is optional, the claims for constitutional protection have failed. Even in those instances where a drug is taken as a sacrament to facilitate an individual's communion with his god, and where individuals have claimed that drug use is "essential" to their religion, courts have concluded that drug use was not sufficiently central to the religion to be protected. These holdings distinguish Native American Church peyote ingestion and other religious drug use by embroiling the courts in theological judgments about the tenets of religious beliefs and their importance to an individual's spiritual development. They have done so even though those inquiries are beyond judicial competence. . . .

The only way courts have "accommodated" religious drug use is to extend constitutional protection on the basis of a narrow, ethnocentric model. Similarly, the few states that have legislatively created exemptions have done so only for peyotists in organized churches, and frequently only for the Native American Church. The tacit reasoning underlying these denomination-based exemptions is that, while government's interest in drug control is sufficiently compelling to justify a total ban on dangerous drugs in society at large, that interest is not significantly compromised if the door is merely cracked open to permit the drug use of one minority religion. The large-scale success of the Native American Church in obtaining exemptions and the wholesale failure of any other church or individual to be extended the same protection also suggests that on some unarticulated basis, Native American Church peyote use has simply achieved a level of political acceptance that no other religious belief has been able to win.

These exemptions also are unmistakably influenced by the incorrect assumption that Native American Church members live and practice their religion as a discrete and insular minority, far removed from the mainstream of American life. The poetic image of a few Native Americans "using peyote one night at a meeting in a desert hogan" is a powerful appeal to our respect for and deference to the ancient ways of the Native American.

But this case illustrates that the image is false. Not all Native Americans are peyotists. Not all peyotists are Native Americans. And Native American Church members are not all refugees from modern society. They are a part of its fabric. They are our lawyers, our doctors, and truck drivers, our teachers and our alcohol and drug counselors. In Oregon, an estimated 89 percent of the state's more than 27,000 Native Americans live and work in urban areas. It is wrong to conclude that religious peyote use can be accommodated on the assumption that its practitioners exist only apart from contemporary society.

Even if the ethnic stereotype of Native American Church members were accurate, it would not warrant an exemption from drug laws only for that single denomination. In matters of religion, the Constitution does not permit cracking the door open in such a way as to permit one government-favored religion to pass through, and to deny passage to all others. Under settled Free Exercise and Establishment Clause principles, government cannot show partiality to any one religious group or promote one religion over the other. Religious drug use must be accommodated, if at all, on the basis of neutral principles that extend the Constitution's protection to all religions on the same terms. Thus, under the Free Exercise Clause, the door to religious drug use must be opened fully if it is opened at all. That result would have devastating consequences for government in its efforts to control dangerous drug use and to enforce its regulations.

Equally important, to hold that religious drug use is constitutionally protected would mean more than simply exempting drug use from criminal prohibitions. Once the Constitution extends protection to religious conduct, it properly extends that protection on several fronts. Society becomes obligated to "accommodate" religious practices in work places, in government programs, and in other public and private settings. . . .

Protection for religious drug use, if it constitutionally attaches, would thus extend to all areas where religion must be accommodated, not just to the application of criminal laws. Stated only in general terms, that conclusion would mean society must "accommodate" religious drug use practices. But more specifically and more accurately, it would require society to tolerate the presence and use of dangerous drugs in settings where it otherwise may insist that citizens remain drug free.

The Free Exercise Clause does not compel that result. It is sometimes an unfortunate reality that to guarantee "religious freedom to a great variety of faiths requires that some religious practices yield to the common good." Religious use of hallucinogens and other dangerous drugs simply is not compatible with society's compelling interest in controlling and eliminating drug use and abuse. Accordingly, for the same reasons that constitutional protection has been denied to members of the Ethiopian Zion Coptic Church, to Hindus, to Tantric Buddhists, to Rastafarians and to the many individual and organized churches that have sought protection for religious drug use, constitutional protection must be denied in this case. . . .

> Respectfully submitted,
> DAVE FROHNMAYER,
> Attorney General of Oregon

SMITH'S BRIEF

[[1. Unemployment Compensation Cases.]] . . . In *Sherbert* the Court stated that while the Constitution permits no governmental regulation of religious beliefs, freedom of religious conduct is "not totally free from legislative restrictions." In such cases, "[t]he conduct or actions so regulated have invariably posed some substantial threat to public safety, peace or order." Where no such threat exists, denial of unemployment benefits is permissible only where: 1. the disqualification as a beneficiary represents no infringement by the State of the constitutional rights of free exercise; or 2. because any incidental burden on the free exercise of a claimant's religion may be justified by a compelling state interest in the regulation of a subject within the State's constitutional power to regulate. . . .

In this case, the Oregon Supreme Court has stated . . . that "[t]he state's interest [in denying respondents unemployment compensation for religious conduct] is simply the financial interest in the payment of benefits from the unemployment insurance fund to this claimant and other claimants similarly situated." . . .

It is because this case is indistinguishable from the *Sherbert-Thomas* line of decisions, however, that petitioners seek to inject a new element into the analysis—the alleged criminality of respondents' conduct. Without it there would be no controversy to be decided by this Court; with it petitioners attempt to create a new issue where none now exists. . . .

The Court in *Yoder* applied the same searching inquiry of the State's asserted criminal interests as it had previously applied in *Sherbert* in a civil context. The Court held that the appropriate constitutional analysis applies not to the state's asserted *general* interest (in the present case the state's general interest in proscribing dangerous drugs), but rather to the far narrower interest in enforcing this interest against a specific group when it burdens the practice of their religion. . . .

[[2. State's Burden of Proof.]] In the present case petitioners have presented no specific evidence showing that exempting the Native American Church's use of peyote would frustrate Oregon's interest in proscribing dangerous drugs. But as *Sherbert* suggests, it is the State's burden to be more specific. . . . Instead petitioners rely on general speculative fears about the drug problem in the

United States in an attempt to lump the highly regulated and limited religious use of peyote by the Native American Church with other drugs that are used almost exclusively for improper purposes.

. . . It is important to note that Oregon stands alone of states with significant populations of Native American Church members in prohibiting religious use of peyote. At least 23 states as well as the federal government exempt the religious use of peyote from criminal proscription. It is disingenuous for petitioners to argue that exempting the religious use of peyote will undermine "[t]he drug laws adopted by the states and the federal government [which] depend on uniformity and comprehensiveness to be effective," when interested states and the federal government *uniformly* exempt the religious use of peyote from criminal proscription. . . .

Second, the facts of peyote use, both legal (religious) and illegal, do not support petitioners' assertions about problems with regulating it. . . . DEA statistics show that a total of 19 *pounds* of peyote was seized during an eight year period while one *million* times as much marijuana was seized during the same period. Respondents include as an appendix to this brief . . . showing that Texas regulations strictly control and account for all legitimate peyote use, without any law enforcement problems. . . .

. . . [[P]]etitioners assert . . . that peyote cannot be safely used by anyone and is a danger to the user and community. Petitioners' assertion is not borne out by experience. Native Americans' religious use of peyote has been documented since the 16th Century. There is no evidence that such use has had any detrimental effect on the users. In addition, petitioners present no evidence from the 23 states which permit the religious use of peyote . . . of any detrimental effect on users or the community. . . . Petitioners' failure to provide any evidence of the alleged detrimental effects demonstrates that no problem exits. Petitioners' assertions are speculative. . . .

[[3. Free Exercise and Minority Religions.]] The Constitutional protection sought by respondents, if granted, would in no way create a broad shield for other drug-based religions and necessitates only a narrow exemption, similar in scope to the existing congressional and administrative exemption for nondrug peyote use by the Native American Church and its members as is the narrow exemption granted to the Amish in *Yoder*. The Native American Church's own tenets dictate that non-religious use of peyote is sacrilegious and prohibit Church members from using or distributing the drug outside of its legally exempted context . . .

The First Amendment to the Constitution exists to protect minority views, beliefs and to some extent practices. . . .

The majority rarely requires protection by the courts. Minority faiths, on the other hand, are in grave danger of infringement without special protection under the Free Exercise Clause.

If the Free Exercise Clause required complete neutrality of treatment among all religions, the Older Order Amish and other minority Christian beliefs would have been subject to outright prohibition by otherwise neutral state laws.

This Court provides for accommodation of minority faiths even if it involves special treatment or accommodation of practices not followed by the majority faiths in this country. The Court must acknowledge its protection of the Native American Church's central ceremony if the Free Exercise Clause is to continue to have meaning for members of minority religions. . . .

The Native American Church shares the strong historic practice circumstances of the Old Order Amish. Originally, Native American Church members practiced their religion in traditional tribal homelands. A combination of factors increased friction between Church members and the greater society, beginning with the use of non-Indian agents and missionaries to run reservations in the early 1900's. The federal Indian relocation program of the 1950's moved many reservation Indians into urban areas. Because of these changes Church members began experiencing prosecution efforts. . . .

Similarly, the majority tolerated the Amish lifestyle until the demands of the urban, technological life of the 20th Century led to increased schooling requirements. If the Free Exercise Clause does not also provide protection to respondents' minority faith as it does to majority religions, respondents, like the Amish, "must either abandon belief and be assimilated into society at large, or be forced to migrate into some other and more tolerant region.". . .

Petitioners raise Establishment Clause issues in their brief for the first time, although these issues are not pressed with much vigor. These claims have been raised before in the Free Exercise cases brought before this Court and uniformly rejected. "Government efforts to accommodate religions are permissible when they remove burdens on the free exercise of religion."

Oregon law is consistent with this principle in providing for exemptions from otherwise valid regulatory laws for the sacramental use of wine. While these exemptions do not specifically name all Christian denominations which use wine, they are directed at one faith. An exemption for peyote use is indistinguishable in theory from these exemptions. . . .

> Respectfully submitted,
> CRAIG J. DORSAY,
> Director, Native American Program.

ORAL ARGUMENT

CHIEF JUSTICE REHNQUIST: Am I correct in thinking that one need not be a Native American to be admitted to the Native American Church, or to participate in its rituals?

MR. FROHNMAYER [[Oregon's Attorney General]]: Justice Rehnquist, I— I would be somewhat hesitant to answer that question, because that is more properly directed, I believe, to the communicants of the church. It is safe to say that the record is somewhat obscure on this point. We know that Respondent Black . . .

REHNQUIST: What about Mr. Black? He was not a Native American, was he?

FROHNMAYER: Mr. Black was not a Native American. We believe it is a fair reading of the record that he believed that he was a member of the Native American Church. There is contradictory evidence in the record concerning whether persons other than Native Americans can be admitted to the ritual, at least if they don't show a certain amount of blood lineage from Native American ancestry. . . .

✻   ✻   ✻

FROHNMAYER: . . . [[T]]he Oregon Supreme Court has concluded, however, that the federal Constitution commands a judicially crafted exemption for sincere adult users of a single church. And this poses for us a dilemma. On the one hand, if the exemption is crafted so narrowly that it applies to one group on a de minimis basis, then that means that our state and federal constitutions have preferred one religion over another, and hopelessly compromised the constitution[[al]] requirements of neutrality. . . .

THE COURT: Can we say the same thing about the result of . . . *Wisconsin against Yoder?*

FROHNMAYER: No, we think not. Because there, in *Yoder*, the church was not singled out by name and by identity and by denomination, and there were no others similarly situated who were clamoring for that particular exemption. *Yoder* is a case which is distinguishable, obviously, on many other important grounds, and I can reach them now.

THE COURT: Well, suppose the Wisconsin legislature had singled out the Amish church. . . .

FROHNMAYER: We think the problem is compounded when a legislature singles it out, because the judicial exemption is free of broader interpretation, whereas, if the legislature in its plenary judgment has singled out a specific church, we believe it has, in many respects, potentially run afoul of the Establishment Clause unless it treats other religions clamoring for equal treatment on similar grounds in similar ways.

THE COURT: Are you arguing that the 23—or it isn't 23 under your figures, but whatever the number of states that grant exemptions, those exemptions all violate the Establishment Clause?

FROHNMAYER: No, we are not. We did not come to this Court to argue that giving an exemption in some form or another is an impermissible state act in the exercise of its plenary authority. Our argument is simply that the Free Exercise Clause does not command every state in this union, as apparently our

Oregon Supreme Court would command, to craft an exemption singling out a specific church. Some of those state exemptions, as we pointed out, Justice Stevens, do speak neutrally with respect to bonafide religious practices.

THE COURT: But some don't. And those that don't you would say are invalid under the Establishment Clause?

FROHNMAYER: I think we would need to know more. And what more we would need to know is whether, if a court were faced with a claim by another religion that, notwithstanding the specific named claim of the particular communicants of one church, if it denied it to another, then perhaps that might implicate the Establishment Clause, because it would have closed the doors to others achieving this equally. So, I believe our position is that we would have to wait for a case-by-case determination to see whether those jurisdictions would open their doors to other claims, if properly advanced by other religions.

JUSTICE SCALIA: You just don't want to have to face up to those problems. You want to be able to—not to have any exemption at all.

FROHNMAYER: That is correct. And this is not a theoretical issue for the State of Oregon, because we have pending in our appellate courts a case which in many ways is on all fours with this, in which sincere religious communicants who believe that their use of marijuana is religiously inspired, have asked for exemption from Oregon's drug laws. And that's part of the problem.

SCALIA: Well, that is also another problem in deciding what the states can do without offending the Establishment Clause. There is a problem in just allowing all religions to use marijuana, or any other hallucinogenic drug, I would assume. Isn't that a problem, too?

FROHNMAYER: Justice Scalia, that is one of the major reasons we have brought this case to this Court for a second time, which is, we are asked, we believe, not merely to see this as one case, but it is in fact the thin end of the wedge in which analytical distinctions are extremely difficult to draw, and in which claims certainly will be made, as they have been made in lower court with increasing frequency, for other drugs and other—

JUSTICE STEVENS: I take it, then, that your flat rule position would permit a state to outlaw totally the use of alcohol, including wine, in religious ceremonies?

FROHNMAYER: That's a different question.

STEVENS: Why is that different.

FROHNMAYER: The issue of sacramental wine is different because, at least at the present, it is not a Schedule I substance. . . .

*   *   *

THE COURT: Well, I think a very good case could be made on the basis of what you say, that there is no risk of its use spreading beyond the Native American Church.

MR. DORSAY [[Smith's and Black's Attorney]]: That is correct.

THE COURT: And that that church has been responsible in its use. But why can't that state say we don't want Native Church members to use it either. We think this is dangerous. It is harmful to people. We don't want children to be brought into this church and taught to use this thing, it is harmful to them. It is a Schedule I substance; we have made that determination.

DORSAY: Because the First Amendment, I believe, requires something more than a mere legislative statement that we believe it may be harmful. States can come up with all kinds of reasons to outlaw all kinds of conduct, as we have cited in our supplemental brief, for instance. That driving of Amish buggies without the reflector warning system is certainly a dangerous act. But if you allow the mere legislative proscription without an actual inquiry into whether harm has in fact occurred, then you are—

THE COURT: But, Mr. Dorsay, under that analysis, is there any—can we possibly defend the state laws that prohibit bigamy? What is the evidence that bigamy is harmful?

DORSAY: Well, I think the evidence that bigamy was harmful in the 1800's perhaps may be different than exists today.

THE COURT: What was the evidence then? It was against a lot of people's religious and moral beliefs, but did anybody ever prove it was harmful?

DORSAY: Well, I would say that the analysis conducted by the Court back in the 1800's was perhaps different, and maybe that statute would not be upheld in the present day. But—

THE COURT: I think that is the logic of your position, that that statute probably falls, too.

DORSAY: I think it is not substantially justified. . . .

           *   *   *

THE COURT: Well, would you—wouldn't you think that the same exemption would be required for other, other sincere claims that the use of peyote is part of their religion?

DORSAY: Well, I have two points of response to that. Yes, I do believe it would be required under normal constitutional analysis, for other peyote churches, such as the Peyote Way Church of God, which have the same exact conditions that the Native American Church does. And there are a number of conditions that go to show that this church, or the use of peyote is unique.

However—

THE COURT: How about marijuana use by a church that uses that as part of its religious sacrament?

DORSAY: Well, see, I think we can get into a lot of examples, and I don't want to go down that road too far because we don't—

THE COURT: I'll bet you don't.
(Laughter)

DORSAY:—have the facts here.
(Laughter)

DORSAY: But the fact is, and a number of courts have looked at marijuana, and they have concluded that marijuana contributes substantially to the law enforcement problem. That has been the distinguishing factor in a number of cases. This drug does not contribute to the law enforcement problem. This substance is used by—as used in its sacramental purposes by the church, does not cause those problems. . . .

SCALIA: But why can't the state consider it itself as the law enforcement problem?

DORSAY: Peyote itself?

SCALIA: The very use, even in religious service. Just as the state may consider the very use of marijuana, regardless of whether it pollutes commerce or anything else, as being itself a problem. We don't want it used. Why can't—

DORSAY: The state can look at it as the problem itself, but we're—it is my position, strongly, that they have to justify that position by showing some actual harm. Otherwise there would really be no free exercise right, because the state could outlaw any kind of conduct and say—

SCALIA: So long as it does it generally, I think—why isn't that right?

DORSAY: So long as it does—

SCALIA: So long as it does it generally and doesn't pick on a particular religion. It has a generally applicable law for good and sufficient reasons.

DORSAY: Well, the problem is . . . this law . . . [[despite]] the "neutral," quote, unquote, proscription, does affect a particular religion only. . . .

THE COURT: Well, I suppose you could say a law against human sacrifice would, you know, would affect only the Aztecs. But I don't know that you have to make—you have to make exceptions. If it is a generally applicable law that the state—

DORSAY: Well . . . a better example . . . is, for instance, cited to a case outlawing the use of dangerous snakes. If there are some snakes that have—are, for instance, are poisonous, but you can show one, that they never bite people, two, that the effect is not really dangerous, that poison is not dangerous, then even in that case I would say you should not outlaw the use of that snake, because in fact it is not causing any harm to people.

THE COURT: And the burden is on the state to show that.

DORSAY: Yes. All of the cases—

THE COURT: So if there were a cult that used rattlesnakes, the state would have to show that in the use of those rattlesnakes somebody has been killed or hurt.

DORSAY: Well, I don't think there is any dispute about the harm that rattlesnakes can cause.

THE COURT: I don't think there is any dispute about the harm that peyote can cause. You haven't disputed that, the general dangerousness of it, have you?

DORSAY: The misuse of peyote, no. We do not believe the circumscribed ceremonial use of this peyote constitute misuse under any circumstances. . . .

THE OPINION

Justice Scalia delivered the opinion of the Court . . .

. . . The free exercise of religion means, first and foremost, the right to believe and profess whatever religious doctrine one desires. Thus, the First Amendment obviously excludes all "governmental regulation of religious *beliefs* as such." The government may not compel affirmation of religious belief, punish the expression of religious doctrines it believes to be false, impose special disabilities on the basis of religious views or religious status, or lend its power to one or the other side in controversies over religious authority or dogma.

But the "exercise of religion" often involves not only belief and profession but the performance of (or abstention from) physical acts: assembling with others for a worship service, participating in sacramental use of bread and wine, proselytizing, abstaining from certain foods or certain modes of transportation. It would be true, we think (though no case of ours has involved the point), that a State would be "prohibiting the free exercise [of religion]" if it sought to ban such acts or abstentions only when they are engaged in for religious reasons, or only because of the religious belief that they display. It would doubtless be unconstitutional, for example, to ban the casting of "statues that are to be used for worship purposes," or to prohibit bowing down before a golden calf.

Respondents in the present case, however, seek to carry the meaning of "prohibiting the free exercise [of religion]" one large step further. They contend that their religious motivation for using peyote places them beyond the reach of a criminal law that is not specifically directed at their religious practice, and that is concededly constitutional as applied to those who use the drug for other reasons. They assert, in other words, that "prohibiting the free exercise [of religion]" includes requiring any individual to observe a generally applicable law that requires (or forbids) the performance of an act that this religious belief forbids (or requires). As a textual matter, we do not think the words must be given that meaning. It is no more necessary to regard the collection of a general tax, for example, as "prohibiting the free exercise [of religion]" by those citizens who believe support of organized government to be sinful than it is to regard the same tax as "abridging the freedom . . . of the press" of those publishing companies that must pay the tax as a condition of staying in business. It is a permissible reading of the text, in the one case as in the other, to say that if prohibiting the exercise of religion (or burdening the activity of printing) is not the object of the tax but merely the incidental effect of a generally applicable and otherwise valid provision, the First Amendment has not been offended.

. . . We have never held that an individual's religious beliefs excuse him from compliance with an otherwise valid law prohibiting conduct that the State is free to regulate. On the contrary, the record of more than a century of our free exercise jurisprudence contradicts that proposition. . . .

The only decisions in which we have held that the First Amendment bars application of a neutral, generally applicable law to religiously motivated action have involved not the Free Exercise Clause alone, but the Free Exercise Clause in conjunction with other constitutional protections, such as freedom of speech and of the press, . . . or the right of parents, acknowledged in *Pierce v. Society of Sisters*, to direct the education of their children, see *Wisconsin v. Yoder*. Some of our cases prohibiting compelled expression, decided exclusively upon free speech grounds, have also involved freedom of religion, cf. . . . *West Virginia Bd. of Education v. Barnette*. And it is easy to envision a case in which a challenge on freedom of association grounds would likewise be reinforced by Free Exercise Clause concerns.

The present case does not present such a hybrid situation, but a free exercise claim unconnected with any communicative activity or parental right. Respondents urge us to hold, quite simply, that when otherwise prohibitable conduct is accompanied by religious convictions, not only the convictions but the conduct itself must be free from governmental regulation. We have never held that, and decline to do so now. There being no contention that Oregon's drug law represents an attempt to regulate religious beliefs, the communication of religious beliefs, or the raising of one's children in those beliefs, the rule to which we have adhered ever since Reynolds plainly controls. . . .

. . . Under the *Sherbert* test, governmental actions that substantially burden a religious practice must be justified by a compelling governmental interest. Applying that test we have, on three occasions, invalidated state unemployment compensation rules that conditioned the availability of benefits upon an applicant's willingness to work under conditions forbidden by his religion. We have never invalidated any governmental action on the basis of the *Sherbert* test except the denial of unemployment compensation. . . .

Even if we were inclined to breathe into *Sherbert* some life beyond the unemployment compensation field, we would not apply it to require exemptions from a generally applicable criminal law. . . .

. . . The government's ability to enforce generally applicable prohibitions of socially harmful conduct, like its ability to carry out other aspects of public policy, "cannot depend on measuring the effects of a governmental action on a religious objector's spiritual development." To make an individual's obligation to obey such a law contingent upon the law's coincidence with his religious beliefs, except where the State's interest is "compelling"—permitting him, by virtue of his beliefs, "to become a law unto himself"—contradicts both constitutional tradition and common sense.

The "compelling governmental interest" requirement seems benign, because it is familiar from other fields. But using it as the standard that must be met before the government may accord different treatment on the basis of race, or before the government may regulate the content of speech, is not remotely comparable to using it for the purposes asserted here. What it produces in those other fields—equality of treatment and an unrestricted flow of contending speech—are constitutional norms; what it would produce here—a private right to ignore generally applicable laws—is a constitutional anomaly.

Nor is it possible to limit the impact of respondents' proposal by requiring a "compelling state interest" only when the conduct prohibited is "central" to the individual's religion. It is no more appropriate for judges to determine the "centrality" of religious beliefs before applying a "compelling interest" test in the free exercise field, than it would be for them to determine the "importance" of ideas before applying the "compelling interest" test in the free speech field. . . .

. . . Precisely because "we are a cosmopolitan nation made up of people of almost every conceivable religious preference," and precisely because we value and protect that religious divergence, we cannot afford the luxury of deeming *presumptively invalid*, as applied to the religious objector, every regulation of conduct that does not protect an interest of the highest order. The rule respondents favor would open the prospect of constitutionally required religious exemptions from civic obligations of almost every conceivable kind—ranging from compulsory military service, to the payment of taxes, to health and safety regulation such as manslaughter and child neglect laws, compulsory vaccination laws, drug laws, and traffic laws; to social welfare legislation such as minimum wage laws, child labor laws, animal cruelty laws, environmental protection laws, and laws providing for equality of opportunity for the races. The First Amendment's protection of religious liberty does not require this.

Values that are protected against government interference through enshrinement in the Bill of Rights are not thereby banished from the political process. Just as a society that believes in the negative protection accorded to the press by the First Amendment is likely to enact laws that affirmatively foster the dissemination of the printed word, so also a society that believes in the negative protection accorded to religious belief can be expected to be solicitous of that value in its legislation as well. It is therefore not surprising that a number of States have made an exception to their drug laws for sacramental peyote use. But to say that a nondiscriminatory religious-practice exemption is permitted, or even that it is desirable, is not to say that it is constitutionally required, and that the appropriate occasions for its creation can be discerned by the courts. It may fairly be said that leaving accommodation to the political process will place at a relative disadvantage those religious practices that are not widely engaged in; but that unavoidable consequence of democratic government must be preferred to a system in which each conscience is a law unto itself or in which judges weigh the social importance of all laws against the centrality of all religious beliefs. . . .

Justice O'Connor, concurring in the judgment . . .

Although I agree with the result the Court reaches in this case, I cannot join its opinion. In my view, today's holding dramatically departs from well-settled First Amendment jurisprudence, appears unnecessary to resolve the question presented, and is incompatible with our Nation's fundamental commitment to individual religious liberty. . . .

The Court today . . . interprets the [[Free Exercise]] Clause to permit the government to prohibit, without justification, conduct mandated by an individual's religious beliefs, so long as that prohibition is generally applicable. But a law that prohibits certain conduct—conduct that happens to be an act of worship for someone—manifestly does prohibit that person's free exercise of his religion. A person who is barred from engaging in religiously motivated conduct is barred from freely exercising his religion regardless of whether the law prohibits the conduct only when engaged in for religious reasons, only by members of that religion, or by all persons. It is difficult to deny that a law that prohibits religiously motivated conduct, even if the law is generally applicable, does not at least implicate First Amendment concerns.

The Court responds that generally applicable laws are "one large step" removed from laws aimed at specific religious practices. The First Amendment, however, does not distinguish between laws that are generally applicable and laws that target particular religious practices. Indeed few States would be so naive as to enact a law directly prohibiting or burdening a religious practice as such. Our free exercise cases have all concerned generally applicable laws that had the effect of significantly burdening a religious practice. If the First Amendment is to have any vitality, it ought not be construed to cover only the extreme and hypothetical situation in which a State directly targets a religious practice. . . .

To say that a person's right to free exercise has been burdened, of course, does not mean that he has an absolute right to engage in the conduct. Under our established First Amendment jurisprudence, we have recognized that the freedom to act, unlike the freedom to believe, cannot be absolute. Instead, we have respected both the First Amendment's express textual mandate and the governmental interest in regulation of conduct by requiring the government to justify any substantial burden on religiously motivated conduct by a compelling state interest and by means narrowly tailored to achieve that interest. . . .

The Court endeavors to escape from our decisions in *Cantwell* and *Yoder* by labeling them "hybrid" decisions, but there is no denying that both cases expressly relied on the Free Exercise Clause and that we have consistently regarded those cases as part of the mainstream of our free exercise jurisprudence. . . .

. . . Even if, as an empirical matter, a government's criminal laws might usually serve a compelling interest in health, safety, or public order, the First Amendment at least requires a case-by-case determination of the question, sensitive to the facts of each particular claim. Given the range of conduct that a State might legitimately make criminal, we cannot assume, merely because a law carries criminal sanctions and is generally applicable, that the First Amendment *never* requires the State to grant a limited exemption for religiously motivated conduct. . . .

. . . As the language of the Clause itself makes clear, an individual's free exercise of religion is a preferred constitutional activity. A law that makes criminal such an activity therefore triggers constitutional concern—and it does not target the particular religious conduct at issue. . . . The Court's parade of horribles not only fails as a reason for discarding the compelling interest test, it instead demonstrates just the opposite: that courts have been quite capable of applying our free exercise jurisprudence to strike sensible balances between religious liberty and competing state interests.

Finally, the Court today suggests that the disfavoring of minority religions is an "unavoidable consequence" under our system of government and that accommodation of such religions must be left to the political process. In my view, however, the First Amendment was enacted precisely to protect the rights of those whose religious practices are not shared by the majority and may be viewed with hostility. The history of our free exercise doctrine amply demonstrates the harsh impact majoritarian rule has had on unpopular or emerging religious groups such as the Jehovah's Witnesses and the Amish. . . .

The Court's holding today not only misreads settled First Amendment precedent; it appears to be unnecessary to this case. I would reach the same result applying our established free exercise jurisprudence. . . .

Thus the critical question in this case is whether exempting respondents from the State's general criminal prohibition "will unduly interfere with fulfillment of the governmental interest." Although the question is close, I would conclude that uniform application of Oregon's criminal prohibition is "essential to accomplish" its overriding interest in preventing the physical harm caused by the use of a Schedule I controlled substance. . . .

For these reasons, I believe that granting a selective exemption in this case would seriously impair Oregon's compelling interest in prohibiting possession of peyote by its citizens. Under such circumstances, the Free Exercise Clause does not require the State to accommodate respondents' religiously motivated conduct. . . .

Justice Blackmun, with whom Justice Brennan and Justice Marshall join, dissenting . . .

. . . I agree with Justice O'Connor's analysis of the applicable free exercise doctrine, and I join parts I and II of her opinion. As she points out, "the critical question in this case is whether exempting respondents from the State's general criminal prohibition 'will unduly interfere with fulfillment of the governmental interest.'" I do disagree, however, with her specific answer to that question.

In weighing the clear interest of respondents Smith and Black in the free exercise of their religion against Oregon's asserted interest in enforcing its drug laws, it is important to articulate in precise terms the state interest involved. It is not the State's broad interest in fighting the critical "war on drugs" that must be weighed against respondents' claim, but the State's narrow interest in refusing to make an exception for the religious, ceremonial use of peyote. Failure to reduce the competing interests to the same plane of generality tends to distort the weighing process in the State's favor. . . .

The State's interest in enforcing its prohibition, in order to be sufficiently compelling to outweigh a free exercise claim, cannot be merely abstract or symbolic. The state cannot plausibly assert that unbending application of a criminal prohibition is essential to fulfill any compelling interest, if it does not, in fact, attempt to enforce that prohibition. In this case, the state actually has not evinced any concrete interest in enforcing its drug laws against religious users of peyote. Oregon has never sought to prosecute respondents, and does not claim that it has made significant enforcement efforts against other religious users of peyote. The State's asserted interest thus amounts only to the symbolic preservation of an unenforced prohibition. But a government interest in "symbolism, even symbolism for so worthy a cause as the abolition of unlawful drugs," cannot suffice to abrogate the constitutional rights of individuals.

Similarly, this Court's prior decisions have not allowed a government to rely on mere speculation about potential harms, but have demanded evidentiary support for a refusal to allow a religious exception. . . .

The State proclaims an interest in protecting the health and safety of its citizens from the dangers of unlawful drugs. It offers, however, no evidence that the religious use of peyote has ever harmed anyone. . . .

Finally, the State argues that granting an exception for religious peyote use would erode its interest in the uniform, fair, and certain enforcement of its drug laws. The State fears that, if it grants an exemption for religious peyote use, a flood of other claims to religious exemptions will follow. It would then be placed in a dilemma, it says, between allowing a patchwork of exemptions that would hinder its law enforcement efforts, and risking a violation of the Establishment Clause by arbitrarily limiting its religious exemptions. . . .

. . . This Court, however, consistently has rejected similar arguments in past free exercise cases, and it should do so here as well.

The State's apprehension of a flood of other religious claims is purely speculative. Almost half the States, and the Federal Government, have maintained an exemption for religious peyote use for many years, and apparently have not found themselves overwhelmed by claims to other religious exemptions. Allowing an exemption for religious peyote use would not necessarily oblige the State to grant a similar exemption to other religious groups. . . . That the State might grant an exemption for religious peyote use, but deny other religious claims arising in different circumstances, would not violate the Establishment Clause. Though the State must treat all religions equally, and not favor one over another, this obligation is fulfilled by the uniform application of the "compelling interest" *test* to all free exercise claims, not by reaching uniform *results* as to all claims. A showing that religious peyote use does not unduly interfere with the State's interest is "one that probably few other religious groups or sects could make;" this does not mean that an exemption limited to peyote use is tantamount to an establishment of religion . . .

Finally, although I agree with Justice O'Connor that courts should refrain from delving into questions whether, as a matter of religious doctrine, a particular practice is "central" to the religion, I do not think this means that the courts must turn a blind eye to the severe impact of a State's restrictions on the adherents of a minority religion. . . .

POSTSCRIPT

The *Smith* decision has proven to be a controversial milestone in the Supreme Court's free exercise jurisprudence. Lower federal courts and state courts have generally interpreted *Smith* broadly, applying its ruling not only to criminal statutes, but also to civil laws and regulations. However, the political reaction to *Smith* has been overwhelmingly negative. Starting in 1990, opponents of *Smith* from across the political spectrum rallied behind the Religious Freedom Restoration Act (RFRA). This legislation, which relied on Congress's power to enforce free exercise rights under Section 5 of the Fourteenth Amendment, reinstated *Sherbert*'s compelling-interest test. If this law was valid, then individuals would have a statutory, rather than a constitutional, right to exemptions from even neutral laws of general applicability that substantially burdened their religious practices, unless those laws were the "least restrictive means" to a "compelling state interest." Such traditional political adversaries as Newt Gingrich (R-GA) and Barney Frank (D-MA) in the House and Orrin Hatch (R-UT) and Edward Kennedy (D-MA) in the Senate formed an unusual alliance in support of the RFRA. Additionally, a diverse group of thirty-five religious and civil liberties groups quickly formed the "Coalition for the Free Exercise of Religion" in support of the RFRA. The Native American Church of North

America, the American Civil Liberties Union, the American Jewish Congress, the Baptist Joint Committee on Public Affairs, and the Presbyterian Church all joined this grand coalition. Despite questions about the law's constitutionality, both houses of Congress passed the RFRA almost unanimously, and President Clinton signed it into law on November 16, 1993.

While Congress was debating the RFRA, the Supreme Court handed down a decision that upheld a free exercise claim, thereby revealing that Justice Scalia's majority opinion in *Smith* had not completely eviscerated the Free Exercise Clause. In *Church of Lukumi Babulu Aye v. City of Hialeah* (1993), the Supreme Court unanimously struck down a series of municipal ordinances that singled out a particular religion for disfavored treatment.[30] The case arose because members of the Santeria faith routinely sacrificed animals as part of their religion. Soon after this group announced plans to open a church in Hialeah, Florida, the city council passed a resolution expressing concern about "certain religions" that were "inconsistent with public morals, peace, or safety." Later, the city council enacted ordinances that banned (with certain exceptions) the slaughter or sacrifice of animals in any kind of ritual. In its decision, the Court concluded that, despite the facial neutrality of the ordinances, the city council's actions showed a clear intent to "infringe upon or restrict practices because of their religious motivation." It therefore concluded that the ordinances were unconstitutional because they were not religiously neutral laws of general application.

Notwithstanding *Hialeah*, it soon became clear that the Supreme Court was not backing away from its holding in *Smith*. In Boerne, Texas, a Catholic Archbishop claimed that a religiously neutral, generally applicable zoning ordinance violated the RFRA because it barred him from enlarging his church, a local historical landmark. He filed suit and won in the lower courts, but the Supreme Court reversed in *City of Boerne v. Flores* (1997). An unusual six-justice coalition of "conservative" and "liberal" justices (which stood in contrast to the unusual bipartisan coalition that produced the RFRA) invalidated the RFRA and generally reaffirmed the doctrine of *Smith*.[31] In justifying the result, Justice Kennedy, joined by Chief Justice Rehnquist and Justices Stevens, Scalia, Thomas, and Ginsburg, concluded that Congress had exceeded its enforcement power under Section 5 of the Fourteenth Amendment. Although that provision of the Constitution gave Congress the power to remedy state denials of free exercise rights, it could not alter the meaning of the Free Exercise Clause by statute. "Congress does not enforce a constitutional right by changing what the right is." Therefore, by requiring that all state and local laws be subject to the compelling interest test, the RFRA in the majority's view unconstitutionally intruded into the police power of the states. In a concurring opinion, Justice Stevens expressed his distinct view that, by giving religious groups "a legal weapon that no atheist or agnostic can attain," the RFRA also violated the Establishment Clause.

In *Flores*, an interesting debate took place between Justice O'Connor and Justice Scalia on the historical intent of the Free Exercise Clause (see box 6.1).

Box 6.1   JUSTICES O'CONNOR AND SCALIA DEBATE THE ORIGINAL INTENT OF THE FREE EXERCISE CLAUSE

JUSTICE O'CONNOR dissenting:

. . . We have previously recognized the importance of interpreting the Religion Clauses in light of their history. The historical evidence casts doubt on the Court's current interpretation of the Free Exercise Clause. The record instead reveals that its drafters and ratifiers more likely viewed the Free Exercise Clause as a guarantee that government may not unnecessarily hinder believers from freely practicing their religion, a position consistent with our pre-Smith jurisprudence.

. . . By 1789, every State but Connecticut had incorporated some version of a free exercise clause into its constitution. . . . The language used in these state constitutional provisions and the Northwest Ordinance strongly suggests that, around the time of the drafting of the Bill of Rights, it was generally accepted that the right to "free exercise" required, where possible, accommodation of religious practice. If not—and if the Court was correct in *Smith* that generally applicable laws are enforceable regardless of religious conscience—there would have been no need for these documents to specify, as the New York Constitution did, that rights of conscience should not be "construed as to excuse acts of licentiousness, or justify practices inconsistent with the peace or safety of [the] State." Such a proviso would have been superfluous. . . .

. . . [[T]]ension between religious conscience and generally applicable laws, though rare, was not unknown in pre-Constitutional America. . . . The ways in which these conflicts were resolved suggest that Americans in the colonies and early States thought that, if an individual's religious scruples prevented him from complying with a generally applicable law, the government should, if possible, excuse the person from the law's coverage. For example, Quakers and certain other Protestant sects refused on Biblical grounds to subscribe to oaths or "swear" allegiance to civil authority. . . . Colonial governments created alternatives to the oath requirement for these individuals. . . .

. . . Quakers and Mennonites, as well as a few smaller denominations, refused on religious grounds to carry arms. . . . Rhode Island, North Carolina, and Maryland exempted Quakers from military service in the late 1600's. New York, Massachusetts, Virginia, and New Hampshire followed suit in the mid 1700's. . . .

To be sure, legislatures, not courts, granted these early accommodations. But these were the days before there was a Constitution to protect civil liberties—judicial review did not yet exist. These legislatures apparently believed that the appropriate response to conflicts between civil law and religious scruples was, where possible, accommodation of religious conduct. It is reasonable to presume that the drafters and ratifiers of the

First Amendment—many of whom served in state legislatures—assumed courts would apply the Free Exercise Clause similarly, so that religious liberty was safeguarded.

JUSTICE SCALIA concurring:
. . . The material that the dissent claims is at odds with *Smith* either has little to say about the issue or is in fact more consistent with *Smith* than with the dissent's interpretation of the Free Exercise Clause. . . .
Assuming . . . that the affirmative protection of religion accorded by the early "free exercise" enactments sweeps as broadly as the dissent's theory would require, those enactments do not support the dissent's view, since they contain "provisos" that significantly qualify the affirmative protection they grant. According to the dissent, the "provisos" support its view because they would have been "superfluous" if "the Court was correct in *Smith* that generally applicable laws are enforceable regardless of religious conscience." I disagree. In fact, the most plausible reading of the "free exercise" enactments . . . is a virtual restatement of *Smith*: Religious exercise shall be permitted so long as it does not violate general laws governing conduct. The "provisos" in the enactments negate a license to act in a manner "unfaithfull to the Lord Proprietary," or "behav[e]" in other than a "peaceabl[e] and quie[t]" manner, or "disturb the public peace," or interfere with the "peace [and] safety of th[e] State," or "demea[n]" oneself in other than a "peaceable and orderly manner." At the time these provisos were enacted, keeping "peace" and "order" seems to have meant, precisely, obeying the laws. "[E]very breach of law is against the peace.". . . "Thus, the disturb the peace caveats apparently permitted government to deny religious freedom, not merely in the event of violence or force, but, more generally, upon the occurrence of illegal actions."
[[Early legislative accommodation of religious practices]] . . . suggests (according to the dissent) that "the drafters and ratifiers of the First Amendment . . . assumed courts would apply the Free Exercise Clause similarly." But that legislatures sometimes (though not always) found it "appropriate" to accommodate religious practices does not establish that accommodation was understood to be constitutionally mandated by the Free Exercise Clause. As we explained in *Smith*, "[T]o say that a nondiscriminatory religious practice exemption is permitted, or even that it is desirable, is not to say that it is constitutionally required.". . .
. . . Had the understanding in the period surrounding the ratification of the Bill of Rights been that the various forms of accommodation discussed by the dissent were constitutionally required (either by State Constitutions or by the Federal Constitution), it would be surprising not to find a single state or federal case refusing to enforce a generally applicable statute because of its failure to make accommodation. Yet the dissent cites none—and to my knowledge, and to the knowledge of the academic defenders of the dissent's position, none exists. . . .

O'Connor claimed that the framers and ratifiers of the Constitution intended to provide religious liberty with more constitutional protection than what was granted in *Smith*. It was more than a mere protection from non-general or un-neutral laws. It was a shelter for religiously motivated conduct from all law, unless there was an important governmental interest that required compliance. If true, O'Connor's historical argument would significantly undercut the validity of *Smith*. In short, it would be profoundly unsettling if religious liberty in the twenty-first century was narrower than what the framers protected in the eighteenth. However, Scalia insisted that O'Connor was simply wrong. The accommodations during the colonial and founding eras were legislatively created. They were "permissible" accommodations that were not constitutionally required. Which of these two justices has the better argument? Which has the better understanding of the meaning of the Free Exercise Clause?

In spite of the Court's insistence on the principle that the Free Exercise Clause did not require exemptions for religiously motivated conduct from general and neutral laws, opponents of *Smith* continued to seek to weaken the decision's import. After *Flores*, eleven states—Alabama, Arizona, Connecticut, Florida, Idaho, Illinois, New Mexico, Oklahoma, South Carolina, and Texas—reinstated the *Sherbert* compelling-interest test for their own laws. Other states, however, refused to follow their example because they feared frivolous lawsuits by prisoners and hate groups seeking religious exemptions from generally applicable laws. At the federal level, continuing opposition to *Smith* resulted in the House passing the Religious Liberty Protection Act (RLPA) in 1999. This legislation would also have provided a federal statutory basis for the pre-*Smith* compelling-interest test, but it relied on Congress's power to regulate interstate commerce under Article I, Section 8 of the Constitution, rather than on Section 5 of the Fourteenth Amendment. However, because of concerns that the legislation discriminated against the nonreligious, undermined civil rights laws and laws against child abuse, and promoted disorder among prison inmates, the legislation stalled in the Senate. In late 2000, Congress unanimously passed and President Clinton signed the much more limited Religious Land Use and Institutionalized Persons Act (RLUIPA). This legislation used the federal commerce power to reinstate the compelling-interest test for two types of laws: municipal zoning laws that restricted use of buildings by religious groups and laws that restricted the religious expression of prisoners and institutionalized persons. It remains to be seen whether the Court will uphold the constitutionality of the RLUIPA against future legal challenges.

Seldom has a Supreme Court decision produced such widespread and enduring political opposition as *Smith* has done The continuing tension between the legislative and judicial branches raises several interesting questions. Is it acceptable for Congress to find ways to legally circumvent an overwhelmingly unpopular decision? Should the Court adhere to its view of the Constitution if public opinion vehemently opposes it? Or should Congress simply accept an unpopular Court decision? And what do the post-*Smith* developments reveal about the workability and desirability of the general applicability free exercise rule? Does *Hialeah* show that the Court's interpretation of the Free Exercise Clause still protects minority religions? Does the public outcry in support of the RFRA demonstrate the desirability of an expanded category of "required" accommodations? Is it proper to let legislatures decide whether or not to grant exemptions to religious groups? Or is it the case that courts are better able to balance free exercise claims against governmental interests?

Compared to what it has done in regard to the Free Exercise Clause in *Smith*, the Court has been far less decisive in its interpretation of the Establishment Clause. During the last ten to fifteen years, the Court has continued to broadly define the category of "forbidden" accommodations in some areas, but more narrowly define it in others. For example, the Court remained skeptical of most forms of school prayer. In *Lee v. Weisman* (1992), a five-justice majority struck down nonsectarian religious invocations at public school graduation ceremonies.[32] Four justices relied on Justice O'Conner's "endorsement" test, while the pivotal judge, Justice Kennedy, ruled that such prayers (in part because students were generally expected to attend graduation ceremonies) constituted a form of psychological coercion of nonreligious graduates. In *Santa Fe Independent School Dist. v. Doe* (2000), the Court extended the holding in *Lee* and declared that student-initiated prayer at football games of public schools also violated the Establishment Clause.[33] However, in *Good News Club v. Milford Central School* (2001), the Court recognized a limited situation in which school prayer was permissible. An evangelical club could engage in prayer as part of an after school program if attendance was completely voluntary.[34]

In contrast to school prayer, the Court has become more tolerant of government aid to parochial schools. For example, in *Agostini v. Felton* (1997), the Court applied the effect-prong of the *Lemon* test so as to allow public school teachers to teach remedial courses to disadvantaged children at religious schools.[35] In so doing, the Court expressly reversed a case decided just twelve years earlier.[36] Similarly, in *Mitchell v. Helms* (2000), the Court overturned two cases from the 1970s and allowed states to provide instructional materials, such as maps and computers, to religious schools as part of a neutral program that also benefited public schools.[37] Finally, in the landmark case of *Zelman v. Simmons-Harris* (2002), the Court ruled that voucher programs that allow parents to pay for public or private school tuition, including tuition at parochial schools, did not violate the Establishment Clause.[38] Religiously neutral educational programs that grant a broad array of benefits to both religious and nonreligious school students, and that only indirectly provide aid to religious schools through the private choices of parents, did not have the "primary effect" of "promoting" or endorsing religion. Vouchers were therefore within the category of "permissible" accommodations.[39] The Court's ruling in *Zelman* overturned decisions from the 1970s and opened the door for dramatic governmental experimentation in school choice programs that included religious schools.

The tension between the Free Exercise and Establishment Clauses has resulted in a complex configuration of required, permissible, and forbidden governmental accommodations of religion. After *Smith* and *Flores* narrowly defined the Free Exercise Clause, the Supreme Court has recognized few required accommodations. Legislatures cannot single out a particular minority religion for disfavored treatment, as the city council did in *Hialeah*, but legislatures are not constitutionally required to provide religious exemptions from religiously neutral, generally applicable laws. Congress and many state legislatures have created such exemptions in certain instances, but they require that religious exemption-seekers win the support of majoritarian legislatures, not always a feasible goal for some minority religions. In regard to the Establishment Clause, the scope of forbidden accommodations has somewhat narrowed since 1990. Aid to parochial schools and public religious symbolism can be legislated by the government, so long as the government is neutral and does not endorse or coerce people to support religion. However, most kinds of organized public school prayer are not permissible, even if legislatures want to support such activities. Accordingly, both the courts and the legislatures of states and federal governments have significant amounts of discretion in defining the appropriate relationship between religion and government.

NOTES

1. Today, since these clauses have been applied against the states by way of the Fourteenth Amendment's Due Process Clause, neither the states nor the federal government can either "establish" a religion or restrict the "free exercise" of religion.

2. I have taken the categories of "forbidden accommodations," "required accommodations," and "permissible accommodations" from Laurence H. Tribe, *American Constitutional Law*, 2nd ed. (Mineola, N.Y.: Foundation Press, 1988), pp. 1166–79.

3. It is also possible for courts to define forbidden accommodations broadly and required accommodations narrowly, or vice versa. In the former case, courts would reject legal accommodations for both mainstream and nonmainstream religions, while in the latter instance, courts would require legal accommodations for both mainstream and nonmainstream religions.

4. Because this chapter focuses mainly on the Free Exercise aspect of religious freedom, the following Establishment Clause cases are meant to convey the basic principles behind the Court's definition of "forbidden" accommodations rather than to provide a comprehensive treatment of Establishment Clause cases.

5. *Engel v. Vitale*, 370 U.S. 421 (1962).

6. *Abington Township v. Schempp*, 374 U.S. 203 (1963).

7. 403 U.S. 602 (1971).

8. *Wallace v. Jaffree*, 472 U.S. 38 (1985).

9. *Everson v. Board of Education*, 330 U.S. 1 (1947); *Board of Education v. Allen*, 392 U.S. 236 (1968).

10. *Lemon v. Kurtzman*, 403 U.S. 602 (1971); *Committee for Public Education v. Nyquist*, 413 U.S. 756 (1973); *Wolman v. Walter*, 433 U.S. 229 (1977).

11. *Mueller v. Allen*, 463 U.S. 388 (1983).

12. *Witters v. Wash. Dept. of Services for the Blind*, 474 U.S. 481 (1986).

13. See *Sherbert v. Verner*, 374 U.S. 398 (1963); *Thomas v. Review Board, Indian Empl. Sec. Div.*, 450 U.S. 707 (1981).

14. However, the Court at times seemed to apply this high standard in a deferential way. It would deny the religious exemption even though it did not seem that the exemption was an "essential" means to a "compelling" state interest. See *United States v. Lee*, 455 U.S. 252 (1982); *Bob Jones University v. United* States, 461 U.S. 574 (1983); *Tony & Susan Alamo Foundation v. Secretary of Labor*, 471 U.S. 290 (1985).

15. Exodus, Chap. 20.

16. *Id.*, 597–600.

17. 319 U.S. 624 (1943).

18. *Id.* at 634.

19. *Id.* at 642.

20. 406 U.S. 205 (1972).

21. 374 U.S. 398 (1963). For a similar later case dealing with unemployment compensation, see *Thomas v. Review Board, Indiana Empl. Sec. Div.*, 450 U.S. 707 (1981).

22. *Wisconsin v. Yoder*, 406 U.S. 205, 221 (1972).

23. *Id.*, at 213.

24. *Id.*, at 222.

25. *Id.*, at 225.

26. *Id.*, at 225–26.

27. *Id.*, at 220.

28. *Id.*, at 220–221.

29. Omer C. Stewart, *Peyote Religion* (Norman: University of Oklahoma Press, 1987), p. 224.

30. 508 U.S. 520 (1993).

31. 521 U.S. 507 (1997).

32. 505 U.S. 577 (1992).

33. 530 U.S. 290 (2000).

34. 533 U.S. 98 (2001).

35. 521 U.S. 203 (1997).

36. *Aguilar v. Felton*, 475 U.S. 472 (1985).

37. 530 U.S. 739 (2000); the earlier cases that *Mitchell* overturned were *Meek v. Pittenger*, 421 U.S. 349 (1975) and *Wolman v. Walter*, 433 U.S. 229 (1977).

38. 536 U.S. 639 (2002).

39. *Zelman* of course did not require states to enact voucher programs. In a recent related decision, the Court ruled that a state could exclude the pursuit of a devotional theology degree from its general scholarship aid program at the undergraduate level without violating the Free Exercise Clause. Just as voucher programs are not mandatory, but permissible, so also are public scholarship programs that support theological training. See *Locke v. Davey*, 124 S. Ct. 1307 (2004).

Index

Note: Page numbers in *italic* type refer to text boxes.

abortion, 93–144; briefs on, 96, 98–104, 121–29; as divisive issue, 93, 113, 119–21, 135, 138–43; health of mother and, 97, 103, 105, 108, 111, 143; and informed consent, 125, 126, 137, 140; judicial confirmation process and, 144; opinions on, 109–12, 118–21, 132–43, 145n8; oral argument on, 96, 97, 104–9, 129–32; "partial birth abortions," 143–44, 146n21; post-*Roe* developments, 112–21; spousal notice concerning, 117–19, 123–24, 126–28, 131–32, 137, 140; trimester framework for, 97–98, 111, 116, 118–19, 136, 140; waiting period for, 117–19, 124, 126, 140
Abrams, Floyd, 212, 232–34
Abzug, Bella, 113, *114–15*
access to Supreme Court, xi
Adarand Constructors, Inc. v. Pena (1995), 65
Aesop, 25
affirmative access, 65
affirmative action, 35–90; briefs on, 37, 40, 43–53, 66, 68, 70, 72–79; early instances of, 36–37; as legislative matter, 41; in military, 68, 78–79; opinions on, 41–42, 56–63, 68–69, 82–90; oral argument on, 40, 53–56, 68, 79–81; racial preferences and, 35; Reconstruction as context for, 51; three principles for assessment of, 65

Agostini v. Felton (1997), 281
Air Force Academy, 79
Akron v. Akron Center for Reproductive Health (1983), 116, 124, 136
Alaska, 94
American Civil Liberties Union (ACLU), 202, 277
American Jewish Congress, 277
American Milk Producers, 202
amici curiae briefs, xi–xii; in *Bakke*, 37, 50–53; in *Grutter*, 68, 77–79
Amish, 253–54
Anti-Defamation League of B'nai B'rith, *amicus* brief in *Bakke* by, 53
Aquarian Brotherhood Church, 260
associational rights, 214–15, 245
Austin v. Michigan Chamber of Commerce (1990), 220, 228, 244

Baca, Joe, *71*
Baird v. Eisenstadt (1972), 99, 128, 134
Bakke. See Regents of University of Calif. v. Bakke (1978)
Bakke, Allan, 37, 61
Barnette. See West Virginia State Board of Education v. Barnette (1943)
Bayh, Birch, 115
Becton, Julius W., 68, 78–79
Bellotti. See First National Bank of Boston v. Bellotti (1978)

Bible, 250
Biden, Joseph, 116
Bingham, John A., 9, 20–21
Bipartisan Campaign Reform Act (BCRA)
    (2002), 208–46, 213; Senate debate
    over, *210–11*
Black, Barry, 173, 174, 176, 183
Black Codes, 10, 20, 26
Black, Galen, 255
Black, Hugo, 8, 17, 95, 96
Blackmun, Harry: on affirmative action,
    42; on flag burning, 155; on freedom of
    speech, 155; opinion on affirmative
    action, 59–62; opinions on abortion,
    96–97, 109–11, 116–17, 120–21, 137,
    144; on religious freedom, 257–58,
    275–76; on retirement, 137, 142
*Board of Education of Oklahoma v. Dow-
    ell* (1991), 32
Boerne, Texas, 277
Bolling v. Sharpe (1954), 129
Bork, Robert, 116
Boulware, Harold, 22
Brandenburg v. Ohio (1969), 162, 191–92
Brennan, William: on abortion, 96–97;
    opinion on affirmative action, 42,
    59–62; on religious freedom, 257, 275;
    on school segregation, 30
Brennan Center for Justice, 222, 233
Breyer, Stephen G.: on abortion, 143; on
    affirmative action, 68, 80; on campaign
    finance regulation, 212, 234; confirma-
    tion hearings for, 144; on cross burn-
    ing, 176
Briggs v. Elliott, 5
Brown, Henry, 2
Brown, Janice Rogers, 144
Brown v. Board of Education (1954),
    1–33, 43, 44, 120, 129, 134–35, 139,
    150, *152*; briefs in, 9–10, 19–25; impact
    of, 12, 28–29; opinion in, 26–28; oral
    argument in, 8–10, 16–19, 25–26; rear-
    gument of, 29; unanimity of decision
    in, 10–11
Buckley, James, 202
Buckley v. Valeo (1976), 202–46
Bumpers, Dale, 224
Bunsel, John, *39*
Burger, Warren: on abortion, 96–97,

145n8; on affirmative action, 41, 64; on
    campaign finance regulation, 204; on
    religious freedom, 251, 253–54, 258; on
    school segregation, 31
Burton, Harold H., 8, 17
Bush (George H. W.) administration, 116
Bush, George W., 65, 144, 146n21, 208
Bush, Jeb, 66
*Buying Time 1998: Television Advertising
    in the 1998 Congressional Elections*,
    222
*Buying Time 2000: Television Advertise-
    ments in the 2000 Federal Elections*, 222
Byrd, James, Jr., 172

Cahn, Edmond, 5–6, *7*
California: Constitution of, 37; on fetus
    and homicide, 101; Proposition 209, 65;
    race-neutral plan for diversity in, 75.
    See also *Regents of University of Calif.
    v. Bakke* (1978)
California Medical Association v. FEC
    (1981), 205
campaign finance regulation, 201–46;
    briefs on, 209–11, 214–30; contribu-
    tion versus expenditure limits, 203–4,
    209; dilemma confronting, 201; opin-
    ions on, 212–13, 235–48; oral argument
    on, 211–12, 231–35; state systems of,
    206
campaign spending, cumulative, 241
Cantwell v. State of Connecticut (1940),
    274
*Carr v. Montgomery County Board of
    Education*, 47
Carter, Robert L., 8, 13, 16–18, 22
cases: analysis of, factors in, xii; number
    of, appealed to Supreme Court yearly,
    xi; process for, xi–xii
Casey. See *Planned Parenthood v. Casey*
    (1992)
Catholic Church, 112
Central Federal Lands Highway Division
    (CFLHD), Department of Transporta-
    tion, 65
Chaplinsky v. New Hampshire (1942),
    147, 162
children, parents' rights concerning, 98–
    100, 122–23, 133

Church, Frank, 115
Church of Lukumi Babulu Aye v. City of Hialeah (1993), 277, 281, 282
City of Boerne v. Flores (1997), 277–78, 282
Civil Rights Act (1866), 9, 21, 23
Civil Rights Act (1964): *Bakke* and, 37, 41, 56–57, 60, 63; *Brown v. Board of Education* and, 12, 29–30; Title VI, 37, 41, 56–57, 60, 90n4
Civil Rights Act (1968), 12
civil rights laws, 1
civil rights movement, *Brown* and, 12
Clark, Kenneth B., 4–6, 8, 11
Clark, Tom, 8
class action suits, 95
Cleary, Edward J., 151, 157, 160–61
Clement, Paul, 212, 234–35
Clinton, Bill, 143, 144, 192, 212, 277, 280
Clinton, Hillary, 192
Coalition for the Free Exercise of Religion, 276
Coffee, Linda, 95–96, 102
Coleman, James S., 31
Collin v. Smith (1978), 150
Colorado I. See *Colorado Republican Federal Campaign Committee v. FEC* ("Colorado I") (1996)
Colorado II. See *FEC v. Colorado Republican Federal Campaign Committee* ("Colorado II") (2001)
Colorado Republican Federal Campaign Committee v. FEC ("Colorado I") (1996), 206, 217
Columbus Board of Education v. Penick (1979), 30
Colvin, Reynold H., 40, 50, 55–56
compelling interests of state: in campaign finance regulation, 228; concerning abortion, 96, 97–98, 100–102, 104, 106, 107, 110–11, 118–19, 122, 124, 125–26, 128, 131–32, 136; freedom of speech and, 148, 159, 166; in racial diversity, 35, 41–42, 44, 48, 50, 58, 60, 64, 66, 68–69, 70, 72, 74–75, 82–83, 88–90; religious freedom and, 251, 253–54, 255–57, 259–60, 272, 275–76, 280; and standards of equal protection, 37
Congress: and campaign finance regulation, 201–46; civil rights laws passed by, 1; hate crime legislation by, 172; judicial appointment hearings by, 116, 144; reaction to *Grutter* in, *71*; and religious freedom, 249–50, 258, 277, 280
contraception, 94, 99
Corfield v. Coryell, 23
corporations: campaign contributions of, 202, 205–6, 219–20, 223, 228; issue advocacy by, 227–29, 239–41, 245
corruption in campaigns, 201, 202–5, 208, 210, *211*, 213, 217, 224–25, 227–28, 237–38, 243–44. See also *quid pro quo*
Court of Appeals for District of Columbia, 202
Cox, Archibald, 40, 53–55
Croson. See *Richmond v. J.A. Croson Company* (1989)
cross burning, 147–98; briefs on, 173–74, 177–87; history of, 170, 180, 183, 187; as intimidation, 170, 176, 177–80, 186–90, 193, 195, 197–98; opinions on, 175–76, 193–98; oral argument on, 174–75, 187–93

Danforth. See *Planned Parenthood v. Danforth* (1976)
Davis, Garrett, 21
Davis, John W., 10, 25–26
Davis v. County School Board of Prince Edward County, 6
Dayton Board of Education v. Brinkman (1979), 30
D.C. Circuit Court of Appeals, 144
Department of Health, Education, and Welfare, 30
Department of Labor, 36
Department of Transportation, 65
Disraeli, Benjamin, 25
dissenting opinions, xii
District of Columbia, school segregation in, 24
doctrine of overbreadth, 149–50, 151, 156–58, 157, 173, 181, 186, 230
doll test, 4–6, *5*, *7*
Dorsay, Craig J., 255–56, 265, 268–70
Douglas, William O.: on abortion, 96–97, 145n8; on rights' penumbras, 94, 95; and school segregation, 8, 16–17

draft card burning, 148–49
Dred Scott v. Sandford (1857), 121, 142
Dreeben, Michael R., 175, 189–90
drug use, religious freedom and, 254–82

education: affirmative action in, 35–90; freedom-of-choice plans for, 29; government role in, 11, 28; history of segregation in, 27; and religious freedom, 250–54, 281; segregation in public, 1–33; speech code implementation, 150, *152–53*, 157
Eighth Circuit Court of Appeals, 171
Elliott, Richard, 173, 174, 176, 178, 183
employment, affirmative action in, 36
Employment Div., Dept. of Human Resources of Oregon v. Smith (1990), 249–82; briefs in, 255–56, 259–65; impact of, 276–82; opinions in, 256–58, 270–76; oral argument in, 265–70
Equal Protection Clause, Fourteenth Amendment: abortion and, 104; affirmative action and, 64–65; *Bakke* and, 37, 41, 42, 56–57, 60; *Brown v. Board of Education* and, 1–2, 8, 9, 11, 15, 28, 29, 134–35; *Grutter* and, 80, 88, 89; hate speech and, 150
equal protection, standards of, 37, 40–42, 47–48, 50, 57
Establishment Clause, First Amendment, 249–82
Estrada, Miguel, 144
Ethiopian Zion Coptic Church, 260, 263
Executive Order 11246, 36, *39*

Fairman, Charles, 23
family, rights concerning, 98–100, 102, 122–23, 133
FECA, Section 323. *See* Title I, Bipartisan Campaign Reform Act (2003)
FEC v. Beaumont (2003), 205
FEC v. Colorado Republican Federal Campaign Committee ("Colorado II") (2001), 206, 216, 232
FEC v. Massachusetts Citizens for Life, Inc. (MCLF) (1986), 205, 219, 228, 239, 242
FEC v. National Conservative PAC (1985), 206

FEC v. National Right to Work Committee (1982), 205
Federal Communications Commission (FCC), 64
federal court judges, appointment of, 144
Federal Election Campaign Act (FECA), 202–3
Federal Election Commission, 201–46
federal election communications. *See* Title II, Bipartisan Campaign Reform Act (2003)
federal money. *See* hard money
Feingold, Russell, 208
Ferber. See New York v. Ferber (1982)
fetus, rights of, 96, 97, 100–102, 104, 105, 106, 107, 110
Fifteenth Amendment, 19
Fifth Amendment, 56, 94, 218, 238
Fifth Circuit Court of Appeals, 65
fighting words, 147–48, 151–54, 156–65, 168–69
First Amendment: affirmative action and, 58; categorical approach to, 169–70; cross burning and, 147–98; freedom of speech and, 147–98, 201–46; and limitations on government, 148–49, 156, 163, 249; political campaigns and, 201–46; privacy rights and, 94; religious freedom and, 249–82
First National Bank of Boston v. Bellotti (1978), 205, 220
527 committees, 213
Flack, Horace E., 23
flag burning, 148–49, 174
flag-salute statutes, 252–53
Florida, 65–66, 75
Flowers, Robert C., 97, 108–9
Floyd, Jay, 96, 106–7
Foley, Tom, 151, 159, 161–63
Fourteenth Amendment: abortion and, 94, 95, 104, 107–8, 109–10, 112, 129–30, 133; *Bakke* and, 50, 51, 59; *Brown v. Board of Education* and, 9–11, 139; Due Process Clause, 94, 95, 104; freedom of speech and, 160; intent of, 20–23, 27, 42; religious freedom and, 276–77; "separate-but-equal" doctrine and, 19. *See also* Equal Protection Clause, Fourteenth Amendment

Fourth Amendment, 94, 112
Frank, Barney, 276
Frank, Leo, 170
Frankfurter, Felix, 8–9, 16–17, 18, 252, 256
Freedmen's Bureau Act (1866), 51
freedom-of-choice plans for education, 29
freedom of speech: briefs on, 155–59, 173–74, 177–87; campaign finance regulation and, 201–46; content-based restrictions of, 148, 149, 151, 153–54, 155–56, 158–59, 161–64, 166–69, 173, 176, 180, 182–83, 193–94, 196–98; cross burning and, 147–98; expressive or symbolic speech, 148–49, 155–56, 182–84; flag-salute statutes and, 252–53; freedom of conduct versus, 148–49, 187–88; hierarchy in, 169; as limited versus absolute right, 147–49, 154; opinions on, 151–55, 163–70, 175–76, 193–98; oral argument on, 159–63, 174–75, 187–93; secondary effects of, 154, 164, 168, 174, 180, 185; speech code implementation, 157; viewpoint-based restrictions of, 156, 160, 161, 164, 165, 171, 172–74, 183
Free Exercise Clause, First Amendment, 249–82, 278–79
Freeman v. Pitts (1992), 32
friends of the court briefs. See *amici curiae* briefs
Frohnmayer, Dave, 263, 265–67
Fullilove v. Klutznick (1980), 64, 65

Garrett, Henry, 6
Gingrich, Newt, 276
Ginsburg, Ruth Bader: on abortion, 143; on affirmative action, 64, 68; on campaign finance regulation, 212, 231; confirmation hearings for, 144; on cross burning, 175, 188, 191; on religious freedom, 277
Gobitis. See *Minersville School District v. Gobitis* (1940)
Gobitis, Walter, 252
Godwin, Mills E., Jr., 177
Goldberg, Arthur, 95
Good News Club v. Milford Central School (2001), 281

Gore, Al, 227
Gratz v. Bollinger (2003), 84, 90n18
Greenberg, Jack, 22, 52
Green v. County School Board (1968), 29–30
Griswold v. Connecticut (1965), 94–95, 98, 99, 100, 128, 129, 134
Grutter v. Bollinger (2003), 66–90; briefs in, 66, 68, 70, 72–79; congressional reaction to, 71; opinions in, 68–69, 82–90; oral argument in, 68, 79–81
Gunther, Gerald, 150, 153

Hagel Amendment, 218
Hanten, Linda, 52
hard money, 206–7, 241
Harlan, John, 2, 95, 96, 139
Harris v. McCrae (1976), 113
Harvard College, 58
Harvard plan for racial diversity, 75, 81, 83, 84
Hatch, Orrin, 113, 116, 276
hate crimes, 171–72, 184
hate speech. See cross burning; speech codes
Hawaii, 94
Hayes, Rutherford B., 19
Hialeah, Florida, 277
Hill, Oliver W., 22
Hindus, 260, 263
Hindu Tantrists, 260
Holman, Craig, 222
Holmes, Oliver Wendell, 139
homicide, fetuses and, 100–101
Hook, Sidney, 39
Hopwood v. Texas, 65
Howard, Jacob H., 21
Hughes, Charles Evans, 139
human life, definition of, 101, 102–4, 106–10, 116
Human Life Federalism Amendment, 113
Hurd, William H., 173–74, 182, 187–89, 193
Hyde, Henry, 113
Hyde Amendment, 113

incumbents, campaign finance regulation as benefiting, 241
Initiative 200 (Washington), 65

integration, court-ordered, 30–32
interest groups, 218–19, 238
interpretation of Constitution, as
    unchanging versus living entity, 24
intimidation, 170, 176, 177–80, 183, 186–
    90, 193, 195, 197–98
issue advocacy, 207, 209–12, 219–22, 227–
    30, 233–34, 238–41, 244–45; sham
    issue ads, 220–22, 244–45

Jackson, Robert, 8, 148, 252
Jeffords, James, 144
Jehovah's Witnesses, 252
Jim Crow laws, 9
Johnson, Andrew, 21
Johnson, Lyndon, 36
Jones, Paula, 212
Jubillee, James, 173
judicial appointments: Bork hearings, 116;
    lower federal judiciary, 144

Kansas, *Brown v. Board of Education* and,
    1–33
Keller v. Superior Court (1970), 101
Kendall, David E., 52
Kennedy, Anthony: on abortion, 116, 118,
    132–37, 143; on affirmative action, 64,
    68–69, 79; on campaign finance regula-
    tion, 212–13, 235, 237, 243–45; on
    cross burning, 175, 188; on religious
    freedom, 256, 277, 281; as swing voter,
    68
Kennedy, Edward, 116, 276
Keyes v. School District (1973), 30
Kilgore, Jerry, 182, 187
King, Martin Luther, Jr., 12, *71*
King, Steve, *71*
Knights of Camellia, 189
Kolbert, Kathryn, 125, 129–31
Kolbo, Kirk, 68, 74, 79–80
Krol, John, 113, *114*
Ku Klux Klan, 170, 173, 178, 179, 183–84,
    188, 189, 191–92
Kurland, Philip B., 53
Kuttner, Bernard, *39*

labor unions. *See* unions, campaign contri-
    butions of
Lawrence, Charles, 150, *152*

LDF. *See* Legal Defense and Education
    Fund
least restrictive means, religious freedom
    and, 251, 253–54
Lee, Bill Lann, 52
Lee v. Weisman (1992), 281
Legal Defense and Educational Fund
    (LDF), 2, 4, 10, 12; *amicus* brief in
    Bakke by, 51; brief in *Brown* by, 9, 13–
    15, 19–22
Lemon test, 250–51, 281
Lemon v. Kurtzman (1971), 250
Leutze, Emanuel, 142
Levin Amendment, 247n19
libel, 148
Lief, Beth J., 52
life. *See* human life
living constitution, 24
Lochner v. New York (1905), 95, 119, 134,
    138–39
Loving v. Virginia (1967), 47, 99, 128, 129
Lucas, Roy, 102
Lynch v. Donnelly (1984), 251

Mahoney, Maureen, 68, 77, 80–81
majority opinions, writing of, xii, 96–97
Margold, Nathan, 2–3
marriage: hardships of pregnancy on, 99;
    privacy right and, 98–99, 102, 133
Marshall, Thurgood: on abortion, 96, 106;
    opinion on affirmative action, 42,
    59–63; on religious freedom, 257, 275;
    on school segregation, 4, 10, 13, 22, 26
Martin, Crawford C., 104
Martinez, Vilma S., 52
massive resistance to school desegregation,
    38, 178
Mazurek v. Armstrong (1997), 143
McCain, John, 208, *210*
McCarthy, Eugene, 202
McConnell, Mitch, 208–9, *211*. See also
    *McConnell v. Federal Election Com-
    mission* (2003)
*McConnell v. Federal Election Commis-
    sion* (2003), 201–46; briefs in, 209–11,
    214–30; opinions in, 212–13, 235–48;
    oral argument in, 211–12, 231–35
McCorvey, Norma, 95–96

MCFL. See *FEC v. Massachusetts Citizens for Life, Inc.* (MCLF) (1986)
McGovern, George, 115
McLaurin v. Oklahoma (1950), 3, 16, 17–18, 28
media companies, and issue advocacy, 212, 235, 240
medical field, minority opportunities in, 44, 61
Meehan, Marty, 208
Metro Broadcasting v. F.C.C. (1990), 64, 65
Metzenbaum, Howard, 116
Mexican American Legal Defense & Educational Fund, *amicus* brief in *Bakke* by, 52
Mexican Americans, educational discrimination against, 52
Meyer v. Nebraska (1923), 99, 128
military, affirmative action in, 68, 78–79
Miller v. California (1973), 148
Milliken v. Bradley (1974), 31–32
Minersville School District v. Gobitis (1940), 252, 256, 258
Minton, Sherman, 8
Mishkin, Paul J., 48
Mississippi Burning (film), 171
Missouri, 3
Missouri ex rel. Gaines v. Canada (1938), 2–3
Mitchell, Clarence, *38*
Mitchell, Todd, 171
Mitchell v. Helms (2000), 281
Montgomery, Alabama bus boycott, 12
Moore, T. Justin, 18–19
mootness, rules concerning, xi
Morse, Wayne, 12
Moslems, 260
Mosley. See *Police Dept. v. Mosley* (1972)

NAACP. *See* National Association for the Advancement of Colored People
Nabrit, James M., 52
National Association for the Advancement of Colored People (NAACP), 2–4, 9–10, *38*. *See also* Legal Defense and Educational Fund
National Rifle Association (NRA), 227, 228, 232–33

National Socialist Party of America (NSPA), 150
Native American Church, and religious freedom, 254–76
nativity scenes, 251
Naval Academy, 78
New Jersey, 102
New Right, 115–16
New York, 94
New York Times v. Sullivan (1964), 148, 221
New York v. Ferber (1982), 163
Ninth Amendment, 94, 95, 104, 109
Nixon, Richard, 202
nonprofit corporations, campaign contributions of, 205, 219–20, 241, 245

O'Brien. See *United States v. O'Brien* (1968)
obscenity, 148
O'Connor, Sandra Day: on abortion, 116, 118, 132–37, 143, 146n21; appointment of, 116; on campaign finance regulation, 212, 235–40, 244; on cross burning, 176, 193–95; opinion on affirmative action, 68–69, 81, 82–85; on religious freedom, 251, 257–58, 273–75, 277, *278–79*, 280, 281; as swing voter, 68
Office of Federal Contract Compliance, Department of Labor, 36
O'Hara hearings on racial preferences, 36–37
Oklahoma, 3
"The Old Rugged Cross" (song), 170
Olson, Theodore, 68, 78, 212, 230, 231–32
O'Mara, Jonathan, 173, 174, 176, 178, 183
opinions: decision process concerning, xii; writing of, xii
overbreadth, doctrine of. *See* doctrine of overbreadth
Owens, Jack B., 48

PACs. *See* political action committees
Parker, John J., 29
Parker, Kellis, 52
Parks, Rosa, 12
parochial schools, 250–51, 281
Pennsylvania, *Casey* and, 117–44

peyote, 254–76
Peyote Way Church of God, 260, 268
Phillips, Carter, 68, 79
Pierce v. Society of Sisters (1925), 99, 128, 271
Planned Parenthood v. Casey (1992), 117–44; briefs in, 121–29; opinions in, 118–21, 132–43; oral argument in, 129–32; strategies in, 117–18
Planned Parenthood v. Danforth (1976), 125, 137
Plessy v. Ferguson (1896), 1–2, 8, 11, 13, 15, 27, 28, 119, 135, 138–39
plurality opinion, xii
Police Dept. v. Mosley (1972), 148, 168–70
Polish American Congress, amicus brief in Bakke by, 50–51
political action committees (PACs), 202, 205–6, 220, 245
political committees, campaign contributions of, 202
political parties, campaign finances of, 206, 218–19, 235–38, 241, 247n19
Polsby, Daniel D., 53
Powell, Lewis: on abortion, 97; as new appointee, 96; opinion on affirmative action, 35, 41–42, 56–59, 64, 66, 69, 75, 83, 84; retirement of, 116
prayer. See school prayer
Preate, Ernest D., Jr., 129, 131–32
precedent: Brown v. Board of Education and, 8–11, 15; Employment Div., Dept. of Human Resources of Oregon v. Smith and, 251–54; Planned Parenthood v. Casey and, 119–22, 128, 134–36, 138, 140; R.A.V. v. City of St. Paul and, 166–67
pregnancy, hardships of, 99, 109–10
Presbyterian Church, 277
privacy, right of: abortion and, 96, 97–100, 102–4, 109–10, 112, 118, 122–23, 128, 132–33; as inferred right, 94–95; marriage and, 98–99, 102, 133
Proposition 209 (California), 65
public education. See education
public opinion: on affirmative action, 37, 70; on court-ordered integration, 31; on religious freedom, 281

quid pro quo, campaign contributions and, 203, 209, 212, 213, 215–16, 237, 242–44
quota systems: denials that Bakke involved, 45–46, 53–54; in higher education, 36; opposition to, 48–50, 53, 73; Powell's disapproval in Bakke of, 36, 42

race: affirmative action and reinforcement of, 46–47; Brown v. Board of Education and, 25–26. See also racial discrimination; racial preferences
race-neutral plans for diversity, 45, 65–66, 68, 75–76, 77–78, 85
racial discrimination, 1–33; Black Codes, 10, 20, 26; briefs on, 9–10, 19–25; Civil Rights Act of 1964 and, 12; de facto versus de jure, 47; Jim Crow laws, 9; Marshall on history of, 62–63; and Marshall's argument in Brown, 10; opinion on, 26–28; oral argument on, 8–10, 16–19, 25–26. See also cross burning; hate crimes; hate speech; racial preferences; segregation
racial preferences: backlash against, 65–66; as factor in decisions, 35–36, 42, 59–60, 83–84; judicial approval of, 47, 59–62; Metro and, 64, 65; remedial use of, 59–61; time limitation on, 69, 85; University of Michigan Law School and, 66
Radical Republicans, 20–21
Ralston, Charles S., 52
Rastafarians, 260, 263
R.A.V. v. City of St. Paul (1992), 147–70, 176; background to, 147–50; briefs in, 155–59; developments after, 170–73; and exceptions to content-based distinctions, 154, 174, 179–80, 184–86, 193–94, 196–98; opinions in, 151–55, 163–70; oral argument in, 159–63
Reagan, Ronald, 114, 116
reargument of cases, 97
Reconstruction: Freedmen's Bureau Act during, 51; politics of, and effect on racial matters, 19
Redding, Louis, 22
Reed, Stanley, 8, 10–11, 18–19
referendums, contributions or expenditures concerning, 205

Regents of University of Calif. v. Bakke
(1978), 35–63; affirmative action after,
63–66, 69–70; background to, 35–37;
briefs in, 37, 40, 43–53; impact of, 43;
opinions in, 41–42, 56–63; opponents
of, *39*; oral argument in, 40, 53–56;
proponents of, *38*; strategies in, 40–41
Rehnquist, William, 174; on abortion, 97–
98, 112, 116, 119–20, 138–40, 143–44;
on affirmative action, 41, 55, 68–69,
85–88; on campaign finance regulation,
213, 234–35, 245–46; on cross burning,
176; on flag burning, 155; on freedom
of speech, 155; on hate crimes, 171–72;
as new appointee, 96; on religious freedom, 256, 265–66, 277
Reidhaar, Donald L., 48
religious freedom, 249–82; accommodations of religion and, 249–52, 256–59,
261–62, 272–73, 280; briefs on, 255–56,
259–65; opinions on, 256–58, 270–76;
oral argument on, 265–70; school
prayer and, 116, 250, 281
Religious Freedom Restoration Act
(RFRA), 276–77
Religious Land Use and Institutionalized
Persons Act (RLUIPA) (2000), 280
Religious Liberty Protection Act (RLPA),
280
Renton v. Playtime Theatres, Inc. (1986),
162, 180, 185
Republican National Committee, 213
Reserve Officer Training Corps (ROTC),
68, 79
reverse discrimination, *38*, 40
Reynolds v. United States (1878), 260, 271
Richmond v. J.A. Croson Company
(1989), 63–64, 65
rights: abortion and, 104, 130; inferred,
94–95; Supreme Court and new, 94–
95, 98, 111, 118, 120, 122, 128. *See also*
associational rights; fetus, rights of;
freedom of speech; privacy, right of;
religious freedom
ripeness, rules concerning, xi
Robinson, Spottswood W., III, 13, 22
Roe v. Wade (1973), 93–112; background
to, 93–96; briefs in, 96, 98–104; *Casey*
and, 117–44; developments after,

112–21; government attempts to overturn, 116, 133; impact of, 94, 134, 141;
opinions in, 109–12; oral argument in,
96, 97, 104–9; reargument of, 97
Rogers, Andrew Jackson, 21
Roos, Peter D., 52
Rudman, Warren, 224
"rule of four," xi

Santa Fe Independent School Dist. v. Doe
(2000), 281
Santeria, 277
Scalia, Antonin: on abortion, 116, 119–21,
140–43; on affirmative action, 64, 68–
69, 80–81; on campaign finance regulation, 212–13, 231–32, 234–35, 240–42;
on cross burning, 176, 187–88, 190,
192; on flag burning, 154–55; on freedom of speech, 153–55, 159–66; on
religious freedom, 256–58, 267, 270–
73, 277–78, *279*, 280
Schnapper, Eric, 52
school prayer, 116, 250, 281
Scott, Charles S., 13, 22
secondary effects of free speech, 154, 164,
168, 174, 180, 185
Section 101, BCRA. *See* Title I, Bipartisan
Campaign Reform Act (2003)
segregation: *Brown v. Board of Education*
(1954), 1–33; constitutional versus
social basis of, 2, 8, 11; *de facto* versus
de jure, 29–30, 32; defense of, 25–26;
effects on individuals of, 4–8, 11, 13–
15, 28, *152*; as established in states and
District of Columbia, 24; in history of
education, 27; indirect attack on, 2–4;
means of remedying, 30–32; post-
Brown situation of, 30–32; Reconstruction as context for, 19. *See also* "separate-but-equal" doctrine
"separate-but-equal" doctrine, 1–10, 15,
16–17, 19, 21–22, 27, 134–35, 138–39
Sereseres, César, *38*
Seventh Circuit Court of Appeals, 150
Shays, Christopher, 208
Shepard, Mathew, 172
Sherbert v. Verner (1963), 253–54, 263,
271, 276, 280
Simpson, Alan, 116

Sixth Circuit Court of Appeals, 66
skepticism, racial discrimination viewed judicially with, 65
Skinner v. Oklahoma (1942), 99, 128
Skokie, Illinois, 150
Smith, Alfred, 255
Smith. See Employment Div., Dept. of Human Resources of Oregon v. Smith (1990)
Smolla, Rodney, 174–75, 186, 190–93
social science, on segregation, 4–8, 11, 14–15, 18
soft money, 206–9, 213, 223–27, 235–38, 243
solicitations for campaign funds, 214, 226–27, 237–38
Soros, George, 213
Souter, David: and abortion, 118, 132–37, 143; on affirmative action, 68; on campaign finance regulation, 212, 232–34; on cross burning, 175, 190–91, 193, 196–98
South Carolina, 25
The Southern Manifesto, 11–12, *38*
Special Subcommittee on Education, House of Representatives, 36–37
speech codes, 150, *152–53*, 157
Stabenow, Debbie, 230
standards, Supreme Court decision: abortion and undue burden standard, 117–20, 123–26, 130–31, 136, 140, 143–44; affirmative action and equal protection, 37, 40–42, 47–48, 50, 57; for campaign finance regulation, 212; rational relationship test, 130; strict scrutiny, 37, 41–42, 47, 50, 57, 60, 64, 65, 66, 68, 86, 88, 117, 121, 130, 137, 167, 209, 212, 215, 222–23, 228–29, 232, 236
standing, rules concerning, xi
Stanley v. Georgia (1969), 128
stare decisis, 120, 133, 134, 137, 138, 139, 140
Starr, Kenneth W., 212, 222, 231
state money. *See* soft money
state political parties, campaign finances of, 225–26, 238, 247n19
states' rights: abortion and, 111, 141; school segregation and, 15, 21, 24, 26. *See also* compelling interests of state

Stenberg v. Carhart (2000), 143
Stevens, John Paul: on affirmative action, 41, 63, 64, 68; on campaign finance regulation, 212, 235–40; on cross burning, 174, 176, 188; on flag burning, 154; on freedom of speech, 152, 154–55, 168–70; on religious freedom, 256, 258, 267, 277
Stevens, Thad, 25
Stewart, Potter: on abortion, 96, 97, 106, 108, 109, 140, 143, 145n8; on affirmative action, 41
Stone Mountain, Georgia, 170
St. Paul Bias-Motivated Crime Ordinance, 150
strict scrutiny: abortion, 117, 121, 130, 137; affirmative action, 37, 41–42, 47, 50, 57, 60, 64, 65, 66, 68, 86, 88; campaign finance regulation, 209–10, 212, 215, 222–23, 228–29, 232, 236; freedom of speech, 167
Sumner, Charles, 22
Supreme Court: changes in late twentieth century in, 64–65; legitimacy of, 135–36, 139–40; and new constitutional rights, 94–95, 98, 111, 118, 120, 122, 128; pro-life movement and, 94, 114–16. *See also* precedent
suspect classifications, 37, 47, 57–58, 60
Swann v. Charlotte-Mecklenburg Board of Education (1971), 30
Sweatt v. Painter (1950), 3, 16, 17–18, 27, 28
symbols, 176, 182–84. *See also* cross burning

Taney, Roger, 121, 142–43
Tantric Buddhists, 260, 263
Tenth Amendment, *38*
Texas: race-neutral plan for diversity in, 65, 75, 77; *Roe v. Wade* and, 95–112
Texas v. Johnson (1989), 149, 154–55, 175, 177
Third Amendment, 94
Thirteenth Amendment, 19
Thomas, Clarence: on abortion, 118, 119–20, 143; on affirmative action, 64, 68–69, *71*, 88–90; on campaign finance regulation, 212–13, 242–43; on cross

burning, 175, 189–90, 195–96; on religious freedom, 277; silence during oral arguments of, 175
Thornburgh v. American College of Obstetricians and Gynecologists (1986), 136
threats, 148
Thurmond, Strom, 12
Title I, Bipartisan Campaign Reform Act (2003), 209–12, 214–19, 223–27, 231–32, 235–40, 247n19
Title II, Bipartisan Campaign Reform Act (2003), 209–13, 219–22, 227–30, 232, 235–40, 242
Title VI, Civil Rights Act (1964), 37, 41, 56–57, 60, 90n4
Title VII and freedom of speech, 154, 165, 168
trimester framework for abortion decisions, 97–98, 111, 116, 118–19, 136, 140
Trumbull, Lyman, 20
Twelve Tribes of Israel (Rastafarians), 260, 263

unborn child. *See* fetus, rights of
undue burden, standard of, 117–20, 123–26, 130–31, 136, 140, 143–44
unions: campaign contributions of, 202, 205–6, 219–20, 223, 228; issue advocacy by, 227–29, 239–40, 245
United States, *amicus* brief in *Grutter* by, 77–78
United States v. J.H.H. (1994), 171
United States v. O'Brien (1968), 148–49, 158, 175, 192
University of California at Davis, *Bakke* and, 37–63
University of Michigan, speech code of, 150
University of Michigan Law School, *Grutter v. Bollinger* and, 66–90
University of Texas Law School, 3

Vinson, Fred M., 3, 8, 10
Virginia v. Black (2003), 173–98; briefs in, 173–74, 177–87; opinions in, 175–76,

193–98; oral argument in, 174–75, 187–93
Voting Rights Act (1965), 12
vouchers, school, 281

Walentynowicz, Leonard F., 51
Warren, Earl: impact on *Brown* of, 10–11; opinion on school segregation, 26–28; on religious freedom, 251
Washington, Bushrod, 23
Washington, D.C. *See* District of Columbia, school segregation in
Washington (state), 65, 94
Watergate scandal, 202
Watts v. United States (1969), 148
Waxman, Seth P., 212
Webster v. Reproductive Health Services (1989), 116–17, 137
Weddington, James R., 102
Weddington, Sarah, 95–97, 102, 104–5, 107–8
West Coast Hotel Co. v. Parrish (1937), 120, 134, 139
West Point, 68, 78
West Virginia State Board of Education v. Barnette (1943), 252–53, 256, 271
White, Byron: on abortion, 97–98, 104–5, 107, 111, 116, 119–20; on affirmative action, 42, 59–62, 64; on campaign finance regulation, 204; on flag burning, 154–55; on freedom of speech, 152, 154–55, 166–68; on religious freedom, 256; on school segregation, 30
white flight, 31, 32
Wilson, James F., 21
Wilson, Paul E., 17
Wisconsin v. Mitchell (1993), 171, 184
Wisconsin v. Yoder (1972), 253–54, 256, 258, 263, 264, 266, 271, 274
Wu, David, 221
Wygant v. Jackson Board of Education (1986), 63–64, 65

Yoder. See Wisconsin v. Yoder (1972)
Young, Andrew, *38*

Zelman v. Simmons-Harris (2002), 281

About the Author

H. L. Pohlman is the A. Lee Fritschler Professor of Public Policy and current chair of the Political Science Department at Dickinson College. Previously he was a Distinguished Fulbright Lecturer in the United Kingdom, a Judicial Fellow at the Supreme Court of the United States, a Reporter of an Ad Hoc Committee of the Judicial Conference of the United States, and a director of the K. Robert Nilsson Center for European Studies in Bologna, Italy. He has received a number of awards, grants, and fellowships. He has published widely in the fields of legal theory and American constitutional law. His work in progress is on law and terrorism.